The Philosophy of the Kyoto School

Tetsugaku-no-michi (The Philosopher's Walk), Kyoto, Japan

Masakatsu Fujita
Editor

The Philosophy of the Kyoto School

Translated by Robert Chapeskie and revised by
John W. M. Krummel

Editor
Masakatsu Fujita
Kyoto University
Kyoto
Japan

Translated by: Robert Chapeskie, Kyoto, Japan;
Translation Supervisor: John W. M. Krummel, Department of Religious Studies, Hobart and William Smith Colleges, Geneva, NY, USA

ISBN 978-981-10-8982-4   ISBN 978-981-10-8983-1 (eBook)
https://doi.org/10.1007/978-981-10-8983-1

Library of Congress Control Number: 2018939131

© Springer Nature Singapore Pte Ltd. 2018
This work is subject to copyright. All rights are reserved by the Publisher, whether the whole or part of the material is concerned, specifically the rights of translation, reprinting, reuse of illustrations, recitation, broadcasting, reproduction on microfilms or in any other physical way, and transmission or information storage and retrieval, electronic adaptation, computer software, or by similar or dissimilar methodology now known or hereafter developed.
The use of general descriptive names, registered names, trademarks, service marks, etc. in this publication does not imply, even in the absence of a specific statement, that such names are exempt from the relevant protective laws and regulations and therefore free for general use.
The publisher, the authors and the editors are safe to assume that the advice and information in this book are believed to be true and accurate at the date of publication. Neither the publisher nor the authors or the editors give a warranty, express or implied, with respect to the material contained herein or for any errors or omissions that may have been made. The publisher remains neutral with regard to jurisdictional claims in published maps and institutional affiliations.

Printed on acid-free paper

This Springer imprint is published by the registered company Springer Nature Singapore Pte Ltd. part of Springer Nature
The registered company address is: 152 Beach Road, #21-01/04 Gateway East, Singapore 189721, Singapore

Preface

The field of academic inquiry referred to as philosophy first became known in Japan following the Meiji Restoration (1868). While attempts to comprehend and digest it had been made earlier, it was only at the beginning of the twentieth century that independent thinking began on the basis of these efforts, a development exemplified by the publication of *Zen no kenkyū* [『善の研究』 *An Inquiry into the Good*] by Nishida Kitarō (1870–1945) in 1911. After authoring this landmark text, along with providing guidance to many students as a professor and chair of philosophy at Kyoto University's Faculty of Letters, Nishida went on to publish many works in a variety of domains and lay the foundation for philosophical inquiry in Japan.

The "Kyoto School" was a group of scholars that took shape around this foundation. Nishida, Tanabe Hajime (1885–1962), who succeeded him as chair of philosophy at Kyoto University, and their disciples such as Miki Kiyoshi (1897–1945) and Nishitani Keiji (1900–1990) were central figures of this school. Philosophy in Japan has come to have a solid foundation thanks to their diverse and fruitful scholarship. They developed their thought creatively and expanded this field of inquiry by both addressing the key issues of Western philosophy head-on and drawing on the traditional thinking of the East. To this day, the appeal of the intellectual products of the Kyoto school has not in the least been diluted. Instead, they continue to offer us numerous suggestions of significance for thinking about the root problems of modern philosophy.

This expression, "Kyoto School", has come to be frequently used in recent years, but it is not entirely clear what the Kyoto school is or who belongs to it. This ambiguity is related to the fact that this school, unlike most schools of philosophy, is not a group that arose out of criticism of a preceding school, or, to put it another way, a group that emerged from the postulation of a particular thesis. Instead, it is a school that arose, so to speak, "spontaneously", at a time when philosophy in Japan that had started with the direct importation of Western thought was beginning to take its first steps on its own, and its assertions and scope possessed no clear boundaries. The work these philosophers engaged in spanned quite a wide range of fields, including not only metaphysics and practical philosophy but also philosophy of history, philosophy of religion, philosophy of mathematics, philosophy of science, aesthetics, pedagogy, and so on.

Indeed, it is not easy to identify any one characteristic feature applicable to Nishida, Tanabe, and all of the disciples who studied under them. If I were to venture a definition of the Kyoto School, it would perhaps be something like "the intellectual network created by Nishida Kitarō, Tanabe Hajime, and all of those who were strongly influenced by them academically and personally."

When we consider the content of their thought, it can be said that they were a group of philosophers who possessed profound knowledge of the Japanese and Eastern intellectual traditions (in particular Buddhism, and, within Buddhism, Zen) along with Western philosophy, and who spun their own original thought in the space between these approaches. In this regard, we can perhaps describe them as a group of philosophers who engaged in speculation by taking the concept of the "nothing" [無] as the axis of their philosophy. And yet among philosophers belonging to the "Kyoto School", there were those who did not positively thematize the "nothing", and there were also those who criticized the theories of Nishida and Tanabe. Miki Kiyoshi and Tosaka Jun (1900–1945), for example, critiqued the perspectives of Nishida and Tanabe from the standpoint of Marxism. And Nishida and Tanabe were in turn influenced to no small extent by their discussions with them. They too came to deepen their thought concerning the issues, for example, of "action" or "history".

In the Kyoto school, there were thus cases of influence not only from mentor to disciple but also from disciple to mentor. There were also cases of mutual criticism. A paradigmatic example of this is Tanabe Hajime's critique of Nishida Kitarō. Tanabe severely criticized Nishida, who was his own predecessor, but at the time he is said to have repeated the words of Aristotle: "Plato is dear to me, but dearer still is truth" (Amicus Plato, sed magis amica veritas). Nishida, for his part, openly accepted this criticism from Tanabe, and went on to expansively develop his own thinking. Their disciples, as well, employed their critique of Nishida and Tanabe as a driving force in the formation and development of their own thought. We may take this kind of relationship that permits mutual criticism, or of taking critique as a springboard or the criticism received as energy for developing one's own thought, to be one characteristic feature of the Kyoto School.

This book was originally published by Shōwadō Publishing of Kyoto in 2001. As I have just noted, in the pre-World War II period philosophers of the Kyoto School produced a large quantity of creative output through mutual critique, but this work has not necessarily been sufficiently carried on in the post-war period. A variety of new ideas have been picked up from American and European philosophy for immediate discussion. But instead of an acquisition of thought, perhaps it is more accurate to say that it has been a case of the latest trends simply being talked about. For this reason I strongly feel that philosophy, standing here at the starting point of a new century, has failed to clearly delineate the direction in which our culture ought to proceed. In this context, the publication of this book arose out of a desire to look back at the thinking of the philosophers of the Kyoto school, who not only actively embraced Western philosophy and laid the foundation for philosophical inquiry in Japan but also created their own distinct thought through an earnest confrontation with Western philosophy, in order to discern from this vantage point a new course of action.

The idea came to me of producing this translation of *Kyoto Gakuha no Tetsugaku* [『京都学派の哲学』 *The Philosophy of the Kyoto School*], the original of which was published in 2001, when hearing that there has been a lot of interest in recent years in Japanese philosophy and the philosophy of the Kyoto school in East Asia as well as in America and Europe, and that many research papers and books on this topic, as well as journals such as the *Journal of Japanese Philosophy*, are springing up one after another. I suspect this interest may have developed out of a desire to obtain from the thought of Nishida and his students, who stood within the interstice between East and West and opened up a new perspective on the world of philosophy, a clue to reassessing the issues of philosophy from the ground up or to drawing new creative possibilities. But at present it seems the materials that have been made available to further realize this kind of intellectual dialogue are far too few. This book is intended to be of some help in this regard.

The themes taken up by the philosophers of the Kyoto school are diverse and numerous. I have tried to select texts that would best illustrate the characteristics of the philosophy of the Kyoto School, and, while their quantity will be insufficient, works that together would outline its shape as a whole so that those who have an interest in Japanese philosophy or the philosophy of the Kyoto School can survey its overall picture. These texts are, of course, quite difficult, and cannot be well understood without sufficient preliminary knowledge. Expository essays have, therefore, been included after each text to provide guidance. In each of these commentaries, a scholar with deep understanding of the philosopher in question has provided an account of his life, intellectual journey, and the significance of the text included in this book. It may be best to read the essay first before turning to the original text it discusses.

It is my hope that through this book a new dialogue of ideas will emerge that, in turn, will engender new developments in philosophy, and thereby further expand the network of philosophical thinking.

In preparing this book for publication, I received assistance in a variety of areas from my colleague Prof. Uehara Mayuko. Mr. Robert Chapeskie translated the original manuscript and Prof. John W. M. Krummel revised and edited the translated manuscript from the perspective of a scholar of Japanese philosophy. This book could not have been completed without their considerable and dedicated efforts, and I would like to take this opportunity to once again express my deepest gratitude to them. I would also like to thank those involved at Springer Publishing, who assisted in this book's publication.

Kyoto, Japan   Fujita Masakatsu
February 2018

Contents

Part I Nishida Kitarō

1. **Place (1)** [場所 (1)] 3
   Nishida Kitarō

2. **The Scope of Nishida Kitarō's Theory of Place**
   [西田幾多郎の場所論の射程] 13
   Fujita Masakatsu

Part II Tanabe Hajime

3. **Clarifying the Meaning of the Logic of Species (1, 4)**
   [種の論理の意味を明らかにす(一、四)] 25
   Tanabe Hajime

4. **What Does Absolute Negation Differentiate?**
   [絶対否定は何を差異化するか] 43
   Nakaoka Narifumi

Part III Miki Kiyoshi

5. **The Logic of Imagination (Preface, Chapter 1 "Myth" 1)**
   [『構想力の論理』(序、第一章「神話」一)] 57
   Miki Kiyoshi

6. **The Philosophy of Miki Kiyoshi** [三木清の哲学] 65
   Akamatsu Tsunehiro

Part IV Tosaka Jun

7. **What Is the Technological Spirit?** [技術的精神とは何か] 81
   Tosaka Jun

8 **On Tosaka Jun's Scientific-Technological Spirit**
[戸坂潤の科学的・技術的精神をめぐって]................ 89
Nishikawa Tomio

Part V Kimura Motomori

9 **Body and Spirit [Mind]** [身体と精神]...................... 109
Kimura Motomori

10 **Reading According to the Context: Kimura Motomori and "Body and Spirit"** [コンテクストから読み解く──木村素衛と「身体と精神」]..................................... 123
Ōnishi Masamichi

Part VI Hisamatsu Shinichi

11 **The Metaphysical Element of the East**
[東洋的に形而上的なるもの].............................. 139
Hisamatsu Shinichi

12 **The Thought and Practice of Hisamatsu Shinichi**
[久松真一の思想と実践].................................. 149
Imaizumi Motoji

Part VII Shimomura Toratarō

13 **The Position of Mathematics in Intellectual History**
[精神史; *Geistesgeschichte*] [精神史における数学の位置]........ 163
Shimomura Toratarō

14 **Shimomura Toratarō: Tracking "Intellectual History"**
[下村寅太郎──「精神史」への軌跡]...................... 183
Takeda Atsushi

Part VIII Nishitani Keiji

15 **Nihility and Emptiness** [虚無と空 (1–5)]................... 199
Nishitani Keiji

16 **Philosophy of Overcoming Nihilism** [ニヒリズム超克の哲学]..... 217
Keta Masako

Part IX Supplementary Essay

17 **The Kyoto School and the Issue of "Overcoming Modernity"**
    [京都学派と「近代の超克」の問題]..................... 233
    Kosaka Kunitsugu

18 **The Identity of the Kyoto School: A Critical Analysis** 253
    John C. Maraldo

Index 269

Editor and Authors

About the Editor

Fujita Masakatsu Professor Emeritus, Kyoto University.
  Major works: *Tetsugaku no hinto* [『哲学のヒント』 *Philosophical Hints*] (Iwanami Shoten, 2013), *Nishida Kitarō* [『西田幾多郎』] (Iwanami Shoten, 2007), *Wakaki hegeru* [『若きヘーゲル』 *Young Hegel*] (Sōbunsha, 1986), "Philosophie und Religion beim jungen Hegel" (Bouvier, Bonn, 1985), etc.

Japanese Philosophers in Recent History

Nihida Kitarō (1870–1945)

Tanabe Hajime (1885–1962)

Tosaka Jun (1900–1945)

Kimura Motomori (1895–1946)

Hisamatsu Shinichi (1889–1980)

Miki Kiyoshi (1897–1945)

Shimomura Toratarō (1902–1995)

Nishitani Keiji (1900–1990)

Authors of Expository Chapters

Fujita Masakatsu, Kyoto University, Kyoto, Japan

Nakaoka Narifumi, Ōsaka University, Ōsaka, Japan

Akamatsu Tsunehiro, Shinshū University, Matsumoto, Japan

Nishikawa Tomio (1927-2010)

Ōnishi Masamichi, Bukkyō University, Kyoto, Japan

Imaizumi Motoji, Ehime University, Matsuyama, Japan

Takeda Atsushi (1934-2005)

Keta Masako, Kyoto University, Kyoto, Japan

Kosaka Kunitsugu, Nihon University, Tokyo, Japan

John C. Maraldo, Jacksonville, USA

Notes on the Translation

- All Japanese names are written in the order they appear in Japanese (family name followed by given name).
- Foreign words appearing in the original text have been left in their original language with a translation provided in square brackets when the meaning in English is not obvious. When an English word appears in the original text this is noted in the translation.
- Titles of Japanese books are transliterated and printed in italics with the original Japanese title and an English translation added in square brackets the first time they are mentioned. In some cases, they are then referred to by their English translation alone. Titles of essays and articles in their English translation are given in quotation marks rather than italics.

Part I
Nishida Kitarō

Chapter 1
Place (1)

[場所 (1)]

Nishida Kitarō

Epistemology today distinguishes three separate aspects [of knowledge], object [対象], content [内容], and act [作用], and discusses their relationship. Yet it seems to me that all that is being considered at the root of this distinction is the opposition between epistemic acts [認識作用] moving through time and the objects that transcend them. To say that objects relate to one another, constitute a single system, and maintain themselves, however, requires that we also consider both that which maintains this system itself and that within which this system is established and wherein it is situated [or: emplaced; 於てある]. That which is must be situated in something, otherwise we cannot make the distinction between "to be" [有る] and "to not be" [無い]. Logically it should be possible to distinguish between the terms of a relationship and the relationship itself, and between that which unifies a relationship and that wherein the relationship is situated. Even when we consider acts, to the extent that in addition to thinking of the "I" [我] as a pure unity of acts we think of this "I" in opposition to the "non-I," there must be something that envelops this opposition between the "I" and the "non-I" and that establishes the so-called phenomena of consciousness. In accordance with the term used in Plato's *Timeaus*, I will call this thing that we may regard as the receptacle of ideas [ἰδέα; forms], "place"[場所]. Needless to say, what I refer to as "place" is not the same as what Plato refers to as "space" or "receptacle" [χώρα].

Although this is an extremely simple way of thinking, we think of physical bodies as existing and interacting in space, and this idea has also long been present in the study of physics. Alternatively, one may think that without any objects there would be no space, that space is nothing more than the relationship between objects, or even, as Lotze maintained, that space is situated within objects. But in

---

Translated from the Japanese by Robert Chapeskie and revised by John W. M. Krummel.

K. Nishida

Fig. 1.1 Nishida Kitaro (1870–1945). Courtesy of Ishikawa NISHIDA KITARO Museum of Philosophy

order to think this, one must believe that the relating things and the relationship are a single thing, something such as physical space, for example. But that which permits the relationship between physical space and physical space cannot itself be physical space. What is required is a place wherein physical space is situated. Or one might say that when that which stands in relation is reduced to the relationship's system, we can conceive of a single complete thing established upon itself, and have no need to think of anything further such as a place wherein it is situated. But to be precise, for any kind of relationship to be established as a relationship, there must be things given as its terms. When it comes to the form of knowledge [知識], for instance, there must be content. And even if we consider them in unison as a single complete entity [(form and content)], there must be some place in which this sort of thing is reflected. Alternatively one may say that this is nothing more than a subjective concept. However, if we are to think of objects as transcending subjective acts and standing on their own, the place wherein objective objects are established cannot be subjective and must itself be transcendent. And when we look at acts by objectifying them we see them by reflecting them upon the place of thought objects. If we are to consider meaning itself as objective, the place wherein it arises must also be objective. Or it may be said that this sort of thing is no more than a simple nothing [無]. In the world of thought, however, even nothing has an objective significance.

When we think about things there must be something like a place in which they are reflected. We can begin by thinking of this as a "field of consciousness" [意識の野]. To be conscious of something it must be reflected in the field of consciousness. We must distinguish, however, between the reflected phenomena of consciousness and the field of consciousness in which they are reflected. One might assert that there is nothing like a "field of consciousness" beyond the sequence of phenomena of consciousness. But in contrast to the phenomena of consciousness transitioning moment by moment, there must also be an unmoving field of consciousness. The phenomena of consciousness inter-relate and follow one another through this field. One might also think of this as a single point we refer to as the "I." Nevertheless, when distinguishing between the inside and outside of consciousness, my phenomena of consciousness must fall within the scope of my consciousness. The "I" in this sense must be something that envelops my phenomena of consciousness. By starting from this perspective of consciousness we are able to recognize the field of consciousness. Acts of thinking, too, are acts of our consciousness. The content of thought is first of all something reflected in our field of consciousness, and objects are indicated through that content. Epistemologists today distinguish between content and object [of knowledge], and think of the former as immanent and the latter as transcendent. They think of objects as transcending all acts to stand on their own. Here we move beyond the field of consciousness. And we think there is nothing like a field of consciousness for objects. But in order for consciousness and object to relate, there must be something that envelops both within itself. There must be something like a place that connects them. What is it that allows for this relation? Even if one says that objects transcend all acts of consciousness, if objects existed completely outside of consciousness we would be unable to think from within our own consciousness that its content indicates objects, and we could not even say that objects transcend acts of consciousness. The Kantian school conceives of a subjectively transcendental subject, that is, "consciousness in general" [意識一般 *Bewußtsein überhaupt*], in opposition to the world of epistemic objects. But can we say that as epistemic subjects we transcend consciousness and step outside the field of consciousness? This may be the limit of the field of consciousness, but the field does not disappear. The field of consciousness conceived psychologically is something that has already been conceived and is nothing more than a type of object. The field of consciousness that is conscious of this field of consciousness, even at its limit, is incapable of transcending that limit. Even behind the field of consciousness that we think of as real, there is always something that transcends reality. The so-called field of consciousness as delimited by experimental psychology is simply nothing more than the domain of sensations that can be measured. But consciousness must include meaning. The consciousness that recalls yesterday must envelop yesterday in its meaning. For this reason we can speak of consciousness as the self-determination of something universal. We can regard even sensory consciousness as a phenomenon of consciousness to the extent that it contains a capacity for reflection after the fact. If we are to regard the universal as incapable of arriving at its extremity, it would be an extremity that the individual fails to reach as well.

The Kantian school conceives of knowledge [認識] as involving the unification of matter through form. Behind this idea, however, lies the assumption of the subject's constitutive act. Form is here conceived as belonging to the subject. Otherwise the meaning of knowledge would not obtain. That which is constituted simply through form is nothing more than a trans-oppositional object [超対立的対象]. And the constitution of objective matter by objective form would be an objective act but would fail to give rise to the meaning of knowledge. We cannot immediately identify the opposition between form and matter and that between subject and object. The constitution of the object of judgment would have to involve a different sort of opposition than the opposition between form and matter. What constitutes the direct content of judgment must be something like its truth or falsity. The place that establishes the opposition between form and matter must be different from the place that establishes the opposition between truth and falsity. At the place that establishes knowledge, not only must form and content be distinguishable, but their separation and combination must be free. In this case we can think of subjectivity as something added from the outside to the trans-oppositional object. Lask also thinks of a completely alogical [非論理的] object of experience as the fundamental matter, in contrast to logical form that is fundamental. But as Lask himself recognized, knowing itself is also an experience. Even if we speak of the content of experience as alogical matter, it is not the same as so-called sensory matter [感覚的質料]. The content of experience is better described as trans-logical than alogical, and is even better described as peri-logical [包論理的]. We can say the same about artistic and moral experience as well. The perspective of knowledge, too, must be one manner in which experience reflects the self within the self. Knowledge is nothing other than experience giving form to the self within the self. The oppositional relationship between form and matter is established in the place of experience. That which endlessly reflects the self within the self, and which contains infinite being by becoming itself nothing, here establishes the so-called subject/object opposition as the true "I". We cannot describe this as same or different, being or nothing, and neither can we determine it by so-called logical forms. Instead it is the place that establishes logical forms. No matter how far you stretch form, you cannot break through and emerge beyond it. The true form of forms must be the place of forms. Aristotle's *De Anima* as well, following Plato's Academy, conceived of the mind as "a place of forms." This sort of a mirror that illuminates itself is not simply a place where knowledge arises; emotion and volition are established here as well. When we speak of the content of experience, in most cases we have already intellectualized it, and consequently we can think of it as alogical matter. True experience must have the standpoint of complete nothing, a standpoint of freedom separate from knowledge. Volitional and emotional content is reflected in this place as well. It is for this reason that we can think of knowledge, emotion, and will as all being phenomena of consciousness.

If we consider place as I have described it above, it seems that acts are relationships that arise between reflected objects and the place where they are reflected. When we consider only that which is simply reflected, it is nothing more than a mere object with no activity of any kind. But behind such objects, too, there must be a mirror that reflects them, a place where these objects exist. Of course, if this place was only a reflecting mirror and these objects were simply placed therein, we could not see objects at work. This is also why we can think of all things as epistemic objects [認識対象], utterly transcending all [our] acts, at the field of consciousness-in-general that reflects them by completely emptying itself. But if there is no connection at all between consciousness and object, we could not speak of its [the object's] reflection or its situatedness. We can thus think of acts of judgment as bridging this gap. Not only on the one hand can we think of objects as transcending acts, but on the other hand we must think of the field of consciousness as transcending acts and enveloping them within itself. When we conceive of the field of consciousness in general as including objects and expanding limitlessly, however, we can think of objects as occupying various positions within it and being reflected in various forms. At this point where the so-called world of meaning is established when objects are variously analyzed and abstracted, we can think of the act of judgment on the other hand to be the reflection of these objects in various positions and various relationships. Yet when the transcendent object and the field of consciousness in general are separated from each other and acts belong to neither, we can think of the so-called epistemic subject [認識主観] as a unifier of acts. If we think in the ordinary manner that things are situated in space, then, to the extent that we can think of thing and space to be distinct, we can think of things as standing in space in a variety of relationships and altering their form and position in various ways. Here we cannot help but think of something like force [力] outside of things and space. And if things possess force as their substance [本体], we can also conceive of physical space by attributing force to space. I would like to consider "knowing" by attributing it to the space of consciousness.

In place of traditional epistemology that takes as its starting point the idea of the subject/object opposition and considers cognition to be the composition of matter through form, I would like to begin with the idea of self-awareness that reflects the self within itself. I think that the fundamental significance of knowing is to reflect the self within itself. This extends from knowing the interior of the self to knowing what is outside. What is given in opposition to the self must, to begin with, be given by being situated within the self. Or we may think of the self as something like a unifying point, whereby knower and known, that is, subject and object, form and matter, stand mutually opposed within the so-called consciousness of the self. But in this case we cannot speak of the unifying point as a knower, for it is nothing more than something already objectified and known. It would be the same even if we considered a vector of limitless unity instead of this kind of unifying point. To know must first of all be to envelop within. But when what is enveloped is external to what envelops, it is nothing other than simply existing in the same way as when we think of matter as situated in space. When we can think of the enveloping and the enveloped to be a single thing, an infinite series [無限の系列] is established. And when we can conceive this single thing to contain matter within itself without limit, we can conceive of pure action, operating without end. Yet we cannot speak of this as being the knower. It is only when we can conceive of what is situated within this thing itself to be further enveloped that we can speak of knowing. Put in terms of the relationship between form and matter, to know is not simply a formal construction but must be an enveloping of the opposition of form and matter. If we regard matter, too, as a lower-level form, we can also speak of the knower as the form of forms. It would have to be a place that transcends pure forms and pure acts to establish them within itself. This is also why, as Lask asserts, we can conceive of the subject as the destroyer of objective objects. Just as physical bodies are thought to be separable within space, we can conceive of the objects of thought as separable within the place of thought. Just as bodies are divisible in space without limit in various senses, objects of thought are divisible in the place of thought. Alternatively, one might say that when thinking of the knower in the above manner, we will lose the significance of the subject/object opposition and that it becomes meaningless to speak of acts or unity in the subject, or even that the very meaning of a subject will disappear. At present I cannot enter deeply into this issue. But in cases where things are merely situated in space, space and things are external to each other, and space presumably would have no sense of a subject. But when the substantiality of things shifts to the relationship of the place wherein they are situated, things are reduced to force. With force, however, we would have to conceive of something like its substance, and with this relationship there would have to be its terms. Where should we seek this substance? If we seek it in the original things we are considering, there would remain things that cannot be completely reduced to force. If we fall back on space itself, we have no choice but to conceive of something like points as the terms of spatial relationships. But if the substance of relationships is simply something like points, force would have to disappear. That which truly envelops relationships of force must be something like a field of force. And upon the field of force every line must have a direction. Even in the place of cognition that can be thought of as enveloping pure acts, every phenomenon must have a direction. We think that we lose the meaning of a subject/object opposition when conceiving the knower as that which envelops, because we think of a place that is external to what is

1 Place (1)

contained [within it]. A simply empty space would fail to truly envelop physical phenomena. What truly envelops various objects must be that which reflects the form of itself within itself, just as when various forms are established in space. Put this way, one might assert that the sense of being "situated" is lost, and that of a place that envelops objects and expands without limit also disappears. But in a field of consciousness that exists separately, even while enveloping all objects of knowledge, we can think of these two meanings as being combined.

If to know is to reflect the self within itself, and acts can be seen in the relationship between the place that reflects and that which is reflected, what becomes of things like Lask's so-called oppositionless object [*gegensatzloser Gegenstand*] that transcend all action? This kind of object must be situated in something as well. When we recognize something that is, we do so in contrast to that which is not. But even what is not that is recognized in contrast to what is is still an oppositional being. True nothing must be that which envelops such being and nothing; it must be the place wherein being/nothing are established. A nothing that negates and opposes being is not true nothing; true nothing must be what constitutes the background of being. For example, that which is not red in contrast to red is still a color. That which has a color, that in which a color is situated, must be something that is not a color. Red is situated in it, and that which is not red must also be something situated in it. To the extent that we delimit it as an epistemic object, I think the same idea can be extended to the relationship between being and nothing. In this way we can think of the "place of emplacement" as a thing in the case of something like colour, and in the manner described by Aristotle we can say that qualities [ποιόν] are situated in things. But in that case it would mean that things possess attributes while losing the significance of a place. In contrast, when we think of things as dissolving completely into relationships, we can think of what contains being and nothing as a single act. But behind the act we must still conceive of latent being. Although we can speak of a substanceless activity or pure act in contrast to substantial being, once this latency is removed from the act there would no longer be an act. We would still have to conceive of a place in the background where such latent being is established. When we think of a thing as possessing a certain quality, the opposing quality cannot be included within it. That which acts, however, must contain opposites within it, and that which changes transforms into its opposite. For this reason, we can think of the place that includes being/nothing itself to be immediately an act. For a single act to be seen, however, a singular genus concept must be determined at its foundation. Opposites can be seen only within a single genus concept. Perhaps we can say that the place lying behind acts is not really nothing, that is, not merely a place, but a place containing a certain content, or a place that has been determined. In an act being and nothing are combined, but we cannot say that a nothing envelops being. In a true place a thing can transition not only into its opposite but also into its contradiction. It must be possible for it to go beyond its genus concept. A true place is not simply a place of transformation but a place of creation and destruction. When we transcend even genus concepts and enter the place of creation and destruction, the meaning of acting disappears as well and there is nothing but seeing. As long as we view the genus concept as place, we cannot eliminate latent being, and we do nothing more than simply look at that which acts. But in the place that reflects even genus concepts we not only see that which acts but also see that which envelops the activity. A truly pure act is not that which acts but that which envelops activity. Actual being must come first, not latent being. Here we are able to see the oppositionless object that combines form and matter.

We can think of this oppositionless object as something that has completely transcended the field of consciousness. But if it is something completely outside of the subject, how is it reflected within the subject and made the end of epistemic acts? I think that even such objects do not lie outside of the field of consciousness in the sense of something like a place; they are always undergirded by a place. When we think of place as simply an oppositional nothing that negates being, we cannot help but think of objects as transcending the field of consciousness and as existing on their own. What is normally referred to as the standpoint of consciousness is the above-mentioned standpoint of nothing in opposition to being. When nothing in opposition to being as a single genus concept subsumes everything, this nothing becomes a single latent being. When we take the standpoint of an endless nothing that negates all being, that is, when the nothing itself stands independent of being, there emerges the standpoint of consciousness. But we can think of all being as reflected and analyzed within that standpoint transcending all being. But the true nothing would not be such an oppositional nothing but that which envelops both being and nothing. To the extent that it is an oppositional nothing, even a nothing that negates all manner of being would still be a kind of being. Even if it goes beyond a determinate genus concept, to the extent that it is something conceived, it cannot escape a single genus-conceptual determination. As a result, we recognize therein the significance of a certain type of latent being in the establishment of a mind-only metaphysics [唯心論的形而上学]. True consciousness must be that which reflects even consciousness as described above. So-called consciousness is still nothing more than something that has been objectified. The true place of nothing must be that which transcends even the opposition between being and nothing in every sense to establish that opposition within itself. We see true consciousness only when the genus concept has been ripped asunder. Even the oppositionless transcendent object fails to transcend consciousness in this sense. Rather, it is seen as oppositionless only by being reflected in this place. Oppositionless objects are objects of our moral consideration, and are the standard for unequivocally determining the so-called content of judgment. If we were to think contrary to them, our thinking would inevitably fall into contradiction, and thinking would thus destroy itself. There is no way to conceive of an oppositionless object divorced from this definition. It may perhaps be thought that when we see such objects we transcend the field of subjective consciousness wherein oppositional content obtains. But this cannot be anything other than progressing from the standpoint of oppositional nothing to the standpoint of true nothing, a progression from a place that merely reflects the shadows of things to the place wherein things are situated. We are not discarding the so-called standpoint of consciousness; instead we are thoroughly penetrating it. True negation must be the negation of negation, otherwise even consciousness in general could not be distinguished from unconsciousness and the meaning of consciousness would be lost. We cannot avoid thinking in this way, for otherwise, when it can be said that we have fallen into a contradiction, this field of consciousness must be something that reflects so-called transcendent objects within itself. Because this standpoint as the negation of negation is the true nothing, it can be said to negate everything reflected in the place of oppositional nothing. By truly emptying itself, the field of consciousness is able to reflect objects just as they are. In this case it may be possible to think of objects as being situated in themselves, but if objects are simply situated in themselves they cannot be the standard for so-called contents of consciousness. The place wherein objects are situated must also be the place wherein so-called consciousness is situated. When we see objects themselves we may think of this to be intuition, but intuition must also be consciousness. So-called intuition, as well, cannot be separated from the field of consciousness that sees contradiction itself. Normally intuition and thought are believed to be utterly distinct, but in order for an intuition to maintain itself there must indeed be something like a "place of emplacement." But this is the same place where thought is situated. When intuition is reflected in the place where it is situated it becomes the content of thought. Intuition must also be included in what is called concrete thought. I do not think that consciousness can ever be thoroughly separated from the background of universal concepts. Universal concepts are always playing the role of a reflecting mirror. Even when we adopt the standpoint of intuition, conceivable as subject-object unity, consciousness is not separated from universal concepts; on the contrary, it reaches their zenith. To break through and beyond universal concepts from a standpoint that is conscious of contradictions implies objectified universal concepts. In this way they are nothing more than what are determined and particular, and do not even possess the sense of knowing. The place that reflects intuition must immediately be the place that reflects the contradiction of concepts.

There may be many arguments against acknowledging something like a place or field of consciousness behind intuition, but if intuition means simply that there is neither subject [主] nor object [客] then it would be nothing more than a simple object [対象]. The mention of intuition already implies that knower and known have been distinguished and moreover combined. And here "the knower" does not mean simply that which constructs or is active; the knower must be that which envelops the known, or indeed that which reflects it inward. To speak of subject-object unity, or the disappearance of subject and object, is simply to say that place becomes truly nothing, or that it becomes a mere reflecting mirror. Although the particular is thought to be objective while what is universal is thought to be simply subjective, the particular is subjective as the content of knowledge, and if we admit the objective givenness of the particular, we can also admit objective givenness in regard to the universal as well. In Kant's philosophy this is thought of as simply an a priori form, but at the root of this idea is the assumption that objective givens are constituted through the subject's constitutive act. But to constitute is not immediately to know. To know must be to reflect the self within itself. The true a priori is that which constructs the content of the self within the self. As a result we may think of a domain category (*Gebietskategorie*), such as that described by Lask, existing outside of the forms of constitution. We see universal concepts determined in the realm of our cognitive objects by means of this place determining itself. What are called universal concepts are instances of place determining or objectifying itself. In Plato's philosophy the universal was conceived to be objective reality, but it did not go so as far as to conceive the universal that truly envelops everything as necessarily being the place that establishes everything. As a result place was thought to be un-real and conceived of as nothing. But this place must also be at the bottom of the intuition of ideas [ἰδέα] themselves. Even the loftiest ideas are nothing more than determined, particular things; and even the idea of the good cannot escape being relative. When we think of the place of mere oppositional nothing as the place of consciousness, we think this place vanishes in intuition and we need not acknowledge a further place wherein intuition is situated. It seems to me, however, that this place envelops intuition itself rather than being enveloped within that intuition. Not only intuition but volition and action are situated therein as well. And this is why we can think of will and acts as pertaining to consciousness. Descartes thought of extension and thought as two kinds of substances, with motion as a mode of extension on the one hand and volition as a mode of thought on the other. But in this sense true extension must be something like physical space, while true thought must be a place in the manner described above. To be conscious and to reflect in the world of epistemic objects might be conceived as immediately identical, but in a strict sense emotional and volitional content cannot be reflected in the world of epistemic objects. The world of epistemic objects can never escape the sense of being a determinate place. The place wherein emotion and volition are reflected must be an even deeper and broader place. Consciousness of emotional and volitional content is not epistemic cognition. The field of consciousness common to cognition, emotion, and volition does not belong to either of them. It expands without limit by enveloping even so-called intuition. Consciousness in its deepest sense must be the place of true nothing. That which reflects conceptual knowledge cannot escape being the place of relative nothing. We already stand upon the place of true nothing in so-called intuition. But the place that establishes emotion and volition must be an even deeper and broader place of nothing. It is for this reason that we can think of an unfettered nothing lying at the root of our will (Fig. 1.1).

Nishida Kitarō (1870–1945). Born in Ishikawa Prefecture. Became an assistant professor at Kyoto University in 1910 (full professor in 1913) after graduating from Tokyo Imperial University's Faculty of Letters and teaching at Dai-shi High School and Gakushūin. During his time at Kyoto University he published numerous works, including Zen no kenkyū [『善の研究』 An Inquiry into the Good] (1911) and Hatarakumono kara mirumono e [『働くものから見るもの へ』 From That Which Acts to That Which Sees] (1927), and served as a mentor to many disciples. His essay "Place" was published in Volume 123 of the journal Tetsugaku kenkyū [『哲学研究』 Philosophical Studies] in 1926 and included in From That Which Acts to That Which Sees the following year. It is also included in Nishida Kitarō zenshū [『西田幾多郎全集』 Complete Works of Nishida Kitarō] Vol. 4 (Iwanami Shoten).

Chapter 2
The Scope of Nishida Kitarō's Theory of Place

[西田幾多郎の場所論の射程]

Fujita Masakatsu

2.1 The Duality of Nishida's Thought

Nishida Kitarō (1870–1945) was not by any means a systematic thinker. It was not that he did not aim to construct a system, but in devoting all his energies to resolving the problems he himself faced directly and those put to him by other philosophers, he did not organize these efforts into a single, unified framework.

With the aim of coming to grips with Nishida's wide-ranging, diversely changing thought, Kōyama Iwao, one of Nishida's disciples, published a book entitled *Nishida tetsugaku* [『西田哲学』 *Nishidian Philosophy*] in 1935. More than a mere explication of Nishida's thought, this text was an attempt to break it down and reassemble it from a systematic perspective. Perhaps this made the non-systematic nature of Nishida's thinking even more apparent. In his forward to Kōyama's book, Nishida explains this shortcoming: "It is not that I did not have this 'construction of a system' as one of my aims; it was simply beyond my ability. I will always be a mere miner. I do not have time to refine the excavated ore. Nor do I have the skill to arrange it neatly in a display window." (*Nishida Kitarō zenshū* [『西田幾多郎全集』 *Complete Works of Kitarō Nishida*] Vol. XIII, p. 221—hereafter cited with just volume and page number.)

This word "miner" very aptly illustrates Nishida's contemplative stance or "style." But Nishida was not always digging; at times he rested for a moment to look back and survey his progress. These reflections provide us the best clues to

---

Translated from the Japanese by Robert Chapeskie and revised by John W. M. Krummel.

M. Fujita (✉)
Professor Emeritus
Kyoto University, Kyoto, Japan
e-mail: fujita.masakatsu.84w@st.kyoto-u.ac.jp

© Springer Nature Singapore Pte Ltd. 2018
M. Fujita (ed.), *The Philosophy of the Kyoto School*,
https://doi.org/10.1007/978-981-10-8983-1_2

forming an accurate overview of Nishida's thought, which is difficult to grasp and progressed through various developments and transformations.

For example, when the new edition of *Zen no kenkyū* [『善の研究』 *An Inquiry into the Good*] was published in 1936, reflecting on his own thought up to that point, Nishida wrote, "In *Jikaku ni okeru chokkan to hansei* [『自覚に於ける直観と反省』 *Intuition and Reflection in Self-awareness*] the standpoint of pure experience progressed to the standpoint of absolute will through Fichte's fact/act [Tathandlung], and in the latter half of *Hatarakumono kara mirumono e* [『働くものから見るものへ』 *From that which Acts to that which Sees*], through Greek philosophy I changed course completely and reached the idea of 'place' [場所]. I think this gave me a key to 'logicizing' [論理化] my own thought. The idea of 'place' was concretized as the 'dialectical universal [弁証法的一般者]', and the standpoint of the 'dialectical universal' was made immediate as the standpoint of 'active intuition [行為的直観]'. What I referred to as the world of direct experience [直接経験の世界] or the world of pure experience [純粋経験の世界] in this book I now think of as the world of historical reality [歴史的実在の世界]. It is indeed the world of active intuition, the world of poiesis, that is the true world of pure experience" (Vol. I, pp. 6–7).

We can see in these words the duality of Nishida's thought. On the one hand, he was able to achieve a series of transformations in the manner just described, moving from the standpoint of "pure experience" to the standpoint of "absolute will," and then from the standpoint of "place" to the standpoint of the "dialectical universal" or "active intuition." On the other hand, however, we must also take note of his statement that "it is indeed the world of active intuition, the world of poiesis, that is the true world of pure experience." Here it can be said that Nishida recognized something clearly consistent within his own thought.

In the forward to Kōyama's book cited above, Nishida expresses this duality as follows. "Ever since *Zen no kenkyū,* my thought has started neither from the subject nor from the object, but rather from a point preceding the subject-object division. Even today, this has not changed. Struggle after struggle, my thinking has simply undergone a variety of changes regarding how to grab hold of this direct, concrete standpoint as philosophy and how to consider various issues from that standpoint." (Vol. XII, p. 219).

It can be said that Nishida's stance of returning to that which is most direct and concrete, described above as "preceding the subject-object division," and attempting to grasp the matter as a whole from this vantage point, remained unchanged from his earliest work to his twilight years. But we can also say that Nishida's thought changed dramatically concerning how to seize what is most direct and concrete, and how, on this basis, to grasp the matter in question as a whole.

2.2 The Position of the Idea of "Place" Within Nishidian Philosophy

As indicated by his statement in the forward to *Zen no kenkyū*, "with a complete about-face I arrived at the idea of 'place'," we can consider the establishment of the idea of "place" as the greatest turning point in Nishida's transformation and development. And as Nishida himself says, we can regard his thought concerning the "dialectical universal" as having the character of the "concretization" of his idea of "place," and his contemplation concerning "active intuition" as "making immediate" his thoughts on the "dialectical universal." In other words, the development of his philosophy from the standpoint of "place" can be thought of as a deepening of this key idea.

The first person to refer to Nishida's doctrine as "Nishidian philosophy" [西田哲学] was Sōda Kiichirō, who had studied under Rickert and had been strongly influenced by Neo-Kantian philosophy. In the same year (1926) that Nishida published his essay "Basho" [「場所」 "Place"], Sōda produced an essay entitled "Nishida tetsugaku no hōhō ni tsuite—Nishida hakase no oshie wo kou" [「西田哲学の方法について—西田博士の教えを乞う」 "On the Methodology of Nishidian Philosophy: Requesting an Explanation from Dr. Nishida"], in which he unsparingly critiqued Nishida's philosophy from the Neo-Kantian standpoint. But on the other hand, he also positively acknowledged that in both this essay ("Basho") and in an earlier essay "Hatarakumono" [「働くもの」 "That which Acts"], Nishida "has entered upon a stage where he can be said to have established a single system." We might regard his reference to Nishida's doctrine as "Nishidian philosophy" to also be an indication of his having perceived the maturity of Nishida's thought in these essays.

In response Nishida immediately published an essay entitled "Sōda hakase ni kotau" [「左右田博士に答う」 "Answering Dr. Sōda"] (1927) in which he replies to Sōda's critique. But in its opening he writes, "Regarding the conclusion of "Basho", I think I arrived at a slightly different idea than I had up to that point" (Vol. IV, p. 290), acknowledging that the essay "Basho" had been a turning point. In fact we can indeed say that this essay possesses a very important significance when it comes to considering the development of Nishida's thought.

One point we must note when trying to understand Nishida's concept of "place" or his "standpoint of place," however, is that these ideas were by no means fixed. Nishida's thinking concerning "place" was constantly being revised and deepened.

In other words, Nishida's idea of "place" was not established all at once and completed with the essay "Basho". On the one hand we can say that it was shaped little by little across the various writings collected in *Hatarakumono kara mirumono e* [『働くものから見るものへ』] (1927), and further developed through sculpting and polishing in *Ippansha no jikakuteki taikei* [『一般者の自覚的体系』 *The Self-aware System of Universals*] (1930) and *Mu no jikakuteki gentei* [『無の自覚的限定』 *The Self-aware Determination of Nothing*] (1932). Nishida's final work was "Bashoteki ronri to shūkyōteki sekaikan" [「場所的論理と宗教的世界

観」 "Placial logic and the Religious Worldview"] (1945), and, as the title of this text indicates, Nishida continued to think about "place" and "placial logic" up until the final years of his life.

Even when regarding the relationship between the standpoint of "pure experience" and the standoint of "place," we ought not to see only change and transformation. It has been asserted that the concept of "pure experience," or the ideas based upon it, rapidly disappeared from Nishida's thought following *Zen no kenkyū*. Yet we can say that Nishida's contemplation always returned to the "concrete standpoint of immediacy" in order to obtain an overarching vantage point. In "Chokusetsu ni ataerarerumono" [「直接に与えられるもの」 "That which is Directly Given"], the first essay in *Hatarakumono kara mirumono e*, Nishida expresses this in the following manner while using the phrase "pure experience [純粋経験]." "What ought to be called truly given experience or pure experience,…must be thought of as possessing an unlimited content. The further we delve into these depths, the more these given realities are present. Subjectively speaking it is the self that cannot be objectified, objectively speaking it is the directly given that resists complete reflection. Here there is an intuition of the unification of subject and object, a consciousness of pure activity, and the source of all knowledge" (Vol. IV, p. 26). It can be said that in all of the essays collected in *Hatarakumono kara mirumono e* Nishida deepens his contemplation concerning what he calls "pure experience," that is, "the self that cannot be objectified" or "the directly given that resists complete reflection."

2.3 The "Logicization" of Thought and the Philosophy of "Place"

On the other hand, however, Nishida has of course also stated, as we have seen, that "with a complete about-face [he] arrived at the idea of 'place.'" He clearly acknowledges a turn in his own thinking. One clue to understanding what sort of change this was can be found in the fact that immediately after these words Nishida adds, "I think this gave me a key to 'logicizing' [論理化] my own thought." These words indicate that at the time Nishida was keenly aware of the necessity of "logicizing" or "providing an overarching logic for" his own thought.

We can assume that behind this stance lay his self-awareness of the inadequacies in his own thought. Nishida expresses this in the preface to *Zen no kenkyū*: "This book's standpoint is that of consciousness, and may perhaps be thought of as psychologistic [心理主義的]. It cannot be helped if it is criticized as such" (Vol I, p. 6). If we take what he writes in the preface to *Hatarakumono kara mirumono e* as a clue, we can think of this as referring to the fact that he had not made sufficiently clear the relationship between experience as the immediate given and conceptual knowledge expressed through judgment.

One might say that Nishida took as his pressing task the clarification of this relationship and "logicizing" of his thought. In thinking about this problem, he focused on Aristotle's concept of the "substratum" [ὑποκείμενον; 基体].

For example, in "Naibuchikaku ni tsuite" [「内部知覚について」 "On Internal Perception"], the fourth essay in *Hatarakumono kara mirumono e*, after noting that Aristotle's "substratum" is "that which is always a subject and never a predicate," or in other words "an individual that is one, never two," Nishida says the following concerning the relationship between substratum and judgment. "The substratum that is always the subject and never a predicate must be a unification of predicates without limit, that is, it must be the limitless unification of judgments. That which unifies judgments must be something beyond judgment. It is the object towards which our acts of judgment are always intentional but which they never reach. I consider this thing to be intuitional [直覚的]" (Vol. IV p. 97).

This passages shows that Aristotle's concept of "substratum" as an individual played an important role in the "logicization" of Nishida's thought, but at the same time it also shows that he attempted to understand it in his own unique sense. Here Nishida emphasizes that at the root of the individual there is always the "intuition of the irrational". It is Nishida's belief that the individual comes indeed from a "conceptualization [概念化]" of this sort of intuition.

Nishida understood the "substratum" not simply as a universal, but rather as something "without action" that is beyond all action and any kind of judgment—the "I" or "self" that is at the root of action and makes action possible. This is "the substratum that does not enter into action" but at the same time "knows the self" or "sees the self." In other words, it is that which maintains the self by "reflecting the self within itself." Judgment carries the meaning of the "self-expression [自己表現]" or "self-awareness [自覚]" of this kind of substratum.

As is widely known, Nishida had already discussed the problem of "self-awareness" in detail in *Jikaku ni okeru chokkan to hansei* [『自覚に於ける直観と反省』 *Intuition and Reflection in Self-awareness*] (1917). It can be surmised that he came to focus on "self-awareness" because, having encountered Neo-Kantian thought, he became conscious of the fact that thinking cannot simply be settled under "pure experience [純粋経験]." How to integrate the autonomy of thought with the idea that direct experience is the only reality became the biggest question for Nishida. What he then came to focus on was "self-awareness." For while "self-awareness" is reflection on the self, at the same time it is itself a single intuition. To put it another way, this was his focus because "reflecting the self within the self" as such is an act of endless self-development [自己発展].

Having obtained this understanding of "self-awareness," in section six of "Naibuchikaku ni tsuite" [「内部知覚について」 "On Internal Perception"], Nishida states that mental acts are, in a strict sense, "that which constructs the self from within the self," and writes as follows: "In our self-awareness, there is no self before the self knowing itself; there is no self before the self acts. The content of the self emerges through the activity of the self" (Vol. IV, p. 127). We can take this understanding of "self-awareness" to be a direct adoption of what was set out in *Jikaku ni okeru chokkan to hansei*. But following this Nishida asks, "In what sort of object-realm does the content of the self develop?" His answer is that "the self reflects the self within itself. The mirror that reflects the self must also be the self itself. It is not projecting the shadow of the self upon things" (Vol. IV, p. 127).

What is notable in the essay "Naibuchikaku ni tsuite" is how Nishida directs his attention in this way toward the place wherein self-awareness obtains. Of course, we can also say that the structure of self-awareness that reflects the self "within the self" already has "place-like" characteristics from the start. It is nevertheless very significant that he directs his attention explicitly to the place wherein the self reflects itself, that is, the place-nature [場所性] of "within the self [自己の中に]" in contrast to "upon things [物の上]." Following the passage cited above, he continues: "'Situated in the self' must be added for the consciousness of self-awareness to obtain. Self-awareness is the oneness of the 'I' that knows, the 'I' that is known, and the place in which the 'I' knows the 'I'" (Vol. IV, p. 127). Nishida here uses "place" with his own unique meaning for the first time.

In this way the formation of Nishida's idea of "place" was closely tied to his taking up the problem of the placial character of "self-awareness." And we can take as its premise his adoption of the concept of a "substratum" and his own unique understanding of it. Nishida expresses the essence of self-awareness, whereby the "I" as a "substratum that does not enter into action" maintains itself and sees itself by reflecting the self within itself, with the statement that "what transcends and envelops the I is the I itself" (Vol. IV pp. 128–9). It seems inevitable that Nishida's attention would be directed towards the place-nature of self-awareness expressed in the phrase "situated in the self" given his understanding of the relationship between "the I" and "that which transcends the I" as this kind of "envelopment." Self-awareness is here assessed anew, no longer as the endless activity of self-development or self-creation, but as a structure wherein the substratum that does not enter into any action whatsoever reflects the self and sees the self within itself.

2.4 That Which Becomes a Predicate but Never a Subject

What is perhaps most striking about Nishida's "logicization" of thought is the fact that he directs his focus toward subsumptive judgments [包摂判断] or the relationship of subsumption between the universal and the particular. In "Hatarakumono" [「働くもの」 "That which Acts"], an essay written before "Basho", Nishida writes as follows: "Knowledge, in its strictest sense, is judicative knowledge.... we may say that the essence of judgment is the subsumption of subject that is particular under predicate that is universal, and that subsumptive judgment is the purest form of judgment" (Vol. IV p. 177).

In line with Aristotle's understanding of the substratum as "that which becomes a subject but never a predicate", Nishida first tried to uncover that which transcends judgment to constitute it through its self-determination in "the direction indicated by the subject" (Vol. IV p. 177). Eventually, however, contrary to Aristotle he came to assert that "the transcendent that is the foundation of judgment" is to be found not in the direction of the subject but in the direction of the predicate. We see reflected here Nishida's idea that the truly transcendent that becomes the foundation of judgment is "consciousness" encountered when advancing the subsumptive relationship between particular and general, subject and predicate, as far in the direction of the predicate as possible. And what we find at the extremity of this subsumptive relationship—what Nishida, inverting Aristotle's phrase, expressed as "that which becomes the predicate but never the subject"—is nothing other than what he refers to as "place." Reflecting on his essay "Basho" in In "Sōda hakase ni kotau" Nishida writes as follows: "When I regarded the predicate aspect of subsumptive judgments as becoming a predicate but never a subject, this was the aspect of consciousness I referred to as 'place', and that 'to be' here is 'to know' was the final thought I arrived at in the essay 'Basho'" (Vol. IV p. 316).

This consciousness as place—not "consciousness that one is conscious of" but "consciousness that is conscious"—is what objectifies the self but can never itself be objectified. In other words, it can never be designated as a subject or conceptualized. In a similar vein, Nishida writes that "this thing [the true self] can neither be said to be the same nor different; it is neither being nor nothing, and cannot be determined by so-called logical forms. Rather it is the place that establishes logical forms" (Vol. IV p. 213). "Consciousness that is conscious" or "the true self" is not the content of knowledge but the place where knowledge is established, and can only be grasped as a "place." Nishida expresses this in particular with the use of the phrase "mere place" (Vol. IV p. 235). For it cannot be defined in any sense as a "being [有]". In this sense place is a "nothing [無]". But of course it is not a nothing that is distinguished from being or which opposes being. Even a nothing that negates all forms of being, to the extent that it has something opposing it, can still be seen as a kind of being. When Nishida refers to place as "the place of nothing", he means not a nothing that opposes being in this way, but rather "that which envelops being and nothing," "that which transcends them to establish them within itself" (Vol. IV p. 220). In other words, Nishida understands "place" in its two-fold nature that reflects itself within itself to establish the "being-nothing opposition" therein while itself remaining nothing (Fig. 2.1).

2.5 The Contemporary Relevance of the Philosophy of "Place"

When knowledge [知] acts as knowledge, the framework for its functioning is simultaneously given shape therein. Knowledge functions as knowledge only within this framework. This framework itself, however, cannot be cognized by means of knowledge. It is the condition that makes knowledge possible and does not belong to the domain of knowledge. Of course, knowledge possesses a dynamic

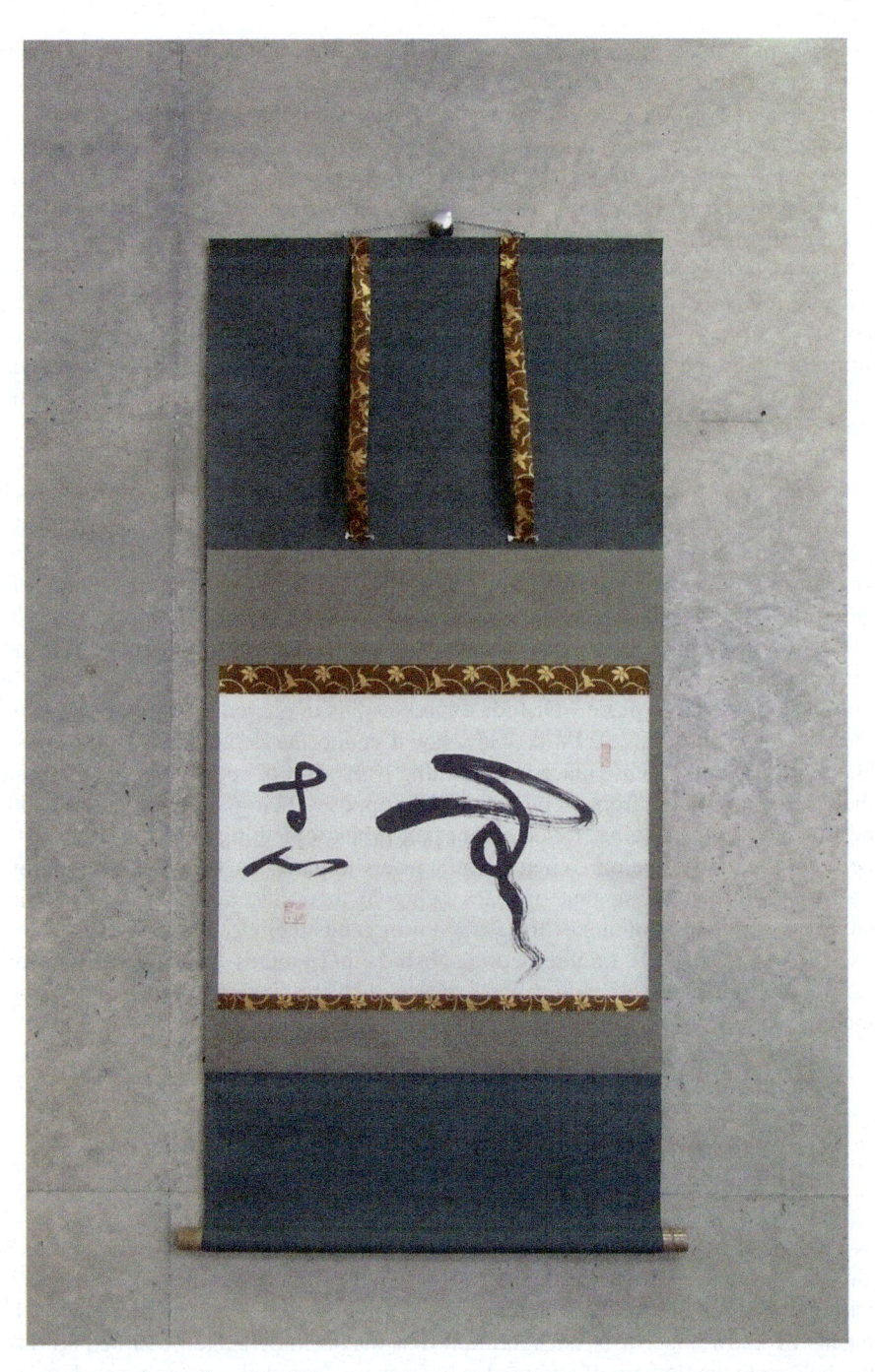

Fig. 2.1 "Nothingness". Calligraphy by Nishida Kitaro. "Sunshin" on the left is the nom de plume of Nishida. Courtesy of Ishikawa NISHIDA KITARO Museum of Philosophy

nature that attempts to bring it into its domain. But there always remains something therein that cannot be drawn into cognitive attempts at subsumption.

Today the issue of how to interrogate this framework or conditions of knowledge that cannot be objectified is addressed in a variety of ways. As examples of this kind of inquiry, the later Heidegger, for instance, spoke of a "step back" from the domain of presence or of beings, and under Heidegger's influence Merleau-Ponty in his later years tried to direct his gaze towards "the invisible" that accompanies "the visible," or that which in principle is hidden.

Nishida's aim, too, was to make this kind of framework of knowledge self-aware, and return to what precedes that framework. This intention is illustrated by the following passage from the forward to *Tetsugaku ronbunshū daisan* [『哲学論文集 第三』 *Philosophical Essays III*]: "Since *Zen no kenkyū*, my goal has been to see things and think about them from the most direct and fundamental standpoint possible" (Vol. IX p. 3).

Zen no kenkyū begins with the lines: "To experience is to know reality as it is. [It is] to know in accordance with reality without any artifice on the part of the self" (Vol. I, p. 9). The "artifice of the self" mentioned here refers to the framework belonging to our knowledge as its premise. To put it more concretely, we sketch out the structure of "subject-object" in advance and undergo various experiences on the basis of its assumption. It can be said that Nishida's theory of pure experience unfolds from his inquiry into the validity of this presupposition.

The cognition of objects on the basis of the "subject-object" structure can easily be tied to the hypostatization [実体化] of objects. Nishida's assertion in *Zen no kenkyū* that "the phenomenon of consciousness is the only reality" is a fundamental critique of this kind of hypostatization. His theory of place carries on this critique. In "Basho" he writes as follows: "When that which is the subject of judgment is place, anything possessing properties disappears and becomes an act without any substratum. And when place itself becomes nothing, acts themselves also vanish and everything becomes a shadow....We can no longer seek anywhere anything like a substance. All there is is that which casts its own shadow within itself by being itself nothing" (Vol. IV p. 247). Everything that is, everything that acts, is understood here as a *shadow*. Everything is understood as the self-determination (reflecting itself within itself) of a "place" that can never be objectified or externally determined.

There is a solid connection between taking states of affairs as involving the relationship between substances and attributes on the one hand, and the fundamental structure of "subject-predicate" seen in various European languages on the other. Nor is Aristotle's attempt to uncover what lies at the foundation of judgment in the "direction indicated by the subject" irrelevant. Traditionally, judgment and knowledge have been understood on the basis of "that which becomes the subject and never a predicate". We might describe Nishida's theory of place as an attempt to approach matters themselves through a dismantling of this "subject-oriented [主語的]" logic. In "Basho" Nishida asserts that a "predicative universal [述語的一般者]" can be thought to lie at the root of all judicative knowledge, and that judgments are established in its self-awareness. Nishida's theory of place aimed to construct this sort of "predicate-oriented logic" [述語的論理].

Nishida was aware that his understanding described above was tied to the traditions of the East. This is illustrated by the fact that he often referred to passages from Buddhist writings, particularly those of Zen, when explaining "the place of absolute nothing" [絶対無] in texts such as *Ippansha no jikakuteki taikei* [『一般者の自覚的体系』 *The Self-aware System of Universals*]. The following passage from the preface to *Hatarakumono kara mirumono e* can perhaps be seen as a direct expression of Nishida's interest in the traditions of the East. "It goes without saying that there is much to respect and learn from in the spectacular development of Western culture that takes form as being and formation as good, but at the root of the Eastern tradition that has nurtured our ancestors over millennia, does there not lie hidden something like seeing the form of the formless, or hearing the sound of the soundless? Our minds [こころ] unceasingly search for this. I would like to provide a philosophical grounding for this yearning" (Vol. IV, p. 6).

Behind his theory of place we can thus see Nishida's intention to philosophically or logically ground this desire that lies at the root of Eastern culture. It is not necessarily appropriate, however, to interpret this passage as one in which Nishida intends an apologetics for Eastern thought. We can see this from the fact that his idea of place was meant to give a foundation to knowledge. Nishida's intention was to problematize knowledge in connection to the invisible, the hidden, and the like to the extent that knowledge is problematized within the framework of knowledge. And we can indeed say that this is something that has been brought into question in a variety of ways in contemporary philosophy. In its relevance to contemporary themes, Nishida's thought presents an extremely important perspective.

Returning to his relationship with Eastern thought, Nishida's aim was not a *regression* to Eastern traditions. His intention rather was to transcend that framework, to release this thought into a wider domain of inquiry, and to concretize and develop within it what the traditions of the East possess as their latent potential. Nishida's focus on these traditions was thus both an attempt to revitalize them and at the same time an attempt to escape from them; his approach must not be understood as simply a return to Eastern thought. And it is in this approach to the Eastern traditions, too, that Nishida's thought remains relevant today.

Fujita Masakatsu Professor Emeritus, Kyoto University. Major works: *Tetsugaku no hinto* [『哲学のヒント』 *Philosophical Hints*] (Iwanami Shoten, 2013), *Nishida Kitarō* [『西田幾多郎』] (Iwanami Shoten, 2007), *Wakaki hegeru* [『若きヘーゲル』 *Young Hegel*] (Sōbunsha, 1986), "Philosophie und Religion beim jungen Hegel" (Bouvier, Bonn, 1985), etc.

Part II
Tanabe Hajime

Chapter 3
Clarifying the Meaning of the Logic of Species (1, 4)

[種の論理の意味を明らかにす(一、四)]

Tanabe Hajime

For the past several years I have worked out what has become "the logic of species" by taking up the issue of the logic of social being. My reasons for undertaking this are, in short, two: the practical and the logical. In the first case, I have come to believe that the ethnic unity and coercive power of the state, which have arisen together quite recently in various countries, include an element that can hardly be comprehended from the standpoint that tries to consider society as nothing but the reciprocal relation of individuals. Not only cannot the coercive power of ethnic states be adequately comprehended under the category of reciprocal relationship in what has been called formal sociology up until now, it cannot be comprehended in terms of the phenomenon of human relationships found in the hermeneutic phenomenology of today. I therefore think we must move beyond the states of psychological phenomena found in the individual's consciousness common to the above approaches, and not halt at so-called ontology but at the same time recognize ontological states. In other words, we must take what the French sociological school calls *chose* [物 thing] to be at the root of national societies. My idea was that society is not a relationship that simply proceeds from individuals or is established at the same time as individuals. Rather, unless it possessed a substratum [基体] unbounded by the generational replacement of individuals and to this extent exist as something preceding them, it would be unable to coercively unify them. And since the social substratum is something species-tribal [種族的], wherein individuals are born and included, I thought it should be called a "species [or: specific] substratum [種的基体]".

Taking the totem tribe as representative of the model of society in which this kind of species substratum appears most powerfully in its relative purity,

---

Translated from the Japanese by Robert Chapeskie and revised by John W. M. Krummel.

H. Tanabe

I attempted to understand the relationship between society and individuals obtained within it through Lévy-Bruhl's "principle of participation" [分有法則]. Of course, I did not believe that the complex ethnic communities of today could be adequately understood by reference to the structure of primitive totem tribes. But as Bergson's *Le deux sources de la morale et de la religion* [*Two Sources of Morality and Religion*] (1932), which was published around that time and that stimulated me, to say the least, in distinguishing so-called closed and open societies, conceived of something like a totem society as a representative of the former, I did not think it necessarily unreasonable to see in it the paradigm [or: model] of what I call the "species society." Furthermore, I believed that since totemism is not something that appears only once in primitive society and then disappears without a trace with the progression of social development, but rather remains extant even in contemporary society as something acknowledged by folklorists, it is not necessarily impermissible to consider the totem society as a comparatively pure form of the species society and to think of this as emblematic of the substrative aspect of ethnic societies. I took this approach because something as complicated as ethnic groups cannot easily be addressed by someone like myself who lacks specialized knowledge in sociology and has not intensively studied the methodology of this field, and because the aspect of this topic that I found problematic lies chiefly on the side of coercion over the individual. Seeing the religious myths and legends of primitive society gradually occupy an important position in recent nationalist cultural studies and their resurgence undertaken as a matter of intellectual policy, I cannot help but believe, now as before, that my amateur intuition was not necessarily mistaken. I want to make it perfectly clear, however, that my intention was not to ignore the work of experts in sociology from this perspective and to assert that ethnic groups could be fully comprehended by relying simply on a concept like that of the species substratum. In any case, in the sense laid out above I conceived the species substratum to be an indispensable moment of society.

Nevertheless, even if we take the coercive power of society over individuals as deriving from this species substratum, we cannot regard the moral obligation of individuals as completely serving this kind of natural coercion. For the rational individual, unless united with autonomy internal to the self, external coercion will not possess a morally binding force. For me, someone who cannot but believe in the rationality of the actual, the coercion of state society must be converted to autonomy through reason. It cannot be mere force but must also possess a rational basis. Reason as I conceive it, however, is not exhausted by the capacity for formal laws of the sort that allows actual individuals to escape every restraint that regulates their being and to simply impose upon themselves universal laws coming from within themselves as the criteria for the maxims of the will. The unrestricted universality of reason must not be simply an abstract universality but a concrete whole. This means that as a consequence of the ultimate regulation of the self as an objective being containing contradictions and falling into antimony, and by means of the self-returning to the nothing, the actual itself must subjectively fill the self as a

3 Clarifying the Meaning of the Logic of Species (1, 4)

whole and unrestricted universality where self-qua[*soku*]¹-actuality obtains. In Kantian terms, ultimate self-negation, in which objective regulation by the phenomenal self's theoretical reason returns to the nothing through the contradiction of antimonies, is, at the same time, nothing other than absolute negation as the subjective self-affirmation of practical reason. It is nothing other than conversion through absolute negation [絶対否定的転換] of pure reason, whereby it dies in theory but lives in practice. Hence we cannot reach the rationality of the actual without first considering the opposition of the individual self that confronts the coercion of the social substratum. The contractual society that is geared toward the self-interest of such individuals, as a society of interests, stands in opposition to the communal society of the species society, and thus gives shape to the model of society corresponding to what Tönnies called *Gemeinschaft und Gesellschaft* [community and society]. With this in mind, I brought to bear the concept of the will to power that usurps for the self the coercive power of the whole in order to regulate the egoity [自我性] of the individual. In referring to the individual's ego that opposes the species society's will to survive, I was of course borrowing Nietzsche's concept of the will to power, but its content is completely different. It is different because what I had in mind was nothing other than the immediate ego or egotism [我執 *ahaṃkāra*] that does not include any of the negative overcoming found in Nietzsche. At the time I was dismayed by the strength of our egotism that is diametrically opposed to the thinking entertained by us intellectuals who know and discuss the baseness of human egotism, and, in particular, the value of no-self, namely the ferocity of our desire for fame and lust for power. And, while anguishing over the fact that the root of this dismay was seated deeply in my own egotism, I discussed the individual's ego and addressed its negative oppositional character towards the social substratum. Rather than developing a dialectic in which the true self is restored by losing itself, that is, the true self attains existence only in absolute negation, my consideration of individuals at that time was instead restricted to the immediate ego of the individual self that ought to be dialectically negated. It was inevitable that this approach could not escape being one-sided, since I had conceived society exclusively from the side of coercion over the individual. It was for this reason that I later revised my account, adding that for the individual to truly become individual it must undergo negation-qua[*soku*]-affirmation [否定即肯定] in absolute negation. The true individual becomes individual within the whole only through the mediation of the universal. It goes without saying that through this absolute negation the species is also negated and becomes the whole society. Generally speaking, it is necessary within dialectical thought for all concepts to have the two-fold meaning of positive and negative. But given my motive in setting

---

¹The term *soku* [即], here translated by the Latin *qua*, is discussed in the essay following this text. The Chinese character 即 has several meanings in Japanese, including "namely" or "that is" [即ち], "immediate" [即時], and "impromptu" [即興]. It is also used together with the character for "self" [自] in the Japanese translation of "in-itself" ("*an sich*" or "*en soi*") [即自], and appears in the word *sōsoku* [相即], which is also discussed in the following essay and has been translated in this text as "mutual unification".

up the problem it was inevitable that the perspective I took as my starting point would be, for the most part, biased towards looking at the side that is immediate and ought to be negated.

That in which the discord between the negatively opposing species substratum and the individual thus transformed into the extremity of their reciprocal negation, that is, the affirmation of the subject in absolute negation, is the mutual unification [相即] of the state and the individual as a subjective whole. On this basis the conversion of substratum-qua[*soku*]-subject [基体即主体] is established and the system of whole-qua[*soku*]-individual [全体即個体の組織] emerges. The state, to the extent it relies on this kind of principle of mediated synthesis, is a whole [made up] of individuals on the basis of a contract, and hence is that which necessarily coerces them. But at the same time it must be a system of self-sacrifice-qua[*soku*]-self-realization [自己犠牲即自己実現], whereby that coercion immediately turns to freedom and the individual, while being negated, is in turn affirmed. The concrete structure of social being as a rational actuality is something of this sort. In general it is something realized from the standpoint of practice that establishes the negative union of the rational and the actual, and is the embodiment of the dialectic of the active subject. Consequently it must necessarily be logical, because being, logic, and action form a unity of three-in-one [三一的統一]. This dialectically elevates Jellinek's thesis of the two sides of the state, and recognizes the essence of the state through a medium [媒介態] that mediates in practice its social and legal aspects. I believe that if we accept this standpoint my view, which at first glance may seem to be nothing other than extreme nationalism, can easily be seen to be not simply the irrational totalitarianism of an immediate nationalism, but rather something like self-sacrifice-qua[*soku*]-self-realization and control-qua[*soku*]-freedom that seeks the construction of the state as the subjective realization of a whole through the autonomous collaboration of each of its members. I called this sort of nation a "human nation" not in the sense of a single nation encompassing all of humanity, but rather because I conceived that each ethnic state, taking the rational individuality of citizens who are its members as a medium, is able to possess human universality through individuals coming together to comprise it while at the same time being ethnic. What I meant was neither the abolition of the specific restrictions of ethnicity (this is impossible), nor the binding together of ethnic states in an international federation, but rather a return to and mediation by an open society in Bergson's sense through the absolute negativity of individuals who are members of an ethnic state so that the nation indirectly obtains the human race. And I suspect that, in this case as well, Hegel's philosophy of right, which possessed instructive significance for my speculations, influenced me through the idea that the world spirit in opposition to the ethnic spirit is borne by the individual. In Hegel's case, the individual who is the bearer of this world spirit is the hero, and would presumably be a so-called leader in today's nationalist states [国民主義国家], but the rational individuals in my thought, each a bearer of this world spirit, must, from the standpoint that "world history is the global court of judgment", become a partial representative of God as global arbiter, and each engage in the establishment of the state as though they were standing before the judgment of world history. History stands between objective spirit and absolute spirit. On the one hand it is the political history of ethnic states, while on the other it is at the same time the cultural history of the human race. And while what belongs to the latter, such as art, religion and philosophy, can transcend the limitations of ethnicity to take up a universal standpoint, the politics and laws that belong to the former do not go beyond the limits of their particular ethnic group. The universal and the particular are therefore characterized in history by the fact that they move between unity and division without being perfectly unified. Therein lies the reason history is taken to be kinesis [動性] without completion and the connection between eternity and time. This is also why it is thought to be the dichotomous unity and at the same time division of so-called rationality-and-irrationality and necessity-and-contingency. But such history is history seen from the standpoint of interpretation, and history viewed practically must always have the sense of the realization of a dichotomous unity in the actions of individuals. From this standpoint political history and cultural history are not separate things but rather something that must be unified through negation, and the practice of individuals must be conducted as though nation and humanity are distinct and yet the same. When it came to the state, too, I must frankly acknowledge that as a result of the motive behind my inquiry being a search for the principles of leadership I was unable to escape this view that stressed one side of its rational humanity divorced from historical actuality as well. The fact that I tended to be partial towards a cross-section of social being in the boundary realms of practice and ignored historical actuality was a limitation derived from the motives behind my speculations. Nevertheless, however, I cannot accept the criticism that in this regard I got no further than proposing an idea of what ought to be done [当為] that ignored actuality. For me, someone for whom Platonism is the path of philosophy, forms [形相] that are the aim of practice are at the same time the principles of actual formation, and are not simply what ought to be, much less pure fantasy. Historical actuality is not something that is simply created separately from action. What first allows the establishment of history is the unity of absolute negation wherein creation takes action as its medium and action takes creation as its medium. This is presumably the reason we think of history as at each stage being connected to God. Unity and division dialectically co-exist as two sides of the same coin, and just as there is no unity that does not include division on its flipside, there is no division that does not anticipate unity on its opposite face. I do not think that conceiving the state as a human state from this standpoint, even if it may have been one-sided, was mistaken. For even if it cannot avoid the abstractions divorced from actual history possessing a divisive kinesis [分裂動性], practice must still take as its end the absoluteness of unity as the medium of such history. The dichotomizing divisiveness of history is an aspect of the alienation [疎外面] of absolute unity, and the actions of individuals must take as their end the sublation [止揚 *Aufheben*] at each stage of this division. In this sense my ontology of the state [国家存在論] was to me inevitable. Some also say that it is precisely because of the fact that the actual state is indeed ensnared in the irrationality of history and is not consistent with this form of the being of the state that the rationalizing acts of practical reason must aim towards the realization of this form [ideal]. If we assume that affirmation is always dialectically conducted through negation and that unity always goes hand in hand with alienation, I think it is perhaps inevitable that we comprehend the side of dichotomous division in historical actuality as the aspect of alienation of unity as I have asserted. I must clearly acknowledge, however, that my not paying sufficient attention to this aspect at the time was inevitable given the motivation behind my inquiry. The fact that my speculative tendency was anti-historical was also a powerful factor. This was nothing but an inadequate sense of history on my part, and it is something of which I am personally ashamed. Moreover, since my goal lay chiefly in confronting state coercion that operates powerfully within the country, and in pursing rational principles to deal with it, the relationship between the state and the individual became the central issue, and today, in an era in which the correlation between intranational and international relationships is intimate, I must acknowledge as another major failing the fact that I did not address the issue of the international relationships between ethnic states. But while discussing questions concerning the state and history in a manner that leaves nothing out is beyond the scope of my present project, since the issue in question was located in social ontology, even today I cannot help but believe that these failings do not directly constitute a reason to reject the logic of species.

The practical motivation behind my social ontology, as mentioned above, was on the one hand to recognize the species substratum of communal society, which is the principle of state coercion, as a so-called "thing" [もの], and on the other hand to simultaneously secure the mediation [媒介性] of absolute negation that accomplishes the conversion of substratum-qua[*soku*]-subject via negation in the act of constructing a state organization that immediately converts coercion into freedom and becomes self-sacrifice-qua[*soku*]-self-realization and control-qua[*soku*]-autonomous cooperation. A standpoint of practice that goes beyond the standpoint of interpretation therefore cannot remain in phenomenology but necessarily demands its own logic. As I stated earlier, being, action, and logic stand in a three-in-one relationship. It goes without saying that this logic must not simply be a logic of identity that expresses being through concepts but rather a dialectic of the unity of negation and affirmation through absolute negation. Since the unity of this dialectic is a unity through negation of being and logic in action, the concepts of logic become forms as principles of the active formation of the actual. The fact that at the same time this is also the form of being is because being is the being of the actual through action. Being neither a substance that exists separate from action and bears no relation to it, nor an expressive existence [表現的実存] without mediation through a relationship to the substrative being of substance, only the active being of a substratum-qua[*soku*]-subject can obtain the status of concrete being that is a so-called "substance" but at the same time a subject. While requiring objective reality, a simple substance, since it conversely bears no relation to a subject, degenerates into a merely posited concept and loses the meaning of being. This is nothing other than the standpoint of the substantialization of concepts found in previous metaphysics and ontology. This what is called substantialism [本体論²]. Reality must be the negative opposite of the subject and must furthermore be its mediating substratum. At the same time, if it loses the mediation of this substratum, the subject's so-called existence will degenerate into a mere potential being of expressive interpretation [表現解釈], and cannot help but wither into a subject of interpretive acts that are mere self-decision without content. This is nothing other than the fundamental ontology or hermeneutic phenomenology adopted today as the new metaphysics. In contrast to previous ontology's standpoint of a substantialist identity of logic and substance that forgets about the mediation of acts, the new ontology takes the standpoint of the unity of formal acts of self-decision that can become content-less through loss of a substratum [on the one hand] and linguistic logic as the interpretation of expression without a substratum [on the other hand]. What is called being here is in fact nothing other than being as interpreted by the subject and capable of self-awareness. In this so-called "fundamental ontology" all being therefore goes no further than potential being interpreted on the basis of potential self-awareness. Here there are no necessary forms [形相] as ends of acts, completed [exhausted] to their ideal limits. While with the latter, the concept of logic becomes the formative principle of being through the mediation of acts unifying the space between affirmation and negation, in the case of the former there is only the potential development of interpretation. It thus follows that here even logic goes no further than the interpretation of linguistic expressions and does not truly arrive at its mediating character. While the new ontology is referred to as existentialism, the fact that it is nothing more than the interpretation of potential being without arriving at real being is of a piece with the old ontology's stopping at posited being. True ontology must be a social ontology serving as the reciprocal mediation via absolute negation between substratum and subject. This is what I have referred to as the third stage of ontology. It is nothing other than the logic of the dialectical unity of being and action. To hold that there is a being of expression that must be interpreted prior to logic is a completely anti-dialectical way of thinking. This can only result in the idea that actuality exists in advance merely as an object of interpretation, separate from the formation of acts. But no matter what sort of actuality, nothing exists unrelated to the formation of acts. To think so is a dogma of the old metaphysics, whereby actuality becomes a mere objective reality, something that possesses no subjectivity whatsoever. Needless to say, we cannot call this a living actuality. It was for precisely this reason that the new metaphysics adopted so-called existentialism and tried to preserve the sense of an interpretation of the actual by maintaining the active subject even while reducing it to the mere formality of self-decision. Actuality is united via opposition with acts, and conversion in negation [否定的転換] between substratum and subject must be what establishes this unity. Nevertheless, because action, like the necessity of the actual

---

²本体論 [hontairon] was commonly used as the Japanese word for "ontology" before the adoption of the current term, 存在論 [sonzairon]. Tanabe, however, uses the term substantialism in his own sense as the way of philosophical thinking that does not pay enough attention to the necessity of negating mediation.

that is the freedom of the self, is an oppositional unity of being and concept mediated through absolute negation, it necessarily possesses the sense of the realization of dialectical logic. Dialectical logic is not a logic that expresses being through identity, but rather a logic united with being through absolute negation while negatively opposing it. That is to say that while it arrives at true affirmation through its negation, at the same time it is a logic the negation of which constantly mediates this affirmation. Because this conversion between negation and affirmation occurs through acts, the being of the actualities formed by acts then becomes the realization of logic. In this sense logic is the principle of active being. Being that precedes logic would not be permitted by transcendental idealism. Moreover, since in the transcendental logic on which this idealism is based the conversion of negation-qua[*soku*]-affirmation is not recognized and the principle of identity is still dominant, the being established by this logic can never go beyond being a mere phenomenon of consciousness and cannot be a thing itself [物自体] opposing the subject's volitional acts through negation. Dialectical logic is what turns into the logic of transcendent being in terms of the thing-in-itself [物自体的] by means of a conversion of acts in absolute negation. By doing so it can become the logic of being. Such being is moreover nothing other than the being of the actual formed and subjectivized [主体化] through acts. Dialectics is a logic of actuality. Logic, as a logic of active actuality, is at the same time nothing other than the ethics of practice. Logic, ethics, and the history of the actual thus reciprocally negate and mediate each other.

(Intervening sections omitted)

In the preceding three sections I have laid out the motivation that led me to consider the logic of species in both its practical and logical aspects. I then explained that these two motives are not separate but in fact possess a necessary connection, and made it clear that the species substratum is the moment of self-negation and the principle of alienation of the dialectic as a logic of absolute mediation, and that this is the mediation via negation of absolute negation. By stating this I believe the logical meaning of species can generally be understood. Necessarily, however, the position of species within this kind of logic of absolute mediation, the task to which it is set, cannot be established without stipulating the content of species and its structure. Having begun by addressing the issue of the logic of social being mainly from [the perspective of] practical needs and hitting upon the concept of the species substratum as the key to its solution, in explicating this [concept] I mainly focused only on the aspect of the logical structure of social being, and did not reach the point of becoming at the same time generally self-aware of the root of this logic's absolute dialectical universal. This kind of generalized reflection naturally tends to be made after one has first obtained a basic overview of the content in question. In my case, too, it was not until after I had written "Shakaisonzai no ronri" [「社会存在の論理」 "The Logic of Social Being"] that I began, in the essay "Shu no ronri to sekai zushiki" [「種の論理と世界図式」 "The Logic of Species and the Schema of the World"], to develop the standpoint of absolute mediation. But once I had reflected on the fundamentals of the logic of species from this standpoint, the concept of species I had first conceived

3   Clarifying the Meaning of the Logic of Species (1, 4)

had to undergo some important revisions. My third paper on social ontology, "Ronri no shakaisonzaironteki kōzō" [「論理の社会存在論的構造」 "The Social Ontological Structure of Logic"], thus describes the results of these revisions. Species as the immediate unity of the substratum opposing the individual's subjectivity, a mere negative moment [否定契機] of social being, as I had first conceived it, now had to be a principle of self-alienation as the negative moment of absolute mediation. In this way the species substratum that had at first been conceived as comparatively simple became endowed with the structure it required as a principle of self-alienation, and the structure of what I had not been able to stipulate with sufficient detail gradually became logically developed. I must now summarize what occurred [in this process]. Through this approach, the concept of species, which at first had merely possessed content of chaotic indefinition described only through a figurative metaphor in the same way Schelling in his essay *Über das Wesen der menschlichen Freiheit* [*On the Nature of Human Freedom*] interpreted matter [質料] in Plato's *Timeaus*, gradually transformed into something possessing logical regularity. Following Plato's precedent, I analyzed this in terms of mathematical physics, employed analogies to the sequent calculus of intuitionism [直観主義の連続論] and the theory of relativity [相対性理論] found in recent approaches to the foundations of mathematics, and ultimately attempted to approach the dialectic of quantum mechanics. My discussing such issues may at first glance seem to be tangential to the study of social ontology, and may be criticized as simply originating in my own bias towards mathematics and physics. I myself would not altogether deny this, as my interest in these areas has indeed led me to pursue these tangents. But I would have to disagree in no uncertain terms if it is suggested that this sort of investigation is nothing more than a digression utterly irrelevant to the logic of social being. If we are to admit the unifying structure of being, the dialectical development of each of its stages, and the relationships of concretization that rises in cycles to form a spiral, it becomes clear that the ontology of mathematics and physics must constitute a certain correspondence to social ontology. If we are to call this relationship of correspondence an analogy, it must by no means stop at signifying the attenuation of the same genus. It may indeed be the case that, if we adhere to the dialectic of identity as a logic of objectivity, analogy would be nothing more than an incomplete argument that does not display the mediating middle term [媒語; *Mitte*] of deduction. But as a logic of the subject, an analogy lacking the commonality of a genus is instead nothing other than the concrete form of mediation of the absolutely negative structure of the active unity of the subject, a mediation common to that unity. An analogy lacking the middle term of being [有の媒語] is in fact a logic of mediation possessing the middle term of nothing [無の媒語]. We can take the inference of being in a deduction of identity to be the state of negation of the inference of nothing in this analogy. Of course, since the meaning of its so-called negation here must always be a dialectical negation, this does not mean that by imposing immediate determination on the analogy and negatively restricting it, deduction will follow. On the contrary, although deduction must have a particular standpoint as the logic of objectivity and must be grasped as if understanding [悟性] as a negative moment of reason [理性]

has its own particular principles, at the same time, in the sense that we can speak of reason as the unity of subjective nothing vis-à-vis the understanding and the unity of the latter's objective being as its negative state, we can understand analogy to be the concrete inference that takes deduction through a common genus to be a negative state. Because the ontology of mathematics and physics as well stands in this sense in an analogous relationship to social ontology, the usefulness of this analogy in subjectively understanding [its] structure is surely beyond doubt. In this sense Pythagoreanism has not by any means lost its foundation even today. I, of course, do not completely support, and indeed on the contrary oppose, the unified science of today's Vienna circle [*Wiener Kreis*] and the assertions, such as those of Neurath's mathematical economics and sociology, that have been made from this standpoint. But in any case it can perhaps be said that in some sense the ideas of this school demonstrate this. It [this view] only possesses a valid foundation to the extent that it is in accord with the spirit of Platonism. In this sense, without any hesitation I roped my scientific interest in mathematics and physics to philosophy, refined my logic from these directions and applied it analogically to social ontology, and, conversely, also attempted to revise the former [my logic] through the mode of this adaptation. My Platonism demanded that I not only consider social structure through analogy to mathematics and physics, but that I conversely also try to advance the logic of mathematics and physics through the logic of social structure. From this perspective I was thus able to logically revise the species substratum.

If I were to say where the gist of this revision is to be found, I would point to species, which I had first conceived simply as an immediate unifying force constituting a mere substratum for the individual subject, and which I then came to understand as a state of self-negation by means of the logic of self-alienation described above. What I mean by self-negation, as we saw in the previous section, is nothing other than to forget the self's establishment upon a unity, thereby losing sight of this unity and causing divisions and generating opposition within the self. As a result, the state of self-negation that alienates the self in relation to itself is an opposition of division in regard to the self's unity, and, at the same time, the opposition of divided moments. In other words, it is a two-fold opposition. The duality of this opposition is nothing other than the fundamental structure of the species substratum. Self-negation as self-alienation occurs through this two-fold oppositionality [対立性]. As a result, without being able to concretely unify this opposition, the alienated unity that therefore simply opposes it as an immediate unity without mediation must itself simultaneously be nothing other than opposition. This is the nature of species that has now been made clear.

What is of particular importance then in this case is that the unity which further stands in opposition to the division of mutually opposing moments is itself in no way something that acts as a unity or is made self-aware as a whole. Although this is clear from what I have previously stated regarding the structure of self-alienation, if we forget this and understand unity itself as existing in contrast to opposition, it will no longer stop at self-negation and hence cannot be non-being [非有 μή ὄν] in Plato's sense. On the contrary, it would have to be being and affirmation. Such a unity is already not simply matter but includes form, and is not the self-alienation of materiality but the spirit's return to itself. For this reason, the species substratum, to the extent that it is not being but non-being, and not self-affirmation but self-negation, cannot be that which is self-aware of its unity. If this unity is made self-aware and in this sense exists, it is no longer a species but a genus [類]. What I mean by genus is nothing other than that wherein self-alienation-qua[*soku*]-self-return attains the so-called self-awareness of self-inhabitation [自家止住の自覚] as the species of self-negation is in this way transformed into absolute negation through acts. Through this [genus] the internal opposition of species is unified into a whole, and if we are to call species only the parallel moments that merely reciprocally oppose each other, then something corresponding to the species-genus relationship found in identity logic appears where what unifies them can be called genus. However, since what originally constitutes the opposition of parallel moments is founded upon the self-alienation of unity, this parallel opposition involves the opposition between parts and whole. For the coercion of the whole that suppresses the parts is, at the same time, the constant coercion of parts by parts. And since, from the standpoint of a species without true unity or absolute whole, it is inevitable that these coerced parts seek to make other wholes opposing this whole their ally, internal opposition and external opposition go hand in hand. Genus must be that which has unified through negation these oppositions that can be thought of as two-fold or even three-fold. At the same time that it is a whole that realizes a concordant unity of individuals through mediation by negation of the opposition conducted internally, externally it is unified with other wholes and itself participates in the absolute whole as a unified individual. This two-fold internal-external unity is the whole of genus, and we can think of it as being itself an individual and at the same time a unity of individuals. Something like the human world, wherein the whole of the state in which the class divisions of ethnicities are sublated and individuals within it cooperate freely forms a whole that is at the same time established through international concord, therefore possesses this structure. In this sense we can think of the state in terms of self-awareness [自覚的に] as a human state [人類国家], and in turn as a member of the state we can think of the individual at the same time as a member of humanity. This is the concrete structure of social being. Because the species as its moment of negation is originally non-being, it is not something that exists on its own. My reason for thinking that the species society first takes shape as something like a totem tribe, too, did not by any means imply that this species substratum exists as this society alone and nothing more. I was simply using "species society" to refer to the form of society in which the immediacy of species as a structural moment of society was superior to other moments. On the contrary, we can consider as significant the fact that even this immediate unity itself, as something that opposes opposition, in itself constitutes an opposition. The flipside of the immediate unity of the tribe is that it will presumably involve intertribal conflict. Of course, divisive opposition is something that arises out of unity, and we can see that divorced from the latter it loses its meaning. But when it comes to the state of self-negation in self-alienation, since unity, too, is included as an opponent opposing opposition, one is not self-aware of it as a unity.

Accordingly it ultimately goes no further than being an oppositional moment as a negated unity and fails to truly unite the opposition. Even if it is a unity merely *in-itself* [即自的に], because non-mediation *in-itself* runs counter to the realization of unity, it is still not something that realizes unity *for-itself* [対自的に *für sich*]. If unity had already been realized it would not be self-negation but instead absolute negation. And even when they are mutually unified [相即する], at the same time they negatively stand in opposition and are mediated only through action. Of course, even a unity being alienated and negated, since this is due to dialectical negation, does not mean that the unity is negated and simply disappears immediately. Because negation is also negation in affirmation, it exists as a moment [契機] at the same time as it is negated, and indeed constitutes a negative mediation that establishes opposition. In other words, it is negated in affirmation. This is why Aristotle's matter, as a substratum, maintains identity before and after the movement that transforms latency [潜勢] into presence [現勢]. If this is reversed, negation is restored as mediation, and [this] is affirmed in negation; because this is already the self-awareness of unity, it is no longer simply self-negation but is nothing other than the active conversion of self-negation-qua[*soku*]-absolute negation [自己否定即絶対否定]. In other words, the species is made into a genus. To negate the substrative nature of matter established by Aristotle and to say on the contrary that it is form that is the substratum must imply this kind of conversion. Aristotle's theory of movement shatters the framework of identity logic and demands a dialectical logic. Furthermore, this must entail the species being made a genus and matter becoming form by means of an active conversion even more thoroughgoing than that found in Hegel. We cannot simply understand this from the standpoint of identity logic as the actualization of latency. It must be the subjectivization in terms of an absolutely negative unity of the self-negating species substratum. To the extent that it goes no further than the self-negating substratum, we lose sight of the unity, unity is alienated, and it cannot itself avoid being nothing more than a moment of opposition. In this way we describe species as a divisive opposition of the absolute that takes even unity itself as a moment of opposition. We can regard matter in the *Timaeus*, which Schelling compared to the open ocean with its agitating waves, as the opposition of the absolute by means of its constitution of the state of self-negation that is a two-fold opposition. On the basis of this structure, species, first thought of as an immediate unity vis-a-vis the individual's subjectivity, instead renders this immediate unity, too, into a moment of negation, and reveals its constitution of the divisive opposition of the absolute. Having now defined species, I can say that unity itself at the same time must be nothing other than opposition. Indeed this would presumably also apply to something like ethnic groups. This is nothing other than what I referred to earlier as the logical revision of the concept of species. And it follows from this that genus means an opposition that at the same time becomes a unity, and the individual is nothing other than the medium through which species as absolute opposition turns into the genus as absolute unity.

If in this way we take the species substratum to be self-negation as two-fold opposition, then the individual that subjectively opposes it cannot be that which immediately opposes species through negation as I had at first thought. For to the extent that species is the divisive opposition of the absolute there can be no opposition outside of the species, and even when it comes to a negative opposition to the species, if this is something that directly engages in reciprocal opposition then this itself belongs to the species and is nothing other than that which we must regard as a relative opposition that constitutes the absolute opposition of the species. Because what truly negates the species in relation to it is the negation of self-negating species, it cannot be anything other than absolute negation. Furthermore, absolute negation as the negation of self-negation, as we have just seen, is nothing other than the act which, as the negation of absolute opposition, realizes *for-itself* [対自的に] the unity that is the mediation of opposition *in-itself* [即自的 *an sich*]. The subjective act of the individual, therefore, is in fact the conversion of the self-negation of species into the genus that is absolute negation, and the individual does not simply oppose the species but instead is established in the transition towards the genus that is mediated by the species' self-negation. Thus individual and species do not immediately oppose each other. The individual is established in absolute negation mediated by the species' self-negation. The medium of the conversion through *for-itself*, in which the unity anticipated as *in-itself* by the absolute divisive opposition of the species is realized as a genus, is nothing other than the individual. It is for this reason that the individual is conceived of as something that acts as a subject. This conversely is established through a holistic unity—in-itself and for-itself—of self-negation-qua[*soku*]-absolute negation. Earlier I took the absolute to be self-inhabiting, took its self-alienating exclusionary aspect to be matter, and described its aspect of absolutely negative return as spirit. But in relation to the material substratum of the species, the individual must indeed constitute a spiritual substratum [精神的基体]. In contrast to the former constituting the absolute's aspect of divisive opposition, the latter constitutes its aspect of unified return. Since in this way the individual is mediated by the species and is nothing other than the negation of the species' self-negation, we cannot think of it as something that immediately negates the species but instead as something established through the unifying restoration of the species' self-negation. As I stated in section two, this is the reason I revised my original conception of the individual's immediate negation of the species, took this to be something mediated by the species, and concluded that it obtains through absolute negation mediated by the negation of the species itself. It should go without saying that this revision was nothing other than the result of revising the very concept of species that had reached the point of clarifying the two-fold oppositional nature of species itself. The individual is thus established through the whole of the genus, and, while simultaneously being a member of the whole, bears and represents the subjective unity of the whole to which it belongs. In this sense the individual [個体] is at the same time the whole [全体], and the whole is at the same time the individual. The two must be mutually unified [相即する]. Because the negation of species is the negation of self-negation, it is the realization *for-itself* of the unity *in-itself* included within the absolute opposition of the species itself, and is thus also the restoration of the whole. The individual is the kinesis of this restoration of the unity of whole and is the process of return. This is why it is an active subject. While the aspect of negation in self-inhabiting absolute negation is the materiality [物質性] of species, its positive aspect is nothing other than the individual's spirituality [精神性]. Just as unity is included *in-itself* as itself a moment of opposition within the absolute opposition of the species, the individual is also immediately included, in turn, in the species' state of self-negation as species. Spirit necessarily takes the body as a moment of negation and is mediated by matter [物質]. The individual as I first conceived it is such an individual *in-itself*, and in turn as an opposite of the species, belonging to the species, is itself nothing other than the species. The fact that in this way what opposes a species is ultimately the species itself is a result of the fact that species is absolute opposition. But because the individual obtains together with the unity of all, and the restorative return of unity occurs through the conversion in negation through absolute negation of the species' self-negation, it goes without saying that both individual and all (genus) take the self-negation of species as mediation. This is why this dialectic must necessarily be the logic of species. I do not think there can be any doubt that the absolute mediation of the dialectic is nothing other than the logic of species.

Alternatively, regarding this point it may perhaps also be thought that, since what is being discussed is absolute mediation, any two of genus/species/individual must be mediated by the remaining third, there is no compelling reason to think that it is species in particular that mediates the other two, and, in this sense, absolute mediation and the logic of species are incompatible. But if what I have stated above is sufficiently understood, this sort of thought will dissolve of its own accord. It is indeed the case that formally, when it comes to absolute mediation, genus/species/individual, like A/B/E [*Allgemeinheit/Besonderheit/Einzelheit*; universality/particularity/individuality] in Hegelian logic, may at first glance seem to imply that all of these elements mediate each other equally. Even in Hegel, however, the three states of mediation are not completely equal. Just as in Aristotle's syllogism [推論式 συλλογισμός] the first term as the most natural in comparison to the other two terms occupies the position of victor, E-B-A unfolds through inference [推論的] the spontaneous primitive structure of the judgment "E is A" as what is most natural. In the natural order of generation, it is inevitable that the particular (B) stand in the position of mediation. But if we add further reflection to this generated state of inference, other forms of inference [推論] are similarly possible, and we can understand inference by taking any one of A, B or E as the mediator of the other two. In this respect so-called absolute mediation is established. In the same way, even when it comes to my logic of species, taking the self-negation and self-alienation of species as the substratum established through a dialectic is the inevitable result of the dialectic being a logic of self-negation. But the twofold oppositional structure of its self-negation at the same time obviously includes *in-itself* the genus (whole) and the individual as moments of absolute opposition. And in this sense, since species is simultaneously mediated by genus and individual, as a matter of course it establishes absolute mediation in which any of the three can mediate the other two. But this is not all. It can also be said that, conversely, any two can mediate the third. It appertains to the necessity of the dialectic that absolute mediation obtains as the logic of species. One doubts this because one does not subjectively comprehend the dialectic. It is just as though time were something absolutely mediated by the three modes of past/present/future, and no one would doubt the indispensability of any one of them as a mediator of the other two. A standpoint that places emphasis on any one of the three modes is possible when it comes to understanding time, and this is why since antiquity we have had telling examples of each approach. Nevertheless, we cannot deny that at the same time the present occupies a particularly select position as mediator in the establishment of time. This is why Augustine's classical theory of time possesses such deep significance. By standing upon this present the kinesis and unity of time are brought together. Not only does the mediating nature of the present not contradict absolute mediation but on the contrary makes it possible. In a similar sense, the logic of species is not only consistent with the logic of absolute mediation but makes it possible. Doubting this, it must be said, is a consequence of objectively making the logic of absolute mediation into formal logic without understanding it dialectically.

One thing we must note here when understanding dialectic as the logic of absolute mediation concerns how we are to understand the nature of inference [推論性] that is the universal character of logic. I indicated the impossibility of claiming to be logic what stops at a mere expressive comprehension by hyper-extending the concept of logic, and asserted the necessity of accurately distinguishing the logos of logic from the logos of linguistic expression. I thereby raised the nature of inference as what characterizes the former [logos of logic]. This is of course in no way an assertion of a new perspective of my own. On the contrary, all I have done is elucidate the meaning found in cases where the concept referred to as logic has been used correctly from the distant past until the present day. But if we restrict the nature of inference to the operation of thought that derives conclusion from premise by simply following its classical meaning, we cannot say that it immediately applies in the case of dialectics. For to derive conclusion from premise would mean the mediation of the conclusion and at the same time the un-mediated immediacy of the premise. Dialectically speaking, however, the premise would also have to be something at the same time mediated if we were to follow the requirements of absolute mediation. This clearly signifies circular reasoning and would not be permitted by identity logic. In this sense some also say that inferentiality and circularity are not compatible. But as the flip side of the principle of contradiction that is the axiom of identity logic, and transcending it through the freedom of the subject in the nothingness of objects, dialectics requires circularity. As a result, if we were to interpret the nature of inference in the ordinary sense, we would have to also say that since the dialectic of absolute mediation is circular rather than inferential [syllogistic] it is not logic.

Nevertheless, even when it comes to identity logic, it has long been acknowledged that, if this logic demands the completion of a system as a method of cognition, it must bring premise and conclusion together [即相] in the way that the premise of a deduction is the conclusion of an induction and establish a circular relationship through the mutual mediation of premise and conclusion. Viewed from this perspective, inferentiality instead combines together [即相] with circularity, the former relating to the whole of the latter as a partial moment. This, generally speaking, is nothing other than the relationship between dialectics and identity logic. Let it be said that the circularity of dialectics is an absolute inferentiality that takes the inferentiality of analytic logic as its negative moment. However, because a negative moment is not an immediate part, if we take a single segment of dialectical circularity (a single direction of mediation, for example) it will not constitute an inference. Instead absolute inferentiality is that which negates the inference of identity and constantly renews it. Alternatively, we might also call this subjective inferentiality that is a negation-qua[*soku*]-affirmation of objective inferentiality. Consequently, in the ordinary sense we cannot say that the logic of dialectics takes inference as its content. Instead it is the motive source of inferentiality that affirms inference by negating it. We could also say that in contrast to how ordinary inference possesses an extensive extensionality that progresses intellectually in terms of identity, it [dialectical logic] signifies an intentionality [内包性] that negatively subjectivizes such inference itself. In contrast to how the inference of identity logic is immediately affirmative, this is absolutely negative. The self-awareness that inference obtains upon this state of absolute negation is nothing other than absolutely negative inferentiality. For this reason we have to understand the nature of inference in the logic of dialectics to mean [意] negative mediation. This is clearly something belonging to the self-awareness [自覚] of an active subject.

Thought of in this way as something that clarifies the negative structure of the middle term constituting the core of ordinary inference, we might easily recognize the nature of inference in dialectics to be nothing other than the concretization of the copula of judgment. My long assertion has been that we can make out the judgment of dialectics, concretely, neither on the basis of the logic of the [grammatical] subject or the logic of the predicate, and that we can understand it only through the logic of the copula. I do not mean to repeat that assertion here. If the dialectic is the mutual unification of negation and affirmation and the mediation through negation of substance [実体] and subject [主体], and therefore the active mediation of being and concept, it is inevitable that the negative mediation of the copula constitute the core of judgment. But within judgment the copula is an immediate unity devoid of content. It is a mere active decision involving negation-qua[*soku*]-affirmation. The unity of predicate and [grammatical] subject does not possess any kind of mediation, and the universality of the concept that signifies the latter [the grammatical subject] combines, unmediated, with the being expressed by the former [the predicate]. This is a mere unity without self-awareness that can even be likened to action without rationale, and we cannot speak of it as sufficiently rational. By thoroughly possessing the self-awareness of reason, rationality would have to be something free. In contrast to this, in the same way that the freedom of conversion of actuality-qua[*soku*]-self [現実即自己] obtains, to be that which is self-aware of the mediation of the predicate is nothing other than the nature of inference. To be that which is self-aware of the species substratum that ought to be the negative medium in relation to the universal of the predicate, and which mediates this in the restoration of the unity that occurs in the subject of the individual expressing the [grammatical] subject, is the nature of inference. In this way the copula of judgment that is without content is able to escape the state of affairs in which, in response to the degeneration of unity into a moment of opposition within the simple immediate state of negative unity, immediate judgment constantly falls into fallacies. [Therefore] it is able to turn [this state] into a state of true reality self-aware of its ground. This is nothing other than the nature of inference. The species substratum is useful as the medium for concretizing the immediate unity of the copula into the unity of absolute negation. It is the inferentiality of the dialectic that is self-aware of this medium of self-negation. The two-fold oppositional structure of this mediation permits us to understand this establishment via negation of judgment, and its self-awareness necessarily concretizes the copula into the content of the middle term. The true content of the middle term is nothing other than the species substratum. We can say that the logic of species that clarifies this is indeed that which realizes the nature of inference. But at this point there should be no need to state once again that this so-called realization is nothing other than the self-awareness of the restoration of unity [統一の回復自覚] in action.

Tanabe Hajime (1885–1962). Born in Tokyo. After graduating from Tokyo Imperial University's Faculty of Letters, worked as an instructor of "Introduction to Science" at Tohoku Imperial University's Faculty of Science. Transferred to Kyoto University in 1919. Took charge of the philosophy program after Nishida's retirement. Writings include *Kagaku gairon* [『科学概論』 *Introduction to Science*] (Iwanami Shoten, 1918), *Zangedō toshite no tetsugaku* [『懺悔道としての哲学』 *Philosophy as Metanoetics*] (Iwanami Shoten, 1946), and four volumes of *Tetsugaku nyūmon* [『哲学入門』 *Introduction to Philosophy*] (Chikuma Shobō, 1949–1952). "Clarifying the Meaning of the Logic of Species" was published in Volumes 259, 260, and 261 of the journal *Tetsugaku kenkyū* [『哲学研究』 *Philosophical Studies*] in 1937. It is also included in *Tanabe Hajime zenshū* [『田辺元全集』 *Complete Works of Tanabe Hajime*] Vol. 6 (Chikuma Shobō).

Chapter 4
What Does Absolute Negation Differentiate?

[絶対否定は何を差異化するか]

Nakaoka Narifumi

Tanabe Hajime established the logic of species as his own philosophical conception, sharply distinguished from the logic of nothing [無の論理] of his mentor, Nishida Kitarō, through which his thinking had passed. Having encountered Marxism's historical materialism, which at the time was enjoying great popularity, he brought the practical dynamism he had learned from it to the logic of nothing.

There is a tendency to view the logic of species as a more or less totalitarian state philosophy and an ideology that supported Japan's war effort. While in previous logical treatments of genus—species—individual species had possessed the role of connecting genus and individual, in Tanabe's conception this species is indeed likened to the ethnic nation-state that mediates the ideal human nation-state (genus) and the individual person (individual). Seen from the perspective of the setting of the period, there is no doubt that the logic of species was completed under the shadow of militarism as it deepened from the Sino-Japanese War into the Second World War and with an awareness sensitive to these circumstances. Nevertheless, it is not as though Tanabe simply showered praise on the ethnic nation-state (in his case Japan). While on the one hand he criticized the individualism and liberalism of the modern West, he also argued resolutely against ethnic nationalism (Japanism) [民族主義 (日本主義)], the vehement discourse and actions of which had silenced and oppressed many people.

In *Shu no ronri no benshohō* [『種の論理の弁証法』 *The Dialectic of the Logic of Species*] (1947), published after the end of World War II, Tanabe recalls the period in which he developed the logic of species as being from 1934 to 1940. The essay excerpted in this book, "Shu no ronri no imi wo akirakanisu" [「種の論理

Translated from the Japanese by Robert Chapeskie and revised by John W. M. Krummel.

N. Nakaoka (✉)
Osaka University, Suita, Japan
e-mail: nar.n@gamma.ocn.ne.jp

の意味を明にす」 "Clarifying the Meaning of the Logic of Species"], appeared in 1937, and in it one might say that the logic of species has by and large been completed. Tanabe would later reach the standpoint of "the philosophy of *metanoetics*" [懺悔道の哲学; "philosophy of the way of repentance"], but this is a philosophy that plumbs further the idea of absolute mediation forming the core of the logic of species and in this sense lies within its theoretical sphere.

4.1 The Source of "Species"—Why Can the State Coerce the Individual?

So, without any further introduction, let us dive into our text, "Clarifying the Meaning of the Logic of Species."

In this essay Tanabe discusses his motivations for formulating the logic of species by dividing them into the practical and the theoretical. In sections one and two he addresses his practical motivations. He then shifts to his theoretical motivations in section three, and in section four explains the kind of revisions he made to the concept of species through the process of adding theoretical reflections to the conception of the logic of species that had sprung from his practical motivations.

We begin by looking at section one. What were the practical motivations behind the logic of species? Tanabe answers this question up front. His answer is also very predictable: noticing the "rise" of the "coercive power of ethnic states" "recently in various states," he had a philosophical interest in the question of the justification of state control. It is common knowledge as a matter of world history that during the 1930s, when the logic of species was being developed, the trend towards totalitarianism intensified in the so-called Axis nations such as Japan and Germany, and civic freedoms were being stripped away by statist control. It is also well known that during this period the slogan "blood and soil [*Blut und Boden*]" was being shouted in Nazi Germany. We must take note, however, of the fact that the accumulated contradictions of modern society would inevitably be exposed even on the side of the Allied nations that had allegedly achieved democracy, above all the United States of America. Recent studies have shown how the New Deal policies enacted under President Roosevelt introduced principles of a different nature than had been implemented in previous democracies in order to deal with these structural contradictions.

Even in today's Japan, where we feel state control to be a thing of the distant past and state authority rarely seems to come to the surface, political and social order does indeed exercise "coercive power" [強制力], whether in the shadows or in broad daylight. This was made particularly clear with the legislation of the national flag and anthem. And facing the phenomenon of truancy in the field of education, we cannot avoid the question of why children must be coerced (the essence of this coercion is the same even when rephrased in terms of children being "guided" or "persuaded") into studying a fixed curriculum. In this sense we can say that Tanabe's inquiry into the source of the "coercive power of the ethnic state" indicates a concern for an exceptional and actual problem. Nevertheless, the fact that he utters "ethnic state" in one breath, and views "ethnic group" [民族] and "state" [国家] as essentially identical, raises our initial suspicion. If we tentatively follow Benedict Anderson in characterizing the modern nation state as "an imagined community," was Tanabe unable to detect the imaginariness of the modern communities referred to as nation states? Was he maintaining, in the shadow of his confrontation with the Japanists [日本主義者], the mythological fabrication of the "Yamato [Japanese] people ruled by an unbroken line of the imperial family"? Although in the first section of this text he explains how even "species" becomes a whole society only by being "negated" and avoids connecting ethnic identity directly to national identity, serious doubts remain.

So from where did the conception of "species" originate? Tanabe mentions the names of French sociologists (chief among them Émile Durkheim), religious studies scholar Lucien Lévy-Bruhl, and French philosopher Henri Bergson. Durkheim points out that a social group is not simply a gathering of individuals, but a *"chose"* [もの thing] of a different dimension than the individual. From this Tanabe concludes that society constitutes a "substratum" [基体] for individuals. Inspiration regarding the species society came from Lévy-Bruhl's theory of totem tribes. Totemism is a belief and social system, seen in so-called "undeveloped" peoples of North and South America and elsewhere, in which a clan regards a particular animal, for example, as its ancestor and recognizes it as its guardian (its "totem"). Along with identifying themselves with the totem, clan members identify themselves through the totem with the tribe as a whole. Lévy-Bruhl saw operating here a distinctive logic whereby the parts that are individuals "share" [分有する] the whole that is society.

4.2 The Logic of the Species Tribe [種族 Ethnic Grouping] and the Negation of Self-interest

So why was Tanabe fixated on the "species tribe"? Is it not too much of a stretch to superimpose the clans of primitive societies on modern and contemporary nation states? Tanabe himself acknowledges this criticism. Nonetheless, encouraged by the fact that Bergson's *Le deux sources de la morale et de la religion* had distinguished between closed and open societies and positioned the totem society as representative of the former, Tanabe concludes that totemic elements remain even in today's societies. He was further emboldened by the ongoing reevaluation of myths and legends amidst the rising tide of ethnic nationalism. "Seeing the religious myths and legends of primitive society gradually occupy an important position in recent nationalist cultural studies and their resurgence undertaken as a matter of intellectual policy, I cannot help but believe, now as before, that my amateur intuition was not necessarily mistaken." As a layman in sociology and religious studies, to find support for his own focus on the species tribe in a political trend that can, to begin with, be described as reactionary, perhaps was not necessarily an appropriate strategy to adopt in legitimizing the philosophical theory of the logic of species.

Compared to philosophy, the discipline of sociology is a much newer field of study, having been created by Comte in the nineteenth century and developed by the aforementioned Durkheim. Tanabe was aware that while he was drawing on the results generated by this new field, he was also simplifying them from his own philosophical perspective. In any case, however, even if society's coercive power over individuals originates in the species substratum (in other words, the emergence of a coercion that is natural), this does not yield an explanation of a morally binding force. For as clarified by Kantian philosophy, morality takes the autonomy of the individual as its premise, and for society (the state) to simply compel individuals to do this or that by force would be nothing but violence and would not establish morality. (Indeed, with a naturally occurring coercion we would not only fail to account for morality, but presumably even the binding force of legal norms.) Tanabe thus turns to the binding force of the species substratum, and calls for an individual with sufficient power to repel it. This individual, however, must self-negate its own power. In Kantian philosophy, the phenomenal self in the field of "theoretical reason" [*theoretische Vernunft*] runs into antimonies, learns the limit of its own cognitive capacity, and must inevitably negate itself. But by advancing to its extremity, a new possibility—"subjective self-affirmation"—is opened, this time in the domain of "practical reason" [*praktische Vernunft*], and Tanabe believed that a "conversion through absolute negation" of precisely this sort was needed here.

On this point he seeks help from Nietzsche's concept of the will to power. In other words, he sees the individual as exercising its will to power by opposing society's coercive power (its will to survive as a collective) and exercising its own "will to power". But Nietzsche's will to power is not simply an attempt to maximize the interests of the self. In some cases it acquires as its nature a "cruelty" that discards even self-protection and births a dynamism from within the self that transcends the individual. In this sense it includes what Tanabe refers to as "overcoming in negation" [否定超克]. The individual Tanabe presents here, however, strives only for self-love and self-affirmation (egoity [我性], egotism [我執]). This individual attempts to seize for itself the coercive power that society as a whole directs toward it and to transform it into its own property. This is the picture that serves as the starting point for the logic of species.

Tanabe states that at first he was disheartened by the baseness of human egotism (particularly intellectuals' desire for fame), but then realized that this lamentation was itself egotism. Society (the state) attempting to make individuals obey and individuals revealing their selfishness pit their powers against each other. This is the view of human beings and society found in naturalism. Tanabe, who had posed as a scholar of Kant, now tries to borrow the language of naturalism. But preceding this point, had not the proposition—in fact more aesthetic than ethical—that "egotism is base" perhaps come to dominate him? The declaration that lamenting egotism is itself egotism may indeed be insightful, but the premise that egotism is something that ought to be negated is never called into question. Tanabe states that Nietzsche negatively overcomes egotism, but the nature of negativity in Nietzsche's account of the will to power is, I think, quite different. To begin with, in Nietzsche there exists no duality of whole/individual as found in Tanabe, nor is there any morally aesthetic sense that views egotism as base.

4.3 The Internalization of Negation: The Magic "*Soku* [即]"

In any case, Tanabe depicts a society that negates the egotism of the individual by force. As the logic of species was revised and developed, this negation became internalized within the individual. In other words, at first the individual resists the force that seeks to negate it from the outside. But human beings are not isolated individuals like animals, and in order to be sublimated into a social being equipped with a view of cultural values, it is necessary that we negate our own egotism and take on universality. To negate the self as an individual is to establish its communal character. Tanabe thus came to believe that "the true self is restored by losing itself."

This true self "restored by losing itself" is described as the antithesis of the trend toward "self-preservation" that dominates the modern Western view of humanity. In contrast to a theory of society focusing on the preservation of the individual's life, liberty and property, here the social order emerges as a "rational universal". As I will discuss shortly, this is close to Hegel's philosophy of the state, but in Tanabe the negative attitude toward the desires of the individual is stronger than in Hegel, and self-negativity or mediation through negation is given the significance of self-sacrifice in the moral or religious dimension. Tanabe is attempting to go beyond the individualistic and quantitative rationality of Western modernity.

On the other hand, however, society (the state) must also pass through the activity of negation. Only by being "negated" does the species community [種的共同体] become a whole society and achieve political legitimation. In this way Tanabe maintains that at first the coercive power of the community over the individual (the species substratum) and the self-interested action s of the individual collide head-on and cause conflict. But then, through the "self-negation" of both community and individual, there arises a social order in which the state (in this case an idealized "human nation") and the individual are unified without estrangement. He describes this in terms of "state-qua[*soku*]-individual person" [国家即個人] and "whole-qua[*soku*]-individual" [全体即個体]. This term "*qua*" or "*soku*" [即], used with the meaning of "mutual unification" [*sōsoku* 相即]",[1] also appears frequently in Tanabe's later works, and here we must pay due attention to this magic word that at a single stroke overcomes both social conflict and logical contradiction.

---

[1] An originally Buddhist term meaning "unity", "combining as one" or "identity" (non-duality) in spite of apparent opposition (duality).

Under this view, the state, while being a "whole [made up] of individuals on the basis of a contract", becomes from the perspective of the individual an intimately familiar entity into which one can throw oneself in "self-sacrifice-qua[*soku*]-self-realization". In a broad sense, this is a view of the state in terms of an organism, in contrast to the social contract approach developed in England. The social contract theory put forward by Hobbes and Locke presupposes the individual as a rational decision-making subject, and holds that such individuals, as a consequence of thoroughly pursuing their own self-interest, will feel an acute need for a social order that protects their own lives and property, and will therefore agree to establish a community to which they will voluntarily transfer or entrust their natural rights. In contrast to this approach, Tanabe tries to harmonize the species "substratum" (the pre-modern community subsisting prior to the individual) and the modern individual. This may be an anachronism inconceivable to Westerners. And yet even in the West circumstances differ depending on the degree of modernization, and in nineteenth century Germany, Hegel, too, constructed a view of the nation in terms of an organism and a pre-established harmony similar to what Tanabe is pursuing here.

Tanabe was unhappy with the fact that the logic of species was seen as supporting state nationalism [国家主義], ethnic nationalism [国民主義], and/or irrational totalitarianism. On the other hand, however, with his mantra of "control-qua [*soku*]-freedom" he also drew a clear line between his view and that of individualist liberalism. His point was that to the extent that Japanese citizens accept the necessity of yielding to state control and consent to it as autonomous individuals, this is in fact the optimal expression of the freedom of the individual. His wariness towards capitalist modernity is apparent here, laying the groundwork for the acceptance of "control" in the economic as well as the intellectual domain. Whether or not the slogan "overcoming modernity" intervenes is presumably not essential. But without discussing in what sense control, that is, explicit control through political authority, is necessary for the systematized society of the twentieth-century, and to what extent it is possible, we cannot come to any conclusion regarding its pros and cons.

4.4 The Ideal International Network

So far we have discussed the relationship between individual (individual persons) and species (existing ethnic states that developed out of species-tribal communities). Next comes genus, namely, the idea of an ideal human state.

Tanabe asserts that "…each ethnic state, taking the rational individuality of citizens who are its members as the medium, is able to possess human universality through individuals coming together to comprise it while at the same time being ethnic." Having forcefully contorted the fundamental discord or conflict between state and individual with his logic of "control-qua[*soku*]-freedom", Tanabe now attempts to logically overcome the conflict between states as well. Taken as they stand, one species (an ethnic state) and another species (an [other] ethnic state) would presumably simply oppose one another. But each species is composed of individuals (individual people = citizens). And individuals are, in Kantian terms, rational beings, and in this sense possess a universality that cannot be confined to a certain species = ethnicity. It therefore follows that "through" these individuals = citizens [国民], an ethnic state "while being ethnic at the same time… is able to possess human universality". This is an extremely dangerous logic. We can perhaps glimpse Tanabe's ambivalence in the way he says that an ethnic state "could possess" human universality. But a tear in his logic is already visible where he has not noticed it. To say that members of an ethnic state are citizens is a tautology. That an individual person who is a citizen possesses "rational individuality," in Kantian terms, is also self-evident. But members of an ethnic state can become intoxicated with patriotism and engage in extremely irrational behavior. Citizen does not *equal* rational individual. Of course, Tanabe is referring to the rational individuality of the citizen "as medium", and is not identifying their national character [国民性] or rationality. And yet this only serves to highlight the ambiguity of his concept of "mediation" [or: medium] and the dubiousness of his theoretical strategy. To put it another way, on the one hand Tanabe overestimates the rationality of the individual (and corrects this later in his philosophy of "metanoesis"), while on the other hand he underestimates the ethnic nature of the species substratum and its irrational potential. Of course, Japanese, Koreans, Serbians, Croatians, and members of all ethnic groups presumably possess "rational individuality", but this does not mean that ethnic conflict did not occur in the past nor does it guarantee it will disappear in the future. Tanabe acknowledges the "impossibility" of "disinheriting the specific restrictions of ethnicity." Yet he jumps straight to the possibility of an international network without adequately theorizing the complex role "specific restrictions" play in the actual world.

Tanabe began as a Kantian or neo-Kantian scholar, but in the context of the influence of Nishida Kitarō and his confrontation with Marxism, finally underwent a baptism in Hegel's dialectic. Regarding the logic of species as well, Tanabe clearly acknowledges the "guidance" received from Hegel's philosophy of right. On the other hand, however, he also spells out his differences with Hegel. For Hegel, the "world spirit", as opposed to the ethnic spirit, is borne by heroic individuals like Napoleon (in the present this would correspond to "so-called leaders"), but Tanabe expects each and every "individual" to transcend ethnicity globally or universally.

4.5 Towards a "Logic" Committed to the Actual: Confronting Heidegger

In actual history, no matter how much people of culture or intellectuals strive for universal conciliation, the heartlessness of politics obstructs its realization. Tanabe assigned himself the serious practical task of "unifying through negation" this duality of culture and politics. As a result of this "motivation for speculation", however, the initial theoretical strategy of the logic of species "was unable to escape a view that focused excessively on the side of rational humanity divorced from historical actuality". I pointed out this flaw earlier, and Tanabe, recognizing it himself, engages in self-critique in the first section of the essay. The logic of species, which attempted to philosophically examine what sort of "rational principle" could be found in the "state control" that had intensified in Japan at the start of the Shōwa era, did not primarily cast its gaze toward "international relations between ethnic states" transcending national borders. Tanabe acknowledges this defect. To add to this, today we would presumably ask: Why limit international relations to only "ethnic states"? Would not regions that do not constitute states, or, conversely, coalitions that transcend [individual] states be objects of "international relations" as well? But let us put aside such questions for now. In any case, even while acknowledging the defect described above, Tanabe firmly rejects "the criticism that the logic of species gets no further than proposing an idea of what ought to be done [当為] that ignored actuality." He does this on the following philosophical grounds.

Regarding the issue of how philosophical theory relates to political and social practice, Tanabe states that he is a follower of Plato and expresses his dissatisfaction with the existential philosophy of his contemporary Heidegger. Appearing at the start of the twentieth century, the logic of species was a new ontology that placed its primary emphasis on "social being" and "substratum", and stands in contrast to the ontology of "substance" represented by Aristotle. Tanabe criticizes [the notion of a] "substance that exists apart from action and bears no relation to it." For even if we assert that a simple substance is an objective reality, since it bears no relation to the subject, it is nothing more than a concept posited or asserted in this way. This would be the "old metaphysics" to which Aristotle belonged, the standpoint of a "noumenal identity" between logic and substance that has forgotten the mediation of acts.

On the other hand, Tanabe also asserts the inadequacy of an "expressive existence [表現的実存] with no mediation in its relationship to the substrative being of substance", in other words, the standpoint of Heidegger. As is widely known, Heidegger held sway over the era in question with his *Being and Time* [*Sein und Zeit*] (1927). Tanabe traveled to Europe as a visiting scholar from 1922 to 1924 and studied phenomenology under Husserl at the University of Freiburg. Heidegger, with whom Tanabe became acquainted at the time, was a few years younger but would continue to be a major focus of Tanabe's attention as a lifelong rival. Tanabe was harshly critical when Heidegger joined the Nazi party and gave his notorious inaugural address as rector of the University of Freiberg (1933). The point on which he again criticizes Heidegger in our text is that [in Heidegger's approach] a subject (existence) lacking the mediation of a substratum becomes a mere "potential being of expressive interpretation" and "cannot help but wither into a subject of interpretive acts that are mere self-decision without content." Heidegger's existential individual can only discover and accept the "content" in which it is hermeneutically involved (here we might rephrase "content" as "cultural values") as something contingent. It therefore follows that however heroic the existential decision may seem, it can only be a "formal act" divorced from content. The fact that beneath the shadow of their shimmering surface the slogans of "being-towards-death [死への存在 *Sein zum Tode*]" and "anticipatory resoluteness [先験的決意性 *vorlaufende Entschlossenheit*]" in *Being and Time* possess a hollow structure capable of absorbing the Nazi mentality has also been pointed out in recent critical studies, and Tanabe's lucid assessment of Heidegger can be said to prefigure this kind of analysis.

But Tanabe had not specifically intended to make an ideological criticism. To the very end he was speaking of a new ontology. This was the standpoint of "absolute mediation", in other words, the idea that every thing-event and every phenomenon exists in correlative relationships or interactions with others. "Beings preceding logic" had already been rejected in Kant's transcendental idealism [*transzendentaler Idealismus*], but Tanabe laments the fact that in Kant the "principle of identity reigns" still and the "thing itself [物自体] that opposes via negation the subject's volitional acts" is not actively grasped. Whatever the nature of actuality might be, it is not something that "exists in advance as an object of interpretation", nor does it exist "separate from the formation of acts".

As noted above, however, if this action were to haphazardly expose the passion of existence it would be empty and dangerous. Aims that are chosen must not be entrusted to "awareness of potentiality" [可能的自覚] as in Heidegger, but rather be properly tied to the content of thought. It is here that Tanabe is a disciple of Plato. The aim of an act is raised by the subject and at the same time possesses the character of a "necessary form". What is needed is not a phenomenology that follows after phenomena, even if only slightly, but a "logic" that penetrates into the principle of the formation of the actual and at the same time raises it as the aim of practice. Tanabe also expresses this as the active being of "substratum-qua[*soku*]-subject". Here he has in mind Hegel's attempts in works like *The Phenomenology of Spirit* [*Phänomenologie des Geistes*] to develop a dialectic which stipulates that spirit is "substance and at the same time subject" and, without haste, stares at actuality in order to grasp and dynamically take part in it. On the one hand modern and contemporary nihilism and decisionism are thus impeached, while on the other hand "linguistic logic as an interpretation of substratum-less expression" (to which we might ascribe all contemporary discourse theories [ディスクール論]) is excoriated.

4.6 Does Absolute Mediation Fully Constitute a Logic of Difference?

Moving on, in the space remaining I would like to undertake a brief survey of section four of the text.

Looking back on the development of the logic of species, Tanabe states that he began by addressing the issue of the logic of social being mainly from practical necessity, and hit upon the concept of the species substratum as the key to resolving it. But he first reached the standpoint of absolute mediation in the essay *Shu no ronri to sekai zushiki* ["The Logic of Species and the Schema of the World"] (1935). From this standpoint he then reflected upon the logic of species at its foundation and added "important revisions" in *Ronri no shakaisonzaironteki kōzō* ["The Socio-ontological Structure of Logic"] (1936). What were these revisions?

At the start, species was conceived to be an immediate unity described in terms of a substratum standing opposed to the subjectivity of the individual. We might picture a pre-modern community suppressing and restraining the freedom of each member as [their] "substratum". But as a result of having logically thought through the fundamental principles of this social contradiction and dilemma, Tanabe was led to extract the "principle of self-alienation" as the negative moment of absolute mediation. In other words, the community itself is not something like a substance that gives birth to individuals while existing without any premise. Nazism invented the slogan "blood and soil", but while this was presented as deeply rooted in immediate life [直接的生命], it was nothing more than an abominable imitation of nature and a fiction. Everything is mediated and subsists in negotiation with other thing-events and phenomena. In the end, absolute mediation is a species of logic of difference that avoids identity logic (supporting some sort of immediacy). This may be a bit easier to picture if we think of it as something that highlights the elements in reciprocal repulsion within a network of reciprocal action and increases the mobility of the whole.

As a consequence of this revision of its trajectory, the species substratum was no longer seen to be an immediate unifying force. The bourgeois state, for example, is a species substratum. This state touts the fabrication that it is a political whole that protects every citizen, when in fact it oppresses one class of citizens, the proletariat, and represents the interests of another class of citizens, the bourgeoisie. As we can see in this example, the species substratum is constantly stirring up division in the shadow of the fabrication of unity. In the sense that while the actuality of division stands in opposition to the idea of unity, at the same time that one moment (the proletariat) stands in opposition to another moment (the bourgeoisie) it contains a two-fold opposition. Because the nature of the species substratum is to generate this opposition, Tanabe stipulates that species is the "moment of self-negation and principle of self-alienation". This division or opposition must be overcome. The state becomes a true whole when class conflict is "sublated" [止揚] internally [domestically] and individuals come to "freely cooperate" with the state. And as such a state it should then presumably be able to work in harmony with other states to concretize the "human world" (corresponding to "genus") as an "absolute whole".

Genus is neither something generated from the unison of species that are forces of negation, uniting them for a common purpose, nor the force of an identity logic that allows such a united front to arise. The self-negation of species is something incomplete [a half measure]. Instead it must be "transformed into absolute negation through action". In that case what exactly is absolute negation? What would a higher principle of negation that sublates the negative social phenomena of human beings (such as conflict) be? Tanabe looks for this not within society in the forces that drive social phenomena but rather in speculative ideas. In Hegel's dialectics, spirit, after first dividing and becoming externalized, then once again restores its self-identity and internally returns to itself. Tanabe, however, revises its processual character and proposes a logic whereby "self-alienation is *qua* [*soku*]{!}-self-return". "So-called self-inhabitation" in Hegel is the idea, strongly idealist in character, that no matter how much spirit stands mixed with other thing-events and at first glance seems "externalized," to the extent that as the subject of knowledge it does not lose cognitive control of its thing-events, it remains just as it is "within" the self. But in the case of Tanabe, who labeled this process with the single word "*qua*" [*soku*], has not the spirit fallen into an even more narcissistic self-occlusion? It seems to have [fallen in], notwithstanding the sense of responsibility felt by Tanabe, who entrusted his sincere efforts to directly address social conflict and logical entanglements to the intensity of the terminology of "absolute negation."

Finally, I would like to take a look at the scientific development of the logic of species. That we tend to think of Tanabe as, in the end, not having departed from the framework of previous metaphysics or ontology is due to his admission of a "unifying structure of being" and assertion that clearly "the ontology of mathematics and physics constitutes a certain kind of correspondence to social ontology". He stipulates this relationship of correspondence as "analogy." This is reminiscent of the Vienna circle's idea of "unified science" that emerged in the 1920s. But Tanabe, by first completing his "social ontology" and then attempting to apply "the logic of mathematics and physics" to this understanding of its social structure, in fact proceeded in a direction opposite to that of the Vienna circle's physicalism. Here it can be noted that Tanabe, having transferred to philosophy after first entering the physics department at the University of Tokyo and having undergone the experience of teaching introductory science courses at Tōhoku University, was a pioneer of the philosophy of science and the philosophy of mathematics in Japan. He writes that he "…invoked analogies to the theory of relativity and the sequent calculus of intuitionism [直観主義の連続論] found in recent approaches to the foundations of mathematics, and ultimately tried to approach the dialectic of quantum mechanics." This expansion into scientific theory, however, was by no means the product of amateur investigation. I should also note here that his interest in this area in fact remained vigorous until his final years; he published *Sūri no rekishishugi tenkai* [『数理の歴史主義展開』 *The Historicistic Development of Mathematics and Physics*] at the age of sixty nine, and *Sōtaisei riron no benshōhō* [『相対性理論の弁証法』 *The Dialectic of the Theory of Relativity*] at the age of seventy.

Nakaoka Narifumi Professor Emeritus, Osaka University. Major works: *Rinshōteki risei hihan* [『臨床的理性批判』 *A Clinical Critique of Reason*] (Iwanami Shoten, 2001), *Watashi to deau tame no Nishida Kitarō* [『私と出会うための西田幾多郎』 *[Studying] Nishida Kitarō to Encounter Myself*] (Demadosha, 1999), Hābāmasu: komyunikēshon kōi [『ハーバーマス: コミュニケーション行為』 Habermas: Communicative Action] (Kodansha, 1996).

Part III
Miki Kiyoshi

Chapter 5
The Logic of Imagination (Preface, Chapter 1 "Myth" 1)

[『構想力の論理』(序、第一章「神話」一)]

Miki Kiyoshi

5.1 Preface[1]

The essays in this book, *Kōsōryoku no Ronri* [『構想力の論理』 *The Logic of Imagination*] *Volume 1*, were first published in the magazine *Shisō* [『思想』 *Thought*]. After having been forced to stop by various circumstances, as I attempted to once again continue its writing I felt the need, as much for myself as for the reader, to gather together the first three chapters that had already been published in a single volume. They originally took the form of research notes, but I have elected to publish them here in this original form with very little revision. A complete systematic account must begin where this inquiry reaches its end. The account here will at first be undertaken in a phenomenological form, but later will probably progress to a purely logical form.

In order to show readers a path through the somewhat complicated text of this essay that was first written as research notes, I will give in this preface a simple statement of my intentions. This will amount to a summary of my intellectual career in recent years. Of course, as I continue writing this essay, I think that changes and developments will probably arise in my trajectory. This is to be expected for someone like me who is in the habit of thinking as he writes, rather than writing after thinking things through.

What captured my interest after the publication of my previous book, *Rekishi tetsugaku* [『歴史哲学』 *The Philosophy of History*] (1932), was the issue of how

---

Translated from the Japanese by Robert Chapeskie and revised by John W. M. Krummel.

[1]This Preface Appeared in *Kōsōryoku no Ronri Daiichi* [『構想力の論理 第一』 *the Logic of Imagination Vol. 1*], First Published in July 1939.

the objective and the subjective, the rational and the irrational, and the intellectual and the emotional can be unified. At the time my main task was formulating this as a question of the unification of *logos* and *pathos*, analyzing all aspects of history as elements in terms of *logos* and *pathos*, and discussing their dialectical unity. The circumstances of this period are clearly illustrated in my collection of essays *Kiki ni okeru ningen no tachiba* [『危機に於ける人間の立場』 *The Standpoint of Man in Crisis*] (1933). Even as I turned my attention toward matters of rationality and *logos*, matters of subjectivity, interiority, and *pathos* were issues I found persistently difficult to avoid. This is also why I was captivated by Pascal (*Pasukaru ni okeru ningen no kenkyū* [『パスカルに於ける人間の研究』 *The Study of Man in Pascal*] 1926) and influenced by Heidegger. Even when my primary interest in historical philosophy led to an intense focus on the study of historical materialism (*Yuibutsushikan to genndai no ishiki* [『唯物史観と現代の意識』 *Historical Materialism and Contemporary Consciousness*] 1928), my pursuit of a human foundation for historical materialism, too, was indeed also a result of the same interest. My demand to not lose sight of matters of *pathos* for the sake of matters of *logos*, and yet at the same time to not forget about matters of *logos* for the sake of matters of *pathos*, eventually took the form of an assertion of humanism. This was, so to speak, a progression from anthropology to humanism, and my collection of essays *Ningengakuteki bungakuron* [『人間学的文学論』 *An Anthropological Theory of Literature*] (1934) stands as a manifestation of my thought in this period.

As I have already mentioned, I tried to unify *logos* and *pathos* dialectically, but already at that point I myself felt that my consideration of this unity, even if not mistaken, was too formal. I am one of those who cannot help but bear antipathy towards the degeneration of dialectics in the hands of many into a kind of formalism, a new formal logic, so to speak, or even an expediency. Even if we take matters of *logos* and of *pathos* to be dialectically united, where, in concrete terms, is this unity to be found? Where is this synthesis, which does not stop at a mere logical composition, given in actuality? Pursuing this question, and remembering Kant's recognition of a function that combines understanding [悟性 *Verstand*] and sensibility [感性 *Sinnlichkeit*] within the imagination [構想力 *Einbildungskraft*], I arrived at the logic of imagination. And so I began writing these research notes while being guided by the premonition that I might be closing in on the solution to my longstanding problem (*Shisō* [『思想』 *Thought*] May, 1937). But at the time when I was writing its first chapter, "Myth" [「神話」], I was conceiving of imagination only as a faculty for the synthesis of *logos* and *pathos*, and I worried that this could degenerate into a kind of irrationalism or subjectivism. We might say that what sustained me amidst this uneasiness was nothing more than the view that "technology" [技術], which is something objective and rational, is, in its universal essence, a unity of the subjective and the objective. Eventually, however, from the time I began to consider "institutions" [制度] it gradually became clear that what I thought of as the logic of imagination was in fact "the logic of forms [形]". The fact that I had been dealing with Greek philosophy recently, in particular, Aristotle (*Arisutoteresu keijijōgaku* [『アリストテレス形而上学』 *Aristotelian Metaphysics*] 1935, *Arisutoteresu* [『アリストテレス』 *Aristotle*] 1938), had advanced my thought in this regard. As the expression "logic of imagination", which is, as it were, subjective, led me to discover the objective (in a manner of speaking) expression "logic of forms", my thinking has, for the time being, attained stability. In this way, having set out from my own, as it were, humanistic question, at the point at which I have presently arrived I have come close to Nishidian philosophy, at least to the extent of my understanding of it. Nishidian philosophy has been constantly guiding me in my research, whether consciously or unconsciously. Yet there are no doubt issues concerning the relationship between the logic of imagination, of which I speak, and the logic of Nishidian philosophy that ought to be considered separately.

In order to avoid misunderstanding concerning the intent of this text and to provide an overview, I will set down the following two or three points here at the start.

What I am attempting to conceive through the logic of imagination is a philosophy of action. Previously when one spoke of the imagination, it was almost always conceived in terms of artistic activities. And when it came to forms, too, in the past they were almost entirely conceived from the standpoint of contemplation. Releasing it from these restrictions, I am now connecting the imagination to acts in general. What is important in this case is to not understand action abstractly as a matter of the will on the basis of subjectivistic idealism, as in the past, but rather as the event of creating things. All acts in a broad sense create something, or, in other words, have the meaning of production. The logic of imagination is the logic of this kind of production. All things made are equipped with form. To act is to make new forms by working upon things and altering their forms (*transforming* them). Forms, as things that are made, are historical and change through history. Such forms are not simply objective, but are the unity of the objective and the subjective, *idea* [*Idee*] and reality, being and becoming, time and space. The logic of imagination is the logic of historical forms. Indeed, even if to act is to make something, history would be inconceivable unless making (*poïesis* [ποίησις]) at the same time has the sense of becoming (*genesis* [γένεσις]). History becomes conceivable when production (*poïesis* [ποίησις]) at the same time has the sense of creation (*genesis* [γένεσις]). The logic of imagination is the logic of forms and of their transformations, but the philosophy of forms I am talking about is not the same as the so-called "morphology" of the past. Morphology is a philosophy of interpretation and not a philosophy of action. And in contrast to many morphologies that are anti-rationalistic, the philosophy of forms of which I speak is instead a unification of the science of forms (*Eidologie*) and morphology (*Morphologie*), and furthermore attempts this from the standpoint of action.

We might say that previous logics, excepting, perhaps, those that have sought grounding in modern science, were all logics of forms. The logic of Aristotle, who can be said to have perfected formal logic, was essentially a logic of forms tied to Greek ontology that saw ideas or forms (*idea, eidos*) as realities. But in this case forms were thought of as unchanging and not considered to be historical. Even Hegel's logic, which can be said to have perfected dialectics, at its core is a logic of forms, and while Hegel did add to it a historical point of view, he too, like Greek ontology, stopped at the standpoint of contemplation and did not take the standpoint of action. His dialectic is a logic of reflection or of cogitation and not a logic of action or creation. As a logic of forms, the logic of imagination is tied to the logic of Aristotle and Hegel, but it grasps forms from the standpoint of historical action. The logic of imagination does not, however, simply reject formal logic or Hegelian dialectics; on the contrary it incorporates them. The logic of imagination as a primordial logic (*Urlogik*) draws them out of itself as forms of concretization of itself.

The logic of imagination takes the standpoint of *active intuition*, and will recognize the primordial meaning of intuition that had been unjustly overlooked by previous philosophy. However this would not be mere intuitionism. True intuition is something that had been mediated by reflection many times over. It is a single point of the present that gathers up the infinite past and leaps into the future. Nevertheless, the logic of imagination is not simply what has been called a logic of mediation. The logic of mediation ultimately remains a logic of reflection, and, to put it bluntly, cannot be a logic of action. It makes all mediation in the end into something abstract and sidesteps the most vigorous leap where all mediation is concentrated in a single form. This is evident in the act of creation in the arts, and also in the invention found in technology in general. And when we see all human acts as operational adaptations to the environment, we must describe all of them as technological. The fundamental idea of technology is form. If we think of the logic of imagination in connection to technology in this way, we may perhaps comprehend the relationship between the logic of forms and science. As technology took science as its foundation, the startling development of modern technology was made possible by the progress of modern science. As this suggests, through the mediation of the logic of science, the logic of imagination is capable of developing into a practical logic.

The idea of science in its proper sense is something that has arisen only in the modern period, but even prior to that technology had always existed. It existed even in the East, where it is said that science did not develop. Together with the culture of the human race, technology is both ancient and universal. Modern science, too, was born out of the demands of technology, and it is constantly being applied to technological purposes. Culture developed on the basis of the idea of form, where form is equivalent to technology, is broader and more universal than culture developed on the basis of the idea of science. Science is also included as an element within the former. We can see that the idea of culture in terms of *Gemeinshaft* that preceded the modern *Gesellshaft* was an idea of form. Today, when the abstractness of modern culture as *Gesellshaft* oriented upon the idea of science is made evident and there is a demand for a new culture as *Gemeinshaft*, the logic of imagination may be able to provide a philosophical foundation for the creation of this new culture. But just as this new *Gemeinshaft* must not abstractly oppose *Gesellshaft* but rather sublate it, the logic of forms as well must not abstractly oppose science but instead be mediated by it.

The logic of forms is not only a universal logic of culture; it also ties nature and culture, and natural history and human history, together. Nature too is technological, and nature also makes forms. Human technology continues the work of nature. In contrast to the view that abstractly separates nature and culture or history, the logic of imagination makes it possible to grasp both in a unified manner through a view to the alteration of forms (*transformation*). Rather than conceiving history from [the perspective of] nature, it conceives nature from [the perspective of] history. From there it should also be possible for the logic of imagination to provide a proper position for the descriptive sciences concerning nature and culture, an approach that has been unjustly disdained in comparison to mathematical natural science.

As is the case with *Gemeinshaft* cultures in general, it can be said that the idea of Eastern culture was also form. Nevertheless, in contrast to Greece where form was viewed objectively, came to mean "concept", and was thus coupled with modern science, in the East form was grasped subjectively, and was thus seen as something symbolic. This subjective perspective was thoroughly adopted through the idea of "form without form", a conception in which the formed is the shadow of the formless. This way of thinking is very significant to us. Form is form in relation to form, and each form stands alone. What lies at the root of these forms and ties them together is not something like laws adopted as ideas of modern science, not something that can be grasped objectively, but instead must be a form beyond form, a "form without form". Even if we say that form is a unity of the subjective and the objective, the logic of imagination is not erected on the standpoint of the so-called subject-object unity, but instead is conceived from a place beyond the subjective and the objective; only then can it be a logic of action, a logic of creation. But even if we can say that Eastern logic takes the standpoint of *active intuition*, we need to be wary of its tendency to go no further than being a state of mind, its technology being a technology of the mind that can easily remain forever in contemplation without stepping forth into practice to act upon things in reality to change their forms and make new forms. Herein lies the need for this approach to be mediated by the concepts of science and the technology of things.

Of course, these ideas need to be more fully developed. For the moment my research is phenomenological, and indeed has only barely begun. To begin I have taken up the three topics of myth, institution, and technology, but since my aim is to address them mainly from the perspective of the logic of imagination, it is inevitable that as independent theories of myth, institution, and technology my account will be insufficient. Even for my purposes there are no doubt various issues concerning these topics that must be considered. I hope to supplement these areas of deficiency as my inquiry progresses.

Tokyo, July 1939.

5.2 Chapter 1—"Myth" 1

Sectionn 1
The term "logic of imagination" [構想力の論理] (*Logik der Einbildungskraft*) derives from Baumgarten. It has also been called the "logic of fantasy" (*Logik der*

Phantasie). According to Cassirer,[2] the concept of the logic of imagination took root in German psychology through Meier and Tetens, disciples of Baumgartner, and it is also connected to the "critique of judgment" (*Kritik der Urteilskraft*) in Kant. Pascal had already discovered a "logic of the heart" (*Logique du couer*) unknown to reason. Today, too, Ribot's "logic of sentiments" (*logique des sentiments*) and Heinrich Maier's "psychology of emotional thought" (*Psychologie des emotionalen Denkens*) both speak of a logic distinguished from the logic of abstract thought. Does this kind of logic that differs from the logic of reason indeed exist? And if it does exist, what is it like? What I have attempted to begin examining here, reviving the term "logic of imagination", are these questions. What sort of connection does the logic of imagination in our sense have to Ribot's logic of sentiments and Maier's psychology of emotional thought? Looking back, in what kind of relationship does it stand to formal logic? An even more significant issue is to clarify the relationship between what is normally referred to as dialectics and what we call the logic of imagination; dialectics is indeed generally acknowledged to be a logic distinct from formal logic.

There are no doubt several reasons that we must consider a logic that differs from formal logic. While I must postpone their detailed description for later discussion, for the moment I will try to give a few of these reasons in order to illustrate the problematic state of affairs in which we stand here at the start of our inquiry.

To begin with, we point to the abstractness of formal logic and demand some sort of concrete logic in response. Where does this so-called abstractness of formal logic lie? At its source, formal logic is intimately tied to Greek ontology that viewed *forms* (*forma*) as real. What is considered as formal in formal logic was originally related to the ontology of forms. Hence if concrete things are constituted from form and matter [質料], one might then say that formal logic is not a logic of things, or that as a logic of things it is abstract. In Aristotle, *logos* or *nous* was conceived as the capacity to receive only forms by stripping things of matter. Put simply, formal logic is logic in terms of *logos*. Nevertheless, it is through our bodies that we come into contact with things themselves in their materiality. We collide with things qua things. If we here give the name *pathos* to the body in its subjectivity, the logic of things is not simply logic in terms of *logos* but at the same time related to things in terms of *pathos*. Previous logic placed perception upon the foundation of thought or upon a previous stage, and hardly reflected upon our sensation of coming in contact with things themselves by means of the above. Even when sensation was addressed, like perception and thought it was only grasped in an intellectual sense. The issue of whether sensation at the same time possesses the meaning of *pathos* was not raised. In cases where one "thinks with the body" as a human being possessing a body and thinking through action, we can say that formal logic is abstract. I believe that here there ought to be something like a logic of sentiments in contrast to the intellectualism of Greek logic.

---

[2]E. Cassirer, *Die Begriffsform im mythischen Denken*, Warburg: Studien der Bibliothek Warburg, 1922, p. 6.

5 The Logic of Imagination (Preface, Chapter 1 "Myth" 1)

Even if formal logic is a logic of the intellect, it presumably cannot be a logic of action. When we act we collide through our bodies with things themselves. Action requires a body, and the objects of action are not abstract universals but rather individual concrete things. The logic of action must therefore be a logic that somehow differs from formal logic. But can this be something like the logic of imagination? When we speak of the logic of sentiments or the logic of imagination, we ordinarily think of the realm of beauty or art. Baumgarten grounded aesthetics upon the logic of fantasy. What Kant sought in the transcendental structure of the faculty of judgment was the ground for the principles of beauty. In this way, even if one acknowledges something like a logic of imagination, one takes it to be a logic of beauty or logic of art and finds it difficult to think of it as a logic of action. Nevertheless, if as I will argue soon all acts in the end possess a sense of *poïesis* (production) or, put differently, a sense of expressive action, then perhaps we can say that the logic of action is the logic of imagination, hitherto conceived merely in regard to artistic expression. We did not originally set out to consent to the standpoint of so-called aestheticism. On the contrary, our issue was to comprehend not only art but all action, including the act of cognition, at its roots by clarifying the fundamental sense of expression to thereby liberate the logic of imagination, as a logic of the expressive world in general, from its restriction to the realm of beauty, and to appreciate it in the relationship of morality and theory and in particular in the relationship of theory and practice.

Action, it should be noted, is essentially social. And it is particularly in regard to group psychology that a logic distinct from formal logic comes to be required. One might say that formal logic is not simply of the individual but rather possesses a supra-individual universality. But by means of this it assumes precisely a human being divorced from historical determination, or humanity as an eternal, abstract essence. The concrete operations of the historical psychology of society, and the psychology of human beings constrained by it, transcend formal logic. Everything that can be seen as a product of group psychology, such as language, myth, manners, custom, institutions, and so on, cannot be grasped by formal logic. Formal logic cannot be the logic of history if the subject of history primarily must be the so-called objective spirit. Even though dialectics has been seen as the logic of history, I am proposing in addition the logic of imagination at this point not because I want to reduce history to something individual. On the contrary, it is quite the opposite. The subject of history, however, is not an abstract universal or mere spirit. It is something equipped with the so-called social body and individually distinguished through corporality. And everything historical exists in an environment, and, while acting upon the environment, is acted upon by it. By both determining the environment and being determined by it, at the same time as a subject it determines itself by means of itself. A historical form [形] thereby emerges. We can think of the logic of imagination as the logic of such historical forms.

Formal logic is a logic of objects, not a logic of [embodied] subjects. To put it another way, it is a logic about something that is already there. We can say that even dialectics in Hegel was still objective or concerned objects. Logic that takes the standpoint of the subject or of action, needless to say, must be one that surpasses not only formal logic but also Hegelian dialectics. In a broad sense, to act is to make something, and, if this means to make something new, then presumably the logic of action must be something like the logic of imagination as a logic of creation. It must take a standpoint of imagination that differs not only from the standpoint of understanding but also from what Hegel calls the standpoint of reason. When we say that the logic of imagination is the logic of history, we are conceiving it not only from the standpoint of understanding history but rather from the standpoint of making history. Indeed Baumgarten's logic of fantasy and Kant's critique of judgment were not only conceived primarily in relation to the realm of beauty, but also took the standpoint of the enjoyment or comprehension of beauty rather than the standpoint of the production of art itself. But the fact that we see the imagination as a faculty peculiar to artists is probably related to the fact that we view artistic activities in particular as original creations. Our job is to elucidate the logic of imagination as a logic of historical creation, while liberating it from its restriction to the realm of beauty and broadly introducing it into the world of action.

As I have already mentioned, formal logic was not only originally simply formal, but was also tied to the Greek ontology of forms; in other words, it was a logic of forms. But this ontology lacked the historicist way of thinking. Hegel's dialectic in a certain sense is also a logic of forms, but possesses the distinguishing characteristic of including a historical approach. But even Hegel's philosophy, like Greek ontology, takes the standpoint of contemplation and does not really take the standpoint of action. The logic of imagination is a logic of historical forms and a logic developed from the standpoint that creates these forms. Even if I speak of this as a logic of things, by things I mean historical things, which as expressive things possess forms. And when I speak of creation, I mean that things with form are made externally. Historical forms are not simply of *logos*, but rather the unity of things in terms of *logos* and *pathos*. The logic of imagination thus stands upon the unity of *logos* and *pathos*.

What then is imagination, and what sort of thing is the logic of imagination itself? Leaving a general answer for later, we shall instead proceed with a phenomenological investigation. Imitating the path Hegel followed from phenomenology to logic, we shall pursue logic amidst the analysis of phenomena.

Miki Kiyoshi (1897–1945). Born in Hyōgo Prefecture. Studied in Germany and France after graduating from Kyoto Imperial University. Professor at Hōsei University from 1927 to 1930. Twice arrested on suspicion of violating the Public Security Preservation Law [治安維持法]. Died in prison in 1945. Writings include *Pasukaru ni okeru ningen no kenkyū* [『パスカルに於ける人間の研究』 *The Study of Man in Pascal*] (Iwanami Shoten, 1926), *Yuibutsu shikan to gendai no ishiki* [『唯物史観と現代の意識』 *Historical Materialism and Contemporary Consciousness*] (Iwanami Shoten, 1928), and *Kōsōryoku no ronri* [『構想力の論理』 *The Logic of Imagination*] (Iwanami Shoten, 1939, 1946). "Chapter One: 'Myth'" of *The Logic of Imagination* was first published between May and July of 1937 in the journal *Shisō* [『思想』 *Thought*]. It is included in *Miki Kiyoshi zenshū* [『三木清全集』 *Complete Works of Miki Kiyoshi*] Vol. 8 (Iwanami Shoten).

Chapter 6
The Philosophy of Miki Kiyoshi

[三木清の哲学]

Akamatsu Tsunehiro

6.1　The Life of Miki Kiyoshi

Miki Kiyoshi was born in 1897 in the village of Hirai (now Tatsuno city) in the Ibo district of Hyōgo Prefecture. After graduating from the local primary and middle schools (in the old education system) he entered the Dai-ichi [The First] High School in 1914.

He seems to have had a passion for literature in middle school, enthusiastically reading Tokutomi Roka's [徳富蘆花] *Shizen to jinsei* [『自然と人生』 *Nature and Life*], novels by Tōson [島崎藤村] and Ōgai [森鷗外] and foreign literature by authors such as Turgenev, attempting to write his own novels and poems, and consulting with a teacher about his desire to become a writer. But eventually he gave up on this ambition and became interested in philosophy.

After entering high school he joined the boat club, became drawn to religion, and was thus passing days of impressionable wandering when he had a fateful encounter. When he was nineteen years old and in his third year of high school, he read Nishida Kitarō's *Zen no Kenkyū* [『善の研究』 *An Inquiry into the Good*, 1911], and, deeply struck by the sense that this was the philosophy he had been searching for, decided to specialize in the study of philosophy under Nishida. The following year, upon graduating from high school, he immediately visited Nishida Kitarō and borrowed a copy of the original text of Kant's *Critique of Pure Reason*. Thus began their master-disciple relationship.

Miki, who entered the faculty of letters at Kyoto Imperial University in 1917, studied philosophy under Nishida, but also received instruction from others such as Hatano Seiichi [波多野精一] and Tanabe Hajime [田辺元]. After graduating from

---

Translated from the Japanese by Robert Chapeskie and revised by John W. M. Krummel.

T. Akamatsu (✉)
Shinshū University, Matsumoto, Japan

the department in 1920 he enrolled at the graduate school and lectured at a private university. Then in 1922 he went to Germany to study, having received funding from Iwanami Shigeo. He first attended seminars given by Rickert of the Neo-Kantian school, but unsatisfied with these studies he moved the following year to Marburg where he attended Heidegger's lectures and seminars and began to receive instruction from him. Miki also interacted with philosophers such as Karl Löwith and Gadamer, and studied the currents of German intellectual history and the new philosophical trends of the time in an intimate setting.

After staying two years in Germany he moved to Paris, where he spent one year devoting himself to reading while studying French. He became captivated by Pascal's *Pensées* after coming across it by chance. He wrote about Pascal, using the hermeneutic method he had learned from Heidegger, and sent one paper after another back to Japan. These papers, originally published in the magazine *Shisō*, were published together after his return as Miki's first book, *Pasukaru ni okeru ningen no kenkyū* [『パスカルに於ける人間の研究』 *The Study of Man in Pascal*] (first published in 1926, and included in Iwanami Shoten's *Miki Kiyoshi zenshū* [『三木清全集』 *Complete Works of Miki Kiyoshi*], vol. 1). Miki became known as an up-and-coming philosopher, worked as a lecturer at the Third High School in Kyoto and as a part-time lecturer at several universities, and provided guidance to students and younger scholars.

In 1927 he moved to Tokyo where he became a professor at Hōsei University while also holding the post of lecturer at one or two other private universities. From around this time Miki began to study Marx and historical materialism, and his writings in which he presented the results of these studies shocked the public. In 1928 these writings were collected and published with the title *Yuibutsushikan to gendai no ishiki* [『唯物史観と現代の意識』 *Historical Materialism and Contemporary Consciousness*] (included in *Miki Kiyoshi Zenshū*, vol. 3).

With this publication Miki committed himself to the Marxist cultural movement that comprised one wing of the socialist movement of the time, and became active as the editor-in-chief of the magazine *Puroretaria kagaku* [『プロレタリア科学』 *Proletarian Science*] while also heading up the Dialectical Materialism Group of the Proletarian Science Institute. He was criticized, however, as an idealist by so-called "orthodox" Marxists. In May of 1930 he was arrested on suspicion of donating money to the Japanese Communist Party. He was released after being sentenced to one year in prison and two years of probation, but it became difficult for him to remain in the teaching profession and he resigned from Hōsei University and his other teaching positions.

From this point on Miki was forced to support himself with just his writing and continued his vigorous activities in this domain, producing several works per month of criticism or commentary on current events as a literary critic and social commentator while continuing to publish [his own] books. Of course, these included many books and essays of philosophy. Ever since his time spent studying abroad in Germany Miki had maintained deep ties with Iwanami Shoten, and worked on philosophy lectures, philosophy library, and completed works planned and published by this publishing house, writing some of these texts himself.

In 1938 he became a member of the *Shōwa Kenkyūkai* [昭和研究会 Shōwa Research Association], formed around the brain trust of Prime Minister Konoe Fumimaro, and was active mainly in its culture division until this association's dissolution in 1940.

Following this he continued to write tenaciously from the standpoint of humanism and liberalism amidst the stifling of freedom of speech under the circumstances of the wartime political system, but in March of 1945 he was arrested on suspicion of hiding suspected violators of the Public Security Preservation Law, taken into prosecutorial custody and sent to a detention center. He was not released even after the war ended on August 15th, and died suddenly in the Toyotama Detention Center on September 26th. At the time of his death he was forty-eight years old.

6.2 A Portrait of Miki's Philosophy as a Whole

Not having been blessed with circumstances that allowed him to devote himself to philosophical reflection within the context of university academism like his teacher Nishida, Miki Kiyoshi was active as a philosopher "out of office" and a critic. In some respects this may have been a choice driven by unavoidable external factors, but he was also the type of person who was more inclined to pour his passion into thinking in accord with concrete actualities than spinning threads of abstract speculation. And because the stance he took throughout his life was one of being committed in some way to social actualities, we might say that this was a way of life that he himself actively embraced. But there was always a consistent philosophical approach behind his journalism and writing of critical essays and social commentary, and he produced many books and papers of genuine philosophy.

Without entering into how Miki understood the circumstances of the time and how he tried to act in relation to social realities, this exposition will focus on his thought as a philosopher and will go no further than extracting its fundamental framework.

The framework of Miki's philosophical thought changed several times, but there are some aspects that remained unaltered throughout these shifts. Broadly speaking, the process of the formation and development of Miki's philosophy can be divided into the following six periods.

(1) The period of his student years when he addressed issues mainly through a Neo-Kantian approach.
(2) The period of hermeneutic ontology after his time spent studying abroad in Europe.
(3) The period during which he approached Marxism and moved from hermeneutic ontology to practical ontology.
(4) The period during which he advocated his own historical social ontology.

(5) The period during which he developed his historical social ontology into a philosophy of the act of technological production.
(6) The period during which he pursued the logic of imagination and logic of forms on the basis of a philosophy of the act of technological production.

Let us take a broad look at each of these periods.

(1) During his university and graduate school years, Miki was interested on the one hand in the issue of what it means for human beings to be individual beings, and on the other hand in the issue within the philosophy of history of how to grasp the progress of human history. Tying these two questions into one they become the issue of "the role of the individual in history", and Miki's question was how to grasp the process by which the accumulation as a whole of individual actions of each free individual person constitutes ethnic culture, civic culture, and, going even further, universal human culture. This was a consciousness of these issue fostered within the educationalist mood of the Taisho era. Using the conceptual apparatus of Neo-Kantianism that was popular at the time and adding to it the concepts of Plato's *idea* and Leibniz' monad, while also being influenced by the studies of his mentor Nishida Kitarō, beginning with his graduation thesis he wrote several essays on this question but could not find a satisfying approach to its resolution.

(2) While studying abroad in Germany, Miki not only directly experienced the state of German society after World War I, but also sensed a major shift taking place in intellectual and philosophical trends. It was no longer the period of Neo-Kantianism. The fact that Miki transferred from Rickert's seminar to Heidegger's seminar is evidence of the keenness of his sense of the trend of the times. But it can also be said that, having borne a *pathos* that could not be quieted by the rationalism of the Neo-Kantian school since his student days, after a long search he had at last found something that would speak to it.

The method of an "ontological hermeneutic of life" that Miki learned from Heidegger was quite different from the method of hermeneutic phenomenology Heidegger refers to in *Being and Time* [*Sein und Zeit*]; the period during which Miki studied under Heidegger was quite some time before this book was published. Miki studied the life philosophy [*Lebensphilosophie*] of thinkers such as Nietzsche and Simmel, the hermeneutics of Dilthey and others, Scheler's philosophical anthropology, and so on in parallel, absorbing these various approaches that mingled together and constituted a single current of thought in Germany at that time. He combined what he learned from Heidegger with these approaches to create his own method of hermeneutic ontology, albeit one that lacked the existentialistic elements found in Heidegger's philosophy. Miki's approach is also distinct in actively affirming the "public aspects" and "social nature" depreciated by Heidegger, a fact that would later play a role in his interpretation of Marx.

Miki used this method of hermeneutic ontology to decipher the ideas of life, death, and love in Pascals's *Pensées*, but he was unable to fully grasp Pascal's religious thought.

(3) In his investigation of Marxism and historical materialism that he began around 1926, Miki employed the same method he had used in his study of Pascal.

In other words, he employed a method of interpretation that clarifies fundamental experience where concepts are given and clarifies concepts where fundamental experience is given. In his interpretation of Marx, however, aspects of this method that were altered under the influence of Marx's thought were also significant. The two-part scheme of "fundamental experience–concept" became a three-part scheme of "fundamental experience–anthropology–ideology", and, conscious of the limitations of the hermeneutical method, Miki began to assert an ontology that takes the standpoint of "practice".

In contrast to everyday experience dominated by an established *logos* (language) and stabilized through its public aspects, what Miki calls "fundamental experience" is an experience that gives birth to a new *logos* from within an "unstable kinesis" without being dominated by an established *logos*. This is also called "the dark" [闇]. What he refers to as "experience" here is not an epistemological concept but rather an ontological concept, meaning the structure of "dynamic correlation", that is, the relationship of negotiation between human beings or between human beings and other entities. From within this relationship, a *logos* is born. The primary *logos* is "anthropology", namely, the *logos* of man's self-comprehension, and the secondary *logos* is "ideology", namely the *logos* of fields such as scholarship, science, social thought, and so on belonging to each epoch.

Miki would go on to interpret various modes of thought and philosophies, starting with Marxism, using this kind of three-part scheme, but the question was originally raised in the context of his self-reflection concerning what sort of fundamental experience his own hermeneutic stood upon as a philosophy. Eventually his goal thus became to erect a philosophy from the standpoint of practice by transcending the standpoints of interpretation and contemplation. Here we see the influence of Marx, but by not taking the standpoint of materialism Miki sets himself apart from Marxism.

(4) Having been arrested under the Public Security Preservation Law, Miki separated himself from the Marxist cultural movement and began devoting himself to the activity of writing. On the basis of his investigations of Marx, he went on to develop an ontology from the standpoint of practice as his own distinct historical social ontology. During this period Miki attempted to elucidate from various angles the process by which human beings make history while being made by history. The act of making history is an act that remakes historical social actualities into new ones even while taking existent historical social actualities as a premise. By taking a fixed form what is made stands opposed to the act of making and transcends it. He calls this relationship of continuity and discontinuity, and of mutual negation amidst mutual assumption, between the act of making history and the actuality made, a "dialectical" relationship, and attempts to clarify its structure. He also claims that the act of making history is a sensory and somatic act, and furthermore that this *soma* (body) is a "social body" and social somaticity is at the basis of the formation of history. A representative work from this period is *Rekishi tetsugaku* [『歴史哲学』 *Philosophy of History*] (first published 1932, included in *Miki Kiyoshi zenshū* [『三木清全集』 *Complete Works of Miki Kiyoshi*, vol. 6]).

(5) From around 1934 Miki began to discuss questions of technology and technological production as important issues to be addressed, and came to grasp the social somatic acts that make history as acts of technological production.

At first Miki addressed technology from the perspective of art. He attempted to clarify the characteristics of artistic creation by contrasting it with technological production, but this gradually broadened into a consideration of technology in general, and he came to argue that human acts in general were in essence acts of production mediated by technology. In this case what he meant by technology includes everything from the manufacture and use of tools to rhetoric as a technology of linguistic expression and the techniques of artistic creation.

Technology is regulated within the relationship between subject and environment. Human beings as subjects stand in opposition to their environment, alter it, and go on making new environments. What mediates this subject and its environment is technology. The concept of the environment is broad, and, not being limited to the natural environment, includes even the social and cultural environments. Correspondingly, technology, too, includes social, conceptual, and mental technologies.

Miki states that the act of technological production is a "creation out of nothing" [無]. That human beings are subjects means that they transcend their environment and are not directly governed by it, and that the ground of human subjectivity is "nothing". Standing upon this nothing, man is seized by demonic and primal urges to undertake creation out of nothing. Here we can see the influence of Nishida on Miki's philosophy concerning the act of technological production. A representative work from this period is *Gijutsu tetsugaku* [『技術哲学』 *Philosophy of Technology*] (First published in 1942; included in *Miki Kiyoshi zenshū*, vol. 7).

(6) The foundation of Miki's philosophy of the act of technological production remained unchanged until his death. But in *Kōsōryoku no ronri* [『構想力の論理』 *The Logic of Imagination*], begun in 1937 he grasps the act of technological production anew as a creation of new forms by means of an "imagination" that unites *logos* and *pathos* (I will discuss *Kōsōryoku no ronri* in the next section). Apart from *Kōsōryoku no ronri*, other important texts from this period include *Tetsugaku nyūmon* [『哲学入門』 *Introduction to Philosophy*] (First published 1940; included in *Miki Kiyoshi zenshū*, vol. 7), *Jinseiron nōto* [『人生論ノート』 *Notes on the Theory of Life*] (First published 1941; included in *Miki Kiyoshi zenshū*, vol. 1), and *Tetsugaku nōto* and *Zoku tetsugaku nōto* [『哲学ノート』 *Notes on Philosophy*, vols. 1 & 2] (First published 1941–42; included in *Miki Kiyoshi zenshū*, vol. 10).

After Miki's death a posthumous manuscript entitled *Shinran* [『親鸞』] (included in *Miki Kiyoshi zenshū*, vol. 18) was discovered. It attempts to clarify the overall picture of Shinran's religion from a variety of angles, but remained no more than a fragmentary draft.

As noted above, there were aspects of Miki Kiyoshi's philosophical thought that were influenced by the intellectual trends of the times and changed in accordance with the circumstances of society. But there is also an aspect that remained consistent and unaltered. If we were to characterize the whole of Miki Kiyoshi's philosophy in a single phrase, we might say that it was a Japanese life philosophy [*Lebensphilosophie*]. During his student years Miki attempted to think through the issue of history and the individual by means of the conceptual apparatus of Neo-Kantianism, but he went beyond Neo-Kantianism's rationalism to emphasize the irrationality of humanity. What Miki encountered when he studied abroad in Germany was the intellectual current of life philosophy in a broad sense, and what he acquired from this was the methodology of the "ontological hermeneutic of life". Even his reading of Marx was conducted from the standpoint of the ontology of life. The claim that when an existing *logos* becomes fixed it contradicts and opposes new fundamental experiences and collapses so that a new *logos* is formed is one of life philosophy rather than Marxism.

Even when it comes to his historical social ontology, its understanding of the relationship between the act of making history and the actuality that has been made fits the framework of life philosophy. Both the philosophy of the act of technological production and the theory of imagination involve the idea of uniting the rational and the irrational, and neither fundamentally go beyond this framework. However, because Miki introduces the concept of "nothing", asserts the groundlessness [無根拠性] of human life, and advocates an ontology of life that takes nothing as its ground, while it is a life philosophy we might also say that it is a life philosophy of a Japanese sort.

Life philosophy does not only address the consciousness or cognition of man, but tries to grasp the being that is man as a whole. In this sense Miki also asserted an ontology. This ontology, moreover, was one developed from the standpoint of action. He shifted from the standpoint of "contemplation" that is hermeneutics to the standpoint of "practice", and from there went on to create a philosophy of action. He emphasized the somaticity of human beings, and tried to clarify the process by which human beings as somatic beings make the world through acts of technological production.

This philosophy of acts was also a philosophy of history. Human acts are undertaken within history, and their results become history. In his philosophy of history Miki's concept of "the subject" was two-fold. Man is a subject and man makes history. History is a subject, and history makes history with human beings as its constitutive elements. The viewpoint that sees history by taking human beings as subjects and the viewpoint that sees human beings by taking history as subject are entangled. Human beings, moreover, are both within history and independent of it.

As noted above, Miki's philosophy of history is a philosophy of history from the standpoint of "action" rather than "contemplation". But because philosophers talk about the relationship between history and human beings who act as though they were standing outside of history, theirs is not a philosophy for the sake of actors themselves taking action, and goes no further than "contemplation about action". In contrast to this, the "logic of imagination" is conceived from a place where actors, while being governed by history, act as independent entities. Herein are the seeds of a philosophy for the sake of actors themselves taking action.

Miki's philosophy was a philosophy that thought through a logic of continuity and discontinuity, immanence and transcendence, in a variety of settings. Unlike his mentor, Nishida Kitarō, he attempted to consider the issues he addressed concretely on the basis of facts, but as a result of his premature death this endeavor will remain forever aborted.

6.3 The Contemporary Significance of *The Logic of Imagination*

The Logic of Imagination is a representative work from the last years of Miki Kiyoshi's life. The first half, initially serialized under the themes of "myth", "institution", and "technology" in the journal *Shisō* from 1937 to 1938, was brought together and published as *The Logic of Imagination Part One* in 1939. The serialization of the next part began immediately, and Miki continued writing on the theme of "experience" until 1943 when he temporarily stopped after announcing his intention to address "language" next. But due to his death in prison his plan was never realized, and the part he had written on "experience" was published alone as *The Logic of Imagination Part Two* in 1946 (in his *Zenshū* [*Collected Works*] the entire work is included in vol. 8).

In the preface and Section One of Chap. 1 of this book, Miki expresses his intentions and understanding of the issues involved in attempting to elucidate the logic of imagination. Ever since publishing *Rekishi tetsugaku* [『歴史哲学』 *Philosophy of History*], Miki had been contemplating "the issue of how the objective and the subjective, the rational and the irrational, and the intellectual and the emotional might be combined", or, more succinctly, "the issue of the unity of *logos* and *pathos*". In order to address this issue, the concept Miki established as the fundamental key to deciphering it was the concept of the "imagination" [構想力]. The "imagination" was conceived of by Kant as a faculty possessing the function of unifying the understanding and sensation. Taking this as his starting point, Miki broadened this concept, calling the faculty that generally operates with the inclusion of both elements of *logos* and *pathos* "imagination" and proceeding to analyze the concrete instances of its operation. Addressing "myth", "institution", and "technology", Miki conceived of the imagination as operating in each case. (Chap. 4, "Experience", is a study of the history of philosophy concerning the concept of imagination).

The imagination is not a cognitive faculty but rather a faculty that operates in the productive act of making things. Miki holds that what is produced by imagination possesses "form". In other words, the imagination is a faculty that produces "forms", synthesizing qualities of *logos* and *pathos* as one. As Miki himself states in the preface, he engaged in an elucidation of the logic of imagination in order to further deepen the philosophy of action he had been developing at the time. He took all human acts to be acts of technological production, but by grasping its "production" (*poïesis*) as the creation of new forms through the imagination he attempted to clarify the essence of human action.

The idea of "a technological production of new forms by means of the free use of the imagination" was not simply a casual suggestion but the result of Miki's long years of philosophical contemplation. And behind it also lay Miki's anxiety over the social circumstances of the period and his desire to somehow commit himself to addressing that situation. In 1937 the Sino-Japanese War began and Japan intensified its wartime restructuring. This was also a time of rupture between *logos* and *pathos*. Any rational discussion on the basis of *logos* was rendered impotent and crushed to oblivion, while *pathos* erupted and flowed freely as ultranationalism. The Shōwa Research Society in which Miki played an active role from 1938 to 1940 was an organization built around technological bureaucrats, or "technocrats", who wanted to somehow avoid a social collapse by reforming Japan's socio-economic system from within (see Arakawa Ikuo, *Miki Kiyoshi*, Kinokuniya shinsho). The aim of this organization was indeed "to produce technologically a new form of system through free employment of the imagination that unites *logos* and *pathos*." This sort of awareness of practical issues was the background against which Miki engaged in the philosophical task of elucidating the logic of imagination.

So do Miki's conception and analysis transcend their era to still possess viability today? To begin with let us consider his analysis of myth. To see myth as a product of the imagination that unites *logos* and *pathos* is perhaps one way of looking at it. But that imagination or fancy is active in the formation of myths is a common-sense view that anyone would acknowledge. Taking this as our starting point, the issue then becomes how to analyze the elements of *logos* and *pathos* contained within myth and establish a viable methodology. Miki's analysis, however, goes no further than giving illustrations of several examples. These examples, moreover, amount to nothing more than pointing out that myths contain intellectual representations and figures as elements of *logos*, and that underlying the figures of myths there are emotions such as the sense of supernatural forces, hope, desire, and fear that exist as elements of *pathos*. *Logos* and *pathos* in myth need to be more clearly defined.

Contemporary analyses of myths do not see in them figures that immediately unite *logos* and *pathos* as Miki did. Lévi-Strauss, for example, held that the logical structure (*logos*) extracted from myth lies in a different dimension from that in which *pathos* operates. Because a myth is a single narrative or *mythos*, *logos* as the narrative's linguistic structure would presumably have to be analyzed at both its surface and in its depths.

Looking next at Miki's analysis of "institutions", his broad grasp of the concept of institution, including in it not only social and legal institutions but also language, morality, and art, is something that is also acknowledged today. And while all institutions are fictions, the posing of the question of why they possess reality in spite of being fictions is an issue that remains meaningful even today. Miki, however, does not provide a convincing answer.

Miki points out that even with artificially established institutions, there are customs and conventions that support them as elements of *pathos* contained within them. Although this is not incorrect, in the current era in which the communities that naturally constitute customs and conventions are disintegrating, the actual issue is how to make artificial institutions that can obtain broad social consent while being temporarily severed from customs and conventions. Leaving *pathos* aside, the issue becomes the validity of *logos* itself.

Miki's project of uniting *logos* and *pathos* suffered in the prewar period from the outpouring and dominance of *pathos* severed from *logos*. Because it is difficult today for *pathos* to constitute the ground of a community, the trend towards consciously putting aside *pathos* and attempting to secure universality through *logos* is strong. This makes Miki's framing of the question difficult to accept in these circumstances that are so different from those of the prewar period. But this does not mean that Miki's theory of institutions is no longer viable at all. For example, when the French sociologist Pierre Bourdieu criticizes both structuralist objectivism and existentialist subjectivism and attempts to elucidate the social behavior of people as conventional behavior based on an acquired "*habitus*", there are aspects of this stance, transcending their considerable separation in time, that accord with Miki's conception.

Turning next to technology, in Miki's account it is defined as the skill used to mediate between subject and environment when there is alienation or opposition between them, and ultimately to make a new environment. While an interesting perspective, this viewpoint alone, even in its account of technology, is probably not sufficient as a theory to provide a course of action to resolve the various issues faced by contemporary society.

Miki's account of technology emerges from the somatic behavior of human beings when they produce things through the use of tools. While he includes within technology conceptual technology and technology of the mind, his basic model is the production of things with tools. Contemporary technology is much more extensive, stretching as far as information technology and technology for the manipulation of biological life. Because Miki's concept of "form" is comprehensive and can include anything, it is necessary to include the concept of information and define the meaning of "form" concretely. Whether or not Miki's account of technology possesses any viability today depends on whether or not it can resolve the fundamental issue of the destruction of nature that our contemporary civilization of scientific technology faces. In order to address this issue it may be necessary to reconstruct it as an account of technology that also incorporates the concepts of "mass" or "matter" vis-à-vis "form".

As stated above, Miki's *Logic of Imagination*, whether as an account of myth, institutions, or technology, cannot be brought into our contemporary world and accepted simply as it is. Miki's elucidation of imagination, however, was a part of the contemplation that constituted his own philosophy. We must therefore evaluate this theory of imagination on the basis of its position within the whole of Miki's philosophy.

As noted above, Miki elucidates the logic of imagination from the standpoint of the philosophy of action. He defines technological productive acts of human beings on the basis of the relationship of the subject and its environment. The difference between human beings and other animals lies in a difference in the relationship between subject and environment. Animals exist within the same dimension or order as the environing world, but human beings transcend the environment. Because there is alienation and opposition between human beings and their environment, human beings reconstruct the environment to better suit themselves. This is a technological productive act. But because in this act man himself is altered as well, the remaking of the environment knows no end. Miki refers to technological production as a "creation from nothing". This is the case because human beings transcend the environment to become "subjects", and the ontological ground of man is "nothing". The production of the environment in a new form comes about through the imagination [構想力], namely the imagination that generates being out of nothing.

If we tie together Miki's philosophy of action and his logic of imagination in this way, what Miki is trying to say is the following: while human beings separate themselves from the natural environment to make the cultural environment, that cultural environment possesses no necessity or ground that would explain it or provide it with reason, and is instead accidental or arbitrary. Although human beings have made new forms called "culture" through acts of technological production, this production occurs through the workings of the imagination. And the forms of culture that have been made are all institutions and fictions, but while being fictions they also possess reality. If we read Miki's philosophy as a theory of cultural formation that explicates the principle of humanity's cultural formation, we can see the value of its deep insight into the essence of human culture.

Miki's philosophy of action is tied to his philosophy of history. Human history is the process of cultural formation through acts of technological production, a process whereby the forms of culture are in continual "transformation". Conversely, we can also say that acts of technological production are undertaken within history. Human beings form history and are formed within it. Following his mentor Nishida Kitarō, Miki takes human beings to be "formative elements of the formative world" (see *Tetsugaku nyūmon* [『哲学入門』 *Introduction to Philosophy*] and *Gijutsu tetsugaku* [『技術哲学』 *Philosophy of Technology*]). Here the "formative world" refers to the historical world as a whole. It can be said that human beings form the world, but conversely it can also be said that as structural elements of the historical world human beings participate in its self-formation. But humanity is also something independent. While being made, as independent entities human beings go on making themselves (see *Tetsugaku nyūmon* [*Introduction to Philosophy*]).

This philosophy of history developed by Miki, when seen from the standpoint of the actor within history rather than from the standpoint of the philosopher standing outside of history or of an observer with a bird's eye view, becomes the "logic of imagination". Actors dwell within a historically formed cultural environment, but even as they are restricted by this environment they are independent of it. They are thus subjects, and as subjects they give birth to new forms of culture. Seen from the standpoint of the actor him/herself, the creation of new forms can only be described as a "creation from nothing". "Creation from nothing" is executed through the imagination, but imagination is not the rational cognitive faculty of an observer with a bird's eye view but rather an imaginative faculty by which the actor internally affected by *pathos* attempts to give this *pathos* form.

New forms birthed by the actor are discontinuous with extant forms that make up the cultural environment. From the perspective of an observer taking in the entire scene, however, there is a "transformation" from extant to new forms. From the observer's perspective, the actor is restricted by the historically formed environment, but for the actor him/herself a leap is made from the existing environment. This, in other words, is "the most vigorous leap where all mediation is concentrated in a single form" (p. 72 of [the Japanese edition of] this book). Miki understood Nishida's "active intuition" by attaching it to his own philosophy of action whereby new forms are created by means of this sort of imagination. While intuition is knowledge mediated by reflection, it is situated in an immediacy wherein that mediation has been extinguished. Moreover, it is not knowledge for the sake of knowledge but rather an operation that generates new forms through action.

Although Miki's philosophy of history is built upon the perspective of transcendentalism, the "logic of imagination" is conceived from the perspective of the actor him/herself who acts within history. Miki is always thinking from this dual perspective of transcendentalist and immanent viewpoints. This method of contemplation transcends epochs and remains alive today.

While on the one hand emphasizing the discontinuity between nature and human culture, once again following Nishida Miki tries to grasp natural history and human history in a unified manner. Here, too, what ties them together are the concepts of "form" and "technology". "Nature too is technological, and nature also makes forms" (p. 73 of [the Japanese edition of] this book). This expansion of the concepts of "form" and "technology" is filled with problems. While form exists in both organic nature and inorganic nature, can we discover "technology" in inorganic nature? We probably cannot call the workings of inorganic nature "technology". In terms of our everyday understanding, among living things perhaps we may be able to say that the behavior of animals with quite a high degree of intelligence, such as primates, is technological. But whether the behavior of all living creatures can be described as technological remains dubious. Miki, however, expands the concept of technology and stipulates that all behavior of organisms possessing a "center" [q. v. Helmuth Plessner] and aiming to adapt to their environment when there is a gap between themselves and that environment is technological. He is saying that the fact that even the inherited innate behavior of living things is not completely determined but possesses a certain degree of freedom is technological. There is indeed a degree of freedom in the behavior of any living creature, and we might grasp human technology as having been formed out of a qualitative change caused by an extension of this degree of freedom. Miki describes this qualitative change as humanity's transcendence of the environment to become "subjects". The environment, conversely, separated from humanity and became an "object". Between humanity as subject and the environment as object lies an abyss of nothing. Here the technology of human beings becomes something different from the technology of nature. It is a technology that makes a cultural environment distinct from the natural environment in order to bury the alienation and opposition between subject and environment. Rather than adapting to the environment it makes an environment compatible with itself. It is, so to speak, reverse adaptation. What works to construct a new cultural environment is the imagination. Although Miki saw "form" and "technology" in nature as well, he did not search for the source of the imagination in natural history.

Miki tries to grasp the continuities and discontinuities between nature and humanity, and between nature and culture, but it is not enough. If we were to make Miki's conception into an abstract logic it would probably be a logic similar to Nishida's "absolutely contradictory self-identity" [絶対矛盾的自己同一], but unlike Nishida Miki's particular strength lay in drawing a logic out of an analysis of concrete phenomena. Miki needed to clarify the logic of discontinuity and continuity in the midst of concretely analyzing the difference and commonality between the forms of nature and the forms of human culture, and between the technology of nature and the technology of human beings, but he stopped mid-way. If we are to bring Miki's philosophy to life today, we must grasp it anew on the basis of the knowledge found in contemporary life sciences and information sciences. In the process the concepts of "subject", "environment", "form", "production", "technology", and "imagination" will inevitably change, but the content of Miki's imagination is worth revisiting in the present era.

Akamatsu Tsunehiro Professor Emeritus, Shinshū University. Major works: *Miki Kiyoshi: tetsugakuteki shisaku no kiseki* [『三木清:哲学的思索の軌跡』 *Miki Kiyoshi: Traces of [his] Philosophical Speculations*] (Minerva Shobō, 1994), Erich Adickes' *Kanto to monojitai* [『カントと物自体』 *Kant und das Ding an sich*] (Translation, Hosei University Press, 1974).

Part IV
Tosaka Jun

Chapter 7
What Is the Technological Spirit?

[技術的精神とは何か]

Tosaka Jun

I believe the technological spirit is the fundamental spirit of modern culture. Let me explain. The protagonist of James Joyce's *Ulysses*, in other words the protagonist of an odyssey story, is Dedalus, and critics state that he corresponds to Telemachus, the protagonist of *The Odyssey* (the one attributed to Homer). According to Professor Doi Kōchi, the name "Dedalus" refers to the Greek "Daedalus" and symbolizes technology.

How deeply significant this observation may be, I myself do not know. But if something related to technology is being recognized in this contemporary adaptation of classical Greece (a description that may not be accurate), this is very interesting. This novel by Joyce, insofar as it engages in an analysis of modern subjectivity or self-awareness (self-consciousness) as a work of so-called "stream of consciousness" literature, belongs, it goes without saying, to a kind of modernism, and with its presentation of some kind of unity in the midst of disorder it communicates something similar to the tempo of modern life. But if that is not all and there is also something that creates an association with certain technological themes, then it must possess a modern meaning in this aspect as well.

What does "technological spirit" refer to? How is it related to technology? What exactly is it that we call "technology"?—We shall address these questions a bit later. There are surely at least a few things understood in common knowledge by the phrase "technological spirit." But in that case it is not necessarily limited to a spirit particular to modernity. Neither can we regard it as a spirit that became dominant only in modern times. On the contrary, the defining characteristic of Thales, whose moral thought first distinguished Greek philosophy from the Epic era of Homer, was nothing other than his technological spirit. What brought him

---

Translated from the Japanese by Robert Chapeskie and revised by John W. M. Krummel.

J. Tosaka

attention from the general public was his genius and special talents for engineering and military technology. Although Plato introduces him as a contemplator of life who fell into a ditch while looking at the stars, Aristotle, a more faithful historian, presents him as an outstanding businessman and moneymaker. It has become a common assumption among historians of science and technology that there was a close historical connection between Greek philosophy and the technological sciences of Babylon and Egypt.

Therefore, if we are to consider the technological spirit quite generally and in terms of its greatest common denominator, it is something neither characterizing nor dominating the modern spirit alone. Speaking from this perspective, I think, to the contrary, that it can even be demonstrated in various ways that this spirit has been a guiding force behind human culture since ancient times. This perspective is fundamentally of great importance, and must also become our fundamental assumption if we are to conclude that this modern spirit constitutes the essence of the technological spirit to the extent that it is the inevitable fruit of the present and the future of the history of human culture. It indeed becomes necessary, to this end, to more or less rewrite the traditional histories of culture and of philosophy, and even of science and of technology. But we cannot present or demonstrate this in brief here. It is sure to become a major, revolutionary topic for historians in the future. Even so, however, to say that the technological spirit represents the spirit of modern culture in particular, to the extent that we consider it by generalizing it to the greatest common denominator, is still lacking in sufficient delimitation. On the other hand, even without necessarily waiting to demonstrate anew each historical fact, this is a relationship that can be sketched out by means of our existing common knowledge regarding the principles of historical narrative.

The fact that the technological spirit began to appear most clearly at the start of the modern era is a basic fact that need not be belabored. This is indeed the case, and no one can deny that it parallels the development of modern industry and its predominance. This being the case, the suggestion that the technological spirit is what characterizes the *Idee* [イデー idea] of modern culture amounts to the suggestion that modern industry determines the character of modern culture.

That modern culture is determined by modern industry (mainly industry after the industrial revolution) is also something widely understood as a matter of common knowledge, and this indeed seems to be the case, but various issues have been raised surrounding this idea, and it is not necessarily a relationship that is plainly self-evident. For example, according to certain types of civilizational critics, the technological spirit or spirit of technology is nothing more than simply the spirit of modern Western culture, and is neither something that will necessarily come to dominate the entire modern world nor something with the proper authority to do so. Such critics say that the spirit of the East (which they arbitrarily consider to be a bizarre mysticism) differs from the technological spirit, and that it will and must become the new leader of modern culture (?) from this point on.

According to this view, the technological spirit is something like the whiteness of the skin of Europeans, and it is not as though skin must be white. Today's elegiac *mythos* of the decline of Western civilization provides an air of exoticism or perverse nostalgia for such theories. In fact, it has indeed been this kind of contemporary civilizational theory that has attempted to simply resolve in the pages of a manuscript the phenomenon of contradiction between capital and technology that has been described as the surplus of technology under capitalism, or in other words the phenomenon of the contradiction of technology itself under capitalism, or (and this again is the same thing) the internal contradiction of capitalism itself that cannot help but give rise to technology. And in the above sense this can also be said of the greater part of the "philosophy of technology"—an actual genre of philosophical texts, many of which are being published. These approaches maintain that what is bad is not the structure of capitalism itself but rather technology, or the technological spirit.

In contrast to these pessimistic theories and apocalyptic visions of technology, there are more cheerful approaches that take an optimistic view, such as those concerning technocracy. An extreme example of this sort of approach states that all resources will have to be converted to energy, and engineers for the calculation of such energy will constitute the brain trust of economy and politics. Of course, Veblen, the economist said to be the progenitor of technocracy, did not offer such facile conclusions. Such conclusions are only drawn by a few cultural hecklers who are half technical experts and half civilizational critics, but they are significant as unpalatable examples that emphasize the modernity of the technological spirit. These optimistic theories of technology originate in several optimistic theories of industry found in America, and the technophilia found in writings such as Ford's *My Philosophy of Industry* (Ford says in his *My Life and Work* that the great achievement of Ford Motors lay in liberating automobiles from being merely toys used for racing) is plausible to the extent that his doctrine of low prices and high wages through mass production is plausible. And to the extent that this optimistic theory on the basis of industry is plausible, so too are optimistic theories of technology. On the other hand, however, when even in America itself the bizarre theory emerges that burdensome public works projects, performed by hand without the use of machines, are necessary in order to relieve unemployment, this optimistic viewpoint cannot but be a mere "philosophy" that has hastily clothed itself by accident in reality. (I regret that I do not have the space here to examine the Ōkōchi school's theory of rural industrialization and the "scientistic" view of industry).

Whether a pessimistic/apocalyptic view of technology or optimistic/evangelical view of technology is adopted, however, in either case these approaches are nothing other than predictions made from a standpoint in which the connection between the technological spirit and modern industry has not been given sufficient consideration. This follows from the fact that they do not appropriately or accurately calculate the more cultural, or cultural-historical, significance of modern industry. Since these approaches simply reduce modern industry in some sense to technology and pass over the issues industry poses concerning the mechanism of social production, the technological spirit in these cases either seem too distressing or too frivolous.

We already know that one of modern industry's fundamental characteristics, when seen from the perspective of the mechanism of social production, is whether or not it is capitalistic modern industry. We can consider the technological spirit, as well, in various ways depending on what sort of mechanism of social production belongs to the industry in connection with which we are addressing it. To the extent we think of it only in connection with capitalist industry, the technological spirit can only appear as a dead-end spirit. This is the typical apocalyptic view of technology. The easiest way to avoid this view is to see it [the technological spirit] as pure technology itself. Doing so results in the typical evangelical view of the technological spirit. In truth, however, the technological spirit must be the spirit of modern industrial *development*. That is, it must be the spirit of social technological development by means of which modern industry breaks through the capitalist dead-end in social structure and progresses beyond it. Is this maturation of markedly objective conditions of *technological development* not in fact modernity in its healthiest sense? The enormous development of capitalist industry in modern times has created this kind of modernity. So called "modernism" (putting aside "Catholic modernism" along with "Ginza[1] modernism" and the like) is indeed nothing more than a shadow cast by this illumination called "modernity".

The technological spirit is the wholesome illumination referred to as "modernity". It is light. Light has possessed a variety of meanings in literature, from the mysterious (as in the Gospel of John), to the mystical (Jakob Böhme) and the metaphysical (Schelling). On the other hand, however, it is only in recent times, and the modern era in particular, that it has been transformed into concepts of civilization (the Enlightenment or *lumière*) and enlightenment (*Aufklärung*). This was the creation of the modern bourgeoisie. But today it is no longer simply a bourgeois spirit. The bourgeoisie has already lost confidence in the technological spirit. What remains is nothing more than a handful of petit bourgeois technicians who somewhat sentimentally worship technology. It is a fact that what truly has confidence in the technological spirit today is the culture of the proletariat. If we want to say, "More light!" and turn the twilight of modernity into a dawn, then the technological spirit may indeed be the solution. It is no coincidence that since the early modern period many utopians and utopian socialists have dreamed of the kingdom of science. For many of them were pioneers of the technological spirit. This is true, to a greater or lesser extent, of thinkers such as Campanella, Francis Bacon, and Saint-Simon. That is not to say, however, that people like H. G. Wells represent the true spirit of modernity.

But what exactly is the content of the technological spirit? I think of it as the other face of the scientific spirit. We have no need here to waste words discussing the fundamental solidarity between science (especially natural science) and technology in general terms. Questions such as whether scientific progress leads to technological progress or technological progress leads to scientific progress, when presented in this kind of straightforward manner, do not seem very meaningful. To find further analysis too bothersome and simply settle things by saying that they act

---

[1]Ginza was an area in Tokyo emblematic of a modernism where new cultural trends and the leading edge of technological civilization were concentrated.

on each other reciprocally does not, of course, resolve the issue. The essential point is whether to conceive science (and in particular natural science) on the scale of the laboratory, so to speak, or to consider it on the scale of society. In other words, the question is whether we think of science as a social product or not, and whether we think of it as a direct phenomenon or not. Although as direct phenomena science and technology of course engage in reciprocal activity, considered in the context of the mechanism of social production the formula which holds that science is *ultimately delimited by technology* is intractable.

To say this is to say that the scientific spirit ought to be reduced to the technological spirit. This is fine for now. What we must keep in mind, however, is that what we call here the technological spirit is not the spirit of technology or the spirit of the technological sciences. It is in truth something that expresses the spirit of *culture*. Thought of in this way, to say instead that the technological spirit is reduced to the scientific spirit would broaden the range of vision and signify that the technological spirit is another face of the scientific spirit.

When it comes to the scientific spirit, today it is being discussed everywhere. To broadly summarize what has been concluded, the scientific spirit is firstly a positivist spirit. Or it is an experiential spirit. Secondly, it is taken to be a rational spirit. It is a spirit of rational inference; in other words, it is a logical spirit. Prof. Tanabe Hajime takes these two stipulations and sees in them two conflicting moments. The opposition between experiment and theory, the opposition between empiricism and rationalism, and other such conflicts are presumably instances of this. It appears that Prof. Tanabe views what unifies these two moments to be something that amounts to action. He states that since history is mediated by action, history is what synthesizes these two moments. The result we arrive at by following this approach is therefore that the scientific spirit is nothing other than the historical spirit.

I also consider the scientific spirit to be the historical spirit. But I do not necessarily think we have to take a circuitous route around the category of action in order to reach this conclusion. The scientific spirit, no doubt, must be a spirit of our everyday life and action. But I do not think that the clarification of the scientific spirit as a historical spirit requires that we pass through the philosophical component of action. The scientific spirit is a positivist spirit. It is a spirit launched from data regarding the actuality of thing-events. Now, to say that these positively actual thing-events exist indicates nothing other than that they exist by conforming to certain laws of progression over time. This is what we generally refer to as the *history* of things. The positivist spirit, therefore, must inevitably acknowledge the historical spirit. But this is not simply a temporal spirit. Mere time or the content of mere time cannot yet be said to be history. History means the law of temporal progression. Only with structure and order in the temporal progression of thing-events does history arise. History is the logic of these sorts of thing-events themselves.

If there is such a thing as a rational or logical spirit, and a truly objective inference (for Hegel believes that reasoning is the essence of logic) exists, it does not lie within the a priori or innate concepts of rationalism but must instead lie within that which is extracted from the structural order of this historical progression.

We may thus state for the present that the scientific spirit is the historical spirit in precisely this sense. I recall Prof. Ogura Kinnosuke attempting to explain the scientific spirit by referring to both the positivist spirit and historical spirit. But these two [concepts] will presumably not be satisfied simply by being juxtaposed.

When we attempt to consider the scientific spirit concretely as a contemporary issue, it turns out that we have to begin by looking at it from the perspectives of the anti-scientific or unscientific spirit of today. For as issues of the current situation, this is how they are presented. Recently I have written quite a lot about these perspectives. I can roughly summarize their main points in three formulations. The first is literature-ism (a way of thinking that dares to engage in analysis through popular literary representations completely independently of scientific categories— as seen in the literary criticism, open discussions, and texts of culturalist metaphysics). The second is philologism (the approach of comprehensive erudition or contrived argumentation basing its thought directly on the results of textual exegesis under the rubric of science— conspicuous in "academic fools"). The third is dogmaticism (an approach that views scholarship as a contribution to education through scripture and the ethical restraint of culture—characteristic of Eastern monasticism and the master-oriented conception of culture).

One characteristic these three anti-scientific or unscientific spirits have in common, although each in its own form, is their complete inability to possess a positivist spirit. Philologism and dogmaticism might seem to be adept at textual proofs, but such proofs are not at all of the positivist spirit of experimental verification. Theirs is an interpretational spirit rather than a positivist spirit. It goes without saying that cultural metaphysics is quite thin in its sense of positivist actuality. It confuses the order of the actual with the order of the potential realm of the heavens and believes that the latter can represent the former. In attempting to replace the real world of the actual with the world of interpretation, it follows the same path as the previous two approaches.

Because of this impotence of the positivist spirit, a valid historical spirit also becomes impossible. Philologism and dogmatism have instead given birth to distorted views of history. Most ultranationalist, feudal, and Japanist social theories are examples of this. The fact that such theories lack a rational spirit is nothing other than the inevitable consequence of their total lack of a positivist spirit and resulting incompetence in arriving at true historical understanding.

It is precisely this positivist spirit that corresponds to living matter in the scientific spirit that ought to be called the "technological spirit". The positivist spirit is the spirit of experimental verification. But here too we must not limit our comprehension of this to the scale of the laboratory. We must comprehend it on the scale of the mechanism of social production. We will then notice that experiments are socially continuous with industry. This is the prototype for human social practice (practice as the political activity of members of society, needless to say, also belongs to this category). It is thus the spirit of industry. This is why it becomes the technological spirit.

True theoretical thought must be capable of being put into practice and verified within social actuality. It is not a realistic truth without being backed by experimentation in this sense. It would lack actuality. Only by having such actuality does this truth acquire practical value. This falls under the motto of the positivist spirit, "see in order to foresee [*voir pour prévoir*]". But the various logical categories used as tools to bring order to this kind of thought also require adequate preparation. Society requires a system of categories suited for proofs and verification. As a result they must be categories in a relationship of solidarity with industrial technology and productive technology. Metaphysical, hermeneutic, philological, literary, dogmatic, and other such categories in actuality are incapable of dealing with even a single aspect of society. If it cannot deal with material things in some sense (and not simply explain this or that about the world), it is not a logic that exists for the daily life of humanity. As it turns out, such categories are, in a manner of speaking, technological categories. And this logic, this rational spirit, is nothing other than the technological spirit. The absolute demand of the technological spirit within thought and culture is, in short, nothing other than the logical, epistemological development of a fundamental understanding that the ideologies of thought and culture can only be properly grasped as a superstructure founded upon the productive mechanism of society. If we are to explain this fundamental dimension of the scientific spirit, we must connect culture and thought to industry and material social production through the technological spirit. Viewed objectively, there is nothing more wretched than culture or thought utterly independent of the industry found within society. Those who do not see its wretchedness are those who are ignorant of world history and who have never experienced the real pressure of thought.—I have already noted how modern thought has overwhelmingly been regulated by modern industry, regardless of whether or not it recognizes this itself. People who say that industry is industry and thought is thought cannot be modern thinkers.

So if I were asked to explain what the scientific spirit is in a single phrase, my answer would be that it is the technological spirit. I would say that it is the unmovable spirit that, by being mediated towards the technology of material production within society, adjusts its categories without neglecting their deduction and verification, makes culture cohere, and characterizes modern culture.

But ultimately there remains the question of what technology is when we speak of the technological spirit. What I call "technology" is not technical skill or means, nor is it art or technique; what I am referring to is "productive technology". That is not to say, of course, that the term technology or technique [*gijutsu*] as it is commonly used cannot refer to anything else. But inescapable confusion arises when we forget the common sense notion that in its proper sense "technology" refers to productive technology. I will not discuss this point at length here because I have already addressed it in a previous text, *Gijutsu no tetsugaku* [『技術の哲学』] *The Philosophy of Technology* (mentioned above).

Concerning what productive technology is, here too I insist on a certain view. We cannot simply adopt the popular view that technology amounts to the system of means of labor. Means of labor are means of labor. Is this not indeed a fully comprehensible phrase? Why should it be necessary to replace it with the common term "technology"? Surely technology cannot be tidied away simply by describing it as a system of means of labor.

I cannot help but sympathize with the main thrust of Saigusa Hiroto's "Gijutsugaku no gurentsu gebiito" [「技術学のグレンツ・ゲビイト」 "Frontiers [Grenzgebiet] of Technological Science"], published in the September, 1937 edition of the journal *Kagakushugi kōgyō* [『科学主義工業』*Scientistic Industry*]. If I were to put this in my own words, I would say it is the assertion that modern philosophy is permeated by nothing other than technological spirit. But I understand that he refers to it as technological science in a much broader sense rather than speaking of the technological spirit. Yes, his phrasing, implying that technological science will replace philosophy, seems to go a bit too far. Would it not be more accurate and reasonable to say that the spirit of modernity must be the technological spirit?

Tosaka Jun (1900–1945). Born in Tokyo. Graduated from Kyoto Imperial University's Faculty of Letters. Formed the Materialism Research Association (唯物論研究会) with Saigusa Hiroto and others in 1932 and began publication of this association's journal, *Yuibutsuron kenkyū* [『唯物論研究』 *Studies in Materialism*]. Writings include *Gijutsu no tetsugaku* [『技術の哲学』 *Philosophy of Technology*] (Jichōsha, 1933), *Nihon ideorogīron* [『日本イデオロギー論』 *On Japanese Ideology*] (Hakuyōsha, 1935), *Kagakuron* [『科学論』 *On Science*] (Mikasa Shobō, 1935). Arrested in 1938 under the Public Security Preservation Law (治安維持法) and died in prison in 1945. "What is the Technological Spirit?" was published in the journal *Kagakushugi kōgyō* [『科学主義工業』*Scientistic Industry*] in 1937. It is also included in *Tosaka Jun zenshū* [『戸坂潤全集』 *Complete Works of Tosaka Jun*] Vol. 1 (Keiso Shobō).

Chapter 8
On Tosaka Jun's Scientific-Technological Spirit

[戸坂潤の科学的・技術的精神をめぐって]

Nishikawa Tomio

8.1 Introduction

Much has been said about Nishidian philosophy. But almost nothing has been said about the left wing, so to speak, of Nishidian philosophy. Of this left wing, Miki and Tosaka both died in prison, one after the other, just before and after the end of the war in 1945. But putting aside Miki for the moment, indeed very little has been said about Tosaka. I myself, while finding Miki's concepts of "fundamental experience" and "imagination" particularly intriguing, have given Tosaka only a perfunctory look without finding anything particularly moving or exciting.

On this occasion, however, having been fortunate enough to be given the opportunity to write this essay, as I reread him I discerned what can be described as "Tosaka's radical criticism" and felt an interest stirring within me quite distinct from what I felt about Nishida and Miki. This interest was further deepened as I encountered Tosaka's "scientific spirit" and "technological spirit".

Since the end of the war, Japanese intellectual history has long been accustomed to evaluating earlier figures using only the dichotomous scheme of "materialism" and "idealism". But it would be difficult to argue that this is necessarily a fair and objective academic stance. I do not want to adopt from the start an uncritical approach that asserts that "materialism" is good while rejecting "idealism". Nevertheless, I would like to examine here the question of why Tosaka persisted in the stance of a materialist philosopher to such an extent, and, through his "scientific spirit" and "technological spirit", I would like to investigate the nature of his relationship to the spirit of his epoch.

Translated from the Japanese by Robert Chapeskie and revised by John W. M. Krummel.

T. Nishikawa

8.2 Why the Scientific, or Technological, Spirit?

It was 1937 when Tosaka wrote "Gijutsuteki seishin towa nanika" [「技術的精神とは何か」 "What is the Technological Spirit?"] (*Kagakushugi kōgyō* [『科学主義工業』 *Scientistic Industry*], October issue). On the topic of technology, he had already published *Gijutsu no tetsugaku* [『技術の哲学』 *The Philosophy of Technology*] (Jichosha) in 1933, and *Kagaku hōhōron* [『科学方法論』 *On the Scientific Method*] (1929, Iwanami shoten), a work into which he put considerable effort, was published even earlier when he was only twenty-nine years old. These were published together in a collection, *Kagakuron* [『科学論』*On Science*] (Mikasashobō) (Vol. 1 of *Complete Writings on Materialism*) in 1935. Building on these earlier works, he wrote "Kagakuteki seishin towa nanika" [「科学的精神とは何か」 "What is the Scientific Spirit?"][1] (*Yuibutsuron kenkyū* [『唯物論研究』 *Studies on Materialism*] Vol. 54) in 1937.

His papers from this period include, for example, "Saikin nihon no kagakuron" [「最近日本の科学論」 "Recent Japanese Theories of Science"] (*Yuibutsuron kenkyū* [『唯物論研究』 *Studies on Materialism*] Vol. 56), "Futatabi kagakuteki seishin nitsuite" [「再び科学的精神について」 "Once again Concerning the Scientific Spirit"] (ibid.,Vol. 59), and "Gendai kagaku kyōikuron" [「現代科学教育論」 "On Contemporary Science Education"] (*Kagaku pen* [『科学ペン』*Science Pen*], April, 1937). In 1941 he published "Kagaku to kagaku no kannen" [「科学と科学の観念」 "Science and the Concept of Science"] (*Keizai jōhō* [『経済情報』 *Economics Report*], politics and economics edition, June issue), and, as essays that further encompass both science and technology, in 1941 he published "Gijutsu to kagaku tono gainen" [「技術と科学との概念」 "The Concepts of Technology and Science"] (*Teikoku daigaku shinbun* [『帝国大学新聞』 *Imperial University Newspaper*], June 9th), "Seisan o mokuhyō to suru kagaku" [「生産を目標とする科学」 "Science that Takes Production as its Aim"] (ibid., September 8th), and "Gijutsu e iku mondai" [「技術へ行く問題」 "The Issue of Moving Towards Technology"][2] (*Miyako shinbun* [『都新聞』*City Newspaper*], September 4th).

As a glance at this list reveals, Tosaka's activity as a writer beginning around 1933 was extremely vigorous; he not only wrote essays and criticism concerning science and technology but also authored numerous texts on ideology.

In 1933 Hitler came to power, and eventually Japan too, along with Germany and Italy, did away with the order of the Versailles-Washington establishment to assert a "new world order". In 1937 the Sino-Japanese conflict, which had gradually escalated into a state of war, finally led to the imposition of wartime measures throughout Japan. A movement for the general mobilization of the national spirit arose. Like it or not, the Japanese intellect could not help getting caught up in this

---

[1]Publication of a collection with this title was planned but never realized as a result of a writing ban, and the finished proofs Tosaka had kept are said to have been destroyed during the war.

[2]This was planned for publication in four parts, but after the publication of the second part a writing ban was issued by the public prosecution authorities.

movement. Kyoto philosophers, too, from Nishida and Tanabe on down, came to be associated with it. Nishida and Miki Kiyoshi's names appear in the list of members of the "Shōwa kenkyū-kai [Shōwa Research Association]". The National Mobilization Law was enacted in 1938, and before that, in 1937, the Ministry of Education [文部省] had published *Kokutai no hongi* [『国体の本義』 *The Cardinal Meaning of National Polity*]". Meanwhile, in 1937 scholars of the "Kōza" faction and people belonging to "Nōrō" [workers and peasants] groups were being rounded up and arrested en masse.

*Arrests under the "Public Security Preservation Law [*Chian iji hō* 治安維持法]"

Year	Number of arrests	Number of indictees
1931	1,187	309
1932	2,489	663
1933	4,288	1,282
1934	2,102	507
1935	654	112
1936	783	149
1937	661	205

(Tōyama, Imai and Fujiwara, *Shōwashi* [『昭和史』 *Shōwa History*], Iwanami shinsho, p. 78)

As this table indicates, in 1932 the number of arrests doubled in comparison to 1931 and reached its peak in 1933. Miki Kiyoshi, who had attended Dai-ichi [第一 The First] High School and studied under Nishida, and who had already made a name for himself as a philosopher and journalist, had himself been struck by the wave of intellectual oppression within the tide of the times. In 1930 he was arrested and detained on charges of having provided funds to the Japan Communist Party, and, being as a result unable to continue his position as professor at Hōsei University, invited his junior Tosaka, whom he trusted, to come to Tokyo and take over his teaching duties.

Tosaka, who had taught at Doshisha Women's College and Ōtani University, had himself already experienced arrest in 1930. The charge was that he had harbored a Communist Party activist. The field of activity would surely be more open in expansive Tokyo than in the much smaller Kyoto. And his doting mother was accustomed to life in the capital. From Tosaka's point of view there was presumably no reason to hesitate. In 1931 he took Miki's place and began teaching at Hōsei University.

This too, however, would not last long. In August of 1934 he fell victim to the "red hunt". In the following year, when the arrest of political activists reached its peak, even those who professed to be engaging only in "research" were taken into custody. The task Tosaka had taken up immediately after arriving in Tokyo was the establishment of the "Yuibutsuron *kenkyū*-kai [唯物論研究会 Materialism Research Association]" (1932) and the publication of its journal *Studies in Materialism*. It was around this time that he began to actively take up a firm stance among Marxist researchers. But in 1937 he was prohibited from writing, and in

February of 1938 the "Materialism Research Association" was ordered to disband. In November of that year he was once again arrested and held at a detention center until 1940.

The situation at the time was sliding from the Manchurian incident into the Sino-Japanese war and eventually into the mire of the Pacific war [World War II] (then referred to as the "Great East Asian War"). The circumstances of this period can be enumerated as follows. (1) Out of a need to build a wartime social structure to elevate the nation, "national mobilization" [国民総動員], and the system of "general mobilization of the national spirit" [国民精神総動員] as one of its constituent parts, were being promoted. (2) Policies promoting science and technology were being implemented as manifestations of this initiative. The Ministry of Education touted the promotion of science and technology and the rousing of the spirit.[3] The rousing of spirit amounted to the establishment of "the morality of the Japanese subject" [臣民道徳] among citizens based on the emperor system [天皇主義]. The promotion of science and technology, too, was in essence something undertaken in order to strengthen the military system.

Tosaka's scientism [科学主義] would, of course, not accept the ignorance of the seeming irrationality of the "way of the Empire". In addition to the critique of this ignorance, the motif of perceiving the crisis of capitalism within a "technology" that wholeheartedly serves military production was also at work in his prolific writings about "science" and "technology" in both academic papers and criticism.[4]

We might furthermore read into Tosaka's work during this period a critique of the academism of the Kyoto school under which he had originally studied. This was a critique of his mentor Tanabe Hajime and of [Tetsuro] Watsuji. He had known Tanabe from when he was still in middle school; Tanabe, whose work thematized the philosophy of mathematics and the philosophy of science, had been a teacher (although of English) at Kaisei Middle School when Tosaka was a student there. And after graduating from Dai-ichi High School Tosaka came to study at [the University of] Kyoto's philosophy department because of having been drawn to the philosophy of Nishida and Tanabe. Considering that after graduating from the science faculty in high school he focused on the "theory of space" [空間論] [as his research topic] in university, Tanabe must, at least academically, have been a closer

---

[3]The second collection of the "*Kyōgaku sōsho* [『教学叢書』 *Teaching and Learning Library*]" published by the Ministry of Education's "Bureau of Teaching and Learning", dated February 1938, states that it "…was edited on the basis of the 'aims of the publication of the Teaching and Learning Library' in order to contribute to the promotion of reform in teaching and learning and a correct understanding of the current state of affairs…"

Similarly, the Bureau of Teaching and Learning's compilation also includes *Shinmin no michi* [『臣民の道』 *Way of the [Japanese] Subject*], which advocates the construction of a new world order, the system of a national defense state, a national polity centered on the emperor, and the way of the national subject that manifests the above. This text was published in 1941.

[4]*Ideorogī ron* [『日本イデオロギー論』 *On Japanese Ideology*], which he wrote around this time, while also criticizing the vulgar culture of the day, essentially took as its motifs the critique of the ignorant "way of the empire" and of a "theory of technology" that would inevitably serve the reinforcement of military power.

mentor to him than Nishida.[5] In his theory of science there are many elements that are in conformity with Tanabe's views.

Whether or not his circumstances were similar to those of Miki, who went to Tokyo after his hopes of obtaining a teaching post at Kyoto University upon returning from studying abroad in Germany were dashed, in the end Tosaka too left for Tokyo after not being given the opportunity to teach philosophy of mathematics at Kyoto University. There is no material we can cite to determine the extent to which this affected him psychologically. But as a materialist, the Tosaka who went to Tokyo, took up the banner of rationalism and the scientific spirit, and developed a critique of current affairs through journalism would have had to turn a critical eye towards Tanabe's scientism as well. *Tetsugaku to kagaku to no aida* [『哲学と科学の間』 *Between Philosophy and Science*] (Iwanami shoten), which collects for the first time in a single volume writings he had published over a period of about two years beginning in 1935, was originally intended to question what the spirit of science is from the standpoint of philosophy, while keeping in mind the national policy of the rousing of this spirit. After stating in the preface that "the recent war harbors a significance that ought to demarcate world history", Tanabe argues that there is a pressing need for a calm "stirring of the scientific spirit" without becoming intoxicated with momentary excitement. From the perspective of a thoughtful person, the period was indeed one of intoxication. As a leading figure in the philosophy of mathematics and a prominent representative of Kyoto philosophy, Tosaka presumably felt something like a calling to discuss "what is the essence of science?" But his spirit of "critique" within the "scientific spirit" appears to manifest in his suggestion that in the end, irrespective of Tanabe's subjective intention, Tanabe too entered into a compromise with the trend of the times on the basis of dialectical thinking.

This razor of "critique" that cut into the flippant trend of the times, and even held his mentor's "scientific spirit" up for critical discussion, bore the character of ideology. Tosaka saw "critique", roughly speaking, as a foundation that essentially constitutes the academic nature of academic inquiry.[6] If academic inquiry loses its "function of critique", it will presumably no longer qualify as academic inquiry. In Tosaka the "critical approach" of the Neo-Kantian school is more radically completed and expanded into an ideological critique. It is for this reason that he added the subtitle "Extending it to the Theory of Japanese Culture" to his essay "What is the Scientific Spirit?".

In broad terms, the "critique" of the Neo-Kantian school, having inherited Kant's "critique," was nevertheless not content to limit itself to the fundamental

---

[5]Tosaka was close to Nishida on a personal level (see "Zadankai Kyoto tetsugaku saha no keiseikatei" [「座談会 京都哲学左派の形成過程」 "Symposium: The Process of Formation of Kyoto Philosophy's Left-wing"], included in Akahide Kakehashi, *Zenshizenshiteki katei no shisō* [『全自然史的過程の思想』 *Thoughts Concerning the Process of Comprehensive Natural History*], Sōjusha, 1980), and at one time Nishida was preparing to invite him to be a lecturer in charge of the philosophy of mathematics.

[6]One of the fundamental positions of *Kagaku hōhōron* [『科学方法論』 *On the Method of Science*]

examination of the right and capacity of reason, expanded its focus to the point of questioning the grounds for establishing academic inquiry itself, and attempted to illuminate the respective horizons for the establishment of natural science, social science, and historical science. In particular, its clarification of the conditions for establishing the scientific nature [科学性] of historical phenomena in relation to the individual nature of events is of great significance. Although he had studied the "critical approach" of the Neo-Kantian school throughout his career, when it came to examining the horizon for the establishment of academic inquiry Tosaka was compelled to take the nature of this inquiry all the way to its "function of critique". This was also a deepening, in Tosaka's own terms, of the rational spirit he had possessed since childhood.

To Tosaka, rationalism referred to a clear-cut way of thinking that says "that is that and this is this"—the thinking of *ratio*, or logic. To "critique" is presumably to thoroughly engage in this clear-cut way of thinking or "thinking that divides". In this sense as well he was not a dialectician [弁証法論者].[7] In Tosaka the thoroughgoing function of critique becomes ideological. During the period when he was writing about "the spirit of science" or "the spirit of technology" he was indeed writing voluminously on "ideology". This discourse was not only directed towards contemporary efforts to instill a "scientific mentality" from the top down, such as, for example, the science and technology policies of the Ministry of Education's "Bureau of Learning"[教学局]. It was also developed as a cultural critique of the trend of the times, which, along with being tinged with a wartime atmosphere, was quite rash and frivolous. And when this critique reached the point of being an ideological critique, he referred to its targets as the "scien*tific* spirit" or the "technolog*ical* spirit". This is where the distinction from what was referred to as the "spirit of science" or the "spirit of technology" lies. In contrast to the latter, where the emphasis of the discourse lay on the realm of objects and method, the former extends further into ideological critique. So how did Tosaka connect this "critique" to materialist philosophy?

8.3 What was the Nature of Tosaka's Materialism?

When attempting to answer this question, I think it behooves us to keep in mind that for Tosaka materialism functioned as an ideology of "critique." The conclusion to be drawn is that in Tosaka materialism was the paraphernalia or apparatus of radical criticism (a fundamental critical approach) that could be used to penetrate every possible field.

---

[7]Thought that rejects dialectical logic as logic can be found anywhere. This is a point on which Tosaka the Marxist differs from other dialectical Marxists. For example, his friend Kakehashi Akihide, a Marxist Hegelian and self-described materialist, dismissed Tosaka's thought as "comprehensionism" [悟性主義].

Why, incidentally, would an urban super-elite, who was also a brilliant scholar specializing in the philosophy of mathematics, hold so stubbornly to the path of materialism and end up dying young in prison? I do not believe that materialism for Tosaka was a view of life and death so necessary that it was worth dying for.[8] Materialism may indeed have been something he needed as equipment for carrying out radical criticism, but his short life that ended in prison, to me, from beginning to end cannot be discussed apart from his unbridled spirit. This spirit was something he received from his mother, known as a woman of firm character[9] and regarded as the clear-headed "Madame Okuni",[10] and going further back we might connect that spirit to his family's origins as major landlords in their region.

As a small child, Tosaka was raised in rural Masuho, Ishikawa Prefecture, interacting with the local landscape and community while maturing with composure as the son of a major landowner. Rinzō (born into the second generation of the Tosaka family), the father of his mother, Kuni, is said to have been intelligent, with an air appropriate to a wealthy farmer and head of the family, and very well liked (Awazu, p. 128). These characteristics seem to have been passed on to the grandson through his mother.

There would have been nothing lacking when it came to enjoying himself on their vast estate. There was a river, woods, flowers blooming in profusion, and insects fluttering about. His world was different from that of the children of the local tenant farmers. Day after day, the intelligent young Tosaka must never have tired of observing nature. If he ever did get bored, he could always go to the workshop run by his uncle and make whatever he wanted. The old handyman would be there, and so would the workers. There would be nothing to stand in the way of the privileged little boy's construction.[11] He would not have felt constrained by anybody. He would have been able to think and act as he pleased. His unbridled spirit seems to have been cultivated by this kind of environment.

Tosaka's seemingly composed but unflappable attitude, which he displayed in later years even while being dogged by the "special political police", and indeed

---

[8]In August of 1945, just before his death, Tosaka, expecting to be released, had his family bring him clothes and ¥500 in cash (this was an extraordinarily large sum, and it has been suggested that it was in fact ¥50). And there are also reports that his direct cause of death was his being deliberately dropped onto concrete by a prisoner on duty who was carrying him to the prison infirmary for treatment of his severe scabies and overall poor physical condition (Mitsunari Hideko, *Tosaka Jun to watashi* [『戸坂潤と私』 *Tosaka Jun and I*], Banrōsha, 1977, p. 354).

[9]"Woman of firm character" [女傑] was the form of address [for Tosaka's mother] used by Tosaka's friends on the left wing of Nishidian philosophy. See the conversation contained in Kakehashi Akihide, *Zenshizenshiteki katei no shisō* [『全自然史的過程の思想』 *Thoughts Concerning the Process of Comprehensive Natural History*].

[10]Awazu Keiyū, *Tosakake no bungaku* [『戸坂家の文学』 *Literature of the Tosaka Family*], Hokkoku shinbunsha, 1994, p. 127ff.

[11]Awazu, ibid. In the countryside, the son of a major landowner would have enjoyed an exceptional status.

even after being forced to live in a detention center and then prison, was presumably related to this ethos. He was never nervous even while being hounded by the authorities. Even when the Materialism Research Association was being investigated by the thought police he remained unfazed. With this fortitude Tosaka must have projected an air of reliability to its members. He naturally came to occupy the position of leader.[12]

Having spent his first five years in the countryside, when it came time to start school Tosaka moved to Tokyo. Needless to say, he was an honor student throughout elementary school and middle school. He also had a good physique. He was not introverted as might often be seen in delicate literary-minded youths. While there seems to have been little direct influence on him [from Tanabe] while in middle school, the path he followed from science to philosophy was the same as Tanabe's. He was an intellectual middle school student. This came across to his classmates as an "unapproachable coolness" (Uchida's Recollection in *Remembering Tosaka Jun*, p. 81). He is also said to have been pejoratively referred to as a "refrigerator".

What was it that motivated this young man's move towards philosophy? No writings remain in which one might decipher the answer to this question. In search of a foundation for the various disciplines, a top-rank prodigy takes the path of philosophy. This was the path, laid out by Miki, of studying in Kyoto. In other words, it was the path of studying under Nishida. It was also the path taken by Kakehashi and Nishitani Keiji.

Graduating from the Imperial University and entering the army, Tosaka applied to become an officer cadet and after qualifying as such was commissioned as an officer. On top of these achievements, his outstanding essay "Kūkanron" [「空間論」 "On Space"], which was based on his graduation thesis, was polished to its final form in the midst of his busy military life as an officer-in-training and published in *Tetsugaku Kenkyū* [『哲学研究』 *Philosophical Studies*]. It seems a bit odd that a graduate of the Imperial University with a Bachelor of Arts degree would apply to be an officer cadet, and it seems quite incongruous that someone who would eventually die in prison as a materialist philosopher had once occupied this role. But Tosaka was just such a man. At the very least he was not a literary young man submerged in internal conflict.[13] He lived through his "moments" with his

---

[12]He is remembered as having the sort of personality that would make him a leader in whatever situation he found himself. See the previously cited "Zadankai Kyōto tetsugaku saha no keiseikatei" [「座談会 京都哲学左派の形成過程」 "Symposium: The Process of Formation of Kyoto Philosophy's Left-wing"]; Tanabe Hajime et al., *Kaisō no Tosaka Jun* [『回想の戸坂潤』 *Remembering Tosaka Jun*], Keisō shobo, 1976. At times when there was anxiety among members of the Materialism Research Association because its members were being prosecuted, he alone would remain composed and for this reason he was seen as dependable.

[13]His close friend Kakehashi writes (Kakehashi's Recollection in *Remembering Tosaka Jun*) that in general Tosaka was not deeply interested in literature. It seems natural that Tosaka, with his scientific sensibility, would not be interested in inward-looking, "I-novel" type literature. Kakehashi even goes as far as to criticize Tosaka for having no literary sensibility whatsoever.

unshakable, unbridled spirit intact. The result can be seen in how he lived his life as a top student. His mother must have been composedly content with him.[14]

Even the stern Tanabe recalls that in spite of being severely criticized by Tosaka, there remained no animosity between them. Tanabe writes, "He lacked the persistent nervousness often found in those who do philosophy" (*Remembering Tosaka Jun*, p. 4). Straightforward and unbridled. And yet open-minded. It was probably for these reasons his friends and juniors regarded him as a "reliable person." (Oka Kunio).

One younger colleague, Kakehashi, writes that "Tosaka was someone who had a sense of self-satisfaction" (*Remembering Tosaka Jun*, p. 54). Water boils at one hundred degrees and that is all there is to it. Tosaka's rationalism lay in adhering to the course of nature. In contrast to Miki's expansion, and, at times, dispersion of the self through pride and "muddy passion," Tosaka does not expand the self outwards, but that is not to say that he submerges it inwards. Kakehashi's analysis was that Tosaka exists in self-satisfaction without there being either inside or outside (p. 56). I think it is an interesting analysis. Tosaka's mien of dignified self-satisfaction comes from his adherence to the course and order of nature. This is an accurate picture of Tosaka the materialist, and, being unable to consent to the irrationality of emperor worship and militarism, he presumably retained his dignity even in detention. Viewed from one side, this was perhaps the reliable naturalism and rationalism of a "Japanese Epicurus". It was also the attitude of life instilled by a mother from an important family. His carefree, comfortable life is attested to by the days he spent skiing before being detained.[15]

At the time he wrote "On Space", Tosaka was not yet a materialist philosopher, nor did he have any inclination toward Marx. It was probably in the midst of his exchanges with people like Miki, Kakehashi, and Kawakami Hajime at the "Ichikō-kai" [Dai-ichi high school graduates circle] that he developed a keen interest in the cutting-edge thought of Marxism that was then in vogue.

---

[14]Even when drinking all night long with his friends of the Ichikō-kai, he [almost] never stayed out all night without notice. This occurred only once, and it is said that Tosaka's mother harshly scolded Kakehashi and his friends, saying, "Jun would never do such a thing". Even when he was detained and sentenced to prison, his mother was not in the least shaken. She may have been proud he would never do anything shameful, but it may also have been a manifestation of self-confidence that had been cultivated within the environment of an important family.

[15]I had previously assumed that being hounded by the special political police and having spent time in detention alone would have been enough to make Tosaka's life miserable. But it felt a bit strange to learn that Tosaka himself seems to have been surprisingly untroubled during this period. During his detention he is said to have received gourmet food from his wife or housemaid every day without fail (Saeki's recollection in *Remembering Tosaka Jun*), and there are also reports that his demeanor was such that he naturally came to be "relied on" by various unconvicted detainees.

During his release on parole there were days he spent mountain climbing and skiing (see *Remembering Tosaka Jun*). When Japan was rapidly rushing from the Sino-Japanese war into the Pacific War [World War II] there were only a very few Japanese youths who would have had the time and money required for such activities. At least to the author [of this paper], who at the time was around fourteen or fifteen years old and taking preparatory courses for teacher's college, this would have been an unimaginable luxury.

Needless to say, while Tosaka became a materialist after arriving in Tokyo, he was by no means a materialist and a Marxist in the sense of someone involved in the revolutionary movement. What gave Tosaka his distinctive character was that, as a critical rationalist, he provided a comprehensively radical critical investigation of ideology, including natural science, social science, and culture.

It was not as though he had detailed knowledge of the lives of poor farmers, fishermen, and laborers. In the case of Funayama Shinichi, who also took part in the activities of the "Materialism Research Association", his acquaintance with the lives of poor farmers gave him a certain sense of sympathetic empathy toward them. In Kakehashi, son of an intellectual pastor, only an abstract sympathy toward poor farmers and laborers was evident. Miki was the prodigy of a wealthy family of the provinces. His intellect possessed a "delicate heart" constantly swayed by his passions. Even while inclining towards Marx, he harbored a human frailty that prevented him from becoming a full-fledged Marxist. This fragility was also appealing. In "Ningengaku no Marukusuteki keitai" [「人間学のマルクス的形態」 "The Marxist Form of Anthropology"] (Included in *Chosakushū daisankan* [『著作全集第三巻』 *Collected Writings Vol. 3*], Iwanami shoten) we notice Miki turning his gaze toward matters of *pathos* [パトス的なもの] after his investigation of humanity in Pascal. Miki exuded human frailty and contradiction. A formulaic Marxist may criticize this as Miki's weakness, but it became part of his appeal and made him attractive to many. In the case of Tosaka the critical rationalist, who at times appeared to be quite cold, there was a soundness in his body and mind. He calmly developed his arguments wherever *logos* may proceed. One might say that even while adopting a severely formal style of writing, for Tosaka, the scientific rationalist, materialism was the fundamental scheme that set the stage upon which criticism was to be carried out. This is why he says, "Indeed, the scientific spirit is the culturally situated form of materialism in the present".[16]

8.4 Tosaka's Scientific and Technological Spirits

8.4.1 Tosaka's View of the Nature of Scholarship [学問性]

Tosaka's fundamental thesis concerning scholarship, briefly stated, can be found in the assertions that:

(a) The academic nature of academic inquiry is to be seen within the function of "critique".
(b) The integrity and unity of natural science and social science are to be sought in materialism.

---

[16]"Futatabi kagakuteki seishin ni tsuite" [「再び科学的精神について」 "Concerning the Scientific Spirit Once Again"], *Zenshū* [『全集』*Complete Works*] *I*, p. 326.

At the time Tosaka was studying in the philosophy department at Kyoto University, the philosophy of the Neo-Kantian school was popular in Japan. Signs of a revival of Kant, who had long been hidden in the shadow of Hegelianism, could be seen towards the end of the nineteenth century, but it was not until the start of the twentieth century that this revival began to flourish under the name "Neo-Kantianism".

In this return to Kant and championing of epistemic critique, and, going further, academic critique in the twentieth century, we can note, broadly speaking, the following three points regarding the questions of the day.

(1) One trigger of these inquiries, along with the development of the various natural sciences, was the flourishing of the various humanities and social sciences. If we bundle the latter together as the human sciences [*Geisteswissenschaften*; humanities], where do the commonalities and differences lie between the two fields? Epistemic critique ought to extend all the way to the roots of scientific methodology and the establishment of science.

(2) At the beginning of the twentieth century, the new understanding of physics developed by people like Einstein and Heisenberg had a major impact on philosophy. Was not the establishment of "absolute space and absolute time" found in Newtonian mechanics endangered by Einstein? Quantum mechanics appears to take simultaneous apprehension in time and space of objects of observation to be impossible. To begin with, is not the circumstance of observation, where light is projected upon an object, an involvement or intervention of the observing subject in the apprehension of the object?

(3) The various natural sciences that had developed rapidly from the second half of the nineteenth century and into the first half of the twentieth century seemed to have brought about the triumph of positivism in the domain of knowledge. This is an approach that limits the realm of knowledge to the scope of experience, and takes opinions concerning realms beyond experience to be of no use. Russel's *Principia Mathematica*, a major work completed in collaboration with Whitehead, was published from 1910 to 1913, and the "Vienna circle [Wiener Kreis]" a group that promoted the "scientific understanding of the world" and hoisted the banner of logical positivism, was formed in 1929. If we are to limit the horizon of the establishment of knowledge to the scope of experience, it goes without saying that the natural and even the human sciences will be confined to empirical science, and the space for the establishment of philosophy as non-empirical or super-empirical knowledge will presumably vanish. If, in the face of positivism, we reject the establishment of metaphysics, where exactly should we expect philosophical knowledge to be established?

On this front line of the debate over knowledge, one motif of the Neo-Kantian movement was to return to Kant's "criticism" and attempt to reexamine anew the ground for the establishment of the natural and human sciences. The critique of reason had to be broadened as far as questioning the scientific nature of not only natural science but also the historical sciences of the humanities and social science.

In the midst of these issues being addressed, Japanese academism, and the Kyoto school in particular, was consciously connected to the philosophy of the Neo-Kantian school under the strong influence of German philosophy.[17] Brilliant young scholars, too, as thinkers engaged in philosophy, must have investigated "what the issues are" concerning various topics. One instance of this was the study group that met in the Rakuyū Hall at Kyoto University to address this topic of "issues" as a theme. It was around 1928 when Tosaka himself gave a report at a colloquium on the abstruse theme of "logic concerning issues".[18]

Perhaps as the circumstances of the era shifted they were gripped by a pressing concern with the question, "What are the issues?" for those who do philosophy. Going out together after Ichikō-kai study sessions, with quick-witted Miki at the center of the group, they must have had heated discussions concerning whether today's philosophers should be permitted to idly devote themselves to writing explanatory commentaries on existing texts.[19]

Tosaka, who had received a baptism in Neo-Kantian criticism, extensively and vigorously pursued his activities as an essayist and critic with *Studies in Materialism* as his main platform (1932–1938) after stepping outside the framework of academism found in Kyoto and moving to Tokyo. There was none of Miki's ornateness in his work. His writing, which took materialism as its foundation and was firmly committed to a critical rationalism, contained aspects reminiscent of the eighteenth century French Encyclopedists (recollections of Oka Kunio).

In Kant, "critique" is always the fundamental examination of the faculty of reason. In Neo-Kantianism, the critique of reason is expanded to the critique of science. In Tosaka, this critique, while succeeded by his theory of science, reaches further into a radical examination of the issues of the day. While on the one hand various fields were being coated in a varnish of militarism or ultra-nationalism, the ideology of a system of

---

[17] For example, Nishida attempts to confront Neo-Kantianism in *Jikaku ni okeru chokkan to hansei* [『自覚における直観と反省』*Intuition and Reflection in Self-Awareness*] (1913–1917), and Tanabe develops a philosophy of science that addresses the issues of space-time and the epistemic issue of the observing subject's disruption of the object posed by Heisenberg's quantum mechanics. Among their disciples on the [political] left, Funayama wrote his graduation thesis on Dilthey.

[18] This seems to have been inspired by Miki's "Toi no kōzō" [『問いの構造』 "The Structure of Inquiry"] (reprinted in volume five of his collected writings), a paper included in his *Shakaigaku no yobi gainen* [『社会学の予備概念』 *Preliminary Concepts of Social Science*] (Tetto shoin, 1929) (Kakehashi, *Zenshizenteki katei no shisō* [『全自然史的過程の思想』 *Thoughts Concerning the Process of Comprehensive Natural History*], p. 286). Tosaka seems to have put together his "Theory of Issues" in response to this text of Miki's (see "Ideorogī no ronrigaku" [『イデオロギーの論理学』 "The Logic of Ideology"] included in *Zenshū* [『全集』 *Complete Works*] vol. 2).

[19] The "Tetsugaku ichikō-kai [Dai-ichi High School Graduates Philosophy Circle]" was a group of seven or eight individuals, including Tanikawa, Tosaka, Kakehashi, and Kaba [?], that formed around Miki after he returned to Japan from his travels abroad in October of 1925. After meeting for about a year, this group became the Aristotle Study Circle. While he did not always attend their meetings, Nishitani's name can also be seen in connection with this group (Kakehashi, ibid., p. 263–264).

governance that would promote the world's degeneration, in other words, its empty false consciousness, also had to be criticized. The discourse of this critique then had to be subjected to considerable refinement from the perspective of materialism, with the question of whether it agrees with reason or not as the criterion.[20] In order to expose the falseness of the actuality of his nation, Tosaka had to become the Encyclopedist of Shōwa-era Japan. He was also the Nakae Chōmin of the Shōwa era. To Tosaka, materialism was a philosophical category that was firmly committed to critique, and which constituted a solid framework for thought.

8.4.2 Theories of Science and of Technology

(a) Let us begin by looking at Tosaka's theory of science. The distinctive characteristic of his theory of science begins with his search in materialism for a unified principle running through both the natural and social sciences. As is widely known, to the Neo-Kantians, and in particular Rickert, the scientific nature of natural science was to be sought in the mechanical chain of cause and effect arising on the basis of the uniformity of nature. If so, then what about the sciences of society, history and culture? In the realm of history events occur only one at a time and are unique. They are not universally nomothetical as in the world of nature. We thus speak of the distinctive character of historical science as the description of individual, unique events, or as an *idiographisch* field of study.[21]

Along with the Neo-Kantians, Tosaka does not place, as Hegel does, the philosophy of "spirit [mind]" above the philosophy of "nature". Idealism pursues, through the speculation of reason [*Vernunftspekulation*], the logical unfolding of *ideas* that transcendentally govern both "nature" and "spirit". As metaphysics, this philosophy naturally turns its back on the empirical sciences. Needless to say, the positivism of the latter half of the nineteenth century avoids this tendency. In this regard both Neo-Kantianism and the logical positivism that came later share a common foundation upon which they were established. Most of the Neo-Kantian school engages in the work of philosophy epistemologically.

On this point Tosaka is a positivist as well. For him the work of philosophy is epistemological and scientistic. He does not dichotomize "nature" and "spirit" (society, history, and culture—what Marxism calls the "superstructure"). He attempts to subsume the natural sciences and the human/historical sciences on a unitary basis.

---

[20]In carrying out this critique Tosaka adopted a lucid "logic of the understanding" instead of an ambiguous dialectical logic (Kondō Yōitsu, "Zenshū geppō" 2 [全集月報二"*Complete Works Monthly Report*"2]).

[21]Tosaka also touches on this in "Kagakuron" [「科学論」 "On Science"] in *Kagakuhōhōron* [『科学方法論』 *On the Scientific Method*]. *Zenshū I* [『全集I』 *Complete Works I*], pp. 70–75. In the end he views natural science as demonstrative scholarship and historical science as a scholarship of discernment, but this [distinction] is fundamentally a Neo-Kantian conception.

But how is this to be done?

The thesis that nature is material existence has long been common among naturalistic thinkers. As a theme this was the case for natural philosophy prior to Socrates, and, in modern times, it was the case generally for the philosophy of eighteenth century French enlightenment thinkers. Tosaka believed that science is established upon a spirit that reflects the world of "things".[22] "Things" conform to temporal and historical laws of progress. If so, we might say that the spirit of science, which takes "things" as its object, is historical. Science, to begin with, takes the positivist spirit as indispensable, but this positivist spirit, after all, is a historical spirit as well. This was Tosaka's view.

Furthermore, Tosaka also believed that, when it comes to a categorical system capable of running through "nature", "spirit", and "history" in a unified manner, the only viable candidate was "materialism". He saw that the singularity and unity of materialist philosophy guarantees the singularity and unity of the academic nature running through all categorical systems and covering both the natural sciences and the social and historical sciences. (*Kagakuron* [『科学論』 *On Science*], *Zenshū* [*Collected Works*] I, p. 134)

(b) What about his theory of technology? In Tosaka, science and technology are not separate. Science anticipates technology, and technology anticipates science. He expresses this as a relationship of conjugation.[23] Experiments that ensure positive proof in science correspond to the technological standards of the period in question, and technology corresponds to the science of the day.

According to Tosaka, broadly speaking the activity of "knowing" and the activity of "making" become one in "creating". For example, while the discoveries of the Curies were of course an expansion of scientific knowledge, at the same time they spurred the development of technology and that which became industrialized. Even if we speak of the autotelic nature of science, it cannot signify pure knowledge. As something operational and practical, it is directly connected to industry. To this extent, scientific knowledge is conjugate with technological knowledge. As a current example, genetic engineering technology is directly conjugated to biological theory when it comes to gene analysis.

In 1930s Japan discussions of technology flourished as a result of two demands of the era. (1) One demand came from the state of affairs and military system that developed out of the progression from the "Manchurian incident" into the

---

[22]The world of actuality [現実の世界]: According to philosophical categories this is referred to as matter (*Zenshū I* [『全集I』 *Complete Works I*], pp. 154–155). For Tosaka, the world of reality [実在の世界] is matter. Epistemologically, the images of the natural-scientific world and of the historical world are established as this world becomes copied and reflected. But in order for this to occur, composition according to categories of natural science and composition according to categories of historical science are necessary. Tosaka's materialism held that "the real world of original things" (ibid.) is "matter" as a philosophical category. If that is the case, however, I think we can still inquire about the ideality of "matter". But I do not know of anyone, both at the time and since the war, who has attempted such an investigation apart from Kakehashi Akahide.

[23]Here I have drawn on Yamada Kō, *Tosaka Jun to sono jidai* [『戸坂潤とその時代』 *Tosaka Jun and his Era*], Kadensha, 1990, p. 31.

"Sino-Japanese war"; it was necessary for the military structure to promote the improvement of productive technology. (2) There was also a demand from the Marxist camp. Marxists held that advanced productive power entering into a fettered relationship with the productive relations of capitalism would inevitably lead to a crisis of capitalism. At the same time, theirs was also an optimistic theory insofar as it held that the productive capacity that had been stifled until that point would then, through the productive relations of socialism, be unleashed and progress by leaps and bounds.[24]

Presumably in response to the latter requirement of the times, discussions of technology flourished among Marxists such as Oka Kunio, Saigusa Hiroto, and Miki. Naturally, Tosaka was also one of those who participated in these discussions. Tosaka's distinguishing characteristic was that he could not be numbered among those in the mainstream who defined technology as a "system of means of labor". The "system of means theory" reifies technology into a "thing". Saigusa instead defined technology as "means as process" and focused on technology's functional aspect, but Tosaka criticized him for falling back into the world of teleology to the extent that he was looking at the purposiveness [合目的性; Zweckmäßigkeit] of means (Zenshū I [Complete works Vol. 1] p. 353).

As for Tosaka, he supported seeing technology not as a "thing" or realm, but rather as power. In other words, he defined it as the "standard of power for the production of things" (Ibid. p. 353, 355). This definition implies the inclusion of elements such as machine technology as a means of production, the capabilities of workers comprising an important moment of productive power as well as those of design engineers. But the question of definition is not so important here.[25]

What is important is that for Tosaka, technology, too, was subject to ideological critique. His theory, accordingly, turns in the direction of (1) and develops into an

---

[24]At the beginning of "Gijutsu no mondai" [「技術の問題」 "The Issue of Technology"], the first essay in Gijutsu no tetsugaku [『技術の哲学』 The Philosophy of Technology], Tosaka discusses the dual demands of the era that constitute the problem of technology. (Zenshū I [『全集I』 Complete Works I], p. 233).

His take on this issue, however, leads to an approach in which optimistic dreams are entrusted to technology within socialist relations of production and a pessimistic crisis is seen in technology within capitalist relations of production. At the time, in the 1930s, Tosaka held that tractors, for example, functioned very differently in the Soviet Union and in America (Zenshū I [『全集I』 Complete Works I], p. 242). If we extend this view as far as the anti-nuclear weapons controversy that broke out for a time after the war, it becomes the strange assertion that Soviet nuclear weapons are "clean" while American nuclear weapons are "dirty". To this extent Tosaka, too, was entrenched in a formulaic way of thinking.

[25]I have previously briefly discussed technology in relation to my own interest in the "metaphysics of poïēsis [ポイエシス; ποίησις]". See my essay "Gijutsu to ningen: poieshisu no keijijōgaku josetsu [「技術と人間 — ポイエシスの形而上学序説」 "Technology and Human Beings: Introduction to the Metaphyscis of Poïēsis"] (Ritsumeikan bungaku [『立命館文学』 Humanities of Ritsumeikan], vol. 315, 1971) and the appended chapter "Gijutsu to hyūmanizumu" [「技術とヒューマニズム」 "Technology and Humanism"] in my book Gendai to hyūmanizumu [『現代とヒューマニズム』The Contemporary Period and Humanism] (Hōritsu bunkasha [法律文化社], 1965).

ideological critique of the theory of technology under the military system. It goes without saying that actual technology "has a certain objective mode of being within certain productive relations and within a certain social system". Tosaka says that this is the material moment of technology.[26] What he calls "material" here also means the social or the objective. This emphasis implies a critique of Dessauer's theory of technology, which was quite influential at the time. According to Dessauer, the world of technology differs from the three worlds whose horizons of emergence Kant had illuminated in his "three Critiques". In other words, Dessauer held that in contrast to the worlds of science, ethics, and beauty, there was a fourth world that involves the activity of creating something new on the basis of some kind of *idea*. He called this the world of technology.

Dessauer's world of the establishment of technology may indeed possess a certain objectivity. To Tosaka, however, this is not the ordinary physical or actual world. It is merely the stipulation of the realm of application of concepts for one thing or another. In that case, one would have to comprehend technology anew as something possessing objectivity and actuality in the process of production and the labor process of production. Tosaka holds materialism to be valid in this sense as well.

Once you position technology within the objective processes of actuality, from that point on critique becomes an ideological critique. For there is no such thing as technology that is purely a process of things. Within technology as a process of labor there is always a "technological system" involving workers and designers. If the authorities engage in the "promotion of the spirit of technology," while exposing capitalism's state of crisis within the context of a trend of rapidly moving towards a wartime structure, ideologically this will clearly transform into a false consciousness.

From the perspective of Tosaka's critical approach, the spiritual movement of promoting science and technology from the top-down that attempts to discover a method for overcoming this crisis by returning to the spirit of the East or the traditional spirit of Japan, insofar as it favors the "heart/mind" over "things", had to be ideologically placed on the chopping board of critique as "false consciousness".

By this point we can see that Tosaka had been distinguishing between "the spirit of science or technology" and "scien*tific* or technolog*ical* spirit". For him, the spirit of science or the business of taking "things" as objects and reflecting their truth, and the spirit of technology that creates "things", were not separate. The positivist spirit that constitutes the essence of the spirit of science is by no means something to be confined to a cramped laboratory. Tosaka states that it exists within the broad framework of the productive mechanisms of society. It is for precisely this reason that, in essence, it is one with the spirit of technology.

---

[26]"Gijutsu no mondai" [「技術の問題」"The Issue of Technology"] (included in *Gijutsu no tetsugaku* [『技術の哲学』 *The Philosophy of Technology*], *Zenshū I* [『全集I』 *Complete Works I*], p. 235).

When this spirit becomes further expanded to the critique of ideology as false consciousness it becomes scien*tific* and technolog*ical*. And the falseness belonging to the promotion of the spirits of science and technology as advanced from the top down can be formulated, according to Tosaka, in three ways.[27] The first is literaturism. Here he may have had Miki, his senior colleague, in mind.[28] "Literaturism" refers to thought formulated in the style of culturalist metaphysics. Even Nishida may perhaps be implicated here. The claim is that cultural metaphysics and Romantic idealism merely replace the actual order of things with supernal desires.

The second formulation is philologism. This is the academic stance of conducting textual commentary in the name of learning. From Tosaka's perspective, the demonstrations of philologists are only interpretations. They are merely replacing actuality with interpretation. In the development of this theory we even see the term "academic fools" being employed. It can also be noted that hermeneutics, which had become quite popular from around this time, abandons the procedure of demonstration and focuses exclusively on the interpretation of semantic associations. To this extent it falls into an anarchic metaphysics (*Zenshū* [『全集』*Complete writings*] Vol. 1 p. 264). To Tosaka, the world of semantic interpretation where originality and curiosity intermingle appears to be lacking in objectivity and a scientific nature. When making such statements Tosaka presumably had in mind Watsuji in particular.[29]

The third formulation is dogmaticism [教学主義]. This is a non-academic stance that takes scholarship to mean the moralistic restriction of culture and its edification by means of scriptures. Tosaka described this approach as characteristic of Eastern monasticism and the master-oriented conception of culture. This presumably refers to the scholars and critics of the "return to tradition" movement who, in response to the flag-waving of the Ministry of Education's "Bureau of Learning", were exhorting an ideology of "Japanese spiritualism".

---

[27] "Gijutsuteki seishin towa nanika" [「技術的精神とは何か」 "What is the Technological Spirit?"], one section of "Kagakuteki seishin ni tsuite" [「科学的精神について」 "On the Scientific Spirit"] (*Zenshū I* [『全集I』 *Complete Works I*], p. 346).

[28] Miki was allegedly mentioned as a representative of philosophy of literature-ism at a lecture meeting organized by the "Hōgakubu gakuyūkai [法学部学友会 Law Faculty Students' Association]" that took place in the University of Tokyo's Faculty of Law during the fall of 1937 (Teruoka Ryōzō, "Kaisō no dampen" [「回想の断片」 "Fragments of Reminiscence"], "Zenshū geppō" 2 [『全集』月報二 "Complete Works Monthly Report" 2]).

[29] A full-fledged critique of Watsuji can be seen in part seven "Nihon rinrigaku to ningengaku" [「日本倫理学と人間学」 "Japanese Ethics and Anthropology"], of the first book of *Nihon ideorogī ron* [『日本イデオロギー論』 *On Japanese Ideology*] (included in *Zenshū II* [『全集II』 *Complete Works II*]). The first edition of *Nihon ideorogī ron* was published in 1935. This was an accumulation of criticism exposing the ideological nature of a thought that, while wearing the guise of liberalism, had aligned itself with Japanism from the period of the Manchurian incident of 1931 onwards and in the end was swept up by the current of militarism. In March of 1934 Watsuji published *Ningen no gaku toshite no rinrigaku* [『人間の学としての倫理学』 *Ethics as the Study of Human Beings*], and in September of that year he was transferred to Tokyo Imperial University.

All three of the above, while conducted in the name of promoting the spirits of science and technology, were in fact approaches that preached an anti-scientific or unscientific spirit. The exposition of this fallaciousness was the point of Tosaka's radical criticism, and the system by which this was incorporated into his philosophy was materialism. Therein lies what Tosaka calls the true scien*tific* and technolog*ical* spirits. Tosaka had once asserted that the academic nature [学問性] of academic inquiry lay in the function of critique. This was, to put it another way, a manifestation of the true scientific and technological spirits.

Nishikawa Tomio Died in 2010. Major works: *Tetsugaku kyōshi no gojyūnen* [『哲学教師の五十年』 *Fifty Years of Teaching Philosophy*] (Kobushi Shobō, 2005), *Kankyō tetsugaku e no shōtai: ikiteiru shizen o tetsugaku suru* [『環境哲学への招待:生きている自然を哲学する』 *Invitation to Environmental Philosophy: Philosophizing About Living Nature*] (Kobushi Shobō, 2002), *Zoku・Sheringu tetsugaku no kenkyū: 'shizen no keijijōgaku' no kanōsei* [『続・シェリング哲学の研究:「自然の形而上学」の可能性』 *A Study of Schelling's Philosophy, Volume 2: the Potentiality of a 'Metaphysics of Nature'*] (Shōwadō, 1994).

Part V
Kimura Motomori

Chapter 9
Body and Spirit [Mind]

[身体と精神]

Kimura Motomori

Human beings, it goes without saying, have been using their bodies since the beginning of their existence on earth. However—strange as this may sound—human thought's discovery of the body as the body, and the start of its comprehension of the body in truth, is by no means ancient but rather a fairly recent occurrence. In fact, we often fail to discover things that are right before our eyes. The Alps certainly existed long before human beings first appeared on the surface of the earth. But it was only with the advent of Romantic literature at the beginning of the nineteenth century that the *beauty* of the Alps was first discovered. Around 1760, even the beautiful Grindelwald valley was being described as a hell-like gorge shrouded in eternal darkness and as the most frightening and uncanny place on the European continent. Even liberators of nature like Rousseau, who himself twice crossed the Alps on foot, never noticed the sublime beauty of the mountain. Just as the Grindelwald was long regarded as the darkness of hell, ever since Plato we have known the body—despite it having been a subject of unsurpassable beauty for Greek sculptors—as the prison of the mind. While the artists of the Renaissance broke through the [perspective of the] middle-ages to rediscover the body's beauty, thinkers as before failed to grasp its true significance. To Spinoza, the body was nothing more than an aspect of material nature. Here the body is sucked into the world of extension. For Descartes, the pineal gland is a particular point that allows mind and matter to reciprocally act upon one another, but not the particular point from which the creative formation of the world occurs. Instead, it is nothing other than the point where Descartes' rationalist philosophical system begins to rupture. If thinkers have had to affix the label of *deus ex machina* to the work of Malebranche and Geulincx, then the body must indeed be an obstacle to those who think.

Translated from the Japanese by Robert Chapeskie and revised by John W. M. Krummel.

M. Kimura

To be sure, evil must often have emerged through the body. The *Ideas* [イデア ιδέα] presumably have been obscured. But does not good appear through the body as well? Moreover, no matter how hard we struggle we can never concretely see the good nor manifest it other than through this body. We are not permitted to complain about the existence of air like Kant's dove. For us the body is an indispensable principle for bringing the good, the beautiful, and the true truly and concretely into existence. For human beings, all things whose existence is desirable and that are worth bringing into existence can only be attained through the body. In this fact we must ascertain the essence of the body. The body is a principle of *expression* [表現].

Expression, however, is the manifestation of the inside on the outside—or, to employ contrasting concepts to which people are accustomed, it is the realization of spirit [the mind] in nature. This, however, is nothing other than causing the inside to exist on the outside. In the world of expression the outside is then the inside. Expression cannot be established at all where this character is lost. If the essential character of expression is established through this kind of interconnectedness between inside and outside, then the path to understanding it must be one that diverges completely from the standpoint of analytic logic that cannot acknowledge that inside is thoroughly inside but at the same time outside and vice versa. That outside is inside is not a state of affairs that can be established by assuming that outside is outside and inside is inside. This being the case, the logic that governs the world of expression must presumably transcend analytic logic and be a logic of a higher level that takes the latter [analytic logic] as its own abstraction. That the route leading there [to the logic of the world of expression] diverges from the rationalism of analytic logic means that this route must therefore involve a leap upwards. In order to understand the world of expression, a methodological leap is required. As a result, if, as stated above, the body is one of the principles of expression, then it must be something that displays its essential structure in the close interrelationship [相即] of inside and outside, or, in other words, subjectivity and objectivity. So to grasp it as simply something belonging to nature, like referring to the body in its everyday usage directly as 'I' and grasping it only subjectively, would surely be a fundamental error. The body is a non-rational entity that cannot be dealt with from the standpoint of an *entweder-oder* [either/or] relationship between nature and spirit. The reason that the dimensional limitation of Cartesian rationalism could not help but expose itself from within lies in its attempt to deal with this sort of entity in an *entweder-oder* setting. Needless to say, to treat the body as a mere modality of extension through the science of physics cannot possibly be a valid approach to understanding its essence, and this goes for approaches based on chemistry and physiology or biology as well. The standpoint of the teleology of nature also fails to rationalize this dialectical entity that constitutes a self-identity of contradictories.

I have stated above that expression is the manifestation of the inside on the outside and the realization of spirit in nature. When I say this, what do I mean by "spirit"? To manifest the inside on the outside is the work of expressive life [表現的生命]. When people refer to the human sciences [*Geisteswissenschaften*;

literally, "spiritual sciences"] in contrast to the natural sciences, the former takes this sort of expressive life as its object of consideration. This work of life, in a broad sense, is the act of expression, and what is manifested in nature as its result is, broadly speaking, a work (product) as something made. For to manifest the inside on the outside, in the essence of its matter, is not simply the inside coming face to face with, and standing opposed to, the outside and receiving it in a purely passive manner. It is nothing other than "to push out" (*express, ausdrücken*) the inner self, and by doing so to see the inside outside and in turn allow the inside to exist on the outside. And to do so is necessarily to remake the outside to some extent. Even in the case of what can be considered purely aesthetic contemplation, in principle this productive nature is never absent. Contemplation, too, is an activity of expressive life, and what is seen assumes the character of what is created and made manifest by expressive life. Moreover, it exists outside, not inside; it exists in nature. Herein lies the reason that the product of an expressive act, as one dialectical entity, in a broad sense ought to be referred to as objective spirit (*objektiver Geist*), and at the same time the reason that an expressive act should also, in a broad sense, be referred to as an act of production. If expression tends to be taken narrowly as simply referring to verbal expression, we may perhaps say that the expression we intend, in its essence and broadness, is more accurately described in terms of what is commonly referred to as *formation*.

This kind of product, then, by being an outward formation, indicates at the root of its being something internal as the movement of an expressive subject. What sort of thing is this? In any case, it must be an internal movement of our mind. That said, however, it cannot be directly equivalent to so-called "psychological (*psychisch*) facts". That would be nothing more than an abstraction seen when, from a certain methodological perspective, true inner life is projected onto the "face of nature". Where we seek the laws governing the occurrence and behavior of such things, a certain psychology as the study of empirical facts is established. When we refer to the essence of the inside as "spiritual (*geistig*)" as opposed to "psychological", we do not simply mean a chaotic stream of representations, emotions, and urges. We mean instead the governance of a self-awareness concerning the demand for some sort of value running through all of these things. The movement of the mind concerned with values: this is what we are accustomed to refer to as spiritual. With deep passion and lofty yearning, the inner movement focuses internally on some manner of desirable figures, shapes worthy of pursuit, or forms that surely ought to exist, and seeks to realize them. A mind that strives while fixing its gaze on ideas—such a mind is spiritual. And extrapolating from this point, we must therefore say that it is in its particularly volitional character that what is internal and spiritual possesses its essence. The will to the realization of values—that is the essence of the internal and spiritual. We thus often ascribe to the spiritual various particular directions, such as the artistic will (*Kunstwollen*), the will to truth, the will to the good, and so on. But the achievements of art, scholarship, and morality are results of such realizations of the will, and as realizations of human values these achievements are referred to in general as "culture". If so, then we can rephrase the internal and spiritual in general as the will to culture, and we can likewise describe the values that we gaze at and strive for as cultural values.

These values are the original ideas of humanity itself, and as such they can always be seen as transcending the demands of mere individuals. That said, however, they do not appear immediately in simple universality. In concrete terms they appear by being determined in a specific form through various restrictive mediations. In this way a national spirit is established among a people, and a spirit of the period is established in historical time. In order to clarify these things strictly in terms of fundamental principles we would probably need to begin by investigating the sort of structures within which human beings exist as social historical entities. At the moment, however, I will not attempt to advance an investigation from this perspective.[1] Let us instead address expression in terms of its universal character. Here it is unavoidable that we determine the perspective of our investigation in advance. If the essential meaning of the body arises at the point where, as is stated above, it is one of the principles of expression, then naturally we must treat it as one moment of expressive life if we are to properly problematize the body. This, however, naturally assumes a holistic structure as a connection of moments. The *body* possesses its unique meaning where it constitutes an expressive *mediating* moment between inside and outside when the *internal* and spiritual that constitutes one moment of expressive life formatively expresses itself on the *outside* that is another moment. I would like to confine our central inquiry, to put it more concisely, to simply clarifying the connection in expressive life between these three moments. In what follows I will attempt a modest investigation into *body* and *spirit* from this point of view.

When we speak of manifesting the inside on the outside, what is this *outside* and what do we mean by it? Is the so-called world of natural things, the world of objects of theoretical (*theoretisch*) cognition, the outside for the world of expression? This world, however, is established upon the standpoint of *theoria* [θεωρία]. As a world itself seen from a thoroughly contemplative (*kontemplativ*) perspective, it is accordingly something itself severed from human action and separated from practical connections, and to that extent established as a solitary, isolated world. The outside for the world of expression is, however, precisely that to which the inside relates in order to formatively manifest itself there. It must therefore be something that cannot be severed from the expressive will and that cannot possess its essential meaning apart from human action. The outside is nothing other than that which is tied to the inside through such a connection and given form by it. We call this *material* (*Stoff*) [素材]. It is the principle of *Materie* (matter [実質]) in contrast to *Form* (form [形式、形相]) as that which is made real by receiving shape through formation [形成]. In this way material affects formation in two senses. Formation acts upon material because form that demands its realization fails to find a reality that satisfies it on the outside, and in this relationship material first

---

[1] I touched on the origin of this investigation in the second half of "Mikeruanjero no kaishin" [「ミケルアンヂエロの回心」 "The Conversion of Michelangelo"].

and foremost opposes form in the negative sense as an obstacle to formation. But by overcoming this negativity of material directed towards itself and breaking down its impediment, formation instead realizes form in this negator. By negating the negation in this way, form affirms itself for-itself [対自的に] in the outside that is fundamentally other [他者] vis-a-vis the inside, and escapes its ideality, that is, its vacancy in relation to matter, to obtain reality. Within this relationship material manifests its positive meaning as a real supporter of form. In this way material is both the negator and at the same time the affirmer of form. The outside in the world of expression is not merely the things of nature, but also must be material, at least in the sense given above. It is not simply *stone* that is the outside; it is *stone material* that is the outside. On the basis of the world of expression, stone in the essential sense of its being is nothing more than what is established as stone material in the abstract low-level plane of being. When the nature of the external world of expression is deprived of its expressive character, stone material falls back into being mere stone.

In this way expression is realized by overcoming the impeding nature of material that is one of its moments. To realize internal forms, that is, the *ideas* seen in the expressive subject, by conquering the outside is nothing other than formative expression. Herein we find the standpoint of idealism. It thus follows that culture means the realization of the ideas of the expressive subject, that is, the ego, by conquering nature as material. Culture is the victory in battle of humanity over nature. Kant and Fichte in principle also shared this way of thinking. Fichte in particular was a paradigmatic thinker who systematically constructed a worldview from this perspective.[2].

To the extent that expression is something that manifests inner life through formation, it is clear that material ought to form one indispensable moment of expressive life. However, is what we ought to call outside in relation to the subject in the world of expression immediately and simply material? When we live concretely in the world of expression, is what we find in our immediate encounters and negotiations outside of ourselves nothing more than material?

What we directly encounter in the concrete activities of expressive life is not simply material. What is external does not stop at simply being formatively processed by the subject. On the contrary, it is something that continuously speaks to the subject. That which constitutes the external moment in the expressive world is not material, but rather the expressive environment that speaks to our expressive will. If history is the expressive life process of human beings then the outside must be nothing other than the historical environment. Prior to encountering material, we encounter that which has been historically created, or what has been expressively made. We are born into this world, we grow up, we ourselves create, and then we perish. Here the outside is a world discovered as something made. Something that is made is, as a matter of course, not something that makes as a subject. It stands in strict opposition to the subject, and, to the extent that it is out of the hands of its

---

[2] See the author's *Fihite* [『フイヒテ』*Fichte*] (*Seitetsu sōsho* [西哲叢書])

maker, it opposes the subject as an other. To this extent it is an object (*Objekt*) and must always be outside in relation to the inside. Nevertheless, it is essentially something that has been made. It is an inside brought to the outside. To this extent it must be spirit that has become *Objekt*. It is for this reason that it speaks. The expressive environment is always speaking to the subject in a language without words. What we directly encounter as the outside is this sort of world. When I say this, people may object by pointing to the ground or a rock and saying that these are outside and are not things that have been made. But before it is material we must first and foremost think of the land as something that incites the human will and its intentionality. There is no such thing as mere land. It is always a particular slope or plane; it may be a mountain range that obstructs human travel or a plain that stretches to a river or the sea. Each piece of lands possesses its own aspect. On virgin soil, there is indeed nothing made by human hands. And yet every piece of land, each with its own type of terrain, incites and speaks to the human will. For this reason we must say that the land and human beings exist in expressive negotiation with each other. We must say that they are in a relationship in which they expressively determine each other, a relationship in which they make and are made by each other. In this sense the expressive environment, in principle and essentially, must take on the character of something that has been made, that is, the character of being spiritual while at the same time being an *Objekt*. We can thus also say that it exists in the character of a *thou* [汝] who speaks to an *I*. To Michelangelo, a piece of stone is not mere material. It is something that deeply calls upon his artistic will. He says that a good artist would not have in mind a work that could not be harbored within a given lump of marble. But it is only the hands obeying the spirit that can bring it out into the light. An artist is thus not someone who engraves his or her spirit on a material that is uninscribed by form. What he or she stands face to face with, on the contrary, is something that houses a will toward a certain shape and compels and appeals to him or her with the demand of a specific figure; it is nothing other than a soul seeking to be born and appear [into the world]. Just as we saw earlier that stone was a low-level abstraction of stone material, stone material, too, is nothing other than a low-level abstraction of *stone-that-calls-to-us*.

It is only as something that relates to its environment in this way that the expressive subject is an expressive subject in its proper sense. The expressive subject is not an expressive subject because it carves itself into lifeless material nature. The subject obtains an expressive subjectivity in its proper sense only as an inside capable of responding to the outside that speaks to it. The expressive world, too, is established in its proper sense only through this relationship between subject and environment. The subject in its originary sense is not the environment. They are mutually other. And it is when these things [subject and environment] are tied together in relationships such as that described above that the expressive world obtains. We must therefore say that the expressive world is a world that contains within itself a principle of negation. The expressive world moves through mutual expressive negotiation between inside and outside that occurs only by mediating them through a negation. This is nothing other than an essentially dialectical world. The inside cannot be the inside without taking the outside as its mediation, and vice

9 Body and Spirit [Mind]

versa. Here the dialectical self-identity of inside and outside obtains in expressive being. This in no sense signifies the neutral identity of inside and outside described by identity philosophy, but rather the inseparable identity of the mutually negating.

To say that the subject responds, by the way, does not mean that it is simply something that listens. That which merely listens is something only determined from the outside, and as such is merely passive without making determinations of its own. The subject must be something that actively responds through listening as its medium. That the subject who is a moment of the expressive world responds, however, must mean that it forms. That the subject responds means that it takes the determination that is a call from the outside as the mediation to formatively determine the outside from the inside in return. If this is the case, however, it becomes impossible for the opposition between subject and environment to be a mere compresent coordination and hence merely a spatial opposition. Even though the outside negatively opposes the inside, the essential character of the subject lies in its formatively determining the outside in return as described above, and in relation to this the outside is always that which is made. That which is made is something that has *already* been seen by the subject. If seeing expressively is fundamentally nothing other than seeing in accordance with formation, then the fact that the outside is something made and that it speaks to the subject would presumably mean that it exists by being given to the subject as something already formatively seen, and that as such a thing it is something that on its own, facing the subject, conveys and imparts itself. In this sense the expressive environment in its essence is thus something that is literally traditional (*traditionell*), and owing to its character of *already* being we must say that it is something past-like [過去的なもの]. There are, of course, things that are important in the expressive environment in terms of the significance it possesses in relation to the subject, but also things that are quite peripheral and inconsequential. Nevertheless, however, it must in principle be acknowledged that this spatial existence as outside is something that in general is established simultaneously through its nature of being-past and through its traditional nature as something that imparts itself. The subject cannot function as subject unless it takes this kind of thing as its mediation. When it comes to this sort of essence we must presumably understand the outside in the world of expression as one of the moments that forms this world. We have already gone beyond the concepts of the idealist philosophy of culture. In this approach the outside remained mere materiality. According to our analysis, material is nothing other than an abstract aspect manifesting the expressive outer realm in its originary sense, not in its concreteness but only insofar as it is viewed one-sidedly as merely something in relation to the responsive determination of the subject.

In contrast to the outside that is an outside, calling out in this way, as what sort of thing does the inside that responds to this call become established? Responding is not simply listening. It occurs when, on the basis of listening, that is, by taking listening as its foundation, the expressive subject acts spontaneously towards the outside. But what sort of content is it that is elicited towards the outside as a response? First and foremost, the subject must see this [content] within itself. As a form that ought to emerge as a response by means of the subject's spontaneity, this is nothing other than the figure of the self that the subject sees within itself as one determination of the self. It sees here the *ideas* [ιδέα] of expression. But the *ideas*, to this extent, remain nothing more than figures seen within. As long as these *ideas* are *ideas* of expression and the subject is a subject of formation, however, the *ideas* cannot stop at simply being seen within. Such a thing [the *ideas*] cannot simply possess the sense of the content of the self for the formative subject of expression. Although it may sound paradoxical, the *ideas* must be something seen on the outside. Herein lies the meaning of seeing the expressive *ideas*. The *ideas* are seen only by being expressively formed and drawn out from the inside towards the outside. For expressive life, seeing, in its essence, is making, and seeing cannot obtain beyond this. But to see in this way only with the eyes is surely impossible. Previously we have distinguished spirit from merely psychological mental activities, defined it in particular as that which operates through a concern with values, and recognized therein the essence of the activities of the spirit. The *ideas* are, to begin with, forms seen within as things with value that ought to be realized. If so, then expressively seeing the *ideas* as described above cannot be possible with merely spiritual activities. Here the unique role of the body in relation to expressive life obtains. To truly see the ideas is not to see them merely spiritually, but, on the contrary, must be to see them somatically. How is it possible to somatically see? We cannot directly address this question quite yet.

If to truly see an *idea* is to formatively see it on the outside, then, to the extent that it is seen on the inside, what ought to be realized outside and become actual, in its way of being of *not yet having reached this point*, must be connected to the subject. Herein obtains the futurity of the *idea*. An *idea*, in its essence, is nothing other than the figure of something that ought to come into actuality but has not yet done so. Time is not something accidental or non-essential to the *ideas*. On the contrary, without temporality the *idea* loses its essential meaning. For mere natural time, the *ideas* are thoroughly transcendent, and how the *ideas* appear within this kind of time is surely an incomprehensibly difficult question. But natural time is nothing more than the dead, abstract side of historical time. Divorced from the expressive will, the *ideas* would degenerate into nothing but mere imaginary concepts. The *ideas* are a reality in the expressive world and are in no way imaginary. This is not to say that an *idea* is something born out of the subject's mere spontaneity, but rather depends on the connection in which the outside as something made that is the pre-determined aspect of expressive life becomes the mediating moment of its spontaneous self-determination [自己限定]. To the extent that expressive life is fundamentally constituted in the dialectic between inside and outside, a determination of the inside that completely ignores the moment of the outside would have to be one that does not possess proper citizenship in the expressive world. Such a thing can do nothing other than drift across the surface of time, dreamlike, as a fictional floating object separated from the practice of expression. The outside, nevertheless, in relation to the inside and enveloping so-called natural matter (*Materie*) as something even broader and also made, is the entire realm of matter (*Materie*). And in relation to it the inside is established as the realm of the ideal (Ideal). From this point of view, we are compelled to say that the expressive *idea* is the subject's self-determination as an idea that ought to appear by connecting itself to the material world while taking the material world as the medium of its own establishment. In this sense the *ideas* are authenticated as a certain reality in the world of expression. Just as it is a mistake to think of the *ideas* as simply a spontaneous self-determination of the inside, it is thus also a mistake to think that they can be brought out through the mere analysis of matter. That expressive life sees the *ideas* by taking *Materie* as dialectical mediation means that the subject determines itself in its mutual conformity with the modality of *Materie*, that is, with its current state. And it is not the mere continuity of determination from outside to inside that is to be found here; on the contrary, negation dominates, and outside and inside are related only through a discontinuous link. Herein obtains the creativity of the inside. The outside must, nevertheless, be something that exists all the more concretely with a traditional character. That determination in terms of the *ideas* must make the outside its mediation, in concrete terms, means that it must therefore make tradition its mediation. Tradition and creation are thus tradition and creation only by mediating each other even while being a negative other to each other. Cut off from each other both lose their respective characters, and therefore must also lose their respective peculiar being-ness.

Consequently, the so-called place where tradition and creation are mediated through negation in this way, where past and future encounter each other and dialectically conform to one another, is nothing other than the present of historical time. We can say that the present bears the meaning of something like a railroad switch that transitionally mediates these two heterogeneous directions. On one side, the present, as the location where a response is uttered in relation to the call of the past, is tied to tradition as transcendent of it and in a discontinuous manner [非連続的に]. But on the other side, in the creative direction, as something that sees that which is *yet* to come, the present is also discontinuously linked to the future as a result of this negativity. In this way, on the one side as that which sees what has already been made but at the same time on the other side as that which looks forward to the yet-to-come, the present itself is thoroughly that which sees and in no way that which is seen as an object, and hence in this sense, as that which lacks the character of being, becomes instead the so-called place of the subject that mediates tradition and creation. We can thus say that individual subjects are each actual points of self-awareness [自覚点] of the historical present. Expressive life reaches the apex of its creative self-awareness in individual subjects. We can see therein a society of self-aware expressive subjects. This is not simply a society of abstract autonomous subjects as in Kant's "kingdom of ends" [*Reich der Zwecke*]. As actual points of self-awareness of the creative will that takes tradition as mediation, the expressive subject here must be an individual entity, the concrete meaning of which from the start is founded upon the historical social whole. And as a result of its self-awareness it necessarily exists as something with free will. This is the case because the fact that the individual subject—as a self-aware point of the expressive will's present that sees the *ideas* in self-determination through creation, taking tradition as mediation—can possess the *ideas* in *self-awareness* means that, assuming it is capable of negating and rebelling against its *ideas*, it can possess no other path than to absolutely affirm them by negating their negation. Resolution is nothing other than what is established in the individual subject through this affirmation. Resolution is not something born out of a merely impulsive will. Nor is it something born out of a mere increase in desire that accompanies *pathos*. The *ideas* are indeed born within the expressive subject as a difficult-to-stop will laden with *pathos*. But for them to become self-aware as *ideas* is impossible without taking double negation in the above sense as mediation. Resolution is the will's self-aware decision. Only through the duplicity of negation, such as in the further negation of the negation of an *idea* as described above, that is, the possibility of freedom towards evil, is the will's practical freedom that takes autonomy as its essence established. And only as the subject of such freedom does the individual and independent being-ness of the individual subject obtain. For this individual the *ideas* must therefore be established as something immanent and at the same time transcendent. As a result of this transcendence the future is discontinuously tied to the present. The individual thus possesses nostalgic yearning through the *ideas*.

Now, if it is the case that the individual subject is something that is established as the practical self-aware point of the present of expressive life that creatively sees the *ideas* by taking tradition as mediation as described above, then we can no longer say that the *ideas* seen immanently-qua [*soku*]-transcendentally by the subject in this way are born through the ego's spontaneous self-determination as mere subject. In relation to this, even culture as the formative expression of such *ideas* cannot be said to be a mere human product produced by the human will taking nature as its material. As noted above, humanity and nature inherently stand opposed to each other in hostility, and culture must signify the subjugation of nature by humanity. Nature sustains culture to the extent that it has been subjugated. The construction of culture is nothing other than the ceaseless struggle of humanity against nature. Idealist philosophy has indeed always conceived of culture in this way. However, according to our investigation thus far mere material nature does not exist concretely and immediately. For self-aware expressive life, the outside constitutes one of its structural moments, as something already made, and is an objective spirit that in principle possesses a traditional meaning and speaks in the direction of the inside. Material nature is nothing other than an abstract aspect of this outside, and nature as the object of theoretical knowledge is thus nothing more than its abstract aspect of an even lower level. Similarly, through its dialectical mediation with this kind of expressive outside, expressive life likewise possesses an expressive inside as a creative moment of itself, and the individual subject, so to speak, is nothing other than the point of self-aware expression of this sort of expressive life. For this reason, the *ideas* of which the individual subject is self-aware are not simply what are established on the basis of the ego's spontaneous self-determination that opposes nature in hostility. They must be what are born and disgorged from the inside of expressive life itself that possesses individuals as points of self-awareness, from the bottom of an expressive world that possesses outside and inside as dialectical moments, and from the depths of a historical reality that possesses tradition and creation in dialectical identity. They must be what possesses historical reality in the modality of immanence-qua [*soku*]-transcendence by taking the individual's self-awareness of free will as mediation. The outside as tradition cultivates the inside, the inside as creative spirit sublates tradition, and in this way historical reality rolls on. That which exists within historical nature that moves and becomes on its own through this kind of negotiation between inside and outside, and which participates with self-awareness in this occupation of expressive life, is nothing other than the individual subject. That which exists within the unfathomable and eternal that comes into being and personally accomplishes with self-awareness the work that ought to be done—that is the individual human being. For this reason culture is not the work of human beings subjugating a nature that is naturally hostile, but must instead, in its deepest essence, obtain when human beings, who exist within historical reality, form reality with self-awareness, or when human beings who consciously exist within historical nature foster nature with self-awareness. We can therefore say that *cultura* in its deepest, truest sense is nothing other than to cultivate historical nature—*agricultura*. In this way education, as one realm of *cultura* in this sense, must possess its deepest, most essential meaning in its aim of cultivating human beings. Just as seeing nature as material was an abstraction, understanding the meaning of culture by taking nature as an enemy was also an abstraction of idealist philosophy. Heaven and Earth continually move while enveloping human self-awareness. We can perhaps say that human beings, like stars in the vast heavens, are its formative points of self-awareness within the expressive universe. Culture is nothing other than the self-expression of this nature that takes human beings as mediation. At the bottom of the struggle between human beings and nature, an *expressive love* of an even deeper reality is operating. But how is it that human beings being the self-aware elements of formative expressive reality in this way can be realized in actuality? If human beings were not capable of formation this would be impossible. But historical nature has been sufficiently accommodating; human beings possess bodies.

What is the body? Whether we conceive of it as mere natural matter or even as a biological entity, the body's essence cannot be grasped. Human beings are essentially formative expressive entities. They are beings that are situated outside to in turn possess an inside; they are spiritual-qua [*soku*]-material entities. The body is nothing other than the dialectical moment of this kind of dialectical entity, concretely making possible its formative realization. Therefore the true essence of the body can hardly be understood from the rationalist standpoint of the *entweder-oder* [either/or] dichotomy of spirit or matter. The fact that in our daily lives we vividly grasp with concrete precision and describe our internal workings and demeanor in accordance with the body is due to nothing other than the fact that human beings are fundamentally expressive beings that are spiritual-qua [*soku*]-material, and are beings wherein something internal displays its concrete form in its material aspect. Not hanging the insignificant upon our *teeth* [not *taking notice* of the insignificant], finding what is extremely difficult unfit for our *hands* [out of our power] and something to which our *teeth* will not stand [something that is too much to bear], we lean on our *knees* towards what pleases the *ear* [*lean towards* good news] and we prick up our *ears* [*are all ears*] to rumors and gossip about ourselves and others. We present our *eyes* to [*wink* at] people, turn up our *noses* at people, we dictate orders with our *chin*, there are times something *stands our stomachs* [irritates us] so much that we rend our *hair* [become angry], when something is of vital interest to us we put our *shoulders* into it [*lean into it*], and when we find that something is not easy we sit our *hips* down [become *focused*].—The hands and the mouth are not the only organs of expression; the eyes, too, often "say as much as the mouth," and the entire body vividly expresses the inside. In this way internal life manifests itself first and foremost directly through its body. Here we can see the first stage in the emergence of expressive life. In concrete terms, in this way the inside directly and immediately possesses itself in the bodily outside. We can see here the in-itself-ness [即自態] of expression in its first stage.

But for a human being, who is essentially a formative expresser, that which is essentially even more important than the fact that the body immediately expresses the mind must lie in its formative nature. The above-mentioned *sitting the hips down* or *presenting the eyes* [*winking*], as well, do not stop at simply manifesting the mind's state or movement, but at the same time display a certain technic. Technics are means that have as their purpose the execution of some act or the formation of some kind of thing. And as a result of this formation a product is brought forth as something made. We can say that, in contrast to the in-itself-ness mentioned above, this is its for-itself-ness [対自態] as the second stage of expressive life. A piece of work in a broad sense—something that is made in general—belongs to this stage. In relation to these stages, the act of making itself, as a dialectical negotiation between inside and outside, must be that which manifests a higher-level self-aware creative activity in relation to them, a dynamic concrete synthesis of both moments of inside and outside. It is here we must say the in-and-for-itself [即かつ対自的な] stage of expressive life is established.

For this reason we must seek the most important essential quality of the body in its formative nature. Speaking from this perspective, we can stipulate that the body is a *will that encroaches upon nature*. It goes without saying that the body belongs to nature as one part of material nature, and all of its movements fall under the laws of nature. Moreover, the body at the same time belongs to the subject and realizes its inner will by moving in accordance with it. Herein lies the dialectical character of the body. It is the self-negation of spirit, and at the same time it is the self-negation of matter. Because the body is thus the self-identity of contradictories [矛盾の自己同一] it possesses the capacity of formation, and expressive life is able to express itself in self-awareness through the mediation of the body. We must therefore say that the body is the apex of the creative will that historical nature drives into its own material aspect. Concrete self-aware formation occurs through the mind functioning at this apex. As the tip of a drill that bores into stone and pierces its surface, we tackle a difficult task by *putting our bodies into* it. The unique character of the body obtains where the mind immediately moves upon it. Here the mind is not spirit of the sort we have stipulated, but, as is illustrated by the expression *hands-mind* [手心 to make allowance/in view of circumstances], exists in the hands in particular and is a mind that functions as hands. Technic is nothing other than this kind of functioning of the mind. Hands-mind, however, as the term itself suggests, arises as the synthesis of these two moments. Outside of the mind it takes the hands as a moment. The mind residing in the hands functions by using them. When this happens the hands become tools, and possess the *adaptability* of application (objective propriety) in relation to an object to the extent it *fits our hands*. In this way the body is established from the synthesis of technicity and instrumentality. Just as a hand that does not work is essentially not a hand, a body that does not work is not a true body. To the essential body, instrumentality and technicity are thus two moments that shape its concreteness, and the mind as technic is not something appended from outside the body. When the hands-mind as this sort of thing moves, *hand-addition/subtraction* [手加減discretion, allowance, consideration, knack] appears, and when *the end of a hand* [手先fingers] grasps a spoon it *extends*, and a *spoon-addition/subtraction* [匙加減discretion, allowance, seasoning, measuring-out] appears. In this way a tool is essentially the end of a hand [fingers], and the body's technicity exhibits itself in tools as extensions of the hand. It is here we find the typical essence of humanity; human beings are entities that make use of tools, the body's instrumentality acquires extensive differentiation and expansion through tools that can be picked up and handled with the hands and at the same time can also be put down, and our technicity also acquires differentiation and extension accordingly. This kind of differentiation and extension of technics and tools is not only based on tools as an extension of the ends of hands for work that *does not fit the hands*, but even more importantly is nothing other than the result of the *hand-dividing* [手分けdividing a job into separate tasks or among multiple parties, specialization] that occurs in relation to work that *does not fit the hands of a single individual*. In other words, hand-dividing is the division of labor, and as extensive differentiation and expansion of technicity and tools occur from that point on, in terms of the subject they must also inevitably establish the *social nature* of human existence. Now the act of formation is essentially nothing other than the workings of historical reality. If so, we must then say that the body that is technological insofar as it uses tools must be something that possesses its essential meaning through historical corporality–or, to put it more thoroughly, historical social corporality.

[Text omitted]

If a tool is established when the body negates itself in the direction opposite the subject, namely the direction of mere naturalness, then this tool itself would have neither a motive nor operative nature. And the tool, in this sense as a corporeal nullity which has lost its corporality, that instead actively recovers corporality as *the negation of a negation* by negating itself in direction even more opposite to the subject, is an automated machine. Upon its establishment, that which stands, as it were, on the side opposite the body even while opposing the body, taking tools as intermediaries, is the machine. If the body is a "+" body, then it follows that a machine must be a "−" body. And in terms of absolute value, it [a machine] is a superior quantitative being incomparable to bodies. Here is the necessary reason that objective bodies overwhelmingly press upon subjective bodies.

Yet here lies the crisis of contemporary times. What will happen if the subjective body, as something under the direct control of the subject, together with the subject from which it is inseparable, entrusts itself to the overwhelming dominance of objective bodies and negates itself on their side? Ought the subject to further regain its footing by taking the objective body as its negative mediation in spite of this crisis? Here we encounter, surrounding this crisis, the issue of worldview, the confrontation of ideologies, contemporary doubt, anguish over contemporary practice, and the root source of issues of contemporary policy and politics. Instead of arriving at some sort of resolution of the issue, our analysis, by analyzing spirit and body, has rather come to face the issue of this contemporary crisis. Issues of even weightier import will now have to be presented anew from the locus to which our analysis has brought us.

Kimura Motomori (1895–1946). Born in Ishikawa Prefecture. Graduated from Kyoto Imperial University's Faculty of Letters. After a stint at Hiroshima University of Arts and Sciences, became an assistant professor at Kyoto University in 1933 and a full professor in 1940. Oversaw the pedagogy program. Major works include *Fihite* [『フィヒテ』*Fichte*] (Kōbundō, 1937), *Hyōgen ai* [『表現愛』 *Expressive Love*] (Iwanami Shoten, 1939), and *Keiseiteki jikaku* [『形成的自覚』 *Formative Self-awareness*] (Kōbundō, 1941). "Body and spirit" was published in *Ningengaku kōza* [『人間学講座』 *Anthropology Lectures*] Vol. 5 (Risōsha) in 1939, and was later included in *Expressive Love* (Iwanami Shoten, 1939). It is presently included in *Expressive Love* [『表現愛』] (Kobushi Shobō, 1997) and *Bi no purakushisu* [『美のプラクシス』 *The Praxis of Beauty*] (Tōeisha, 2000).

Chapter 10
Reading According to the Context: Kimura Motomori and "Body and Spirit"

[コンテクストから読み解く——木村素衛と「身体と精神」]

Ōnishi Masamichi

10.1 Kimura Motomori as a Scholar of Education

Kimura Motomori was born in Ishikawa Prefecture in March of 1895. His progress through school was delayed due to illness, but at the age of twenty-five he entered the elective program in the Department of Philosophy [哲学科選科] of the Faculty of Letters at Kyoto Imperial University. (Also attending were Mutai Risaku and Miki Kiyoshi as his seniors, Kōsaka Masaaki in the same class, and Nishitani Keiji one year below him.) He completed his courses in March of 1923. After stints at Otani University and Hiroshima University of Humanities and Science he became assistant professor at Kyoto Imperial University Faculty of Letters in May of 1933. In 1939 he was put in charge of the pedagogy and teaching methods course. In 1940 he received his Doctor of Letters degree and became full professor in the same field. In February of 1946 while on a lecture tour he died suddenly in Ueda, Shinshū. He was fifty years and eleven months old. His major works include *Fihite* [『フィヒテ』 *Fichte*] (1937), *Kokumin to kyōyō* [『国民と教養』 *Nation and Cultivation*] (1939), *Hyōgen-ai* [『表現愛』 *Expressive Love*] (1939), *Doitsu kannenron no kenkyū* [『独逸観念論の研究』 *A Study of German Idealism*] (1940), *Bi no katachi* [『美のかたち』 *The Shape of Beauty*] (1941), *Keiseiteki jikaku* [『形成的自覚』 *Formative Self-awareness*] (1941), and *Kokka ni okeru bunka to kyōiku* [『国家に於ける文化と教育』 *Culture and Education in the State*] (1946). In addition to his scholarship, we must also not forget his deep connection to teachers in the class-

---

Translated from the Japanese by Robert Chapeskie and revised by John W. M. Krummel.

M. Ōnishi (✉)
Faculty of Education, Bukkyō University, Kyoto, Japan
e-mail: m-onishi@bukkyo-u.ac.jp

© Springer Nature Singapore Pte Ltd. 2018
M. Fujita (ed.), *The Philosophy of the Kyoto School*,
https://doi.org/10.1007/978-981-10-8983-1_10

room; over a twenty-year period he gave lectures, talks, and instruction, while touring roughly a hundred locations in Shinshū.[1]

Although Kimura Motomori has occasionally been addressed from the angle of aesthetics, in this essay we shall examine him as a scholar (philosopher) of education. But this does not signify a biased approach shedding light on only one side of his work, because Kimura philosophized from the principial depths of *praxis = poiesis* underlying both the undertaking of the practice called "education" and the act of creating a work of art, and the terminus at which his approach arrived must be sought among his thoughts on education.

10.2 Text and Context

Kimura Motomori's text included in this book is "Body and Spirit". This essay was completed in November of 1938 and included in *Ningen no shomondai (ningen-gaku kōza V)* [『人間の諸問題（人間学講座V）』 *Various Issues of Humanity (Anthropology Lectures V)*] published by the Rishōsha Publication Department. It was later revised in several places and graced the opening pages of his *Hyōgen-ai* [『表現愛』 *Expressive Love*] published by Iwanami shoten in September of 1939. It is worth noting here that this text was positioned as "part one" of *Expressive Love*, in which its larger framework was established, and an essay written subsequently, "Hyōgen-ai no kōzō" [「表現愛の構造」 "The Structure of Expressive Love"] was made its "part two".

When it comes to Kimura Motomori's body of work as a whole, what position does this essay occupy and what is its significance? In order to ascertain the answer to these questions, we must have in hand a rough sketch or "bird's eye view" of the development and evolution of his thought. We must also take into consideration the various factors that surrounded him. Each individual essay (text) is written under particular circumstances and at a specific stage in an individual's life. In other words, a text, irrespective of one's self-awareness or intent, is interwoven upon a definite context and woven into that context. Each individual text is colored by a

---

[1] See Maeda Hiroshi, "Kimura Motomori kyōjyu no shōgai to gyōseki" [「木村素衛教授の生涯と業績」 "The Life and Accomplishments of Kimura Motomori"] (*Kyoto daigaku kyōikugakubu kiyō* [『京都大学教育学部紀要』 *Kyoto University Department of Education Bulletin*] 4, 1958; Chō Satsuki, *Chichi Kimura Motomori kara no okurimono* [『父・木村素衛からの贈りもの』 *Gifts from my father Kimura Motomori*], Miraisha, 1985. Kimura Motomori sensei Gojukkaiki kinen kankōkai-hen *Kimura Motomori sensei to shinshū* [木村素衛先生五十回忌記念刊行会編 『木村素衛先生と信州』 Professor Kimura Motomori Fiftieth Anniversary Commemorative Publication Committee, ed., *Professor Kimura Motomori and Shinshū*], Shinano kyōikukai shuppanbu, 1996; and Kobayashi Kyō, ed., *Hyōgen-ai* [『表現愛』 *Expressive Love*], Kobushi shobō (Kobushi bunko 21), 1997. Murase Yūya, ed., *Bi no keisei* [『美の形成』 *The Formation of Beauty*], Kobushi shobō (Kobushi bunko 26), 2000; Iwaki Ken-ichi, ed., *Kimura Motomori "Bi no purakushisu"* [『木村素衛「美のプラクシス」』 *Kimura Motomori: "The Praxis of Beauty"*], Tōeisha (Kyoto tetsugaku sen sho 7), 2000 (see also the commentaries given by each editor).

variety of internal and external contexts, and a cluster of texts together interweave to create a single texture and stitch together their own internal context. At the same time, reversing their direction, these texts merge together and return to the synchronic and diachronic contexts surrounding them to shape a new context. Each text, therefore, together with its context, must be read with a compound eye that sees its multiple layers from both the angles of the context or circumstances in which it is placed (its external context) and of the development of its author's fundamental thought (its internal context). This chapter is an attempt to spin a new context *out of* Kimura, patterning it after one such "texture" of Kimura's thoughts on education and deciphering it from the various contexts that interweave to create it. In order to explicitly draw out the various contexts related to Kimura Motomori, then, let us once again pick up the trail of his research and writings.

Kimura Motomori studied under Nishida Kitarō and started out as a scholar of German idealism. We can say that his footing as a scholar was established, more than anything else, through his translation and investigation of Fichte. His doctoral dissertation, entitled "Jissenteki sonzai no kisokōzō—kyōikutetsugaku no kōsatsu ni mukeraretaru fihitetsugaku no hitotsu no kenkyū" [「実践的存在の基礎構造―教育哲学の考察に向けられたるフィヒテ哲学の一つの研究」 "The Basic Structure of Practical Existence: An Investigation of Fichte's Philosophy Directed toward a Consideration of the Philosophy of Education"], was completed in 1937, and the greater part of it was published in the same year as *Fihite* [『フィヒテ』 *Fichte*], part of the Kōbundō shobō's Western philosophy series. This was Kimura's first book. It dealt with Fichte's early period, but by this time Kimura had already detected, through Fichte, the limitations of German idealism as a whole (particularly in regard to its understanding of "nature").[2] In other words, the task of "the critical surpassing of German idealism" had begun to occupy his mind.

On the other hand, we must not overlook the fact that the phrase "philosophy of education" appears in the subtitle of his doctoral thesis. Kimura's involvement in pedagogy began suddenly. When Konishi Shigenao, who had been professor in charge of the pedagogy and teaching methods course at Kyoto Imperial University Faculty of Letters, was appointed president [of the university] in February of 1933, Nishida Kitarō nominated Kimura Motomori as his intended successor. Kimura himself, however, had no desire to abandon philosophy and aesthetics, and

---

[2]In *Fihite* [『フィヒテ』*Fichte*] (the preface) and his last major systematic work *Kokka ni okeru bunka to kyōiku* [『国家に於ける文化と教育』 *Culture and Education in the State*] (the end of Chapter 2), Kimura enumerates three problems with German idealism and the idealist view of human culture. The latter in particular played a pivotal role in the development of his own discourse. For an analysis of his understanding of the world and the framework of his thought that takes these problems he points out and his approach to overcoming them as hints to understanding his thought, see my essay "Kimura Motomori ni okeru hyōgenteki sekai no kōzō" [「木村素衛における表現的世界の構造」 "The Structure of the Expressive World in Kimura Motomori"] (Otani daigaku tetsugakukai *Tetsugaku ronshū* [Otani University Philosophy Society *Collection of Philosophy Essays* vol. 43], 1997).

"anguished for a hundred days" over his transition to pedagogy.[3] Here we can extract two themes (internal contexts) found in the narrative of Kimura's career as a thinker. One is his "intellectual self-establishment through a confrontation with German idealism", and the other is his "conversion to pedagogy and independence as a scholar of education". These two themes would go on to guide the formation of Kimura Motomori's thought on education.

10.3 *Ichida no Nomi* [「一打の鑿」 "The Hit of a Chisel"] and "Body and Spirit"

According to the preface to its first edition, *Expressive Love*, the book containing "Body and Spirit", "is not a work that was written by systematically laying out the issues from the start, but rather one written by constantly returning to the identical original theme and each time starting from there anew". "Herein a consistent motif is in operation" and "the parts written later, while 'sublatively' including the earlier parts, gradually broaden and deepen them, and, at the same time, proceed by grasping the structural connectivity of the whole with greater intimacy." In other words, while each of the included essays is an independent work, at the same time they are linked together as a whole. Each possesses a unique, irreplaceable individuality, but at the same time they are further deepened while resonating with each other. In *Expressive Love*, to use a musical analogy, the relationship between context and text is like that between *basso continuo* and motif. As a whole it forms a canon-like structure. Yet it is not simply a repetition of "more or less the same tune" [同工異曲] for it [the essays] "proceed by grasping the structural connectivity of the whole with greater intimacy". And the essay that was written last and corresponds to the *coda* was "Expressive Love".

It is thus clear that the essays included in *Expressive Love* must be read as a cycle, or connected series of works on a theme or motif. "Body and Spirit", in particular, in addition to being a stand-alone essay, for Kimura also comprises "part one", or the first half, of his writings on "expressive love". In other words, it ought to be read as part of a single unit or set, along with "Expressive Love Part Two" ("The Structure of Expressive Love") that comprises its second half.

That said, among all of these essays, "The Hit of a Chisel" and "Body and Spirit" warrant particular attention. We can see that "The Hit of a Chisel" was for Kimura a manifesto, a declaration of his independence as a thinker. The idea for

---

[3]Kimura overcame his "anguish" by positioning pedagogy as one of the "principle subjects" for his "inquiry into the philosophy of practice". See my "Kimura Motomori—jissen ni okeru sukui no kyōiku ningengaku" [『木村素衞—実践における救いの教育人間学』 *Kimura Motomori: A Pedagogical Anthropology of Salvation in Practice*] (Sumeragi Norio and Yano Satoji eds., *Nihon no kyōiku ningengaku* [『日本の教育人間学』 *The Pedagogical Anthropology of Japan*], Tamagawa daigaku shuppanbu, 1999).

"The hit of a chisel" "was suddenly revealed" [4] to Kimura in the spring of the year he turned thirty. It can perhaps even be described as a "divine revelation". Kimura incubated this idea for several years, and wrote the following in his diary in the spring he turned thirty-six (1931)[5]:

> I got the idea of someday writing an essay called "A Hit of the Chisel". There I would express my own life. Until now I have privately been giving an account of myself, hidden behind figures such as Kant, Fichte and Hegel. With "A Hit of the Chisel" I will cast aside all masks. I will expose my raw self. By unsealing animate life with the flash of a mallet, the hit of a chisel, a sculptor will reveal the mystery of life. …/As a thinker, I hope to fully express myself through "A Hit of the Chisel" to the point of not regretting even death/Oh, this hit of a chisel!/Everything attains Buddhahood [悉皆成仏]/…

Kimura finished the manuscript of an essay on the theme of "the hit of a chisel = the dialectic of the productive act" in November of the same year, presented it once, and eventually completed it after polishing it for another year and a half. "Body and Spirit" and "The Structure of Expressive Love", along with "The Conversion of Michelangelo", were then written within the context of taking "The Hit of a Chisel" as their starting point.

When Nishida Kitarō read "The Hit of a Chisel," he immediately sent a letter saying, "Kimura, this is a great essay…", and after obtaining a copy of *Expressive Love* he wrote to him again, saying, "I think your idea of seeing the concrete existence of human beings in expressive formation most fully comprehends what I mean by expression."[6]

"Expressive love" is the core of Kimura Motomori's thought and its fundamental principle. While "grasping with greater intimacy" the issues and themes of the whole structural connectivity, starting with "The Hit of a Chisel" Kimura accomplished his own unique principial formulation of it as "expressive love". If "The Hit of a Chisel" was a turning point for him, "Expressive Love" (taking "Body and Spirit" as part one) was a monumental work that established and confirmed "my [Kimura's] own path".[7] In the preface to *Keiseiteki jikaku* [『形成的自覚』 *Formative Self-awareness*], written two years later, Kimura states, "The central focus of my intellectual interest for the past few years has been to proceed toward various specific issues from *the standpoint of expressive love*, and through its concrete development, …" [emphasis added]. In other words, Kimura had established his own "standpoint" in *Expressive Love*, and the next act of his drama had already begun.

---

[4]*Bi no katachi* [『美のかたち』 *The Shape of Beauty*], Iwanami shoten, 1941, preface p. 3.

[5]*Akai mi to aoi mi* [『紅い実と青い実』 *Red Fruit and Blue Fruit*], Kōbundō (Atenebunko 48), 1949, pp. 21–22.

[6]*Nishida Kitarō zenshū* [『西田幾多郎全集』 *Complete Works of Nishida Kitarō*], Vol. 19, Iwanami shoten, 1966, p. 70, 88.

[7]According to the preface to the first edition of *Expressive Love*, "For me the investigation has in no sense reached its destination. When I look back at the road I have travelled, however, I feel as though at some point I had been *walking my own path* unawares, and that at any rate to continue walking down this road is to take my *own path*" [emphasis added].

Nevertheless, the fundamental terms and concepts out of which Kimura's discourse is woven cannot be described as purely original. "Historical life" [歴史的生命] and "historical nature" [歴史的自然] were Nishida's terms, and, in fact, the framing of issues in terms of "expression" was shared by those surrounding Nishida at the time.[8] In this we can discern the story of Kimura's intellectual development as one of establishing his own intellectual standpoint on the basis of Nishidian philosophy and in doing so moving beyond German idealism.

10.4 The Internal Context of the "Structure of Logic"

While it may sound paradoxical, the essay "Body and Spirit" does not directly discuss the body and the spirit. Kimura explains the "perspective of the investigation" as follows. "The *body* possesses its distinct significance where it constitutes a moment of expressive *mediation* between inside and outside whereby the *internal* spiritual that comprises one moment of expressive life formatively expresses itself on the *outside* that is another moment" [emphasis in the original]. "The central issue" is to clarify the "connection of these three moments in expressive life". The body is "one principle of expression", and, along with the spirit, constitutes "one moment of expressive life".

Kimura Motomori's "Body and Spirit" is not a mere theory of the body and the mind. It goes without saying that it does not comprise a mind-body dualism, but neither is it, conversely, a theory that advocates the oneness of mind and body [身心一如]. Its framework is fundamentally distinct. The body is a moment that mediates expression between inside and outside, spirit and nature, and the "three moments" of spirit, nature and body are connected *in* "expressive life". We must begin by coming to grips with this unfamiliar compositional scheme itself in the manner in which it is presented to us. In doing so, the key point is to grasp *what*, or rather *what sort of situation*, Kimura is trying to hit upon with the phrase "expressive life".

But in addition to "expressive life", other terms such as "expressive entity", "historical life", "historical reality" and "historical nature" also make their appearance, and Kimura carries on with his discourse without defining any of them. This can be a stumbling block for readers first encountering his work. Kimura's method of argument, moreover, does not take the form of a deductive accumulation of reasons step-by-step. This makes it all the more apparent that we must take the following approach. That is, we must grasp the logical structure that gives rise to Kimura's discourse as a *gestalt*; we must understand it as a compositional schema.

---

[8]When Kimura speaks of "formation" [形成], Nishida's "historical acts of formation" deeply permeate his thought, and the same can be said of the concepts of "expression" [表現] and "self-awareness" [自覚] in Nishidian philosophy when Kimura speaks of "expressive self-awareness" [表現的自覚] and that of "thou" [汝] when he speaks of "the outside as *thou*" [汝的外].

When we take this approach, what enters our field of vision as an important clue is the logic of "the reciprocal and mutually identical relation of negative mediation between individual mediation and universal mediation",[9] or, to put it another way, "the dialectic of mediation between individual and universal", that Kimura propounds. We can view this as a reassessment and logical treatment of the world of expressive love and its principial structure from an ontological angle. It is a formulation unique to Kimura that, while standing upon the foundation of Nishidian philosophy, takes one step beyond it. Kimura found here the basic scheme of his own original thought, and to him this was at the same time the logical structure that gives rise to the world of actuality and is living and operating within it. And herein others (society) and history are also included.

The "*standpoint* of expressive love" thus obtains the backing of *logic*. When we reread "Expressive Love" in light of this compositional schema, we understand that "expressive life", "historical nature", and "historical reality" are all of a single series as things standing on the side of the "universal" in "universal mediation", or rather signify the whole of the connection of moments or the movement of mediation, and in the final analysis are all different terms referring to the same state of affairs. This being the case we can also grasp the above-mentioned "connection of moments in expressive life" between spirit, nature, and body, in terms of a multi-sided structure.

10.5 The Positioning of Education

The "intellectual independence" of Kimura Motomori discussed so far, however, does not necessarily mean "independence as a scholar of education". So what about this second theme, his "independence as a scholar of education"?

Whenever Kimura deals with "education" he always views it in connection to "culture". In other words, he deals with it within the context of "culture and education". This is immediately obvious if we look at the titles of his works. These include, for example, "Bunka no honshitsu to kyōiku no honshitsu" [「文化の本質と教育の本質」 "The Essence of Culture and the Essence of Education"],[10] "Bunka no tetsugaku to kyōiku no tetsugaku (jyō/ge)" [文化の哲学と教育の哲学 (上・下) "The Philosophy of Culture and the Philosophy of Education (Parts One

---

[9]See the second half of "The Conversion of Michelangelo" (in *Expressive Love*); *Kyōiku to ningen* [『教育と人間』 *Education and Human Being*], Kōbundō, 1948, pp. 25 ~ 9; *Kokka ni okeru bunka to kyōiku* [『国家に於ける文化と教育』 *Culture and Education in the State*], Iwanami shoten, 1946, pp. 61~65. I have previously attempted to decipher Kimura's views as assertions shot through with this logical structure. "Kimura Motomori ni okeru 'Keisei/hyogen' ni tsuite [「木村素衛における「形成・表現」について」 On 'formation/expression' in Kimura Motomori]" (*Kyoto daigaku kyoikugakubu kiyo* [『京都大学教育学部紀要』 *Kyoto University Department of Education Bulletin*]32, 1986).

[10]Completed in November of 1939. Included in *Keiseiteki jikaku* [『形成的自覚』 *Formative Self-awareness*], Kōbundō, 1941.

and Two)"],[11] and his last work, *Kokka ni okeru bunka to kyōiku* [『国家に於ける文化と教育』 *Culture and Education in the State*], the final chapter of which, moreover, is entitled "Kokuminbunka to kokuminkyōiku" [「国民文化と国民教育」 "National Culture and National Education" [or: "The Culture of the People and the Education of the People"].

Furthermore, if we delve into its discursive content, we see that this context is actually already present in "Body and Spirit". Here, upon ascertaining that the essence of culture is "the cultivation of historical nature", Kimura situates education in relation to it. (The deepening of his grasp of "nature", as part of his "surpassing of German idealism", had settled on a Nishidian conception of "historical nature".[12]) At this stage, however, he went no further than to take education as "a single domain[13]" of culture, its "special case taking human beings in particular as objects[14]". In other words, he dealt with education here as being in the same phase as culture, and as simply one of its constituent parts. It was not until a bit later that he would grasp the relationship between education and culture in terms of its multi-sided structure.

Moving beyond his flat understanding of education as simply "one domain" within culture, Kimura arrives at a multi-sided grasp of it as "something that cultivates culture from its subjective root[15]" and "rears reality from the roots of its subjects".[16] There had been a "turn" within the context of "culture and education". What had brought about this "turn"? "Reality" in the phrase cited above is nothing other than the previously discussed "historical reality", or, in other words, "historical nature". Kimura did not stop at simply borrowing this concept from Nishida.

---

[11] Completed in April and in August of 1941. Published as part of the *Iwanami kōza—rinrigaku* [『岩波講座 倫理学』 *Iwanami Courses: Ethics*] series.

[12] Kimura gave a lecture entitled "The Concept of 'Historical Nature' in the recent Nishidian Philosophy" on Nishida's "Ronri to seimei" [「論理と生命」 *Logic and Life*] (*Shisō* [『思想』 *Thought*], July, August, and September 1936) in Shinshū (in June of 1937). A printed booklet from this event remains. This is another indication of how Kimura's inquiry shared its path with Nishidian philosophy of the later period.

On the concept of "historical nature" in Kimura, and how it ultimately came to mean the "expressive universe", see my previously cited "Kimura Motomori ni okeru hyōgenteki sekai no kōzō" [「木村素衞における表現的世界の構造」 "The Structure of the Expressive World in Kimura Motomori"].

[13] *Hyōgen-ai* [『表現愛』 *Expressive Love*], Iwanami shoten, 1939, p. 23. Nansōsha, 1968, p. 43. Kobushi shobō, 1997, p. 31. The sentence that includes this phrase was, moreover, added to "Body and Spirit" when it was published later as part of *Expressive Love*. At the time he wrote this essay Kimura's interest in education seems to have still been only peripheral or incidental.

[14] *Hyōgen-ai* [『表現愛』 *Expressive Love*], Iwanami shoten, 1939, p. 86. Nansōsha, 1968, p. 106. Kobushishobō, 1997, p. 83.

[15] *Kokka ni okeru bunka to kyōiku* [『国家に於ける文化と教育』 *Culture and Education in the State*], p. 194.

[16] *Kyōikugaku no konponmondai* [『教育学の根本問題』 *Fundamental Problems of Pedagogy*], Reimei shobō, 1947, p. 22. This was a written record of the 1942 pedagogy and teaching methods course [教育学教授法講座] "standard lectures" ('Introduction to Pedagogy') taken by Oda Takeshi.

He deepened his understanding of it on his own to take hold of it as a multi-sided structure. This lies at the bottom of the "turn" mentioned above. "Nature taking form while including the accomplishments [of human beings][17]"—that is "historical nature". For "the human subject to go on fostering its work in self-awareness by existing within it[18]"—that is "culture". And to raise human subjects that accomplish this—that is "education". Education thus is the fostering of "culture", "reality", and historical nature itself from the root that is the "human subject". The work of education is positioned in this way as an indispensable structural moment that gives rise to historical nature = the expressive universe.

Incidentally, around the same time he was steering Kimura towards the study of education, Nishida Kitarō was himself writing a paper called "Kyōikugaku ni tsuite" [「教育学について」 "On Pedagogy"] (originally entitled "Tetsugaku to kyōiku" [「哲学と教育」 "Philosophy and Education"]) in which he quotes the phrase "support the transformation and nurturing of Heaven and Earth [santenchinokaiku 賛天地之化育]" from Chūyō [Zhōngyōng 『中庸』 The Doctrine of the Mean]. Years later Kimura would take this a step further, defining education as "the task of supporting the transformation and nurturing of Heaven and Earth by cultivating those who can support the transformation and nurturing of Heaven and Earth (human beings)".[19] Here we can see another "turn" or "development". And this way of connecting education to the transformation and nurturing of Heaven and Earth [i.e., all that is], or, in other words, this state of affairs that is not direct but mediate, is found in exactly the same structure as the mediating nature of the work of education within historical nature. They are parallel. Or rather, for Kimura, "the transformation and nurturing of Heaven and Earth" is indeed the functioning of historical nature itself.

In this way the relationship between nature, culture and education was grasped in terms of structure, and education was properly positioned. The understanding of "nature", the understanding of the relational structure of "culture and education", and the relationship between "the transformation and nurturing of Heaven and Earth" and the work of human beings: these three smaller contexts interweave to form Kimura Motomori's thought on education, each of them displaying their own internal "turns" and calling back and forth to each other. And in the depths of this thought flows the unbroken context of his connection to Nishida Kitarō.

---

[17] *Keiseiteki jikaku* [『形成的自覚』 *Formative Self-awareness*], p. 39. Text in parentheses was added.

[18] *Hyōgen-ai* [『表現愛』 *Expressive Love*], Iwanami shoten, p. 55. Nansōsha, p. 75. Kobushi shobō, p. 58.

[19] *Keiseiteki jikaku* [『形成的自覚』 *Formative Self-awareness*], p. 51. Text in parentheses has been added. For a detailed discussion of the "development" mentioned here, see my previously mentioned essay "Kimura Motomori – jissen ni okeru sukui no kyōiku ningengaku" [「木村素衞 ― 実践における救いの教育人間学」 *Kimura Motomori: A Pedagogical Anthropology of Salvation in Practice*], note 20.

10.6 Toward a Theory of National Education
[国民教育論]

When it comes to the internal contexts present within Kimura Motomori, there are indeed still others I have not yet discussed. We must not overlook his orientation toward a theory of national education. This orientation can be thought of as having two causes. On the one hand there was the fact that Kimura's study of Fichte extended to the latter's late period. What Kimura saw there was that, in contrast to having taken the standpoint of human culture during his Jena period, during his Berlin period Fichte converted to the standpoint of national culture and national education. On the other hand, there were also the circumstances of the era (external context) following the Manchurian incident of 1931. These circumstances pushed him towards the question of how to consider the "culture and education" of the Japanese people. While superimposing himself on Fichte of the later period, there is no doubt that Kimura took the problem of "the principial grounding of the education of the nation" as one of his tasks as a scholar of education.[20]

We can well understand these factors as a backdrop or set of circumstances. But the problem then seems to have been what sort of principle or logic should form the basis upon which to carry out this task. What was the stance Kimura adopted as he tried "to critique Fichte while surpassing him"?[21]

Kimura did not directly take part in the "dispute over the meaning" of the war. But when it came to his fundamental standpoint or point of view for dealing with the current state of affairs he did have something in common with thinkers in the so-called Kyoto school. What he shared with them was a philosophy of "world history". To Kimura, this meant a "world historical standpoint as a higher-level *synthesis* of the human *universal* and the national *species* [or: *specific*]" [emphasis added].[22] Kimura saw the relationship of "humanity—nationality (ethnicity)—individual person" as one of "universal—species—individual". The standpoint of "world history" then had to be a logic that would "synthesize" in a high-level manner the "universal" and the "species" among these elements.

Kimura also understood the relationship of "humanity—nationality—individual person" by reframing it as a relationship of "genus—species—individual". Kimura's distinctive logic, to begin with, was, as we have seen, the "dialectic of mediation between individual and universal". But here there is no place for the "species". In order to position "national specificity," another logic is needed. Was it not then Tanabe Hajime's logic of "species" that he invoked there? Did not the standpoint of "world history" that was supposed to become the basic principle of national education for Kimura, in the final analysis, go no further than being a

---

[20]See the preface to *Kokumin to Kyōyō* [『国民と教養』 *Nation and Cultivation*], Kōbundō (kyōyō bunko 21), 1939).

[21]*Kokumin to Kyōyō* [『国民と教養』 *Nation and Cultivation*], preface, p. 3.

[22]*Kokka ni okeru bunka to kyōiku* [『国家に於ける文化と教育』 *Culture and Education in the State*], preface p. 2 (p. 6 in the third printing).

compromise between "Nishida–Kimura" and "Tanabe"? A compromise, however, is not a synthesis. Ultimately a logic that grounds a "specificity" that is a nationality, and further a "broader specificity" that is the Great East Asia Co-prosperity Sphere, through synthesis with "the universal of the human race," was not found. Did not this incompleteness in the investigation of fundamental principles in the end become a weakness in Kimura's theory of national education, resulting in its failure? Considering the fact that his thoughts on education converged and resulted in his theory of national education, this becomes a significant issue in the overall evaluation of Kimura Motomori. Taking stock of this is a task that remains for us to carry out.[23]

10.7 Contexts Emerging from Kimura Motomori

Thus far we have looked at the various contexts woven together into the single texture that was Kimura Motomori's thought on education. So what sorts of contexts can we then unwind from Kimura's work? There are several strands we may consider.

The viewpoint of "I and thou" can naturally be developed in the domain of issues concerning pedagogical relations. Kimura himself, starting from "expressive love", then examined "educational love" as a "specification" or "one determination" of this concept. The root of education must be not only the act of progressively assisting students' development, but also a love that absolutely affirms their existence. A renewed taking up of Kimura's theory of educational love is especially necessary today, when the establishment of authority and respect has become difficult. Kimura also developed a theory of "teaching materials" within the context of the "expressive environment" or, in other words, the context of the "outside as *thou*" [汝的外]. On the other hand, in the essay "Body and Spirit" he refers to tools and machines and therein discerns discorporality and transcorporality (this section of the text was not included in this book). Today, as the mass media environment envelops children and has even begun to be incorporated into school education, these perspectives come alive when we think about these issues. The issue of the media can be approached from both the angle of "educational materials" and that of "educational tools", that is, from both its aspect "as an 'outside as *thou*'" and its aspect "as a tool or machine". This is the case, in short, because this category of devices, as *mech*anized teaching *tools*, have themselves already become an "environment that calls out" to children.

---

[23]See my "Kimura Motomori ni okeru kokumin kyōikuron no kōzō" [「木村素衛における国民教育論の構造」 "The Structure of the Theory of National Education in Kimura Motomori"] (Wada Shūji ed., *Kyōikuteki nichijyō no saikōchiku* [『教育的日常の再構築』 *The Reconstruction of an Educational Daily Life*]. Tamagawa daigaku shuppanbu, 1996). Here I have been looking at Tanabe Hajime's influence on Kimura, but one is also reminded of the fact that one of the factors that spurred Kimura's research on Fichte was his participation in Tanabe's reading seminars.

In any case, however, here we are not considering which part of Kimura's thought on education we should investigate, but rather the fact that we ought to be receptive to his thought as a whole, taking up the full magnitude of its compositional scheme that deals with education.

In today's industrial society, the "school" is heading toward a collapse. Stopgap measures are of no use. Fundamentally new principles must be found in order to rebuild school education as a system.

Modern schools mainly take intentional education as their content. At the core of school education lies the "subject curriculum". This curriculum is an apparatus for the "transmission of culture", and school education is conducted with a focus on the "teaching—learning" of the curricular content. Here the "content" is determined preceding the child's "life" and then handed down to the learner. The rest is a question of the "method" of education. Attention shifts toward technical discourse on how children can be made to master the content most efficiently. The acquisition of knowledge and technical skills is seen as the main "purpose", and "academic attainment" is measured according to the degree to which this is achieved. The formation of "character" is considered separately. In other words, the modern school is erected on a dualism of academic attainment and character, and thus adopts as its methodology a dichotomy between cultivation [陶冶] and moral education [訓育]. It also maintains within its depths a dualism of development and education along with that of nature and culture (artifice).

In contrast Kimura Motomori adopts a monistic view of the historical *nature* that envelops *culture*, "the dialectic of mediation". Not the *mastery* of extant culture, but rather the activity of human subjects who *do culture* by taking it as *mediation* and an education that fosters this from its roots are clearly positioned within this [perspective]. With this as a starting point, our view of education, its fundamental composition, how to set up and assemble a pedagogy—all of this would change. If we take as the origin of education not a Platonic but rather a "Kimurian" theory of the *ideas*, in which the *ideas* are born out of the midst of an expressive negotiation between *I* and *thou*, out of the depths of expressive life = historical nature, then education (its "purpose") comes into view as something with a fundamentally distinct character. If this view is taken, the idea of a "subject curriculum" itself, put together on the basis of purpose and content, can no longer be realized. Conversely, however, education itself is freed from that framework. The expressive negotiation between *I* and *thou*, the mediating connection between call and response, in other words, the "life" structure of human beings just as it is, becomes the structure of "education". The education of the self, the education of others, school education, and lifelong education can all be conceived directly from the ontological principle of human beings existing within the world structure of expressive love.

[Otto Friedrich] Bollnow once broadened the denotation of "education" and expanded the scope of pedagogy with *Existenzphilosophie und Pädagogik* [*Existential Philosophy and Pedagogy* 『実存哲学と教育学』] and *Die pädagogische Atmosphäre* [*The Educational Atmosphere* 『教育的雰囲気』, published in Japanese under the title *Kyōiku wo sasaerumono* [『教育を支えるもの』 *That which Supports Education*]. But what is required in pedagogy today is not an expansion of its domain. Instead what is needed is to create a new paradigm for education and pedagogy akin to how quantum mechanics subsumed and sublated Newtonian mechanics. In this context, once we take up Kimura Motomori's thought on education as something that appeals to and awakens our own creative imagination, we will find it has the capacity, beyond simply being one alternative form of pedagogy, to become one of the triggers of a broader paradigm shift.

Ōnishi Masamichi Professor in the Faculty of Education, Bukkyō University. Major works: *Shōgaikyōiku ningengaku no tame ni* [『生涯教育人間学のために』 *For an Anthropology of Lifelong Education*] (Bukkyo University, 2013), *Hyōgenteki seimei no kyōiku tetsugaku: Kimura Motomori no kyōiku shisō* [『表現的生命の教育哲学:木村素衞の教育思想』 *A Philosophy of Education of Expressive Life: Kimura Motomori's Thoughts on Education*] (Shōwadō, 2011).

Part VI
Hisamatsu Shinichi

Chapter 11
The Metaphysical Element of the East

[東洋的に形而上的なるもの]

Hisamatsu Shinichi

Although in recent times phrases like "Eastern culture" and "Eastern spirit" have been conspicuously promoted, the semantic content of these phrases appears to be diverse and lacking uniformity, varying according to the intentions and underlying motives of those employing them. There are cases in which, out of a situational consciousness related to recent events [wars] or an ethnic consciousness, these phrases are recited like slogans or headlines in order to control and uplift the hearts and minds of the general public via group psychology; cases in which they are used to describe a project assigned to the East in the sense that we in the East must create in the future some sort of a distinct culture, different from the West; cases in which they are employed in a historical context in an effort to obtain comprehensive knowledge of extant cultural facts belonging to the East; and cases in which they are employed in the philosophy of culture in an effort to go beyond simply knowing these elements, extract from them those that are particularly distinct from the West, and investigate their characteristics, foundations, and even their value. It thus follows that even though in all cases they invoke Eastern culture, the focus of interest and approach taken are distinct. For my part I would like to proceed in this essay by focusing on the question of what it is that the culture particularly characterized as "Eastern" in contrast to the culture of the West is based upon.

I think it is perhaps not impossible to say that something of a metaphysical nature (not in the sense of belonging to [the Western academic discipline of] metaphysics) that differs from [such things in] the West was discovered particularly in the East, and that a great cultural system, involving metaphysics, philosophy, religion, ethics, art, and so forth has flourished on its basis. I believe it can be said that if this peculiar metaphysical element had not been found in the East and transmitted throughout this region then the cultural system that can be characterized as distinctly Eastern would not have been established. I would therefore suggest

---

Translated from the Japanese by Robert Chapeskie and revised by John W. M. Krummel.

S. Hisamatsu

that coming to grips with this metaphysical element is indispensable if we are to internally understand the Eastern cultural system.

When we speak of "the metaphysical element of the East" it may seem to imply that this metaphysical element is somehow regional, but that is not the meaning of "Eastern" at all. Needless to say, there is no distinction between East and West in this element itself; it is exceedingly universal. But because this universal element was discovered in and transmitted throughout the East, the philosophy, metaphysics, ethics, and so on concerning it arose in the East, and we therefore refer to it as "Eastern". Just as natural science, even though it is valid not only in the West, is described as "Western" because it was developed in the West, what I refer to as the metaphysical element of the East, although it happened to have been discovered in the East, has the right to demand recognition as something genuinely metaphysical in the West as well. It must indeed be said that the metaphysical element of the East is not merely different from the metaphysical element of the West but something markedly deeper. Rather than discuss this point here, however, I would like first to elucidate the character of this metaphysical element.

When you think about it, what we normally refer to as the "actual world", both the external world and the internal world, is the world of "being" [有]. You and I, conceived as possessing a body and a spirit, can never exit the world of "being". The world of "being" is a world in which the many [多] reciprocally determine and contradict one another. The world of "being" is inconceivable without reciprocal determination and contradiction. That which is something that necessarily determines others and at the same time is determined by others. Just as there is no being that only determines others, there is no being that is only determined by others. Even when it comes to the spirit there is none that is not determined by others at all, and when it comes to matter there is none that does not in any way determine others. To the extent that it is constantly determined by others, we must therefore say that what is, even while it is said to be, is something that is not. In this sense we must say that what is, as a whole, is at the same time what is not. Furthermore, we can also say that without it being something that at the same time is not, it cannot be something that is. There cannot be something like a being that is simply and exclusively being. Something like a being that is only being is nothing more than a mere concept or abstraction. That which concretely is must be something that is constantly in conformity with nothing. Without nothing, being is inconceivable. It goes without saying, however, that since what concretely exists is not the mere concept of being, when I say that being is inconceivable without nothing, I do not mean this simply in the formal-logical sense that the concept of being is a relative concept vis-à-vis the concept of nothing and is inconceivable without the concept of nothing. Rather I am talking about that which concretely exists in actuality. In this way we must say that what concretely exists in actuality is that which exists in terms of being-qua [*soku*]-nothing, or that which is not while constantly being. In this sense, that which exists is that which is always faced with nothing. But since this nothing is the determined aspect of being, and indeed the future direction of being, it is not the absolute nothing. Nothing is the being of some other thing that exists. We can also say that the nothing of one thing that exists is the being of another thing that exists, and the being of one thing that exists is the nothing of another thing that exists. We ordinarily speak without difficulty about something existing or not existing, but we are unable to strictly distinguish between being and nothing. We can say nothing forces its way into the places where something that is exists without any gaps, and conversely it can be thought that nothing does not exist in places where there is no being. We can also say that something like a nothing where there is no being whatsoever is inconceivable. What we call being or nothing, however, are the affirmative and negative aspects of that which exists in actuality. Divorced from that which exists there is neither affirmation nor negation, or, in other words, neither being nor nothing. At the same time that nothing is the negative aspect of that which exists it is the direction of self-affirmation. At the same time that being is the affirmative aspect of that which exists it is also the direction of self-negation. Where that which actually exists is not simply nothing but also being we find its afferent nature and self-preservational character, and where it is not simply being but also nothing we find its efferent nature and developmental character. Being is the existence of that which is; nothing is its course, the future contained within its existence. Due to the fundamental character of that which exists in actuality, in dialectics we conceive of no being that is not mediated by nothing and no nothing that is not mediated by being.

Both the idea found in Greek philosophy that what exists in actuality is neither purely form nor matter but rather the unity of form and matter, and the idea in modern dialectical philosophy that what exists in actuality is neither purely affirmation nor negation but rather negation-qua-affirmation, must also be said to derive from this character of being-qua [*soku*]-nothing. We must therefore say that what exists in actuality is nothing while at the same time being, and being while at the same time nothing. It thus follows that in actuality being is the being of nothing [無的有] and nothing is the nothing of being [有的無]. We must say that being and nothing are always mutually identical and interpenetrating. Neither can be conceived apart from the other. We must say that being is always confronting nothing and nothing is always confronting being. This fundamental character of that which exists in actuality must be characteristic of all that exists in actuality. Human beings, too, to the extent that we exist in actuality, cannot escape possessing this character. Human cognition and action, society and history, everything [human] must ultimately be said to be delimited by this fundamental character. To the extent that we are beings possessing this character, whether thinking about things or doing things we can never depart from this standpoint. Not only actual thing-events but things described as metaphysical or as transcending actuality are nothing more than things that are conceived *from the standpoint of this fundamental character* of humanity and *on the basis of this fundamental character of that which exists in actuality,* either in the direction of being, in the direction of nothing, in the direction of the unity of being and nothing, or in the direction of the mutual mediation of being and nothing, either temporally or logically, and as either causes, results, ideals, ideas, or bases for argument. Even the conception of metaphysical elements in the ancient philosophy of the West as either nothing, being, pure form, or the first cause, or, in modern philosophy, as the first principle, the thing itself [*Ding an sich*;

物自体], the postulated God, absolute ideals, absolute ideas, or absolute identity, as either the limit, absolute mutual mediation, or absolute unity, do not, generally speaking, escape this [perspective]. Such metaphysical elements, whether transcending actuality by separating from it, or transcending actuality in their mutual identification with it, in either case, as objective things distinct from ourselves, stand in contrast to us human beings who necessarily cannot but be things existing in actuality, and can never become subjects of ourselves. It may be thought that what is metaphysical, since it constitutes the ground of actuality while transcending it, is something subjective rather than objective, and must be something subjective. Even so, this subjectivity, to the extent that we ourselves are not these metaphysical things, is nothing other than something facing us objectively as a subjective thing. That which is nothing but a mere conceptual subject, needless to say, differs from a substantial subject, but in either case, to the extent that it is something metaphysical it must be something transcending us and standing in contrast to us. Even in cases where something like an ideal we have created can be thought of as a subject that moves us in actuality, we ourselves are not this ideal. And even in cases where the first cause can be thought of as the subject that causes us in actuality, we ourselves are not this first cause. Even if we cannot define the God of Christianity as something that ordinary metaphysics would call metaphysical, as something that absolutely transcends humanity we may be allowed to regard it as metaphysical. And yet to believers in God, like the saying that it is no longer I who live but Christ who lives in me, as the subject of one's entire life God comes to have a far more intimate relationship to the believer than what metaphysics regards as metaphysical. And yet even for the believer, God stands in contrast to him/her and the believer is not God himself.

In this way, even in cases where the metaphysical is conceived in terms of a subject, as something transcending us, in its distinction from us we can discern the character of what is metaphysical in the West. This follows from the fact that no matter what we do we cannot exit the standpoint of that which exists in actuality. Here the metaphysical is that which transcends actuality on the basis of the standpoint of that which exists in actuality. Someone may still say that the metaphysical is something that transcends even the standpoint of that which exists in actuality itself. But this person him/herself, to the extent that he/she has not transcended the standpoint of that which exists in actuality, is making this claim, as before, from within that standpoint of that which exists in actuality. Since this is the case, to speak of transcending the standpoint of that which exists in actuality is equivalent to dreaming that what I have dreamed is a dream. But can there ever be a case in which we transcend the standpoint of that which exists in actuality?

We can probably say that there are hardly any such cases in the West. In the West there has been no experience of transcending that which exists in actuality, in other words, that which possesses the character described above. As a result, in the West everything is based on that which exists in actuality and its self-awareness. In the West, not only everything that exists in actuality and the science of these things, but even that which transcends what exists and its science as well, are developed within this standpoint of that which exists in actuality. This must be the fundamental meaning of the assertion that the West is a world of "being" and Western culture is a culture of "being". Western philosophy and metaphysics, too, never escapes this fundamental constraint that is the standpoint of that which exists in actuality. In the West it is not known that there is such a thing as escaping the standpoint of that which exists in actuality and ceasing to be a being. This fact that is unknown in the West is known in the East, and we find the fundamental character that distinguishes the East from the West where culture and scholarship are founded upon this fact. Of course, as I have already mentioned, I am not saying that all culture that exists in the East has this as its basis without exception. I am simply saying that in the East there is some culture, and moreover a broad cultural system of religion, philosophy, morality, and art, that is based on this [standpoint] and cannot exist without it, and that can be said to be Eastern since it possesses a character that differs distinctly from that of the West. In other words, in the East there is a standpoint that transcends that of the West, and because there is a distinctive culture based on this standpoint that is absent in the West, I call it "Eastern". Of course, in the East as well, in cases where we are unable to escape the fact that we exist in actuality, we do not exit the standpoint of being as in the West. But [Eastern] culture founded on the standpoint of being cannot be compared with the intricate complexity of that found in the West. When it comes to philosophy, too, even when we happen to find in the East something taking the same standpoint as that taken in the West, or even something that could be thought to surpass what is found in the West, it is simply an extension of something Western and nothing that ought to be distinguished from what is Western as constituting the basic character of the East. What should be described as Eastern philosophy possesses its originality in taking a standpoint different from that of the West. Even if there are cases in which what we are trying to call Eastern philosophy is seen from a Western standpoint and in its extension is found superior, this would be something incidental and not essential. There is a heterogeneous standpoint in the East that Western philosophy has failed to reach, and what is essential to Eastern philosophy is found where philosophy takes this standpoint. Because Eastern philosophy is something of this character, it cannot be understood from the standpoint of Western philosophy. On the contrary it is something that can be understood only through a conversion from the standpoint of Western philosophy. Eastern culture, not limited to philosophy, can only be internally and fundamentally understood by our ceasing to be that which exists in actuality. Because this conversion of standpoint involves becoming something that is not "being", we call it "nothing", and if we are to call it more specifically an "Eastern nothing", then this "Eastern nothing," as can be inferred from above, is neither nothing as a moment of that which exists in actuality nor the nothingness of all conceived from the standpoint of "being". Nor is it the nothingness of humanity in comparison to God. This "Eastern nothing" is something that cannot be fit into the category of what exists in actuality. Without being something metaphysical from the standpoint of all beings or "being", it is something metaphysical that negates and transcends being itself. In this case, however, that which is metaphysical is not conceived from the standpoint of that which exists as something that transcends what exists without our thoroughly departing from this standpoint of what exists. Rather, because we truly depart from this standpoint of what exists and transcend what exists, and because it is neither being based on nothing, nor nothing based on being, nor something metaphysical thus derived, but instead something that is beyond determination or contradiction, this metaphysical element is subjective and existent. As was mentioned above, ordinarily metaphysical things, even when they are described as subjective, are not subjective in this sense but rather objective. Therein lies the fundamental difference between what I refer to here as the metaphysical and things that are ordinarily referred to as metaphysical. Here it is not what exists in actuality but rather the metaphysical that is existent as a subject. It goes without saying, however, that the subject we are referring to is not a subject in contrast to an object, and the existence of which we speak is not a temporal existence. Here the subject is a subject beyond all interrelations, and the existent possesses an eternal existence. Even when I speak of the metaphysical, therefore, it implies no special opposition between the metaphysical and that which exists in actuality. This is why we can speak of "the true world having one form [法界一相]". Can we not thus call the metaphysical element that is distinct from the metaphysical elements of Western metaphysics and that of Christianity and unique to the East, "the metaphysical element of the East"? What is referred to as "true emptiness" [shinkū真空], "nirvana" [涅槃], and "the dropping away of body and mind" [身心脱落] is nothing other than this "metaphysical element of the East ". It goes without saying that just as what we have called "Eastern nothing" does not mean that there is simply nothing, "true emptiness" [shinkū真空]" does not mean simply being empty. Whether we speak of "true form" [実相], "suchness" [shinnyo真如;tathatā; "reality as it is"], or "ultimate truth" [第一義諦], what we are describing is neither the concrete form of that which exists in actuality itself nor the reality or first principle found in the metaphysics of the West, but on the contrary assumes the total negation of such things. Crisis theology asserts the absolute negation of humanity, and in relation to this negated humanity God is something thoroughly transcendent. On the other hand, *Buddha* [仏], *Dharmakāya* [法身] and the like ought to be described as subjective; they are not simply transcendent but rather the existence of transcendence. Since the Buddha is nothing other than we who have ceased to be something existing in actuality, or in other words "the Eastern metaphysical", to us who have ceased to exist in actuality the Buddha is existence. The Buddha as an object, which in terms of time is in the future and in terms of space is in another world or which exists in the present and in this world, is not the true Buddha. The Buddha is not absolutely other like the God of crisis theology. While it is absolutely other from [the perspective] of that which exists in actuality, being absolutely other is not the ultimate nature of the Buddha. While not the same as the actual self, insofar as the Buddha is a subject, we can say that it is instead the absolute self. This is why it is said that the Buddha is self-nature [自性], the true self, or "one's original face before the birth of one's parents", and that the true Buddha is the self-Buddha [自仏].

In this way, "the Eastern metaphysical" is neither the transcendental moment of that which exists in actuality nor something deduced from that which exists in actuality as what transcends the limit of everything existing in actuality. Instead, because it presupposes the negative conversion of that which exists in actuality itself, it is not something that we can attain through our knowledge, reason, actions, or emotions while still remaining as something that exists in actuality. This is why in the East there are special methods whereby we can cease to be something that exist in actuality. "*Parnirvāṇa*" [滅度], "*śamatha*" [止calming the mind], "the great death" [大死], "*dhyāna*" [静慮 meditation or concentration], "dedication to spiritual improvement" [工夫], "*samādhi*" [三昧 meditative absorption], and "*zazen*" [座禅sitting Zen meditation], are all examples of this kind of method. Whether "*parinirvāṇa*", "*śamatha*", or "the great death", none of them are mere logical negation or mere death, but methods by which we can cease to be that which exists in actuality. Whether "*dhyāna*", "dedication to spiritual improvement", or "*zazen*", they are neither ways of thinking logically nor ways of acting ethically but rather methods of transforming what exists in actuality itself, or that which is the subject of thinking and acting, into "nothing". They go beyond all thought and action that take as their subject a thing that exists in actuality. For thought and action are endlessly bound to the complications of "being". This is why in *The Awakening of Faith* [*in the Mahāyāna*] [『[大乗]起信論』 [*Mahāyāna*] *Śraddhotpāda Śāstra*] it is written that in the practice of *Samatha* "without relying on perceptions of the senses and consciousness, you must purge all ideas whenever they arise, even the idea of purging ideas."

The meaning of the following passage from [*Fundamental*] *Verses on the Middle Way* [中論 *Mūlamadhyamakakārikā-śāstra*] is the radical uprooting of actual being and a reversion to the true form of emptiness of all:

> Normal people, because they cover their eyes with what belongs to them [我我所], cannot see the truth, but holy people, because they have no belongings, extinguish egoistic afflictions [煩悩] and see the true form of all things…

Ōbaku [黄檗 Huángbò] says, "Both body and mind becoming nothing; this is called the great way", and Nyojō [如浄 Rújìng] even goes as far as to say,

> The practice of Zen is the dropping away of body and mind, earnestly sitting [and meditating] without burning incense, worshipping, calling the Buddha to mind, repenting before Buddha, or reading sutras.

Dōgen [道元]'s so-called *shikantaza* [simply sitting], is, as he puts it,

> Severing worldly ties, respite from all things, not thinking about good or bad, disregarding right and wrong, stopping the movement of the conscious mind, and ceasing internal reflection and assessment…

This involves neither thinking nor acting, but rather the dropping away of body and mind through reflection in the light of wisdom. True sitting is neither the sitting of a person's body nor the sitting of a person's mind, but rather has to be a sitting that is the shedding of the person. As Nyojō says, there is no *zazen* [sitting meditation] other than body and mind dropping away, and since the one who is sitting through this dropping away is, in other words, the Buddha, there is no true sitting that is not Buddha sitting, and no truly sitting person that is not a sitting Buddha. This is why it is said that only the Buddha realizes Buddhahood [唯仏与仏]:

The truth of the Buddha is not something that can be known by human beings, and this is why from ancient times it has been impossible as an ordinary person to understand the truth of the Buddha.

To know the Buddha or to understand the Buddha, too, is not to possess information about the Buddha or comprehend the Buddha but to make yourself the Buddha [作仏]. There is no understanding the Buddha without becoming the Buddha, and there is no seeing into one's nature [*kenshō* 見性; initial awakening] without becoming the Buddha. The Buddha that is known as *noema* apart from the one who knows is not the [true] Buddha, and neither is the Buddha that knows through *noesis* as something that stands apart from what is known. The Buddha must be the extinguishing of both outward objects and consciousness [境識雙泯]. Ōbaku also says, "Forgetting both the mind and outward objects [心境雙忘] is the real truth [真法]." The thirty-two forms and eighty secondary characteristics [of Buddha], too, are outward objects and cannot escape from falsehood. It is said, "If correct awareness is realized, everything is extinguished silently like an emptiness, with neither detritus on the outside nor consciousness and thought on the inside." A Buddha with consciousness and outward objects is not the [true] Buddha. Since the Buddha is without outward objects it is unborn [不生], and since the Buddha is without consciousness it is formless [無相].

In this way, the fact that the method of knowing the Buddha is neither cogitative, rational, deductive, nor even intuitive in the manner of Western metaphysics, nor through faith as in Christianity, is due to the Buddha's character being metaphysical in an Eastern way. The fact that thinking and reason have been emphasized in the West from ancient Greece onward is due to the fact that what is metaphysical in the Western way is cogitative and rational. If what is metaphysical had been cogitative in the East as well then it would now be necessary to place more emphasis on thinking. But the fact that in the East thinking has been disregarded and even believed to impede the truth is due to the fact that in the East what is metaphysical is not cogitative. The fact that thinking did not develop in the East is due to its impotence in the face of the metaphysical element of the East, and is by no means a coincidence. The dim view of thinking taken in the East is neither the result of the primitive mentality of the people of this region nor simply a misunderstanding, but rather came about because of a fundamental critique of thinking. Thinking, as described earlier, is based on the fundamental character of that which exists in actuality, or, in other words, "being", and can never be separated from it. As a new mode of thought emerges "irrationalisticaly" by means of a new pre-cogitative state of "being", and a new state of "being" is drawn out "rationalistically" by means of a new pre-ontic [有前的] state of thought, it [thinking] is always in a relationship of mutually prosperous coexistence with "being". Thinking is thinking only to the extent that "being" continues, and without thought "being" necessarily cannot persist. Thought, seemingly independent and free from "being," critiques and guides "being", and yet conversely is always being tested by "being". Even if thought critiques and guides "being", it can never critique "being" itself since it is primarily something that subsists on the basis of the fundamental character of "being". This is as analogous to a blade being unable to cut itself. Because the destiny of "being" itself is the destiny of thought, thought is not in a position to provide salvation when it comes to the absolute crisis of "being" itself. "Being" is always faced with large and small crises. The fact that "being" is always faced with crises is, in turn, the reason for its subsistence. "Being" without crisis is not "being". And yet the crises that make it possible for "being" to be "being" are found in the fact that none of them is an absolute crisis. While these are crises of "being", they are also, conversely, crises that maintain "being". "Being," while continuing in existence, is that which faces crises. In other words, as we have already stated, "being" is nothing even as it is being, and is being even as it is nothing. The fundamental character of "being" is that although "being" must be thoroughly being, to this end it must also always be nothing. Being actual we cannot escape such "being".

But can people not critique this "being" by digging up the root of this "being" itself? Ordinary critique is nothing more than the critique of specific states of "being" from the standpoint of "being". The critique of "being" itself can be conducted only upon the absolute crisis of "being" itself. The absolute crisis of "being" itself is encountered in the absolute tension between being and nothing within "being". In the absolute tension between being and nothing, being becomes a concrete, pure being that can never be abstract. At the same time, however, being can no longer be being. This is a being confronted with the absolute nothing, life confronted with absolute death. We can also call this absolute tension an absolute contradiction. But even if we speak of an absolute contradiction, it is a contradiction only in terms of logic. But because substantially it is not logical but holistic, in terms of the will it is an absolute dilemma and in terms of emotion it is absolute agony. An ordinary contradiction is a contradiction and not a contradiction, an ordinary dilemma is a dilemma and not a dilemma, and [a normal agony is an] agony and not agony. Contradictions, dilemmas, and agony can only be said to be pure upon absolute tension. In absolute tension, contradiction must be not only logical but at the same time volitional and emotional. This absolute tension is not an event that "being" simply encounters by accident; it is an inevitable pitfall lying in wait within the fundamental character of "being". We must therefore say that "being" already has hidden within itself a necessary moment that cannot be "being". Here lies the fundamental reason that "being" must dismantle "being" itself to become something that is not "being". The passage to the metaphysical element of the East is nothing other than this moment hidden within "being". This is why the metaphysical element of the East is the dismantling of "being" itself on the basis of a deep critique of "being" itself. The fundamental approach of the East is for "being" to become that which is not "being," in other words, "nothing," through the dismantling of "being" itself. This is why the East is religious and tends to take leave of actuality. But even if we speak of "taking leave", this only refers to a reorientation away from "being" towards "nothing". And we ought not to forget the autonomous and independent freedom of "nothing" itself that is beyond being/nothing and life/death. Even if we speak of taking leave of "being", this does not refer to moving away from "being" to go outside of it, but rather to become that which is not being by dismantling "being" itself as though being resurrected after death [絶後に甦る]. This is therefore, on the contrary, something positive. To cease "being" is to become a free body that has escaped from all determinations and contradictions. It is the presencing of free flowing and unhindered great action [無滞無礙の大用の現前]. Without form [無相] it presences all forms, and presencing all forms it does not dwell in any single form. This is what is referred to as "creating a mind that does not dwell in a place" [応無所住而生其心]. Herein lies the great act [大行] without defilement [無漏] that radically differs from all acts undertaken from the standpoint of "being". In the *Rinzairoku* [『臨済録』 *Record of Linji*] we can see, more than anywhere else, a vigorous [活溌溌地] example of an undefiled act. Among the records of the sages there is nothing that surpasses the *Rinzairoku* in the vividness of its unimaginable great action of no form [無相の大用]. In this way, even when we mention "taking leave," it by no means implies the cessation of breath, extinction, or so-called seclusion. Since it is the dismantling of "being" through the fundamental critique of actual "being" and the obtaining of a new life, we must instead say that it is something deeper than "being".

Hisamatsu Shinichi (1889–1980). Became an instructor at Kyoto University in 1935 and a full professor in 1946 after graduating from Kyoto Imperial University's Faculty of Letters and teaching at various institutions inluding Rinzaishū University and Ryūkoku University. Major works include *Tōyōteki mu* [『東洋的無』 *Eastern Nothing*] (Kōbundō, 1939), *Zettaiteki shutaidō* [『絶対的主体道』 *The Way of the Absolute Subject*] (Kōbundō, 1948), and *Zen to bijutsu* [『禅と美術』 *Zen and Aesthetics*] (Bokubisha, 1957). "The Metaphysical Element of the East" was first published in the journal *Shisō* [『思想』 *Thought*] in 1939, and was later included in *Eastern Nothing*. It is presently included in *Zōho Hisamatsu Shin'ichi chosakushū* [『増補 久松真一著作集』 *Collected Writings of Hisamatsu Shin'ichi: Expanded*] (Hōzōkan) Vol. 1 and *Eastern Nothing* (Kodansha Gakujutsu Bunko).

Chapter 12
The Thought and Practice of Hisamatsu Shinichi

[久松真一の思想と実践]

Imaizumi Motoji

12.1 Life

The life of Hisamatsu Shinichi was one lived from the standpoint of awakening [覚], involving the elucidation of the "religion of awakening" through the "philosophy of awakening". The various stages in the developmental paradigm of human modes of being that he spoke of from his early period onward were also the stages he himself personally lived through. The ultimate stage he reached in this process was that of the "religion of awakening". In elucidating the content of this awakening, he first spoke of an "Eastern nothing" [東洋的無], and then expressed and clarified it with other terms such as active nothing [能動的無], existence as nothing [即無的実存], the way of the absolute subject [絶対主体道], and the formless self [無相の自己].

Hisamatsu was born in the twenty-second year of the Meiji Era (1889) in Nagaramura (now part of Gifu City), Inabagun, Gifu Prefecture. He was born into a family of farmers who were fervent believers in the True Pure Land sect [浄土真宗] [of Buddhism]. Having been raised in this religious atmosphere, from a very young age he harbored the desire to become a religious leader. At first his interest in religion took a passive form through the external influence of his family, and he even considered entering the Buddhist University (now Ryūkoku University) established by the Nishi Hongan-ji temple, the head temple of his family's religion, to become a priest. He has described this childhood faith in True Pure Land Buddhism as a life governed by a medieval heteronomous theonomy. After entering Gifu Middle School and acquiring knowledge of science, however, he began to harbor doubts about his faith in True Pure Land Buddhism. He would later say of

---

Translated from the Japanese by Robert Chapeskie and revised by John W. M. Krummel.

M. Imaizumi (✉)
Ehime University, Matsuyama, Japan

that time in his life, "I experienced a transition from the religious life of a naïve, medieval faith that avoids so-called rational doubt to the critical way of life of the modern human being founded upon the autonomous judgment of reason and empirical proof" (I, 418[1]). Through this experience he arrived at the decision to pursue philosophy based on reason.

The consciousness of sin was present in Hisamatsu from an early age, and this became a major motivation towards [his interest in] religion. He states that even when he discarded medieval faith his "rational awareness of sin" (I,429) only deepened, and this sentiment is also evident in a letter he wrote to Nishida Kitarō after Nishida had admonished him for acting rashly when he tried to drop out of university just before graduation in order to practice Zen: "Until I obtain freedom all of my acts are sinful" (I,429). This consciousness of sin was further clarified and set down in *Zettai kiki to fukkatsu* [『絶対危機と復活』 *Absolute Crisis and Rebirth*]. In this text he states that while sin is ordinarily thought of as sin in terms of morality, that is not all there is to it. Sin must instead be extended as far as truth/falsehood and beauty/ugliness: "in sum, broadly speaking, the concept of sin must be amplified to include sin that arises between being rational and being anti-rational" (II,149). Sin as a conflict between the rational and the anti-rational is established on the basis of the fundamental structure of reason and cannot be overcome through reason. Hisamatsu calls this conflict intrinsic to reason itself absolute antinomy, and describes it as the predestined limit of reason. Modern humanity, which takes the standpoint of reason, cannot help but run up against this limit. We can presumably say that the root of what was earlier referred to as the "rational self-awareness of sin" is to be found here. This consciousness of sin led Hisamatsu to religion. And the sin to which he referred when he stated that until he obtained freedom all actions were sinful was to be elucidated, and at the same time completely eradicated, by obtaining freedom and being able to live in truth.

When Hisamatsu resolved to pursue philosophy founded on reason, the principal of his middle school, Hayashi Hachizō [林釟蔵], counseled him to enter the University of Kyoto, where Nishida Kitarō, who would ultimately come to have the greatest influence upon him, was teaching at the time. With the aim of entering the University of Kyoto he advanced to Dai-san [The Third] High School, and it was during his final year of study there that [Nishida's] *Zen no kenkyū* [*An Inquiry into the Good*] was published. Hisamatsu immediately bought and read it. His attention was drawn mostly to section four, "Religion", because it contained a "religion that does not contradict reason, and to which reason can also consent" (I, 422). His interest in religion that had previously been obliterated by rational critique was thus reborn. Right around this time Nishida gave his only lecture course on the study of religion. Hisamatsu later states that this lecture course of Nishida's awoke in him the strongest and most profound fascination he experienced

---

[1]Note: All citations are from *Hisamatsu Shinichi chosakushū* [『久松真一著作集』 *Collected Writings of Hisamatsu Shinichi*] (Risōsha). Roman numerals indicate the volume and Arabic numerals the page.

during his three years at university. He would later recall, "I had my religious eyes philosophically opened through this lecture course" (I, 425).

When he was on the verge of graduating from university, however, he found himself confronting "various living issues" (these are Hisamatsu's words, but if we look at the letter to Nishida mentioned earlier it is clear that the central issue was the problem of sin), and with these particular problems as moments he drove himself in the direction of the universal source of all problems. Instead of viewing these issues objectively, he deepened them into the issue of the subject itself. Hisamatsu could not but be aware of the fact that philosophy, to the extent that it is the pursuit of truth by means of objective understanding, is impotent when it comes to resolving this issue of the subject. He therefore sought its resolution in Zen. He looked for a solution in a Zen that was "neither mere religion nor mere philosophy, but rather a subject-knowledge through practice [行的な主体知] and a practice engaging the subject [主体的な行]" (I,426). Following the recommendation of Nishida Kitarō, who was himself a longtime lay practitioner, he began to practice Zen [meditation] under Ikegami Shōzan [池上湘山], a master at Myōshin-ji meditation hall. Hisamatsu's "*kenshō* [initial awakening, lit. 'seeing into one's nature']" was brilliant. Perhaps it was simply fortunate timing, but only a month after first meeting Master Shōzan, on the third day of "Rōhatsu-sesshin" [an intense meditation practice] Hisamatsu, his "entire body blackened with a vast, great doubt" [通身黒浸々の一大疑団],

> …suddenly dissolved completely from within, and at the same time it was as though Shōzan's formidable 'silver mine iron wall' [銀山鉄壁] had collapsed without a trace; there was not even a hair's breadth between them. Here he [Hisamatsu] realized for the first time his formless and free true self, and at the same time he was also for the first time able to encounter Shōzan's true face (I, 433).

This experience of *kenshō* occurred in December of 1915. Hisamatsu continued practicing Zen under Shōzan and his successors Hiramoto Tokujyū and Hayashi Ekyō until 1938. He also held teaching positions at a series of institutions including Ryūkoku University, the University of Kyoto, and Kyoto City University of the Arts before passing away in Nagara, Gifu City in 1980. Having awoken to his true self in this way, he states that his eternal destiny is:

> …to live this true self, practice subject-knowledge through such living, express the self in its various aspects through this practice, develop these activities into a religion of awakening, objectify the self through the true self becoming conscious of itself as an object, and therein obtain object-knowledge of the self to establish a philosophy of awakening (ibid.).

In this way the "religion of awakening" and the "philosophy of awakening" constitute two sides of the same coin: the so-called philosophy of awakening is the theoretical elucidation of awakening and the religion of awakening is its practical enactment. As constituting two sides of the same coin, the philosophy of awakening and the religion of awakening are difficult to separate, but if we were to forcibly pry them apart we might say that the philosophy of awakening is found in the essays included in volumes one and two of his collected works (the Risō shuppan edition), *Tōyōteki mu* [『東洋的無』 *Eastern Nothing*] and *Zettai shutaidō* [『絶対主体道』 *The*

Way of the Absolute Subject], in which we find a theoretical elucidation of awakening, while the religion of awakening is mainly discussed in volumes three and four, *Kaku to sōzō* [『覚と創造』 *Awakening and Creation*] and *Sadō no tetsugaku* [『茶道の哲学』 *The Philosophy of the Way of Tea*]. The philosophy of awakening can thus be divided into two periods corresponding to *Eastern Nothing* and *The Way of the Absolute Subject*.

12.2 Eastern Nothing

"Eastern nothing", which describes what we might consider the seminal core of the content of awakening, is also the title of Hisamatsu's first book, and expresses the latter's distinctive character in a single phrase. It is a phrase that Hisamatsu first used in 1938. According to Hisamatsu, he chose the title "Eastern nothing" because "Eastern nothing" is "the fundamental moment of that which specifically characterizes Eastern culture in contrast to Western culture" (I,29) and "is the source of distinctly Eastern culture, and also its able expresser" (ibid.) "The metaphysical element of the East" in *The Metaphysical Element of the East*, the essay included in this volume, is this "Eastern nothing". Hisamatsu says that in the West,

> …not only everything that exists in actuality, and the study of these things, but even that which transcends what exists, and the study of these things, is developed within this standpoint of that which exists in actuality. This must be the sense of the fundamental meaning that the West is a world of 'being', and Western culture is a culture of 'being'. Western philosophy and metaphysics, too, never get beyond this fundamental restriction of the standpoint of that which exists in actuality" (I, 20).

In contrast, in the East it is known that "there is such a thing as ceasing to be a being by escaping the standpoint of that which exists in actuality" (ibid.). This thing unknown in the West but known in the East is the metaphysical element of the East, or, in other words, Eastern nothing. So what is Eastern nothing? Eastern nothing is "not nothing [non-being] as a moment of that which exists in actuality… nor is it the nothingness of all conceived from the standpoint of 'being'" (I, 21). Instead,

> …because we truly depart from the standpoint of that which is and transcend it, and become neither a being in conformity with the nothing nor a metaphysical thing derived from it, but instead that which is beyond determination as well as contradiction, this metaphysical thing is subjective [主体的] and existential [現存的] (ibid.).

In referring to the subjective, however, Hisamatsu does not mean the subject vis-a-vis the object. On the contrary, it is a subject that exists as neither a subject nor an object. Eastern nothing is something subjective, while the elements of Western metaphysics are objective. In the context of Buddhism the Eastern nothing as something subjective is the Buddha, and

> …because the Buddha is nothing other than we who have ceased to be something that exists in actuality, or in other words 'the metaphysical element of the East', the Buddha for ourselves who have ceased to be what exists in actuality is existence (I, 22),

and is also referred to as "self-nature" [自性] or "the true self" [真の自己].

In the East there is a method for ceasing to be what exists in actuality, and this method is referred to, among other appellations, as "*zazen* [sitting meditation]". This method does not rely on Western metaphysical or rational thinking. Rational thinking is impotent when it comes to the Eastern nothing. Western thinking is thought undertaken from the standpoint of "being", "it is a thinking that arises only to the extent 'being' continues, and without thinking 'being' necessarily cannot continue" (I, 25). In this way Western thinking is inevitably tied to "being", but this "being" is also always tied to "nothing". The crisis of "being" lies in its always being capable of becoming "nothing". We cannot resolve this crisis of "being" by means of "being" itself, nor through Western thinking. The absolute critique of "being" can only be conducted through the absolute crisis of "being" itself. The absolute crisis of "being" is the absolute tension between "being" and "nothing". Being in absolute tension is being confronted with absolute nothing, life confronted with absolute death. Absolute tension is the absolute contradiction of "being" itself:

Herein lies the fundamental reason that 'being' must dismantle 'being' itself and become something that is not 'being'. The path to what is metaphysical in the East is nothing other than this moment hidden within 'being'. This is why the metaphysical element in the East means the dismantling of 'being' itself on the basis of a deep critique of 'being' itself. The fundamental orientation of the East is that 'being' becomes something that is not 'being', that is, 'nothing', through the dismantling of 'being' itself (I, 27).

While this fundamental approach is to become that which is not "being", namely, "nothing", because this "nothing" is absolute nothing and absolute nothing is beyond the nothing that opposes being, we must not forget the autonomous, independent freedom this "nothing" possesses. "To cease to be 'being' is to become a free body [自由体] that has escaped from all determination and contradiction" (I, 27). Hisamatsu later uses the term "active nothing" [能動的無] to more clearly express the active nature possessed by this free body (see *Nōdōteki mu* [『能動的 無』 *Active Nothing*] (I, 67~)).

This is how Hisamatsu explicates the Eastern nothing in *The Metaphysical Element of the East*. In its final passages he concludes that the Eastern nothing is a "free body" or a "subject engaging in free flowing and unhindered great action [無 滞無礙の大用]", and that what will further elucidate this subject is the way of the absolute subject.

12.3 The Way of the Absolute Subject

For Hisamatsu, the way of the absolute subject is the true and ultimate mode of being for human beings. In order to elucidate this true mode of being, in the preface to *The Way of the Absolute Subject* for the first time he divides the human mode of being into five types and examines each in detail:

The first is an unreflecting and facile human absolutism that is unaware of the absolute death that dogs the footsteps of humanity, an uncritical and naïve self-reliance. The second is an absolutely negative nihilism that is critical but without any kind of affirmation. The third is existentialism, whose affirmation is critical but fails to obtain any escape from absolute anxiety. The fourth is an absoluteotherpowerism [絶対他力主義] that escapes absolute anxiety, but loses independent autonomy due to relying on others. In contrast to these, the fifth can be described as an absolute-self-power-ism (II, 10).

While it would undergo slight modifications, it is safe to say that his later thought follows this initial way of thinking. These five modes of being are not simply considered in parallel. Rather, their relationship is such that each is critiqued by the following mode, with the fifth being the true mode of being of human beings and Hisamatsu's own standpoint. By classifying human modes of being, Hisamatsu thus attempted to clarify his own standpoint while at the same time critiquing others. The slight modifications mentioned above were the inevitable result of attempts to critique and reposition the thought that emerged [in this process]. Along with these alterations, the description given to Hisamatsu's own standpoint was also modified from time to time.

Let us now take a brief look at this classification [of modes of being]. Human absolutism, the first mode, which can also be called the idealistic conception of humanity, is an anthropocentrism that emerged from a critique through human reason of the theocentricism of the medieval West. In this standpoint what is rational has value and what is irrational is without value. Accordingly, the direction in which we ought to proceed is to overcome the valueless and irrational by living rationally. The aim of a rational life is to thoroughly overcome the irrational. But this aim is ultimately an ideal and will never be realized. For as already mentioned, "The opposition between the rational and the irrational is the fundamental structure of reason, and to adopt only the rational while removing the irrational is already impossible on the basis of the structure of reason itself" (II, 149). Ideals are natural demands of reason, and they presumably give rational human beings the aspiration to live. But reason includes within itself what Hisamatsu calls "absolute antinomy" and is established on its basis. Lacking awareness of this absolute antinomy, the standpoint of human absolutism endlessly pursues an ideal that will never be realized.

Today the limitations of human absolutism have become apparent, and two [further] modes [of being] have emerged, namely the standpoints of absolutely negative nihilism and existentialism. Nihilism, the second mode, emerges by knowing—subjectively rather than objectively—that an absolute antinomy lies at the root of the rational human being. In it there is only an absolute negation without any positivity or affirmation whatsoever. The nihilist image of humanity reflects an awareness of the absolute negation at the root of the structure of human existence. But this does not imply an overcoming of this absolute negation or a transcendence of the limits of modern humanity. An absolute nothing that is absolutely negative and without any overcoming of absolute negation, however, is not the true absolute nothing. True absolute nothing is subjective nihility, but subjective nihility cannot be realized without the overcoming of absolutely negative absolute nothing. While aware of the absolute nothingness of humanity, to a certain extent nihilism still views it by objectifying it and has not yet arrived at a subjective nothing. Its nihility therefore remains a certain kind of being. A nihilism that fails to overcome absolute negation cannot help but descend into despair. Even despair, if it is true despair, has the potential to free those who have fallen into it, but because the nihility of nihilism is still a kind of being it provides no escape from despair.

Existentialism, the third mode, while aware that absolute negation is something for which for human beings are fated, nevertheless continues to pursue something affirmative. Existentialism senses the absolute death that human beings cannot escape, and yet attempts to live by discovering a rationale [for being] within the bounds of this absolute death. It is a deeper understanding of humanity than the idealism that is ignorant of the absolute death of human beings, but within this standpoint one cannot be freed of absolute death. Adopting it one does not reach a state of salvation but remains lodged in a state of anxiety.

Absolute other-power-ism, the fourth mode, is a conception of humanity that escapes the state of anxiety found in existentialism and reaches a state of great relief [大安心]. It is a conception of humanity that is aware both of the limits of absolute negation and absolute death possessed by human beings and of the fact that it is impossible to get away from this absolute death under one's own power, and thus escapes it by leaning on something absolute that is other [to the self]. This mode is reminiscent of the crisis theology of [Karl] Barth. Ever since the dawn of early modernity, it has only been through absolute other-power-ism that autonomous humanity could be saved from the absolute death it bears within itself. But this salvation was attained through the negation of the autonomy that had constituted the essential nature of modern humanity. "While crisis theology and the like are oriented towards the negation of modernity, these approaches fail to completely negate atheistic perspectives" (II, 59). Contemporary human beings are unable to accept the negation of human autonomy. Hisamatsu presents a new image of humanity in terms of autonomy, asserts that this is the true image of humanity, and through this image attempts to formulate a fundamental solution to various contemporary issues. This conception of humanity is the fifth mode, absolute-self-power-ism.

Absolute-self-power-ism has been called by different names, including the absolutely autonomous conception of humanity, the late modern conception of humanity, the Zen conception of humanity, the atheistic conception of humanity, the "true emptiness wondrous being" [真空妙有] conception of humanity, the formless self [無相の自己], and so on. The first mode, human absolutism, or, in other words, the early modern rational [conception of] humanity, runs into the absolute antinomy of reason, and out of an awareness of the limits and frustrations of early modern humanity the conceptions of humanity found in the second and succeeding types emerge as attempt after attempt is made to escape this absolute antinomy. Hisamatsu states that the true method of escaping absolute antinomy is "awaking to our selves that are neither valuable/valueless nor ontic/meontic [or: existent/non-existent]" (II, 74). Ordinarily this awakening is blocked, and what blocks it is the fact that we are rational beings. When we who are rational beings are plunged into absolute antinomy,

> ...taking this as an opportunity, our essential selves awaken by passing through adversity. This awakening is an awakening that, from a position at the limit of reason, penetrates and goes beyond it. ...[T]o the extent that we affirmatively remain in the standpoint of reason, we cannot understand the limit of reason. But when we deeply reflect upon reason and critique it we become aware that an absolute antinomy lies at its foundation. We become aware of this, moreover, not as an object but rather subjectively. It is a self-awareness and an awareness of absolute antinomy itself, but we become aware here also of that which has passed through it [absolute antinomy] (II, 174f).

This awakened state is the self who is neither "being/non-being" nor "valuable/valueless"; this is the human being of absolute self-power-ism. Hisamatsu calls this self the "formless self". This formless self is the conversion of the antinomous human being into a human being who has passed through antinomy from within and has awakened from the depths of absolute antinomy as a self who has overcome it. The formless self "does not exist outside of absolute antinomy, or, to put it another way, does not exist in the manner of a separate other in regard to absolute antinomy, but instead awakens from within absolute antinomy by dropping away of it" (II,175). Release from absolute antinomy can therefore never occur through that which is absolutely other. "Salvation occurs when absolute antinomy is overcome by the awakening of the true self– the true self that has not awakened although it has always been awake" (II,176). The formless self, "is an autonomy that had dropped away of and passed through the limit boundaries of rational autonomy to be an autonomy, so to speak, of a deeper dimension. This is an originary absolute autonomy that has dropped away of the fateful absolute antinomy of rational autonomy" (II, 176). The self who has awoken to the original self, who is originary absolute autonomy,

> ...fills the self who has not yet awoken as a self by flowing back into it. In other words, the original self becomes the source, and the way of being of the self up to now becomes that which had emerged from this source. ...Previously there was the continuity of self-negation proceeding from the unawaked self to the awakened self, but now there is realized, in reverse, the continuity of affirmative positing, proceeding from the awakened self to the unawakened self (II, 178).

Here the awakened self affirmatively restores the actual. The world up to now in which the unawakened self (the rational self) was the subject is converted just as it is into the world in which the awakened self (the formless self) is the subject. Because the world in which the awakened self is the subject is not a world distinct from that in which the unawakened self is the subject, it is not a world that is released from actual history. The awakened self "creates history, while transcending it, from within history without leaving the world of history" (II, 179). In this way Hisamatsu sought to overcome the absolute antinomy of modern rational humanity and create the true world (the world of awakening) through "FAS", an approach that involves awakening to the real self (the formless self), standing on the standpoint of the entire human race, and making history by transcending it.

The above is the theoretical elucidation, in terms of object-knowledge, of the content of awakening that Hisamatsu calls "the philosophy of awakening". "The metaphysical element of the East" was the initial explication of the content of awakening as "Eastern nothing". This Eastern nothing was then dubbed "active nothing" as something subjective and active, and this in turn was finally presented in its ultimate form as the "way of the absolute subject" of absolute-self-power-ism.

12.4   FAS Zen and Mind-Tea [Shincha 心茶]

Since Eastern nothing is subjective and is the way of the absolute subject, it naturally of a single body and indistinguishable from its practice. Eastern nothing is the self itself, and as Hisamatsu indicated in the citation above, he wanted to found a "religion of awakening" through "living this true self, practicing in subject-knowledge through living, and expressing the self in every aspect through practicing" (I,433). A "religion of awakening" is to be put into practice through the support of this kind of "philosophy of awakening". For Hisamatsu this practice consisted of FAS Zen and the way of mind-tea.

The religion of awakening was first put into practice in 1944 at the University of Kyoto's "Gakudō dōjō". The Gakudō dōjō was a *dōjō* [training hall] founded by an organization within the University of Kyoto and open to the public. The Gakudō dōjō was transformed into the FAS Society on the occasion of Hisamatsu's trip abroad in 1958. The platform of the FAS Society is comprised of four guiding principles, the first of which is "This *dōjō* engages in the study and practice of the absolute great path, and, through these efforts, participates in the holy project of the revitalization of the world" (III, 160). On the basis of these guiding principles a "Vow of Humankind" was created, and this vow can be said to encapsulate FAS Zen as a whole. FAS Zen arose through a critique of traditional Zen. The core of this critique is embodied in these words of Hisamatsu's:

> If Zen stops at this sort of mere awakening of the self and awakening of others, then we would have to say that it is something that falls into the deep pit of deliverance from this world [*mok ṣa*; *gedatsu*] through mutual collaboration of self and others, but it is not the true attainment of complete awakening. It is not enough for the self and others to become enlightened; the important issue of [religious] practice [行] is what to do after enlightenment has been obtained. The great agency and great action [大機大用] of Zen, along with its emanation in the direction of helping each individual attain enlightenment, must also emanate towards the actual world, that is, towards the formation of the world as well as of history (III, 73).

To put it the other way around, since early modernity traditional Zen has lacked practical efficacy in regard to the historical world. Hisamatsu emphasizes self-awakening as a human being who possesses in unison depth (F), breadth (A) and length (S). He criticized traditional Zen with its bias towards a self-awakening of mere depth, and emphasized the "awakening of the *dōjō*" over the awakening of individuals. He took FAS Zen to be the overcoming of the state of humanity since early modernity, as discussed above, in the three dimensions of depth, breadth and length. To put this in terms of the acronym FAS, traditional Zen lacks A = "to stand on the standpoint of **A**ll humanity[2]" ("let us stand on the standpoint of all humanity") and S = "to create **S**uperhistorical history" ("let us create history by transcending history"). And the fact that A and S are lacking means that F = "to awake to the **F**ormless self" ("let us awake to the **F**ormless self"), too, cannot be consummately attained. When it comes to the formation of the world and of history, Hisamatsu uses the expression "Superhistorical history". "Superhistorical history" means what Christianity speaks of as the end times [終末 *eschaton*] being not in the future but in the present. "Although in Christianity, too, what is described as real history begins with the end, that end in Christianity occurs not in the present but in the eternal future" (III,286). The S of FAS Zen refers to the creation of history, where the end is in the present. It means the formation of history through what traditional Zen refers to as the method of "building all that exists without wavering from the truth" [真際を動せすして一切法を建立す].

Hisamatsu also founded the "Mind-Tea Association" [*Shincha-kai* 心茶会]. The Mind-Tea Association was founded in 1941 as an organization within the University of Kyoto, and was then opened to the general public after being restructured in 1956. Hisamatsu says that "Mind-tea is *wabi*-tea [*wabi-cha* 侘茶; "refined tea"]." He then defines this term as follows. "*Wabi*-tea is a synthetic system of cultural life that is characterized by *wabi* [侘: quiet elegance, refinement], whereby *wabi*—Zen that has infused the tea ceremony, tea in which Zen becomes the subject—acts as the primordial subject and creates values and entities as their fundamental standard" (IV,104). *Wabi* is Zen's ground that has nothing [無一物底], subject that has nothing [無一物的主体], the absolute subject, and the true self. It follows that the world of mind-tea is the world of *wabi*-tea, the world that creates the true self:

> *Wabi*-tea, by taking Zen as its fundamental subject, fundamentally altered the world of tea ceremony as it had existed in the past, created the ethics of *wabi*, the manners and etiquette of *wabi*, the art of *wabi*, and so on, and constructed a new, unique and synthetic cultural system spanning the entirety of human life in which the 'Buddha *dharma* is within the tea ceremony' [仏法も茶の湯の中], thereby creating the distinctly Japanese cultural asset of the way of tea, [a practice] abundant with form and formlessness, incomparable to anything in the West (IV,120).

This *wabi* is the "mind [*shin* 心]" of "mind-tea". The world created by the mind of mind-tea is the "tea [*cha* 茶]" of mind-tea. "The 'mind' of mind-tea is the self. And it is a self that is unobtainable. It is nothing other than the mind when the ordinary mind has become unobtainable, namely the subject that is nothing. The 'tea' of mind-tea is tea as the expression of this kind of subject, and this is nothing other than the tea ceremony of *wabi* [侘の茶の湯]. The world of '*wabi*-tea' is the world of the subject who is nothing, or, in other words, the world of the original face of humanity, expressed in connection with the tea of the everyday. It...is the model

---

[2] This phrase and those following "S" and "F" are written in English in the original text.

world of the system of human dwelling" (IV, 55). While he speaks of a model world, it is not something that is fixed. As it is a world created by a subject who is nothing, it must be a world that is renewed every day. To live the way of mind-tea means to "return to the expressive subject itself through *wabi*-tea, and, from there, as one who is primordially expressive, to participate in the historical world while regulating one's own life" (ibid.). Here lies the indistinguishable unity of everyday life and the world of mind-tea. Hisamatsu emphasizes the indistinguishable unity of the historical world of actuality and the world of mind-tea, and says that we must not confine the way of tea to the tea-ceremony room as its specific place. *Wabi*-tea "brought Zen from the temple to the layman's garden and hut, and transformed the Zen monk into a tea-ceremony practitioner as a lay person" (IV, 19), transforming Zen into *wabi*-Zen. *Wabi*-tea tried to secularize the Buddha *dharma*, and thereby make manifest the singular world of truth. *Wabi*-tea must therefore further transform the so-called *wabi*-tea of today, narrowly confined to the so-called world of tea, into "mind-tea". *Wabi*-tea must become mind-tea. Zen must become mind-tea Zen. Hisamatsu further states that the mind of mind-tea must become a subject and create the historical world as the world of truth. But as mentioned in the description of FAS Zen above, this means that in the sense that the end of time is not in the future but in the present, this creation occurs in such a way that

> ...the present is the world of religious creation, or, in other words, the present is the world of *bodhisattva* practice [菩薩行], and when it comes to something like the divine creation of the world, too, this means neither that God created the world in the past nor that the kingdom of God will begin at the end of time, but rather that the world of God's creation obtains in the present, continually renewed (III, 287).

In this way FAS Zen and mind-tea, for Hisamatsu, were of one body and indistinguishable. Having begun by taking the acts of philosophy and of living as of one body and indistinguishable, Hisamatsu put this into practice over the course of his own life through FAS Zen and mind-tea.

Imaizumi Motoji Professor Emeritus, Ehime University. Major works: "Testugaku to shūkyō" [『哲学と宗教』 "Philosophy and Religion" (*Ehime daigaku hōbungakubu ronshū* [『愛媛大学法文学部論集』 *Ehime University Faculty of Law and Letters Essay Collection*], 1995), "Tetsugakuteki kojikyūmei toshite no *Zen no kenkyū*" [『哲学的己事究明としての『善の研究』」 "*An Inquiry into the Good* as a Philosophical Examination of the Self"] (*Zen to tetsugaku* [『禅と哲学』*Zen and Philosophy*], Zen bunka kenkyūsho [Institute for Studies of Zen Culture], 1988).

Part VII
Shimomura Toratarō

Chapter 13
The Position of Mathematics in Intellectual History

[精神史; *Geistesgeschichte*]
[精神史における数学の位置]

Shimomura Toratarō

13.1 The Position of Academic Inquiry Within a Cultural System

Any culture significant enough to have had its existence noted in world history necessarily forms a cultural *system* endowed with religion, academic inquiry, art, law, technics, and so on. A culture completely lacking in any one of these presumably would not exist in actuality. Any culture, of course, is unique and original in the manner of organizing its system, but it is particularly through the individual parts of such systems that the distinctive character of each culture comes into being. Upon carefully observing the specificity of each culture once again after tentatively acknowledging these universal aspects of culture in general, however, we discover that religion, academic inquiry, art, and so on, which had earlier been thought of as universal elements indispensable in any culture, are in each case unique and hardly aspects that can be said to be religion, academic inquiry, and so on in the same sense. For example, when it comes to the self-reflective stage, putting aside for the moment the naturally spontaneous so-called "primitive" stage, looking at cases in which "imitation" is taken to be the essential character of art and cases in which "the discernment of true form" [実相観入][1] is taken to be its essence, even if we cannot say that they share nothing in common whatsoever it is difficult in practice to refer to both of these aspects of culture as "art" in the same sense. Likewise, it is

---

An Excerpt from *Philosophy of the History of Science* (1941).

[1]This phrase refers to a poetics in which the self is thrown into the object of the poem and describes a world in which self and object become one (translator).

T. Shimomura

questionable whether both Buddhism and Christianity can be called "religion"[2] in precisely the same sense. In regard to our immediate topic, academic inquiry, we can probably say that what has been referred to as "*Science*"[3] in the West, strictly speaking, has not existed in the history of the East, including India, China, and Japan. Even in the West, while "*Science*" in the Western Europe of *modernity* generally referred to the "natural sciences" that constituted the typical avenue of academic inquiry, in *ancient* Greece "*Mathemata*",[4] the "subject of study", meant "mathematics", and therefore mathematics in particular was taken as its paradigmatic model. The *character* of the "academic inquiry" that took physics as its model in modernity is completely different from its counterpart that took geometry as its model in antiquity. And of course "academic inquiry" [*gakumon*学問] in our mother tongue, if we follow its classical usage, meant something close to that which takes "statecraft" [治国平天下] or "moral conduct for living" [修身処生]—ultimately things of a religious or political-moral, generally practical nature—or "practical inquiry" [実学] as its subject matter. Here, in addition to differences in the character of the actual academic inquiry conducted, the *idea* of academic inquiry itself also differs. Of course, to the extent that all of these undertakings are referred to as academic inquiry, they indeed possess some commonality. Nevertheless, differences exist that make it difficult to refer to them as academic inquiry in precisely the same sense. These differences probably derive from differences in the character of the culture itself, or, more profoundly, the conception of the world itself, that each [form of] academic inquiry takes as its background or foundation. A psychological typologization of "intellectual" or "rational" aptitudes or tendencies of various ethnic groups of the sort that has become common, for example, does not exhaust them. On the contrary, this is a question of historical social-cultural systems, and, going further, the worldviews that lie at their foundations. It is thus more an issue of *intellectual history* than *the history* of *psychology*. It is not a question of *consciousness* but a question of *worlds.*

Today the belief that all academic inquiry is originally motivated by the needs of everyday life, and thus that astronomy and mathematics, for example, were motivated by practical issues in navigation, agriculture, and so on, has become a commonsensical view. But even if the so-called necessities of everyday living constitute the motivation behind the establishment of academic inquiry, we cannot say that this immediately determines the *character* of academic inquiry, for example, or its individuality. We cannot simply deduce *individuality* from universal formal principles. Moreover, to say that something is produced or results from a mere demand or a mere necessity is no different from a mysticism that claims, "He said, 'let there be light', and there was light." The so-called necessities of everyday

---

[2]The English word "*Religion*" is added in parenthesis following "宗教 [religion]" in the original text (translator).

[3]"Science" is written in English in the original text (translator).

[4]Words such as "*Mathemata*" that are written in languages other than Japanese in the original text have been left untranslated. The author's capitalization has also been retained (translator).

living are themselves neither simply subjective demands nor external needs. Academic inquiry, like all other cultural formations, is nothing other than the product of an internal resolution mediated by external needs. It is not the product of mere spirit or of mere nature, but the self-formation of the "world" in which it realizes itself through the opposition of spirit and nature. The so-called ethnic [folk] spirit, too, is fundamentally not something that simply exists as "nature", but rather a "world" that historically realizes itself through an ethnic group that forms a nation in a particular place.

Religion, academic inquiry, and art, too, as products of this ethnic spirit, thereby form a system of culture, and, through the mediation of the ethnic spirit, express the world; the world thus realizes itself in them. As things of this nature none of them originally exist independently and separately in advance. They form a system by reciprocally differentiating and mutually combining. The character and originality of the spirit of each ethnicity resides in the manner of this differentiation and formation. Among the peoples of antiquity, for example, the Israelites formed their characteristic culture by placing religion in the most prominent position, the Greeks by establishing the "*polis*" (city-state) and *civitas*, or, in other words, *civilization*,[5] and the Phoenicians through an economy built on commercial trade. Each of them expressed their own world within these characteristic cultures. The character of their "spirit"[6] obtains *in* the manner of formation of these worlds. In each case their own spirit is formed through the formation of a "world", and its character is determined by the manner of this formation.

Europe indeed formed the character of its own spirit and culture through its formation of "academic inquiry". Or, to put it the other way around, that which established its own character through the formation of academic inquiry is the European spirit. The concept of Europe is not simply a geographical concept but a historical concept, and it is only through this [concept] that it obtains a unified and complete meaning. There is no direct cultural continuity between the Greece of antiquity and the Europe of modernity; their politics, religion, and social organization are not the same, nor do they overlap either ethnically or territorially. Is it not then the culture of academic inquiry that, possessing a unity in its European character and having maintained itself consistently from antiquity to modernity, stands in contrast to, and is distinguished from, the East?

The concept of culture (*Kultur*)[7] itself was in fact originally a European concept. It arose in Europe and is a concept unique to Europe. Today the concept of "culture" is used quite universally, in referring to "Egyptian culture", "Indian culture", or "Japanese culture", for example, and is thus understood to be something

---

[5]"*Civilization*" is written in English in the original text (translator).

[6]The Japanese word translated here as "spirit" [精神] is also found the term translated as "intellectual history" [精神史]. A literal translation of the latter as "spiritual" or "psychical" history would be misleading given its usage in Japanese, but the connection should be noted. "Spirit" is used here in its broadest English sense (translator).

[7]The German "*Kultur*" is added in parenthesis following "文化" [culture] in the original text (translator).

common to both East and West. But *"Kultur"*, in its classical sense, originally meant παιδεία [*paideia*] (*Bildung des Menschen*), referring to the full attainment of human potential or human perfection (ἀρετή [*arete*]) as a universal idea, and "culture" thus defined is a concept unique to Europe. In contrast, the various cultures of the East must be said to be of a different character, whether as that which, being *primarily* moral or *primarily* spiritual, disregards sensibility and the present world to take withdrawal as its ultimate goal, or as that which, being *primarily* religious, ignores creative production in this world. These cultures, in their one-sidedness, are essentially distinct from the original concept of *Kultur*. For it [this concept] recognizes the ideal of culture in the perfection prescribed by the essence of humanity itself in its totality and the harmony of its parts, manifests in the historical formation of a people as a whole, and functions as a formative force in the formation of its individuals. Anything other than this cannot be said to be "culture" in the same sense (W. Jaeger, *Paideia*, I, S.6ff).

The unity and completeness of Europe obtains under this idea of culture. It also gave rise to the concept of "history". We can probably say that history in the sense found in Europe does not exist in any other culture. Taking this culture and history as its backdrop, the idea of academic inquiry in Europe arose through an internal connection to them.

It is said that the concept of "Europe" in the sense of something in contrast to "Asia" originally comes from Asia. It is pointed out that in Assyrian carvings "*asu*"—(the land of) sunrise—is often contrasted with "*ereb*" or "*irib*"—(the land of) darkness or sunset, and it is inferred that these [phrases] were brought to Greece by the Phoenicians and thus gave rise to the names "Asia" and "Europe". Geographically Europe is nothing more than a peninsula of Asia. Historically, however, from ancient Greece to the present era, Europe has been a complete world distinct in character from adjoining Asia. What is it that forms Europe's consistently unified nature in spite of the fact that it lacks a common identity when it comes to language, ethnicity, religion, and customs? We might think of Greek culture, the Roman Empire, and the Christian religion as principles that unified and organized the Europe of their respective eras. But what is it that unifies these three principles and thereby forms the continuous unity of Europe? This, and indeed precisely this, is surely the fundamental question of the intellectual history of Europe. Apart from the question of whether Europe itself is conscious of this, we can clearly detect it in its contrast to ourselves. The psychological domain that is not yet *self-aware*, namely, that which exists as natural material, is, precisely because it is natural, by and large universal, common through East and West. Needless to say, there are differences, but because they are natural differences, they are not issues of importance to us. A specifically European character must, however, be sought in what they [Europeans] produce with self-awareness. When it comes to self-awareness, we must say that it is indeed academic inquiry that, in terms of its fundamental nature, serves as its prototype. And it is indeed in academic inquiry in particular that we sense not only a difference in kind from our own character but a contrast to it. It seems that what unifies Europe by vertically rendering it continuous and horizontally organizing it, and at the same time also constitutes a contrast with the East, indeed lies in the idea of academic inquiry and its tradition. At very least, to us a psychological account of this difference that describes it as a mere intellectual or rational tendency is overly vague, tinged with arbitrariness, and insufficient to provide an objective, historical characterization. In principle, too, this presumably goes no further than merely describing differences in natural history.

The character of a culture is determined according to the position academic inquiry occupies within the system of that culture in relation to religion, morality, politics, and so on. Indeed, the existence of academic inquiry itself, as distinguished from religion and morality, already anticipates an original cultural character. As a result, the concept of academic inquiry is itself problematic. In the Eastern tradition, aside from academic inquiry that *is* religion or academic inquiry that *is* morality there is in general no academic inquiry as academic inquiry itself—academic inquiry as *philosophia*. To put it the other way around, generally speaking, academic inquiry that is *not* at the same time religion or morality is an idea of academic inquiry that is distinctly European. Even under Christian dominance during the medieval period, *studium* stood independently in contrast to *sacerdotium* and *imperium*. In other words, the independence of academic inquiry was acknowledged in relation to religious and political authority. The *artes liberales* were recognized as rivals of theology. Ultimately the establishment of this idea of "academic inquiry" was a single event in history and not something natural or universal.

Moreover, it was through the formation of academic inquiry of this character that Europe first gained independence from Eastern thought. It is a fact that Western learning owes its motivation and the acceleration of its development to the more advanced nations of the East. The academic inquiry of Babylon, Assyria and Egypt played a triggering role in the establishment of academic inquiry in ancient Greece. Thales, Democritus, and even Plato—according to legend, at least—studied abroad in the East. At the beginning of modernity, too, Western academic inquiry was spurred by that of Arabia and Persia. But although each of these [other traditions] still served as its impetus, they did not constitute its moments. There is nothing Egyptian in Greek geometry. On the contrary, they [the Greeks] were aware of this contrast from the start. The mission of Thomas Aquinas was to *distill* the academic inquiry of Aristotle from the Arabic and Jewish traditions. No further explanation is needed when it comes to the academic inquiry of Galileo. The academic inquiry of Europe is both purely and completely European.

What was it that allowed the academic inquiry of Europe to become independent from that of the East and form its own character? To give a preliminary answer, the idea of European academic inquiry is established on the basis of a three-in-one relationship between "metaphysics", "physics", and "mathematics". Metaphysical speculation as well as mathematical scientific knowledge, in themselves, not only were not absent in the East, but on the contrary were [developed] earlier and in some cases even more prominent [than in the West]. But nothing like the formation of a system of academic inquiry through the interrelationships of these three academic fields, even with their mutual differentiation and independence, ever occurred in the East. This means that in the East science distinguished from metaphysics, mathematics distinguished from science, and metaphysics distinguished from science did not exist, and, ultimately, that philosophy, science, and mathematics in a strict sense did not exist either. In other words, metaphysics as metaphysics, physics as physics, and mathematics as mathematics were nowhere to be found.

Astronomy that was *Astrologie* in the East became *Astronomie* in Greece. But when Alexander's Eastern expeditions gave rise to Greek academic inquiry in the East, Western *Astronomie* again became *Astrologie*. The later *revival* of *Astronomie* during the Renaissance was a revival of the Western spirit. What formed the background of *Astrologie*, however, was not necessarily mere "superstition" but rather academic inquiry of a different character. It assumes as its fundamental experience an Eastern naturalism or Eastern sympathy that intuits the *Sympathie* of all beings in the world—the sympathy of heaven and earth—whereby celestial phenomena correspond to human matters. In this sense it is a metaphysic that is also a physic, and at the same time even an ethic. To put it the other way around, here there is no metaphysics (*Meta-physik*) that transcends physics (*Physik*) and no physics distinguished from metaphysics. Any kind of academic inquiry is physics and at the same time metaphysics, metaphysics and at the same time physics. Thus in a strict sense this is neither metaphysics nor physics but rather *practical learning* [実学]. Academic inquiry, in the end, has a completely different genealogy and a completely differing character in the East and in the West.

The subject of our investigation, then, to begin with, is this branching of academic inquiry into physics, metaphysics, and mathematics, and its meaning, and in particular the character of mathematics as distinguished from physics and metaphysics and the significance of its establishment [as an independent field of inquiry]. We must first recognize the distinctness of this mathematics. As will be made clear later, physics and metaphysics were separated and distinguished through the establishment of mathematics as their mediation, and moreover came to form a three-in-one system through their interrelationships while mutually standing in contrast to each other. The establishment of mathematics, accordingly, becomes the impetus behind the formation of the European idea of academic inquiry. For this reason it will be our focus. The issue we are addressing here is not simply one of external social constraints or the natural aptitudes of this ethnic group, but rather one of its spirit, or, in other words, its intellectual history.

13.2 Concerning the History of Mathematics as Intellectual History

Today mathematics is a discrete, autonomous science and constitutes a purely formal field of inquiry independent of philosophy and other qualitative sciences. In theory today's mathematics is composed of the formal manipulation of pure thought independent of all empirical content. Such a mathematics, however, is a *result* of the development of modernity. And this is not a fact that *exists* everywhere but rather a particular occurrence that arose historically. The ordinary history of mathematics is the history *of* mathematics. It is the history of the development of mathematics that already exists as mathematics. But this presupposes the establishment of mathematics itself. Or, rather, there is no awareness of its genesis. Our concern is not the history of mathematics, but the history *towards* mathematics. It is not simply a history of the natural occurrence of mathematics, but a history of the spirit of the formation of mathematics. In this case, however, what sort of thing is this "spirit"?

In the modern era, culture in general, as something that has been cultivated and formed, has been contrasted with "nature" that exists on its own. That which creates this culture is nothing other than "spirit". Culture is nothing other than spirit made objective. Although spirit is persistently internal, as something that always expresses itself through what is objectively formed and not as an individual subjective consciousness it is "objective spirit". The form of existence and character of spirit are only *substantiated* through culture as its product. It is indeed through the creation of this culture that spirit itself takes form. There are no objective grounds for interpreting the character of spirit apart from its artifacts. This being the case, however, because these artifacts that are the only clue to interpreting spirit are not "things of nature" but rather "things of civilization" [文物], they are essentially historical. The products of spirit are never completed. Put plainly, they are living and moving. Even works of art that exist as things, such as, for example, paintings and sculptures, cannot be said to have been completed once the artist stops working on them. Works, independently of the artist's will, and in some cases in opposition to the artist's intent, give rise to transformations with the passage of time. This is not limited to *natural* alterations in their pigments or other materials. At the same time these natural alterations themselves give rise to qualitative changes—such as a *"deepening with age"* [蒼古]—and come to be appreciated in different ways. A work's external alteration at the same time results in its internal alteration, that is, in the transfiguration of the work's spirit. This alteration in a work is therefore not merely a *becoming* but at the same time possesses a formative character. This is why such a work truly differs from "things of nature". An artifact of the spirit is never ultimately completed. Even "ruins" possess beauty.

This incompleteness, however, becomes something particularly *essential* within products of culture that, like academic inquiry, do not simply exist as an objective thing but are always being subjectively, historically, socially, collaboratively, and continuously carried out. This alteration is not at all natural, but rather artificial and consciously formative. Such a cultural product not only undergoes transfiguration but qualitative change due to constantly being reflected upon and critiqued. For this reason it is impossible to directly *surmise by analogy* its origins from its current state. Because this is something formed and not something that has simply emerged, the issue is not simply its origin but the spirit lying at the root of its formation and the spirit's development in that formation. Even if the origin of probability theory is in the game of *sugoroku* [a board game similar to backgammon], this is irrelevant to the question of the spirit of the formation of probability theory.

This kind of approach is therefore necessary when we attempt to address the intellectual history of mathematics. It is not an approach concerned with the *psychological* process of the establishment of mathematics, nor does it simply take external social restrictions as the issue to be addressed. In either case this is nothing other than *natural history*. The issue in intellectual history is history experienced by spirit in which mathematics, which had originally been merely a technique for calculation and measurement, came to be understood as an indispensable [part of] the education of sages and national leaders, and became a field of inquiry that could be said to display divine wisdom and eternal features. It is the tracing of the self-awareness and development of spirit through the establishment and transfiguration of mathematics. In the intellectual history of mathematics, the issue is not the "mathematics of nature" that is directly related to technics, but rather the "mathematics of spirit", so to speak, and its establishment. To begin with, what sort of spirit is this spirit that forms such a mathematics? What is its significance in terms of intellectual history and what sort of conclusions does it lead to? We are attempting to trace the phenomenology of the spirit of European academic inquiry in this *genesis* of mathematics. This is thus to all extents an intellectual history rather than a psychological history of mathematics.

But for what reason has mathematics in particular been chosen? For what reason is the genesis of mathematics a phenomenon of the academic spirit?

"Counting" or "measuring" are the most fundamental [modes of] thought and the most primeval methods of thinking. But the primeval nature of numerical thinking is fundamental and not simply viewed in its genesis. Numerical thought is as mundane and everyday as can be, and at the same time is connected to the most otherworldly [彼岸的]. *Zahlenmystik* [numerology] was not simply a particular idea unique to the ancient Pythagorean school, but is a universal phenomenon. In any case it is a fact that even in some corners of our civilized society a *Zahlenmystik* that recognizes in numbers a fateful magical power continues to exist. Even if not consciously so, this must be said to be at least the remnant of a universal *Zahlenmystik*. Here numbers are not mere forms of thought but to all extents a category of being, or indeed symbols of transcendent being. What indicates this fact is that numbers in essence are not limited to simply the everyday and the technical, but at the same time also possess the character of being symbols of fate and the superhuman. To generally notice in numbers only a technical and practical meaning as is the case today is on the contrary a modern development, and indeed something that characterizes modern thought. The existence of a large number of mathematicians and the publication of a large quantity of papers on mathematics is something very recent. The relationship of numerical thinking to what is most primeval, and indeed transcendent and mystical, in human beings is not based simply on the primeval and undeveloped nature of [this] thinking. We ought to remember that numbers have in fact been thought of as ultimate principles by the great philosophers of each period. The domain of numbers extends from the mundane and technical art of calculation to mathematics as a form of academic inquiry, and beyond them to the domain of metaphysics. Not limited to simply abstract, formal questions, it relates to issues of reality. To put it another way, thinking involving numbers is not a domain of thinking specifically human, but rather a universal domain and a fundamental [type of] thinking. The domain related to mathematics is in the end being in general, or the world. This is why there is an especially close connection between mathematics and philosophy. This is why the metaphysical genealogy of mathematics must be explored.

What is important here, however, is that counting is not directly [equivalent to] the counting of *numbers*. Numbers are *formed* in the standpoint that abstracts the individuality of individual things and sees them as simply something abstract, a universalizing standpoint. Only by having their individuality or particularity abstracted and removed and by being universalized can individual things each be counted simply as "a single thing". This is why uncivilized people and infants can only count things of the same kind. Although when engaging in such unsophisticated ways of thinking they assume universal or abstract numbers of some sort, they are simply anticipating them rather than being immediately aware of them or forming them. Unsophisticated numbers are the numbers of things. Here the distinction between number and the thing counted does not yet obtain. Only through this conscious distinction are numbers formed. Although counting as the most primitive form of thought exists in ethnic groups and societies of any level [of development], the concept of number as independent of that which is counted is not something that necessarily always exists; indeed, to formulate this concept with self-awareness, organize a system around it, and construct "mathematics" as a purely academic field is an extremely rare historical occurrence, which in actuality was only undertaken by the Greeks. Mathematics carves out numbers as thoughts or concepts and forms them into a system. The systemization of numbers is the numericicization of the system of being, and eventually a numeric formation of the world. Presumably this must in the end again anticipate the formation of "logic". While every ethnic group engages in numerical thinking, not all of them possess *mathematics* in this sense. We must strictly distinguish everyday numerical thinking and mathematics as an academic inquiry. It was the genius of the Greeks that formed mathematics as an academic inquiry. Although pieces of mathematical knowledge had probably existed in abundance among various ethnic groups from ancient times, the idea of "mathematics" as an academic inquiry had never existed before. As a result such fragments cannot be compared, as a systematized academic field, to the mathematics of Greece and of the West that inherited it. Confusion often arises on this point. Mathematics as an academic inquiry is indeed something that requires ingenious, logical formation and is not an occurrence that arises naturally. This is to all extents a formation of thought in general in, or through, numbers. Mathematics is the conception of the world through numbers. At the same time, as a philosophical issue it is something that presumably requires the speculative labor of philosophers for its constitution. It was indeed first achieved through the participation of the philosophers of [ancient] Greece. This was indeed what Plato's Academy took to be its own task. The intellectual history of mathematics therefore necessarily possesses an internal connection to the history of philosophy.

The fact that philosophy was internally and essentially related to mathematics constitutes the most fundamental characteristic of the Western philosophy that has inherited the tradition of Greek philosophy, particularly in contrast to Eastern philosophy. But this fact in itself was not limited to being a merely accidental occurrence in the history of Western philosophy. On the contrary it formed its essence and defined its character.

This fact, however, does not necessarily mean that "philosophy" and "mathematics", academic disciplines that were established and have existed independently of each other, have always influenced one another or were combined with one another. To attempt to assert this would not only evidently amount to hyperbole, but by itself would still not allow us to say that a particularly internal and essential connection necessarily exists between them. For example, a relationship such as that which exists between contemporary philosophy and mathematics does not appear to be one that can necessarily be described as an internal and immediate connection. On the contrary, contemporary mathematics and philosophy are independent of each other; there is no place where mathematics and philosophy are immediately combined apart from so-called "mathematical philosophy". Even this, from the start, was not a complete union of philosophy and mathematics; to philosophy, it is nothing more than a set of *particular* philosophical questions, not the very question of philosophy itself. Nevertheless, contemporary mathematical philosophy, as the so-called "grounding" of mathematics, presupposes as a fact the mathematics that already exists without relying on philosophy. Ultimately this means the rejection here of an original, essential relationship between mathematics and philosophy. If we limit ourselves to this kind of relationship, we can say the same in regard to all other domains of academic inquiry, and there would be no need to postulate an internal relationship with mathematics in particular. For this reason it is clear that this is not the position from which we seek to recognize the internal relationship between philosophy and mathematics in particular.

Indeed, even today mathematical philosophy does not simply amount to a "grounding" of mathematics in this sense. But at the same time, it cannot be denied that this sort of relationship, to a certain extent at least, possesses a necessity in the history of philosophy and constitutes an actual state of affairs. But recalling the period of Descartes or Leibniz, for example, should be enough [to confirm] that this is, strictly speaking, a *singular* historical relationship, a singular historical *state of affairs*, and does not exhaust the relationship between philosophy and mathematics in general. We cannot say that they were philosophers *and* by coincidence *also* mathematicians. It is clear from the fact that mathematical methods were directly connected to philosophical methods that in their time philosophy and mathematics were not necessarily two independent academic fields. Spinoza's *Ethica ordine geometrico demonstrata* [*Ethics, Demonstrated in Geometrical Order*] was not simply an *application* of mathematical methods to philosophy. Only in Kant's period does the distinction between mathematics and philosophy become an *issue*. One of the central questions in his discussion of the transcendental method in *The Critique of Pure Reason* was, as is widely known, the distinction between philosophical knowledge and mathematical knowledge. "The essential difference between these two kinds of rational cognition consists in their form, and does not rest in their matter, that is, their objects" (K.d.r.V., B.742). Mathematics throughout these periods, in the end, was in the process of *becoming*. And to this extent we must also say that philosophy, too, was connected to this genesis of mathematics and was at the same time in the process of *becoming* towards its own form. It was in the nineteenth century that this distinction between philosophy and mathematics was no longer an *issue* but had become a *fact*.

This state of affairs is not limited to a unique and particular *trend* of the times found only in modernity. We can indeed discover something analogous to this even in the history of ancient Greek philosophy.

Mathematics—mathematics as an independent academic inquiry—was indeed only *established* after passing through this process. Mathematics did not *exist* beforehand as mathematics but was *established* by *coming into being*. Moreover, philosophy was involved in this genesis of mathematics, and this fact conversely was the development of philosophy itself, its self-formation. It is only at the point where the formation of philosophy and mathematics is reciprocal and mediating that we can begin to recognize the essential internal connection and union between philosophy and mathematics.

In any case, the state of affairs in which philosophy and mathematics exist by and large independently such as pertains today—although, of course, not only today —is without doubt also an actual historical fact. But this too is ultimately only the relationship of a single historical stage, and goes no further. Here the "mathematics" that already *exists* in itself is an *outcome* of becoming. Today we cannot help but acknowledge the existence of mathematics as mathematics—mathematics that subsists without relying on philosophy. But have we not perhaps become too accustomed to the existence of mathematics? Are we not then inclined to neglect the *establishment* of mathematics itself and its significance? But the development of mathematics is not simply a development *within* mathematics. Mathematics has not only developed simply *as mathematics*; there was development not only *inside* mathematics but also *towards mathematics. Mathematics itself came into being.* The issues we actually address in the history of mathematics today all generally remain confined to developments within mathematics as though there were no issues to be addressed concerning the historical *establishment* of mathematics itself. This is the general *assumption* of today's history of mathematics. If anything, it is a dogma. It is not simply the dogma of historians of mathematics, however, but indeed one of the current era in general.

In other words, an analogous assumption exists in our history of philosophy as well. It goes without saying that the systematization of our history of philosophy was first formed in Hegel, or at least upon Hegelian foundations. This history of philosophy is nothing other than a history of the development of philosophy out of philosophy. It is also a fact that the concept of philosophy we actually possess is in some sense based on this. And in quite the same way this [assumption] itself is also problematic. But I will not get into this right now.

The same can also be said of the relationship between philosophy and science. It is certainly one consequence of historical becoming that philosophy and science exist side-by-side while being mutually independent as they do today, and this is not a state that is universal and constant. Indeed, science itself came into being and was established correlatively with philosophy. But of course this is not to consider philosophy and science to be at different stages or phases of development as Comte did, for example, or to take the establishment of science as the ultimate stage [in the development of philosophy]. Science was not originally something that emerged *separately from* and *outside of* philosophy. For example, when the natural science of modernity took an excessively antagonistic stance towards medieval Aristotelian, scholastic *philosophy*, at the *same time* it advocated a different *philosophy*, the so-called *"new philosophy"*.[8] In this way the active organization of modern science had to wait for the conscious formation of metaphysics of the seventeenth and eighteenth centuries in order to be established. Above all, what characterized, typified, and patterned *modern* science as *natural* science was nothing other than the concept of "nature" that was discovered and established by the metaphysics of this period. The natural science of modernity was first *established* by taking this as its fundamental principle. Its fundamental categories, no doubt, originate in the ontology first established by the metaphysics of modernity. To this extent natural science is indeed the *fruit* and *product* of modern philosophy. As a result, the establishment of a "science" that possesses an awareness of method—the *establishment* of natural science—occurred in the nineteenth century when the development of modern philosophy had been more or less completed. What had existed previously in early modernity was a physics that had not yet been distinguished from metaphysics, and a metaphysics that had not yet been distinguished from physics. A philosophy that takes science as a premise but takes a distinctive standpoint by opposing science—"transcendental philosophy"—is indeed something that belongs to the period of Kant. The relationship between philosophy and science thus cannot be unambiguously, mechanically stipulated. It is always correlative at the stage of "the period of the history of philosophy".

In this relationship between philosophy and science, however, mathematics intervenes and mediates [them].

As *mathematike*, mathematics in ancient Greece referred to the *subject of study* in general. Even when it came to mean a *particular* subject of study instead of "subject of study" in general, it still meant music, astronomy, arithmetic, and geometry. Each of these was a subject of study possessing a definite concrete content. In other words, this *Mathematik* was still *Physik*–physics. At least it was not independent of physics. It was not even exceptional for philosophers to be mathematicians. Nevertheless, only after passing through this *process* was pure mathematics—mathematics as mathematics—established. It was in Plato's later years that *mathematike* came to refer to the study of numbers in particular, and it was in Aristotle's school that this became firmly established. Its further compilation and organization would occur (passing through various preliminary periods in history) a half century later in Euclid's *Elements* [『原論』] (*Stoicheia*). The core sections of this text, however, are indebted to people like Archytas, Theaetetus, and Eudoxus, individuals who were connected to Plato or Plato's Academy. Euclid

---

[8] *"new philosophy"* is written in English in the original text (translator).

himself was a member of the Academy. From Plato onward, mathematics in principal became independent of philosophy; in other words, it became specialized. This signifies nothing other than the establishment of mathematics as mathematics.

In Plato mathematics is distinguished and made independent of physics, but it is still not necessarily distinguished from metaphysics. On the contrary, it is often numerical metaphysics. In Plato's successor, Speusippus, it is sheer numerical mysticism. But in the establishment of these distinctions mathematics was indeed in the process of becoming. Or, to put it another way, these distinctions themselves were nothing other than mathematics' process of becoming. In this way the formation of mathematics was *at the same time* its differentiation from physics and metaphysics, and its formation as itself.

This occurrence is also analogous to what took place in modernity. Within Descartes himself there was no awareness of his "analytic geometry" as a new "mathematics"; it was simply a technical method. *Consequently*, his *Principia philosophiae—Principles of Philosophy*—also includes such topics as the creation of the world and principles of meteorology. The modern idea of pure mathematics was first realized by Leibniz. It was through *this* Leibniz and Kant that modern "metaphysics", "science", and "mathematics" became distinctly established, and a unity through their respective divisions, namely, the organization of modern academic inquiry, emerged. To this end, Leibniz, like Plato, formed a logic of modernity and sought to *establish an "Academy"*—a global academy intended to organize the academic fields of modernity. This was not simply the fleeting inspiration of a genius.

The fact that these philosophers were at the same time scientists and mathematicians should not be attributed to the mere *personal* circumstance that the ancients happened to be *geniuses*. Rather, during that period philosophers themselves possessed such a character, and were at that stage [in their development]. The fact that this no longer happens in the modern period and "philosopher" no longer has a direct connection to "mathematician" is not due to the *quantitative* development of the various fields of study as they became broadly and diversely differentiated and specialized, but is rather entirely owing to the fact that these various fields of study themselves underwent a qualitative change. Therefore, as stated above, Descartes and Leibniz were not philosophers who were also mathematicians by happenstance. Philosophy, science, and mathematics were *directly* combined during their period, and, to put it plainly, mathematics, not yet independent as mathematics, was still in the process of becoming. The *differentiation* of philosophy and mathematics was still a question even in the era of Kant, and long after Newton and Leibniz the issue of the differential method continued to be a *metaphysical* issue in its relation to the "infinitesimal". The establishment of pure mathematics would have to wait another hundred and fifty years for the period of Cauchy and Weierstraß. It was not until the latter half of the nineteenth century that modern mathematics was at last able to obtain complete independence from philosophy. But this complete independence was then nothing other than the formation of pure mathematics. It was indeed at this point, too, that natural science became independent as natural science. Needless to say, the distinction between philosophy, mathematics, and science is not an issue today. But it has *ceased to be* an issue *at last*. To put it another way, mathematics has *finally* became established as mathematics. The history of mathematics must address not only the development of mathematics but also this development *towards* mathematics.

If mathematics was thus not something that had originally existed as mathematics in advance, but rather something that came into being and was established, we can and must distinguish *Vor-mathematik* [pre-mathematics] and *Meta-mathematik* [meta-mathematics] in contrast to *Mathematik* [mathematics]. But what does this distinction mean? What sort of significance exists in this distinction itself? Therein lies the impetus behind the intellectual history of mathematics.

Mathematics is something that comes into being. But what is especially important to keep in mind is that this is not a mere becoming but one in which philosophy too is involved. Conversely, *in* participating in this formation of mathematics and *by means of* participating in it, philosophy itself is *also becoming*, and the establishment of mathematics as mathematics eventually comes to mean at the same time the establishment of philosophy as philosophy. Mathematics that comes into being through its connection with philosophy, and philosophy that in turn comes into being in the formation of mathematics—both are academic developments particular to the West. This is the character of Western academic inquiry itself, or rather forms the character of Western academic inquiry itself.

As I mentioned earlier, in ancient times *Mathemata* primarily referred to "subject of study" in general and secondarily to the particular subjects of astronomy, music, arithmetic, geometry. While by extension it therefore encompassed the "physics (*Physik*)" that dealt with celestial bodies, musical scales, calculation, and land surveying, it was still not directly equivalent to the "study of numbers" [数の学]. Moreover, this "physics" was still not necessarily one that had been distinguished from "metaphysics" (*Metaphysik*). It was only when these natural entities could be reduced to principles of number that *Mathematik* became mathematics as the study of numbers independent of *Physik*. Mathematics did not originally exist as a science *dealing* with mere numbers but rather became established with the reduction of nature to number. This indicates that even "number" itself was not something that existed as a ready-made concept but rather something that could take shape only after laborious contemplation. To understand mathematics or numbers as spontaneously or naturally existing in advance is the result of either thinking of numbers as things, or at least of not conceiving of numbers as distinguished from things. A mathematics that is pure, however, is established here only by means of distinguishing a "one" itself that is not *one* stone, a "two" itself that is not *two* desks, forming a pure science of numbers (*arithmetike*) that is not simply a technique of calculation and measurement (*logistike*), and reducing the various disciplines of physics to a unified and single academic inquiry that takes numbers as its principle. These numbers are the product of formation through thought, and mathematics is the conception of the world by means of such numbers.

Through this establishment of mathematics, so-called formal entities transcending, and existing outside of, the entities of physics are discovered and classified. By means of this process, natural entities, in turn, at the same time came to manifest themselves as purely natural entities. When an entity's *form* is exposed, its *matter* is made distinct. We become aware of material nature that has as its essence motion and becoming in contrast to formal entities that are unmoving and constant. The formation of the mathematics of forms at the same time mediates the formation of the physics of matter. Here being is divided and split into natural entities and supernatural entities. A mathematical entity, as transcendent of natural entities, is itself a metaphysical (supernatural) entity. Herein lies the impetus that internally links mathematics to metaphysics. Mathematics is itself a metaphysic. This approaches the school of the Academy that Aristotle critiqued. But to distinguish mathematics from metaphysics is truly the establishment of mathematics as mathematics, and at the same time the formation of metaphysics as metaphysics. To put it another way, the method of transcending natural entities is not limited to this so-called mathematical transcendence. This is transcendence towards universal entities (that is, mainly ideal or possible entities) while including natural entities as *specific instances*. Within this standpoint natural entities have neither their own being nor their own significance. It only recognizes [in them] a merely negative and passive meaning. They exist only to be negated and transcended. In addition to this *idealist transcendence*, there is a method of transcendence that recognizes the realization of transcendental being in these natural entities themselves, namely the method of so-called *realist* transcendence, the sort that takes natural entities as *individuals* without simply negating them and recognizes in them the realization of the transcendent. This realism is of course no mere naturalism. It is a realism that, passing through the transcendence of nature, returns and reduces to nature with mathematical idealist transcendence as mediation. It is an immanentism that takes transcendence as mediation. Herein we discern the existence of a two-fold method of transcendence. This is what eventually distinguishes metaphysics in principle from both mathematics and physics and is nothing other than the self-awareness of the standpoint of philosophy as philosophy. It is the standpoint of the sage who, after emerging from the darkness of the cave, returns to it once again.

In this way the establishment of "mathematics" not only establishes "physics" but at the same time also establishes "metaphysics" (supra-physics). When mathematics is not formed as mathematics, neither a pure physics nor a metaphysics distinguished from physics is formed either. For this reason, through the establishment of mathematics, academic inquiry is split into mathematics, physics, and metaphysics, and together they form a system of interrelationship while remaining independent of each other. Here philosophy and science serve as the medium for the establishment of mathematics, and conversely mathematics serves as the medium for the establishment of philosophy and science. It is *in* the establishment of mathematics that philosophy as philosophy and science as science are established.

The idea of an academic inquiry with this kind of structure—namely, the idea of academic inquiry in which mathematics, physics (science), and metaphysics (philosophy) mediate each other and thereby constitute a triune structure—is a characteristic of Western academic inquiry, established only within the tradition of the Greek spirit and having existed nowhere else. Because in the East mathematics was never formed as mathematics, neither were physics formed as physics nor metaphysics as metaphysics. In the East there was academic inquiry as [*soku* 即] religion, morality, or political science. Metaphysics was immediately [equivalent to] physics and mathematics. Herein there clearly lies a fundamental difference in the character of the conception of academic inquiry. That is why we must reconsider the historical significance of the establishment of mathematics. This not only concerns mathematical thought but Western academic thought as a whole. An intellectual history of mathematics is thus required.

As I have repeatedly stated, if mathematics is simply knowledge or technics concerning numbers then there is no time or place in which it is absent. The same goes for religious or metaphysical speculation. These [forms of] thinking are the most fundamental and universal elements of human thought. But a pure mathematics distinguished even from physics and metaphysics, and moreover possessing, at the same time, an internal connection to them, is the inheritance of the tradition of Western academic inquiry and that which defines its character. This is also the underlying reason that [Western] philosophy and science differ fundamentally from those of the East. To begin with, throughout its history nothing directly corresponding to what is called "philosophy", "science", or "mathematics" in the West existed in the East. These terms [in Japanese] are all translations or neologisms.

In the end, the formation of a mathematics in which philosophy and science mediate each other was a development unique to Western academic inquiry. The characteristic distinction between academic inquiry in the East and that in the West lies here and derives from here. This establishment of "mathematics" was therefore *a world-historical event*, and we can say that it is here that Western academic inquiry became independent of the East. In the history of culture it is indeed the nations of the East that were more advanced. A culture of arts and sciences had already matured in Egypt, Babylon and Assyria long before the arts and sciences flourished in ancient Greece. But with the formation of this characteristic mathematics, the West for the first time obtained independence from the East.

This state of affairs remained unchanged in the modern period as well. Modern Europe, too, spurred on by the cultures of the East, such as that of Arabia and Persia, eventually set about forming its own academic inquiry, but what constituted the cause of this independence was indeed the spirit that takes the formation of this kind of mathematics as its guiding moment.

If, as described above, mathematics was formed through intermediation with philosophy, we must acknowledge that it is something not simply motivated by the technical issues of calculation and measurement but rather takes as its motive and content the issues of being in general—"the world".

The establishment of mathematics has as its origin the distinction and extraction of *arithmetike* from *logistike*. Numbers, which are the objects of mathematics, here are not "things" but "numbers" as first established through their formation in thought. Numbers as distinguished from things are the "form" and "essence" of things themselves. The organization of a *system* of pure mathematics is therefore the formation of the world's form in numbers. Mathematics is the "mathematics of the world". Mathematics is the conception of the world by means of numbers.

A metaphysical genealogy must be sought in mathematics. In actuality, religious or moral elements have existed within the content of mathematics as well.

As is widely known, the Pythagorean School, which became a hotbed of Greek mathematics, was originally a religious group, and its motivations for engaging in mathematics and central interests had an intimate relationship with music. In [ancient] Greece music was something that possessed a mystical, religious character and concealed within itself the truth of the world (see the next chapter).[9] Furthermore, unlike the sort of music found in modernity that is left up to free creation on the basis of individual inspiration, it was something determined and enacted by the *polis* and in general possessed a political and ethical character. It was even thought that innovation in music would entail political reform. The transformation of *Musikethik* [music ethics] into *Musikästhetik* [music aesthetics] was seen as the degeneration of music. The discovery that the structure of this sacred music was composed by simple numerical ratios was for them a most astounding realization. We can thus freshly comprehend their devotion to the mathematics involved in this and its prestige. *Logistike—the art of calculation—*was therefore indeed "something for merchants", but *mathematics* was truly the refinement of philosophers and statesmen. Mathematics was a noble academic inquiry associated with the study of political ethics. Greek mathematics was in fact formed out of Pythagorean and Platonic, that is, religious and ethical, motives. We can likewise also find geometrical mysticism among the motivations behind the formation of modern geometry.

If mathematics as an academic inquiry was established on the basis of the numerical formation of the world, this would suggest that historical typological differences in mathematics have also been established in relation to this [formation]. Owing to different conceptions of the world and different ways of understanding it, different formations of logic establish different mathematics.

The Greeks grasped being, and thus the world, in terms of forms. This world in general is therefore finite. Their thinking was an intuition of forms. The method of Greek mathematics was also in general intuitionistic. The concepts of numbers and geometrical figures each had their own forms and were isolated and discrete. Methods of authentication were conducted correspondingly.

Modernity, however, grasps true being—the world—in general as *infinite* (here I will not get into the issue of whether or not what lay behind this approach was the Christian worldview). Infinity, to the extent that it is infinite, cannot possess an immediate form, and as a result we are unable to directly intuit it. There can be no positive proof concerning infinity through intuition. The thinking of the infinite requires a "pure thinking" separate from the intuition of forms—pure thinking as a uniquely *modern* concept. To grasp the infinite in general is the fundamental issue of modern philosophy. It thus follows that the central issue of modern mathematics also lies in infinity. This is why the main branch of modern mathematics is the

---

[9]*Sūgaku no keijijyōgakuteki keifu* [「数学の形而上学的系譜」 "The Metaphysical Genealogy of Mathematics"], not included in this book (translator).

analysis of infinity. Presumably neither the fact that the method of differential calculus that is a fundamental method of [mathematical] analysis was not formulated until Newton and Leibniz, nor the fact that this topic was not simply a specialized, technical issue, but rather, as a question of the infinitesimal, a matter possessing an internal connection to the philosophical speculation of this period, should require any more detailed explanation.

Although previously infinity had been abandoned as something beyond the reach of the human intellect, in modernity it became positively grasped as something immanent within the finite. Leibniz's "monad", while itself a finite being, *expresses* the infinite universe. It does not simply possess an image of the infinite but represents within itself the infinite. The dignity of the "person" in Kant is an ethical expression of this ontology. An *objective* cognition of the infinite in Kant is an "idea"–an extreme transcending the limits of the empirical and actual. The practical standpoint makes it possible to accomplish this transcendence. The thesis of an idea itself is indeed something of a volitional, practical character. That which ventures to intuit what cannot be directly intuited is indeed the will. Or rather belief. Its ground is not something that exists on the side of objectivity, but rather something that can only be sought in the arena of the subjective. There is no guarantee other than internal certainty or internal consistency. The immanence of infinity within the finite and its volitional demand—this is what modern ontology entailed. To put this standpoint in epistemological terms, it is an idealism in which the subject is independent of, and superior to, the object. "Pure thinking" is indeed the character of the thinking found in this idealism.

"Pure thinking" is an internal thinking inside consciousness. It is thinking within subjectivity of a subjectivity that is independent of objectivity. It is a thinking that is possible solely within itself, and thus a thinking that takes *consistency* (*Konsequenz*) as its fundamental principle. It is therefore also a thinking independent of intuition and positive proof. Modern mathematics hangs on the *composition* of pure thought. The establishment of non-Euclidean geometry was probably what motivated the full awareness of modern mathematics as this sort of thing. The negation of the "axiom of parallels" can only be postulated principally and purely by taking up the standpoint of the possibility of thought rather than relying on positive proof through intuition. The non-intuitiveness, formality, abstractness, and so forth of modern mathematics derive from this character of *pure* thought as well. Grasping the infinite presumably becomes possible only with such modern thinking.

The immanence of infinity within finitude does not mean that the finite is immediately the infinite but rather that it is the *expresser* of the infinite. This concept of "expression" is directly linked to the concept of signs (symbols). The symbol renders the non-sensible into sensation, the non-intuitable into intuition. It is the finitization of the infinite. The infinite can only be grasped semiotically and symbolically. Modern mathematics of infinity had to become semiotic, algebraic rather than geometrical. The method of proof also had to be a formalism rather than an intuitionism. Here lies the historical reason that modern mathematics had to be a formalistic axiomatics.

Through the formation of this modern "mathematics" as "pure mathematics" founded upon *pure thought*, the "physics" of modernity was at the same time formed as an empirical and practical *positive science*. In contrast to pure mathematics as exclusively the thinking of a subject, the physics that became "natural science" took as its method experimentation as the cognition of objects. The experimental method is cognition among objects by means of objects. Truth here is not demonstrability = universal validity but positivity = objectivity. Herein is established the idea of empirical science as modern physics. Here the character of "reason" is not *logo-logical* [ロゴス的] = demonstrative but experimental = technical. Put plainly, this so-called experimental reason manifests itself not in "argument" but in the formation of "machines". Machines are not mere nature, nor are they an extension or imitation of nature; they are in truth the recomposition of nature. Or rather a "makeover"—a recreation. In time this becomes the transcendence of nature. It also eventually becomes the establishment of a metaphysics that transcends physics. The metaphysics of modernity is not the metaphysics of forms found in antiquity; not a metaphysics of the standpoint of intellectual intuition, but instead one characterized by the standpoint of volitional practice. Practice, according to Kant, is something made possible by freedom. [He] distinguishes and contrasts internal subjectivity from external objectivity and recognizes the predominance of the former over the latter in the freedom of subjectivity from objectivity. If freedom is established in this transcendence over the object or nature, and if "spirit" (*Geist*) is established on this basis, then we can presumably say that the formation of machines is indeed its complete transcendence. The so-called mechanization of society in modernity must be conceived as having an internal connection to the metaphysics of modernity, *Geistesidealismus* [the idealism of spirit]. To think that this mechanized society threatens or dominates human beings is an *archaic* idealism that still thinks of it as objective nature.

Can we not perhaps find here as before, at the root of the branching and opposition in the conspicuous difference in outward appearance between mathematics, science, and philosophy in modernity, a triune system of all three?

To concretely trace in history what I have formally and schematically posited above is the next issue we must address.

Shimomura Toratarō (1902–1995). Born in Kyoto Prefecture. Graduated from Kyoto Imperial University's Faculty of Letters. Professor at Tokyo Arts and Sciences University (Tokyo University of Education). After reaching the age of retirement, became a professor at Gakushūin University. Writings include *Raipunittsu* [『ライプニッツ』 Leibniz] (Kōbundō, 1938), *Kagakushi no tetsugaku* [『科学史の哲学』 *Philosophy of the History of Science*] (Kōbundō, 1941), *Runessansu no geijutsuka—seishinshiteki kenkyū* [『ルネッサンスの芸術家——精神史的研究』 *Artists of the Renaissance: A Study in the History of Spirit*] (Chikuma Shobō, 1969). "The Position of Mathematics in the History of Spirit" was first published in *Sekaiseishinshi kōza* [『世界精神史講座』 *Lectures on the History of the World Spirit*] Vol. 7 (Risōsha, 1941), and was later included in *Philosophy of the History of Science*. It is included in *Shimomura Toratarō zenshū* [『下村寅太郎全集』 *Complete Works of Shimomura Toratarō*] Vol. 1 (Misuzu Shobō).

Chapter 14
Shimomura Toratarō: Tracking "Intellectual History"

[下村寅太郎――「精神史」への軌跡]

Takeda Atsushi

14.1 The Man Who Brought the "Kyoto School" to a Close

Allow me to begin our discussion with some personal reminiscences and emotions.

Today, the day on which I begin writing this text, is the fifth anniversary of Shimomura Toratorō's death. That is to say that he passed during the middle of the night on January 22nd, 1995 at his home in Zushi, Kanagawa Prefecture, at the age of ninety-two. Now, five years later, to refer to my teacher simply as "Shimomura" and write his name here is one stage in the inevitable process by which a man of the actual world, once possessing flesh and blood, now becomes merely a "person's name" and is gradually historicized and objectified. This period of five years may well have been the minimum time required for the transition from individual to universal, from reminiscence to assessment.

But the confirmation of this kind of "transition" is of course not merely something born out of my own personal feelings toward Shimomura. Shimomura lived later—in other words, until more recently—than not only the "major figures" featured in this book, such as Nishida and Tanabe, but indeed any of the philosophers included in the so-called "Kyoto School". In other words, he was the *last* to die. By living for ninety-two years, Shimomura, in a manner of speaking, took on the role of bringing the "Kyoto School" to a close. If this is indeed the case, then the "Kyoto School" that was drawn to a close with Shimomura's death must also encounter here its period of complete historicization and objectification.

To what extent was Shimomura himself conscious of this role? In his later years, amidst the passing of his senior, junior, and contemporary colleagues one after the

---

Translated from the Japanese by Robert Chapeskie and revised by John W. M. Krummel.

A. Takeda

other, Shimomura spent his days with composure, reading, writing, and producing numerous works, the last of which was *Burukuharuto no sekai* [『ブルクハルトの世界』 *The World of Burckhardt*]. At the same time, however, hearing the news of the deaths of his old friends one after another as his years multiplied, his sense of loneliness gradually deepened (I often heard him reminisce, "Prof. Tanabe used to ask us, 'Can you understand the sorrow of old age?', but now I am beginning to experience it myself"). The diary he left behind tells of how with each passing of a friend, in spite of the distance and despite his advanced age, he would rush to their funeral wherever it was being held. The last of these deaths during Shimomura's lifetime was presumably that of Nishitani Keiji, who passed away in 1990 (November 24th). The following day Shimomura set out immediately for Kyoto to "pay respects to the body". The next day, on the 26th, "Funeral service at two o'clock at Shōkoku-ji temple. I was the only one to offer a message of condolence".[1] We cannot explain these actions of Shimomura simply by referring to his conscientious character or the depth of his friendship and loyalty. As he began to have premonitions of the "fatality" of his long life, Shimomura presumably became increasingly aware of his "duty" as the one who would likely bring this school of philosophy to a close. If so, how was the "Kyoto School" understood in Shimomura's own mind, and how did he position himself within it?

14.2 Up to *Kagakushi no tetsugaku* [『科学史の哲学』 *Philosophy of the History of Science*]

Shimomura Toratarō was born in 1902 in Kyoto's Shimogyō ward (now Higashiyama ward). After graduating from a local elementary school, he followed the standard course of talented students, attending the Dai-ichi [The First] Middle School, Dai-san [The Third] High School, and Kyoto University. Oddly enough, of all the major philosophers belonging to the Kyoto School he was the only one born and raised in Kyoto. Needless to say, the appellation "Kyoto School" derives from Kyoto "University" and is not rooted in the geographically area bearing this name. Nevertheless, philosophy, though a universal science, cannot escape the influence of its milieu, and this is even truer when it comes to "philosophers". To the aesthetic sensibility of Kyoto native Shimomura Toratarō, the countrified manners of Noto peninsula native Nishida Kitarō must have been a shock. Conversely, as an encounter with someone antipodal to himself, this may well have engendered in him a deep sense of awe.

Regarding Tanabe Hajime, Shimomura himself writes in his diary, "I can sympathize with Prof. Tanabe's dislike of Kyoto people. But…the Kyoto people he

---

[1] "Chronological History", *Shimomura Toratarō chosakushū* [『下村寅太郎著作集』 *Collected Writings of Shimomura Toratarō*] (hereafter abbreviated as *Collected Writings*), Misuzu shobō, vol. 13, p. 630.

knows ... are outsiders and rustics who have come to Kyoto from elsewhere, and what surrounds him is not 'Kyoto' but its 'margins'".. "Kyoto people are not Osaka people—they are calm and quiet but uncompromising. Kantō [including Tokyo] people are assertive but surprisingly compromising. Professor Tanabe himself has this quality. The *Reflexibility*[2] of his thought is one manifestation of this." (October 25th, 1934).[3] Its name notwithstanding, the "Kyoto School" was indeed formed by what Shimomura referred to as "outsiders who came to Kyoto". The tendency to regard Shimomura as a figure easily overlooked within the "Kyoto School" may ironically have been the result of his having been a native of Kyoto. We shall return to this point later.

As for why Shimomura, a young man born "downtown" who would normally have been expected to enter a trade school, chose academia as his path in life, various explanations, such as his sense of incompatibility with the life of a merchant, an innate love of reading, and the influence of his older brothers who died young (he was the third son born to his family), can be offered on the basis of his own statements. But what made this vague orientation ultimately sublimate and condense in the direction of the philosophy of mathematics? Shimomura has often stated that although his true passion was history (Nishida had advised him to pursue the philosophy of history) and he had no aptitude whatsoever for mathematics, he nevertheless took the bold step of choosing the philosophy of mathematics in order to overcome an innate sentimentalism or romanticism. But at the same time he may well have sensed that in fact this stoicism was simultaneously an inversion of romanticism, and that within this very world of mathematics he had chosen there moreover existed a marmoreal romanticism of the highest degree.

Behind young Shimomura's decision there was also the backdrop of the rapid development of mathematics and physics in the West that ushered in the twentieth century, and the rise of the philosophy of mathematics that followed in its wake. If I may be permitted to give a rough summary of these developments, perhaps the crowning achievement in these fields was Einstein's discovery of the "principle of relativity" (1916), and in 1922 Einstein himself came to Japan (he had been awarded the Nobel Prize the previous year). Shimomura, twenty years old at the time, attended one of his lectures in Kyoto. An "Einstein boom" was erupting throughout Japan, but Shimomura, who had previously attended a lecture by Einstein's translator and interpreter, Ishihara Jun, would later say, "I was very shocked {by the fact that in his lecture Ishihara had said that he could not explain further without the use of mathematical formulas}.[4] Why couldn't he explain in ordinary language? Why was it possible to do so using mathematics? This may have been one of the triggers that led me to pursue the philosophy of mathematics".[5]

---

[2]"*Reflexibility*" is written in English in the original text (translator).
[3]Ibid., p. 586.
[4]Text in { } added by the author (Takeda Atsushi) (translator).
[5]Ibid., p. 575.

But the path ahead for Shimomura was by no means even. He received guidance from the autodidact Iemura Seiichi,[6] a mathematical genius. But he had not yet found favor with Nishida at Kyoto University and Tanabe was studying abroad. As the latter fell ill shortly after returning to Japan and had already moved away from the leading edge of the philosophy of mathematics, Shimomura's situation at the time was no doubt indeed as he later recalled it. "[Mathematics and physics today have already]created a magnificent, robust and elaborate system that towers like an impenetrable wall. Stepping suddenly inside, it is as though one is lost in dense and deep woods, unable to find a way out or even a direction in which to head. There didn't even seem to be any space into which a philosopher might stick his nose. My gloomy wandering continued".[7]

Shimomura graduated from Kyoto University's Philosophy department in 1926, but he often recalled being the last among both his seniors, including Miki, Kimura, Kōsaka (Masaaki), Tosaka, and Nishitani, and his juniors such as Kōyama (Iwao) to be "accepted" by both teachers (Nishida and Tanabe). His graduation thesis was not published in *Tetsugaku kenkyū* [『哲学研究』 *Philosophical Studies*], regarded as the gateway to success for promising young scholars. (What occasioned Shimomura's self-awareness that he had been "accepted" by Nishida for the first time was the essay "Benshōhōteki sekai no sūgakuteki keitai" [「弁証法的世界の数学的形態」 "The Mathematical Form of the Dialectical World"] (1936).) Following this he made his claim for wider recognition with his first book, *Raipunittsu* [『ライプニッツ』 *Leibniz*] (1938), published as a volume of the *Seitetsu sōsho* [西哲叢書 *Western Philosophy Library*], followed by *Shizen tetsugaku* [『自然哲学』 *Philosophy of Nature*] (1939), and finally *Kagakushi no tetsugaku* [『科学史の哲学』 *Philosophy of the History of Science*], of which the text included in this book is a chapter. It was published in November of 1941, when Shimomura was thirty-nine years old.

14.3 *Philosophy of the History of Science*: The History Toward Science

The publication of *Philosophy of the History of Science* was framed, coincidently, by two events, one public and one private. The latter was a significant shift in Shimomura's own academic circumstances: in the spring of that year he was appointed assistant professor at Tokyo University of Arts and Sciences [東京文理科大学] and moved to Tokyo. This was the end of the "*Lehrjahre*" (training period —a favorite expression of Shimomura's) of his career, and, at the same time, a

---

[6]Iemura Seiichi (?–1948) is a figure worthy of detailed study, not only as someone who supported Shimomura's research on the philosophy of mathematics but also as an individual whose scholarship and abilities were held in high regard by Tanabe Hajime.

[7]"Dokusho manroku" [Reading Notes], *Collected Writings*, vol. 13, p. 44.

parting from his hometown of Kyoto as well as a mild form of desertion from his longstanding personal relationships with others in the "Kyoto School". The personal relationships that awaited Shimomura in Tokyo and its environs would greatly contribute to new developments in his academic life.

The public, external circumstance that framed *Philosophy of the History of Science* was the outbreak of the Pacific War [World War II], which followed closely on the heels of its publication. Amid the extraordinary increase in interest in science and technology as the key to modern warfare, the view that this great war was not simply a clash of military powers but a struggle between Western mechanistic civilization and the Japanese spirit was rampant, partly as a result of [state] coercion. From a bird's eye view, wars are often said to be a clash of civilizations, and this sort of understanding cannot necessarily be dismissed as nonsense. But in this case such arguments were for the most part quite superficial and myopic, and amounted to nothing more than, for example, trotting out a "Japanese science" in contrast to modern science and dwelling upon its superiority in a manner that can only be described as exemplifying the madness of state power that smothers academic inquiry. It was this book's fate, for better or for worse, that at the time of its publication its content was inevitably given a reception that was above all "timely", that is to say, *un*-"timely". It goes without saying that the gist of what its author, Shimomura, was asserting remained consistent from start to finish. Put simply, this corresponds to Shimomura's incisive remark given during the infamous "Overcoming Modernity" symposium held the following July: "The spirit that made machines—that is what we must problematize".[8] (Later on Shimomura would often say that he had been so astonished by the "frailty" of intellect and "shallowness" of the understanding of the West belonging to a portion of the symposium's attendees, including figures such as Kobayashi Hideo and Kawakami Tetsutarō who proudly flaunted the "Japanese spirit", that he stopped reading their works from that point on).

The composition of *Philosophy of the History of Science* is as follows: (1) The character of European academic inquiry (preface); (2) The position of mathematics in intellectual history; (3) The metaphysical genealogy of mathematics; (4) On the methodology of the theory of science; (5) The concept of the human being today/ the position of the human being within nature.

Let us begin by attempting to extract the main thrust of this text from its preface. The book "attempts to reflect upon the character of academic inquiry [of European culture] as one moment" of European culture, and "the particular focus on mathematics …" is "…because… [Shimomura] thinks that the unique character of European academic inquiry can be discovered through this [field]". Above all "the formation of *pure mathematics* was not only a unique event in Europe, but a *world historical* event".[9] In Chapter Two the intellectual history of mathematics is defined

---

[8]For a discussion of *Kindai no chōkoku* [『近代の超克』 *Overcoming Modernity*], see Chap. 17.
[9]*Kagakushi no tetsugaku* [『科学史の哲学』 *Philosophy of the History of Science*], *Collected Writings*, vol. 1, pp. 143–144.

as "a history experienced by the spirit wherein mathematics that was originally a mere technique of calculation and measurement became mathematics as an academic inquiry that came to be understood as [part of] the essential education of the sages or leaders of the nation-state and said to display divine wisdom and an aspect of eternity". He then poses his central question: "What sort of a spirit is this spirit that forms mathematics?"[10]

The conception of a "history *toward* science before the history of science" and an "*intellectual history* that addresses the becoming and establishment of fact"[11] was indeed itself an "event in intellectual history" within this country's academic circles. The opening of the preface is pregnant with tension: "For us, Europe is indeed the other. But it is an other with which we are mutually bound together in mutual opposition".[12] Then in Chapter One Shimomura writes, "Europe is for us already not the other side but this side... not a 'thing' but a 'thou'". And "it is particularly in us Japanese that the 'world' in the sense of East vs. West ...including intellectual culture becomes universally and completely an *issue*".[13] The understanding that Europe is *already* the "issue" of "us Japanese" ourselves, while constituting a sharp critique of the "timely" trends mentioned above, at the same time goes far beyond this, becoming the fundamental motif of Shimomura's subsequent "intellectual history".

14.4 "Philosopher" as "Historian"

The project Shimomura undertook after *Philosophy of the History of Science* is revealing. In comparison to his previous work that had thematized the establishment of Greek mathematics, in the subsequent *Mugenron no kōzō to keisei* [『無限論の構造と形成』 *The Structure and Formation of the Theory of Inifnity*] (1944) he gave modern mathematics the same treatment. (Until the end of his life Shimomura regretted stopping at set theory and not being able to address continuum theory). The excellent environment at his new place of employment, Tokyo University of Arts and Sciences (which later became the Tokyo University of Education), and his close companionship with mathematicians and physicists he met there, including Sugawara Masao, Nakamura Kōshirō, Tomonaga Shinichirō, and Fujioka Yoshio, as well as others such as Suetsuna Joichi who lived nearby, all of whom were around his own age, provided him with knowledge and a free and generous academic atmosphere he had been unable to find in Kyoto. It was such to his liking that

---

[10]Ibid., p. 193.
[11]"Chosaku henro" [『著作遍路』 "Pilgrimage Through Writing"], *Collected Writings*, vol. 13, p. 304.
[12]*Kagakushi no tetsugaku* [『科学史の哲学』 *Philosophy of the History of Science*], *Collected Writings*, vol. 1, p. 143.
[13]Ibid., pp. 147–148.

Shimomura would later reminisce, "This was a delightful time in my university life"[14]. (Over time the intellectual exchange that developed with these figures at its core broadened, became multilayered, and culminated in the founding of the Japan Association for Philosophy of Science in 1953).

In 1945, two months after Nishida Kitarō's passing Japan surrendered unconditionally, and the so-called post-war order rapidly took shape. Replacing the Right and its ultranationalists that had been running rampant, the Left and its pseudo-modernists reveled in their spring in all corners of academia and the press. Shimomura once again had to struggle against another current of "timely" violence. At the same time he also participated in the editing of *Nishida Kitarō zenshū* [『西田幾多郎全集』 *Collected Works of Nishida Kitarō*], completing it after seven years, and engrossed himself in his own distinctive understanding and interpretation of Nishidian philosophy.

Taking the fruits of his previous research as its foundation, Shimomura conceived "a historiology of modern science" [近代科学史論], placing Newton at its pinnacle as the consummator of the scientific revolution. In the end Shimomura was only able to realize this vision in an extremely incomplete form, and this too became one of his lifelong regrets. Later Shimomura became increasingly haunted by the idea of "incompleteness", eventually realizing that this was something that corresponded to his own disposition, and become deeply engrossed in it as a topic of contemplation. In this case, however, the "incompleteness" of his project was made inevitable by the most significant event in the "intellectual history" of Shimomura himself. Before I discuss this event, however, let me first present another issue concerning the direction of Shimomura's own research.

As we have already seen, the starting point of Shimomura's scholarly career was the philosophy of mathematics. But from there Shimomura gradually shifted his focus to the history of science, and, drifting further still, to individual historical figures in the history of culture. Shimomura later reflected on his own spiritual orientation that "naturally bent in the direction of the history of science and the history of philosophy while aiming at a pure, originary philosophy of science", and, borrowing the words of Whitehead, explained that "the force of gravity is undeniable, and the spine is bent without awareness of it".[15] In Shimomura's case, this "gravity" was, of course, "history". "Interpreting" this, Shimomura later states, "Profs. Nishida and Tanabe, in each case, were logicians and not historians. ...but is it impossible for a philosopher to be a historian? ...I came to think that perhaps I am a historian instead of a logician, and this awareness grew stronger by degrees. Even when considering the issue of logic, I began to face the issue of the historicity of logic. Whether the philosophy of mathematics or the philosophy of science, they are both in fact the philosophy of the history of mathematics or of science; not the

---

[14]"Kōki" [「後記」 "Postscript"], *Collected Writings*, vol. 1, p. 486.
[15]Ibid., p. 484.

history of mathematics and the history of science, but the philosophy of the history of mathematics and of the history of science".[16]

The most momentous event in Shimomura's own "intellectual history" was his first visit to Europe, lasting three months, in 1956. Here too Shimomura is subtly influenced by "timeliness". What if the Second World War had never broken out and Shimomura had studied abroad when he was still young? (Nishitani Keiji, who graduated from Kyoto University two years before Shimomura, left to study in Germany in 1937.) This "what if" conjures images of youthful excitement. In actuality, however, Shimomura Toratarō set foot in Europe as a fifty-four-year-old middle-aged tourist carrying a single heavy trunk.

Regarding the overall picture of this trip, many details can be gleaned from *Yōroppa henreki* [『ヨーロッパ遍歴』 *Wanderings in Europe*] (1961), a work that can be said to have been written for a specific "avid reader": Tanabe Hajime.[17] In just one hundred days of rushing from place to place, Shimomura grasped in his own hands the "spirit" of Europe that he had imagined and groped for through his reading and contemplation. It was "like receiving a momentary flash or reflection", but here Shimomura turns the adverse circumstances into something positive, saying "impressions that have been obtained at a glance cannot necessarily be said to be any less deep or intense". "Mere knowledge" became "fact", and "[my] heart was filled with abundant and enormous 'existence' to the point of bursting. Now the task will be to digest and ruminate on this. It will be a task the end of which is difficult to gauge.[18]"

Later one and then another "task the end of which is difficult to gauge" were undertaken, and [his inquiry] continued to deepen. As a historian, Shimomura then began to openly display his inclination toward "history". Beginning with *Reonarudo da vinchi* [『レオナルド・ダ・ヴィンチ』 *Leonardo Da Vinci*] (1961) as a "*coup d'essai*", after *Asshishi no sei furanshisu* [『アッシシの聖フランシス』 *St. Francis of Assisi*] (1965), he discerned a point of contact between the history of science and art in *Runessansu no geijutsuka* [『ルネッサンスの芸術家』 *Artists of the Renaissance*] (1969, awarded the Japan Academy award) and [developed this] further through *Mona riza ronkō* [『モナ・リザ論考』 *A Study of the Mona Lisa*] (1974) and *Reonarudo, enkei to kinkei* [『レオナルド 遠景と近景』 *Leonardo: Background and Foreground*] (1977). In the meantime he published *Suēden joō kurisuchina* [『スエーデン女王クリスチナ』 *Christina, Queen of Sweden*] (1975), *Runessansuteki ningenzō* [『ルネッサンス的人間像』 *The Renaissance Image of Man*] (1975),

---

[16]"Chosaku henro" [「著作遍路」 "Pilgrimage Through Writings"], *Collected Writings*, col. 13, p. 344.

[17]While they were being serially published in the journal *Kokoro* [『心』*Mind*], Tanabe eagerly awaited each installment, and after reading it would immediately set down his impressions in detail and send them to Shimomura. Encouraged by this, Shimomura continued his writing as if addressing himself to his former teacher as his only reader. A total of twenty-two letters from Tanabe are included in the monthly report of each volume of the *Collected Writings*.

[18]*Yōroppa henreki* [『ヨーロッパ遍歴』 *Wanderings in Europe*], *Collected Writings*, col. 8, pp. 273–274.

Seishinshi no naka no geijutsuka [『精神史の中の芸術家』 *Artists in Intellectual History]* (1981), and other works before finally arriving at his dense masterwork *Burukuharuto no sekai* [『ブルクハルトの世界』 *The World of Burckhardt*] (1983). Shimomura had always professed that he was strongly drawn to what other people do not address. In regard to the above, hardly any of the topics he explored in these texts would have been subjects of "research" for most philosophers (at least not in Japan). But Shimomura was only interested in an approach to intellectual history that would address these figures.

Even though he employs the same term, "intellectual history", Shimomura's works after his European "experience" are of a markedly different character to those preceding it. In *Philosophy of the History of Science*, for example, intellectual history was "history" experienced by the "spirit [精神]" on the basis of the formation of mathematics as mathematics. But his interest now was not to address the formation of a science, but to advance closer to the lofty peaks of the histories of thought and of culture. Regarding this point, Shimomura would later write:

> Once a conclusion or an 'image' is completed regarding a certain issue or thinker, it is as if it separates from that process and begins to stand on its own feet within the author's mind. It often separates from its original form and takes its own independent journey. It moves towards logical simplification separate from facts... in a development not necessarily based on facts. To use my own phrase, towards 'axiomatization'. This image is reached through various processes, but once this endpoint is attained these processes are removed as superfluous, and we can say that it has been formalized or sculpted. By means of this... things such as deduction from axioms are frequently fashioned. Here a tendency towards separation from originary historical features arises. In my studies of Leibniz, Leonardo and Francis, this is what happened in each case.

Thus, "history of thought [becomes] intellectual history, ...[and] each thinker becomes a single *Typus* of spirit in intellectual history. They become 'heroes'. To me they are 'understood' in this way. The individuality of each is not erased, but typified and generalized". "In the case of Francis, imitation of Christ through poverty and owning nothing became the axiom of my image of him. ...I came to believe that the entirety of his life, words and actions could be derived from this".[19]

Once the "image" is fixed, it then "separates from its original form" and starts down the road toward "logical simplification separate from fact", or, in other words, "axiomatization". And once the "axiom" is established, "deductions" in turn are derived from it, and we arrive at the creation of a "*Typus*" through the "typification and generalization of individuality". This approach to "intellectual history" does indeed speak to Shimomura's origins in the philosophy of mathematics. At the same time, this approach was also presumably a theoretical pillar supporting Shimomura as he endeavored to be a "philosopher who is at the same time a *historian*".[20]

---

[19]"Chosaku henro" [「著作遍路」 "Pilgrimage Through Writing"], *Collected Writings*, vol. 13, pp. 364–365.

[20]"*historian*" is written in English in the original text (translator).

In the passages quoted above, the names of Leibniz, Francis and Leonardo are mentioned as objects of this [approach]. In the case of Leonardo, whose activities were far more multifaceted than those of St. Francis, and who, moreover, left behind *extraordinarily* brilliant works of plastic art and other disciplines, a one-dimensional application of this "approach" is difficult. In the end Shimomura wrote three volumes of books and many additional articles concerning Leonardo, but naturally in taking on this great genius of tremendous versatility he must have suffered from a frustrating sense of an unreachable itch. Nevertheless, the demonstration that in Leonardo "scientist", "artist", and "philosopher" constitute, so to speak, a *singularity* rather than a composite of A, B, and C, must be considered a major contribution of Shimomura's "intellectual history" to the study of Leonardo. A favorite phrase of Shimomura's was "Burckhardt saw Spain in Murillo and the Netherlands in Ruisdael",[21] and in this sense Shimomura himself indeed saw the Renaissance in Leonardo. This understanding then naturally led Shimomura to Burckhardt.

The World of Burckhardt was Shimomura's magnum opus written in his final years. Shimomura felt a kinship spanning a hundred years to the existence of Burckhardt as a human being, and at the same time I think he found in Burckhardt's philosophy—*his* "philosophy" that did not profess to be a "philosophy"—a foundation for the "philosophy of world history" he had been formulating for many years. "Among the various types of history", Shimomura writes in his notes, "only the history of art is an exception. The past *exists*[22] in the present. Works are not fragmentary but perfected and complete. They are existing in front of everyone."[23] There were many issues Shimomura would have wanted to unravel even if it meant taking them to the "next world", but chief among them were the "philosophy of world history" and magic as the root of the Renaissance (regarding the latter he left behind two enormous cardboard boxes of unfinished manuscripts).

14.5 A Philosopher of Kyoto

Now we return once again to the issue of the "Kyoto School" and Shimomura Toratarō.

To discuss this is difficult in two senses. First, when it comes to what the "Kyoto School" is in the first place, its conception is extremely unclear. Books like this one, of course, may provide us with some guidance. The selection of philosophers to be addressed alone may point us in the right direction. When it comes to this selection,

---

[21]"Kēgi *Burukuharuto to yōroppazō*" [Kaegi *Burckhardt and the Image of Europe*], *Collected Writings*, vol. 10, p. 328.

[22]"*exist*" is written in English in the original text (translator).

[23]*Rohen kūgo (shō)* [『炉辺空語(抄)』] *Fireside Conjectures (extracts)*], *Collected Writings*, col. 10, p. 566.

however, with the exception of Nishida and Tanabe the other names could all be replaced, and many other lists thereby compiled. The origin of the appellation "Kyoto School" is thought to go all the way back to Tosaka Jun, but to begin with how meaningful is the conceptualization itself of this kind of grouping of human beings that, to put it in commonly used terms, includes individuals from both the "Right" and the "Left"? Although it is a somewhat vague articulation, I would like to tentatively propose the following as a definition of the "Kyoto School":

> The whole intellectual network, centering around the two figures of Nishida and Tanabe, intimately and reciprocally formed over a period of three-quarters of a century by those who received the influence of both *directly*, both academically and personally (including after their passing).

To the extent that we remain within the customary interpretations of the "Kyoto School", Shimomura's influence is weak—or at least has been thought of as such. The lack of a "systematic nature" of the kind belonging to Nishida, Tanabe, and the school's other members has been raised, and this has been taken as equivalent to a lack of "originality". In addition, when Shimomura extended the domain of his own work from its origins in the philosophy of mathematics to include Francis, Leonardo and Burckhardt, it received the critical assessment from some (including even some of his students) that not only did it not belong to the "Kyoto School" but it was not even "philosophy". Putting aside the former criticism for the time being, as for the latter Shimomura would presumably not have deemed it worthy of a response. In labeling himself, Shimomura had no other term than "philosopher".

The assignments Shimomura took up in his later years, in addition to the two mentioned above, included the reexaminations of Leibniz, Newton, and Nishida, his uncompleted theory on landscape and portrait painting, and the issue of the history of philosophy. The establishment of a *history* of philosophy was an "event" that was first accomplished in Hegel, and it was Shimomura's heartfelt view that the consideration of this establishment itself was an important issue for philosophy to address. He planned to reconstruct the existing framework of the history of philosophy and work out how the "philosophy of world history" was to be positioned within it.

In regard to the "philosophy" of Nishida and Tanabe, while he acknowledged his deep intellectual debt to them, he could not help but become increasingly aware of their differences with himself. These differences were rooted in (what might be described as) distinctly Shimomura-like "logical" and "psychological", or rather, "physiological" traits.

> Professors Nishida and Tanabe are both *logicians*.[24] Their historical *sense*[25] is weak. ... How can history be established in the 'eternal now' [永遠の今] that is the fundamental standpoint of Nishidian philosophy? It is the continuity of the discontinuity of points [点の非連続の連続], from moment to moment. /In Tanabean philosophy as well, historicity is the 'moment that turns the past into the future.'[26]

---

[24]"*logician*" is written in English in the original text (translator).

[25]"*sense*" is written in English in the original text (translator).

[26]Ibid., p. 565.

Shimomura, having thus reaffirmed his own status as a "philosopher and a *historian*", then declares, "My own historical interest can be thought of as being connected to the demand to understand from the source. Because it is an understanding it is not a creation. However, my private conceit is that this understanding from the source makes it philosophical."[27] The following recently published "prediction" of Ōhashi Ryōsuke expresses an assessment [of Shimomura] by a member of a later generation that is full of expectation regarding the "demand to understand from the source": "With the publication of *Dirutai zenshū* [『ディルタイ全集』*Complete Works of Dilthey*], Dilthey's speculative system, called the 'philosophy of life' and forming one of the main currents of twentieth century thought, began to make its appearance",[28] and:

> I believe that circumstances similar to those found in the case of Dilthey, or conditions that gave rise to these circumstances, have now arisen with the publication of *Shimomura Toratarō chosakushū* [『下村寅太郎著作集』 *Collected Writings of Shimomura Toratarō*]. And in content, too, this [text] overlaps with Dilthey's thought.[29]

At the start I noted that among all of the members of the so-called "Kyoto School", Shimomura Toratarō was, surprisingly, the only one born and bred in Kyoto. The "Kyoto School" was in fact a circle formed by outsiders who had come to Kyoto from other regions, in other words, quasi-Kyotoites. Of course, as we have already seen, the "Kyoto" in "Kyoto School" perhaps ought to be read as "Kyoto University". Nevertheless, however, the history and milieu of the land that constitutes Kyoto is also of great importance.

I have no recollections of Shimomura actively addressing the topic of the "Kyoto School". (But he did mention several times, with the mischievous glint in his eyes he often displayed in his later years, that a book called *Kyoto-schule* or something of the sort had been published in Germany.) But Shimomura (as might be expected) loved Kyoto. Although he rejected repeated invitations from Kyoto University, and ultimately realized his desire to pass away in the Eastern region of Japan, his heart always remained in Kyoto. What then exactly was "Kyoto" in this case?

If I may dare to put it in so bold a term, it is "civilization" as symbolized by this eternal capital. It is a delicate yet formidable aesthetic intelligence that longs for "understanding from the source". When a (mathematics) conference was held in Kyoto not long after the war, Shimomura played the role of a tour guide for the "prominent figures of the world of mathematics", and after visiting Ryōan-ji temple he decided to introduce them to a "philosopher of Kyoto". He was referring to Hisamatsu Shinichi.[30] In this case, "philosopher of Kyoto", needless to say, did not

---

[27]"Pilgrimage Through Writing", ibid., p. 416.

[28]Ōhashi Ryōsuke, *Shimomura Toratarō—Seishinshi no naka no nihonkindai* [『下村寅太郎 — 精神史の中の日本近代』 *Shimomura Toratarō: Japanese Modernity in the Intellectual History*], Toeisha, 2000, p. 462.

[29]Ibid., pp. 454–455.

[30]"Hisamatsu Shinichi – aru hi no" [「久松真一――ある日の」 "Hisamatsu Shinichi —One Day of"], *Collected Writings*, vol. 13, pp. 144–145.

simply refer to philosophers residing in Kyoto. But neither did it *particularly* refer to "philosophers of the Kyoto School". Although the pages Shimomura devoted to Hisamatsu were few and he almost never spoke of him, his deep sense of respect [for this thinker] remained unshaken until the end of his life.

<Addendum>

A testimony more precious than any other for tracing Shimomura Toratarō's career as a "philosopher" and "writer" has been left by Shimomura himself. It is "Chosakuhenro aruiwa jigajisan" [「著作遍路あるいは自画自賛」 "Pilgrimage Through Writing or Self-Praise"], cited several times in this text, and it was published as an eighteen-part series in the journal *Sōbun* [創文] from 1982 (when Shimomura was eighty years old) to 1985. I would like to make two additional points about this text.

First, a general issue: the danger inherent in a work that documents the development of one's own thought as, so to speak, a "retrospective summary" written later (late) in life. As has often been said of Descartes' *Discourse on Method* [*Discours de la méthode*], for example, when an author attempts to depict his own "life" of decades past from the single point of the *present*, a powerful "ordering" is at work. The act of summarizing over a gap in time in relation to the *life* of the present gives the past, which was originally darkly amorphous, chaotic and disordered, shape, order, and meaning. "His" life that we know through this work is a life that has been given meaning after the fact and not the true state of his life at each point in time. Even in the case of this essay, which in many respects is based on "Pilgrimage Through Writing", the reader probably ought to be *wary* if it seems as though the tracks of Shimomura's life and thought are being traced too clearly.

Second, a certain "wariness" is necessary in regard to "Pilgrimage Through Writing" itself. Although, as noted above, this work was published serially in a journal, when an extensive ordering of Shimomura's library and study was undertaken after his death a "manuscript" in which all of the published pages have been heavily revised and amended was discovered. (This may have been because there was a plan to release the text as a book; such cases concerning other works are not uncommon.) The problem is that along with this discovery a considerable number of "supplementary" unfinished manuscripts were also "unearthed". As editor of the *Collected Writings*, I inserted these into this text at my own discretion while bearing in mind their period and content, and concerning what could be added or supplemented I dealt with them without concern for format or presentation (see *Collected Writings* vol. 13, "Concerning vol. 13").

In short, this means that the entire volume of "Pilgrimage Through Writing" is an *unfinished* manuscript, and as a result ultimately Shimomura does not bear full responsibility for what it says. At the same time, however, this also presumably raises the possibility that it contains Shimomura's otherwise unrevealed "true intentions".

In the final endnote I have also included the entire text of a postcard sent to the author by Tosaka Jun at the time this book was published.[31]

Takeda Atsushi Died in 2005. Major works: *Meijijin no kyōiyō* [『明治人の教養』 *The Culture of the People of Meiji*] (Bungeishunjyū, 2002), *Monogatari "Kyoto gakuha"* [『物語「京都学派」』 *The Story of the "Kyoto School"*] (Chūōkōronshinsha, 2001), *Nishida Kitarō* [『西田幾多郎』] (Chūōkōronshinsha, 1979).

---

[31]"Dispensing with the preliminaries, thank you, belatedly, for *Philosophy of the History of Science*. I want to say right away that although I actually read it for the first time only recently, I was very impressed. Excluding your Watsujian methodology, I am in whole-hearted agreement with your emphasis on "intellectual history". If I may say so, culture, for example, exists everywhere (even in the Andaman islands and New Guinea), but the spirit of culture, the conscious formation of culture, is probably quite rare. And because there are indeed many places in which my own ideas have been put in order, I think this is a book that I will have to keep and not sell. There are places that today's light-headed bunch need to read slowly and reflect on deeply. Surely one who 'recommends' this book brings honor not to the author but to himself. I think there are points remaining concerning the issue of science and technology, but I will give them some thought [before sharing them with you]. (Give my regards to your wife). April 1st, 1942."

Part VIII
Nishitani Keiji

Chapter 15
Nihility and Emptiness

[虚無と空 (1–5)]

Nishitani Keiji

One of the greatest, most fundamental issues all religions are now facing is their relationship to science. The worldview found in science, or the scientific view of things in general, appears to be fundamentally incompatible with the worldview and ontology that religions have on the whole taken as their foundation. Some may perhaps object that these worldviews and ontologies are not religion but metaphysics or philosophy, and bear no relation to the essential life of religion. There is an element of truth to this, but it cannot be said to be the whole truth. Every religion, when concretely established, that is, as a historical actuality, always includes, even if in an unconscious form, some kind of worldview or ontology as its foundation. For a religion, such a "philosophy" is not comparable to a suit of clothes that can be changed at will. It is an essential condition, like water is to a fish, for it to be established in actuality. Water is neither the fish's life itself nor its body, but it is essentially connected to both of these things. A change in worldview or ontology would be as fatal to a religion as being moved from salt water to fresh water would be for a fish. Therefore the assertion, often repeated, that religion and science each has its own domain and the two will thus never come into conflict as long as they remain within their own fundamental boundaries, is untenable. The boundary between the two domains divides them but at the same time belongs to both, and it is indeed at this boundary that the root of the problem lies. In fact, it can be said that from ancient times metaphysics and philosophy have consisted in the investigation of this boundary between science and religion. There is no buffer zone between science and religion. And today the issue of boundaries has reached the point of becoming a question of whether or not a boundary even exists. For today, from the standpoint of science itself, the boundary of its standpoint is, by and large, not an issue. In other words, the scientific standpoint displays, perhaps as an

---

Translated from the Japanese by Robert Chapeskie and revised by John W. M. Krummel.

K. Nishitani

essential component, the tendency to overlook not only religion but also philosophy —at least if we exclude the kind of "scientific" philosophy that makes the scientific standpoint itself directly into a philosophical one. That is to say that science seems to view its own standpoint as one of absolute truth from which to assert itself categorically. As a result, today we can no longer content ourselves with the customary method of drawing boundaries. The issue is even more deeply critical than the proponents of so-called "crisis theology" believed.

The basic reason that science can view its own standpoint as absolute truth lies in the complete objectivity of the laws of nature that are both the premises of scientific cognition and its content. No discourse from any other standpoint can interpose when it comes to elucidating the laws of nature accomplished by science. Criticism and corrections of this elucidation must be carried out exclusively from the scientific standpoint. Thus, even when such an elucidation has an essentially hypothetical character, its content is always presented as objective fact. This may account for the unique power that science enjoys, the intrinsic authority of being scientific. But if so, does this mean that religion, philosophy, art, and the like are no more than subjective opinion in virtue of the absolute character affixed to scientific cognition? Is scientific truth, with its absoluteness, the all-encompassing truth? Is it really impossible that along with the absoluteness of scientific truth, absolute truths might be established in each of these other domains? The establishment of multiple absolute truths may seem preposterous. We think of two absolute truths as entailing a contradiction, and that only one of them can be true at a time. But is this indeed self-evident? Is it not, on the contrary, based on a certain fixed, and merely specific, conception of things like absolute and relative? Is a new way of thinking concerning absolute and relative, whereby absolutes can be mutually co-established, utterly impossible? Have we no other way to conceive relativity than through delimitation, such as is seen, for example, when we divide a sheet of paper into two parts by drawing a line through it? Might we not also think about absolute and relative in such a way that two things, despite both being absolute, or rather because of this, can in turn also be relative, as in the case of looking at a sheet of paper from the front and then looking at it from the back? In order to consider such matters, I would like to approach the issue of science and religion from a slightly different angle than that from which it has ordinarily been addressed up to now.

What first becomes an issue, assuming that the objectivity of these laws of nature is beyond doubt, is the sort of horizon on which these laws are encountered or the sort of dimension wherein they are received. For instance, when someone tosses a piece of bread and a dog leaps to catch it in its mouth in mid-air, all of these "things", the bread, the person, the dog, and even all of their movements, are subject to physicochemical laws. From this point of view, the concrete particularities of these "things" and their movements can each be dissolved and reduced to homogeneous and impartial relationships between atoms and molecules. We may then conclude that the true nature of these concrete things and their movements lies in these relationships and the laws governing them. We suppose, needless to say, that in addition to the physicochemical domain there is the biological domain, and beyond that lies the psychological domain, as well as the domains of "spirit" and "personhood", but we may still regard all phenomena in these domains as reducible to physicochemical relations and laws, and explicable in their terms. On the other hand, however, it is also an indubitable fact that "things" such as the bread, the dog, and the person each exist in their own particular way of being and their own particular "form". Not only that, these "things" also form specific relationships with one other. To the dog, for example, the bread and the person belong to its "environment", while to the person the same is true of the bread and the dog. And the particular properties, manner of moving, structure of the body, and so on of the dog and the person presumably cannot be considered in isolation from the particularities of their own environments. Moreover, it can also be said that within this kind of relationship between "things" and their environment the laws of nature have been "received" in various ways that differ in terms of, so to speak, their "dimension". In the case of the example just mentioned, the dog and the person *live* the laws of nature in their actions. Here the laws of nature are lived laws. For all living "things", the laws of nature appear as laws that are lived in their day-to-day lives. Furthermore, in the case of creatures like dogs or persons, when these laws are lived in their day-to-day lives—for example, in the act of tossing the bread or the act of leaping towards it—these acts at the same time imply what in some sense can be regarded as a realization of these laws. Namely, it is the kind of comprehension referred to ordinarily with the vague term "instinct", or a comprehension prior to comprehension. Here we cannot enter into an examination of the "instinct" that was deeply investigated by Bergson among others. But in any case, on the one hand it is based on the relationships between individuals and the environment that regulate the properties, movement, and somatic structure of living things, while on the other hand it is based on the way of being of the "species" [「種」], transmitted as the "form" of the individual from the individual parent to the individual offspring. We can probably say that what we call instinct is established at the dynamic intersection of these two vectors. These generalizations do not even begin to cover the fundamental distinction between plants and animals, but for now I will not delve into this any further. Indeed, from the standpoint of natural science, we must say that the laws of nature govern and are "at work" even in the above-mentioned behavior of living beings. What I want to point out here, however, is that these governing laws become manifest in living beings as laws that are lived and acted out through a kind of "instinctive" realization. Laws of nature become manifest only by being lived, acted, and furthermore embodied and realized by living beings. In the world of concrete "things", the hegemony of these laws manifests only by being realized by "things". That is, the rule of these laws, in the case of living beings, is encountered in the dimension of instinct. We can also say that the nature of this encounter in living beings itself, the manner of this manifestation, that is, the very fact that the laws become laws that are lived and acted out, is nothing other than what we call instinct. Instinctive behavior is the manifestation of the laws of nature. The fact that the activity of living beings occurs only in accordance with these laws means that these laws are "at work" within, or as, that activity. The laws of being become manifest in the dimension of living "things" as laws that are embodied and realized. This manner of the manifesting of these laws displays on the whole a "purposive" character. The site where living things are established and instinct becomes active is the site where the laws of being take on a teleological character. Therein the various physicochemical laws are synthesized within a teleological structure to become, as it were, its material.

In the case of human beings, what is unique is technology. Our comprehension of the relationship between the particular goal we intend and the specific means necessary for its realization involves a knowledge of these laws. Unlike mere instinct, technology implies some sort of intellectual comprehension of the laws of nature. We might say that when primitive people learned to make tools and use them, for example, to make fire, this grasp contained in embryo an understanding of the laws of nature as laws. To act technologically by means of tools is possible only through such knowledge. Conversely, knowledge advances and develops through technological activity. And progress in such knowledge advances technology. Therein laws become understood as laws, and, being understood, they become laws that are lived and acted out through instrumental technology. In this case as well, the fact that human beings, in their technological activity, act in accordance with the laws of nature means that these laws are "at work" in and as this activity and are made manifest. In this case, however, unlike in the case of instinct, these laws become manifest in activity by being refracted through knowledge. And technology is nothing other than this manifestation. In technology laws become manifest where knowledge and action are at work together and develop together, and it is in such sites that the rule of law is received and encountered. The same thing also occurs in cases where knowledge becomes scientific and technology becomes scientific. In natural science a law is known purely as a law through its abstractness and universality. And technology that involves this kind of knowledge, too, becomes a mechanized technology. When this occurs, the development of technology, by improving the equipment of observation and experimentation, promotes the development of scientific knowledge, and, conversely, the development of knowledge in turn allows for the development of technology. The tempo of this development has been accelerating sharply since the mechanization of technology. And the significance of the fact that human beings act in accordance with the laws of nature, and that the laws of nature become manifest through and as human activity, is most thoroughly visible in technology dependent on machinery. In other words, we can say that the laws of nature emerge in the form of laws most manifestly at the site of mechanical technology, where knowledge and purposive activity make their greatest advances and work as one body. We encounter laws most directly at this site. Mechanical technology and machinery are the ultimate embodiment and realization of the laws of nature in human beings.

The laws of nature thus become manifest in a variety of dimensions and a variety of sites. And we encounter laws in all of these dimensions. We encounter laws not only at the site of technological activities, where we use tools and machines, but also at the site of instinct where we are on equal footing with dogs and at the site of material inertia where we are on equal footing with a piece of bread. And we have even come to regard the history of human "progress" as enfolded within this discrimination of dimensions. In other words, we have given our blessings to the trend towards the rationalization of humanity's understanding of nature, as well as of the intellect itself, by means of science, and at the same time to the rationalization of the entire day-to-day living of human beings.

Within the kind of process we have been discussing we can see two states of affairs tied together as one. One is that the laws of nature govern all things, from inanimate objects to human beings, in correspondence to the mode of being proper to each dimension. We can see therein how the governing force, the law exercised over things, permeates and extends to them through their various dimensions. While inanimate objects are merely material, living things are material but at the same time biological, and human beings are material and biological but also intellectual. But we may say that the fact that laws of nature permeate all of these dimensions as they internally unfold in their beingness, that is, in the fact that things exist, and thoroughly govern them illustrates the depth of control these laws exercise upon being. The order of being displays a superposing perspective, and as it ascends through the different stages of being its "teleological" nature intensifies and ultimately attains its complete realization in machinery, where the purposive activity of human beings functions in a purely "mechanical" manner. It can be said that therein lies the final deepening of the rule of the laws of nature. The other state of affairs mentioned above is that, in proportion to the deepening of the governing power of these laws, the force of "things" that make use of them manifests, by degrees, with greater profundity. This second aspect implies an escape from the laws of nature, or release from the fetters of these laws, through the use of these laws, and therefore that freedom gradually becomes manifest with greater profundity in these "things". It goes without saying, moreover, that these two aspects are bound together as one. In other words, as we ascend through the dimensions of beings, on the one hand the rule of the laws of nature deepens, while on the other hand the freedom of the "things" that employ these laws becomes more fully realized. Inanimate objects are completely passive vis-à-vis the laws of nature, and to this extent we can think of the rule of these laws in their case as direct but also shallow and superficial. In the instinctive behavior of living things, these laws manifest as laws that are lived and acted out. This means that the rule of these laws is deeper than in the case of inanimate objects, and manifests in an internalized form. Even if living things cannot take so much as a single step away from the laws of nature in their the day-to-day lives and behavior, at the same time in the sense that they live these laws they already manifest a step beyond their rule. In short, the sense that subordination to these laws also directly entails release from them is vaguely discernable in the mode of being of living things. We can say that the manifestation of the laws of nature and their utilization become immediately one in "instinctive" life and behavior. But to the extent that this unity is immediate, the world of living things is a world bound by the laws of nature. On the other hand, in cases where human beings use tools and act technologically, while the rule of law appears all the more internalized, at the same time the fact that these laws are being used also manifests with greater clarity. This is because the laws become manifest in human behavior through the intellect. Only in human behavior is it clearly apparent that submission to the laws of nature also directly implies freedom from their constraint. This appears in its most thoroughgoing form at the stage where technology becomes mechanical. Looked at from one side, the emergence of machinery demonstrates that the laws of nature have become manifest most profoundly, and, at the same time, most openly, in, and through, the activities of human beings. In machinery we can say that the activity of human beings transcends its own character, is itself objectified, and takes on the character of the direct functioning of the laws of nature themselves. Machinery is to all extents a pure product of the human intellect, something that human beings manufacture for their own specific purposes and that cannot be found within the natural world (as products of nature are). Yet it can furthermore be said that machinery expresses the activity of the laws of nature most purely, even more purely than the products of nature itself. In machinery the laws of nature act with an immediacy not seen in the products of nature. We may say that in machinery nature is brought back to itself or purified (abstracted) to an extent not possible within nature itself. As such, the work of machinery becomes an expression of the work of human beings. An expression of the laws of nature, possessing an abstractness more pure than what is seen in the products of nature, that is, an abstractness that cannot arise spontaneously, has become the expression of the work of human beings. This shows the *depth* of the governance of the laws of nature. That is to say that the laws of nature manifest their governance most deeply in penetrating the day-to-day life and work of human beings, so deeply that they transcend the barrier of the "human" to return once again to nature itself (as abstracted nature). Therein lies the deepest manifestation of the governance of the laws of nature over "things" in general. Looked at from the other side, however, the emergence of machinery marks the greatest release from the rule of the laws of nature. It is the greatest manifestation of freedom in making use of these laws. In machinery the work of human beings becomes completely objectified, and artifice that possesses a certain purpose is, so to speak, "inserted" into nature so that it becomes as though it were a part of nature itself, thereby rendering its governance over nature complete. It is a governance over nature that is more thorough than the governance of nature over itself. As a result, most distinctly manifest here is a relationship in which submission to the governance of a law immediately implies release from it. This site itself finds direct expression and emerges as machinery.

Importantly for us, a major issue has arisen ever since the relationship between the laws of nature and "things" I have just described entered its final stage with the emergence of machinery. This issue, briefly stated, is that the relationship discussed above is in the process of undergoing a reversal. This reversal is a state of affairs in which, in a manner of speaking, the governing is becoming the governed. In the account given above, the fact that the rule of the laws of nature governing "things" intensifies the higher we ascend the stages of being at the same time meant that "things" in their being are increasingly released from the control of these laws, and conversely come to use them for their own "purposes". In this sense we see a relationship of governance on both sides: a relationship in which laws rule over "things" and one in which "things" rule over laws. But as these relationships reach their zenith in the emergence of machinery, a new state of affairs arises. Looked at from one side, at the site where machinery emerges, that is, the site where the rule of the laws of nature deeply manifests in the day-to-day life and work of human beings, human life and work become completely mechanized and depersonalized. The site where human beings stand having produced machinery, which has been growing increasingly powerful ever since it first appeared—although it is a site where two factors are in mutual correspondence: the abstract intellect demanding scientific rationality on the side of human beings, and a "denaturalized" nature on the side of nature that, as was mentioned above, is purer than nature—is gradually coming to look like something that leads to the loss of humanity. When the relationship described above, namely, the relationship in which "things" govern the laws of nature through the laws of nature governing "things", reaches its zenith in the emergence of machinery, it becomes a relationship at a site beyond the original and natural ties between human beings and the natural world. It becomes a relationship in the kind of site that shatters the barrier between the humanity of human beings and the naturalness of nature. As a result this relationship becomes most thoroughly radicalized. But at the same time a profound inversion also arises in this extreme situation on the basis of this relationship. In other words, a relationship in which human beings govern the laws of nature through the laws of nature governing the day-to-day life and work of human beings inverts at a more fundamental level, and the laws of nature once again resume governance over these human beings who govern the laws of nature. This is nothing other than the state of affairs referred to as the tendency toward the mechanization of human beings or the tendency toward the loss of humanity. And it goes without saying that today this state of affairs constitutes one aspect of what is referred to as the crisis of culture.

Looked at from the other side, we can see another state of affairs tied to the mechanization of human beings in this inverted relationship. Namely, just as the mechanization of human beings is the inversion of the rule of human beings over the laws of nature, an inversion arises in the rule of the laws of nature over human beings as well. This manifests at the extremity of the profound rule of the laws of nature in human beings where it opens up a human mode of being in which it is as if human beings stood completely outside of the laws of nature. This mode of being human is, to put it simply, the mode of being open to nihility at one's root. The site where machinery appears, the site that, as mentioned earlier, can be described as the correspondence between the abstract intellect demanding scientific rationality and denaturalized nature, eventually opens up nihility both at the root of human beings, who rely upon that intellect, and at the root of the natural world. Only by taking a stance on this nihility can human beings escape the thorough governance of the laws of nature and find complete freedom from it. This is, in a manner of speaking, a standpoint that views the laws of nature as entirely external to the self. Therein the human mode of being of living in submission to the order or laws of nature as it has been described since ancient times is completely shattered. In its place, a mode of being human arises in which it is as if one were making use of the laws of nature from a position entirely outside of them while standing upon the freedom of nihility. It is an impulsive and orectic mode of being of a subject conforming itself, in a word, to "life" in its raw, unmodified form. In this sense it presents a form close to "instinct", but, as the mode of being of a subject situated upon nihility, it is in fact a mode of being diametrically opposed to "instinct". This mode of being of a subject that adapts itself to raw life while standing upon nihility is undoubtedly presented in various forms depending on its depth. Nihility lurks, for example, beneath the tendency towards absorption in things like sports, *keirin* [bicycle racing on which bets are placed], and entertainment within today's general public. It is merely drifting through the atmosphere of day-to-day living without rising to the level of awareness, but therein lies a "crypto-nihilism" (Helmut Thielicke, *Nihilismus*). There is also, on the other hand, nihilism as existence, shunning the trends of the general public to choose nihility with clear awareness and deliberation. And between them various other forms have also come into being. All of them, however, are of the same mode of being that we may describe in terms of a subjectivity given over to raw life and standing in nihility. It is a mode of being wherein one uses the laws of nature as if standing completely outside of them. The fact that laws of nature govern human beings has thus inverted at its extremity into a human mode of being. The fact that the laws of nature govern human beings while becoming manifest through the work of human beings signifies the rationalization of human life, which from the Age of Enlightenment in the eighteenth century until today has been regarded as human progress. In fact, however, a raw life completely preceding rationalization gradually emerges from the roots of this rationalized mode of life as one resting on a nihility that opens up in a place that rationalization, on the contrary, utterly fails to reach. Parallel to the progress of the rationalization of life, the affirmation behind it of a completely non-"rational", non-"spiritual", pre-reflective human mode of being, namely, the standpoint of a subject that pursues its desires without limit while standing on nihility, continues to gather strength. And this fact is also one of the fundamental aspects of what is referred to as the contemporary crisis of culture.

Accordingly, from whichever side we look, an inversion in which the governing becomes the governed comes into view. At the extremity of their freedom where they govern the laws of nature, human beings display a tendency towards losing and mechanizing their humanity. At the extremity of their comprehensive rule over day-to-day human life, the laws of nature conversely become something governed by human beings as subjects of orectic freedom existing as though outside all laws and principles. The mechanization of day-to-day human life and the transformation of human beings into completely non-"rational" subjects of orectic freedom are bound together as one at their root. For this reason, in mechanical technology—that is, in the emerging of the site where machinery comes into being in the interior of day-to-day human life—the state of affairs mentioned above, wherein submission to the laws of nature immediately implies release from these laws, manifests in its most thoroughgoing form. At the same time, however, the true form of this situation is distorted and remains deeply hidden. In human beings the form this situation fundamentally ought to assume manifests conversely as its opposite. This is what is meant by the common remark that human beings are dragged along by the machinery of their own creation. And it is a matter lurking at the root of the problem described as a lack of coordination between the progress of science and the moral progress of human beings. What is seen at this root is indeed not so much an uncoordinated progress but a regress. It goes without saying that these issues manifest together in the problem of nuclear weapons. Moreover, if we further broaden the mechanization and orectic subjectification of human beings and extend them to historical and social issues, we can also discuss the various forms of political systems that exist today within the context of the same problem. The political systems of communist states, for instance, display a tendency towards totalitarianism that implies an orientation towards the mechanization of human beings along with the mechanization of institutions. In liberal states the individual freedom found in democracies takes the orientation of transforming into the mere freedom of orectic subjectivity. But these differing orientations, at their root, are bound together as one. Moreover, viewed as a whole, the issues of mechanized civilization and political systems have at their base the same source. This root is where contemporary nihilism arises, whether in an overt or cryptic form.

Nihilism today, accompanying both the emergence of the mechanistic worldview of science that began in early modernity and the trend toward the mechanization of humanity that increasingly permeates not only the social structures of modernity but the inner lives of human beings, originates—as I stated earlier—from an awakening to the meaninglessness at the root of this world and of human beings. We can say that in the midst of this trend toward the the mechanization of day-to-day human life, both socially as well as psychologically, and toward day-to-day human life being perceived as a mechanism, it was only as an orectic subject standing in the nihility (whether with self-awareness or not) opened at the bottom of this mechanization that human beings could escape dissolution of their own existence into these mechanisms both inside and outside of themselves. As I stated earlier, the inversion that arose upon the originary relationship between the laws of nature and human beings manifests as a fundamental intertwining of the mechanization of human beings and their orectic subjectification, and at the root of this intertwining nihility has opened up as its meaninglessness. This nihility, accompanying as it does the situation human beings find themselves in today, has opened as something that had to be opened and thus is not something that can escape being brought into our awareness. If we look directly at our own existence without deceiving ourselves, we will naturally become aware of it. This is also the reason many existentialists today, through integrity towards their own existence, resolutely proceed to plant themselves upon nihility. The positive nihilism found in such existentialism displays the intention to take a step away from the mechanization of human beings as well as from their degradation into orectic humanity found in unawakened nihilism. In other words, it signifies an effort to climb up out of the pit of inversion into which humanity has today fallen. But at the same time one cannot escape this inversion to the extent that one plants oneself upon nihility, for it was precisely through this inversion that nihility was disclosed, and the pit that opens at the bottom of this inversion is indeed nothing other than nihility itself. For nihility cannot be rid of nihility. As a result, nihilism's intention mentioned above is hampered by the very nihility upon which it is planted. We can say that this is the standpoint of the dilemma that nihilism and the realization of nihility entail. Moreover, if this nihilism is something that arose from the rule of the laws of nature, the manner in which they operate on the world and human beings, and the regulating role of science and technology, we can then say that the issue of science and religion appears in a condensed yet fundamental form within this nihilism and the dilemma it contains.

We can say that in relation to these contemporary issues—the guidance of science and scientific technology discussed so far, or, more fundamentally, the fact that the site of correspondence between the abstract impersonal intellect and the mechanistic image of the world has opened as the site of their establishment, and, as a result of the factors discussed above, the appearance of a tendency towards the mechanization of the inner life and social relationships of human beings and simultaneously towards their orectic subjectification (in short, the tendency toward the loss of humanity)—the standpoint of traditional religion based upon a personal relationship between God and human beings conceived as persons, as was touched on earlier, faces a single fundamentally difficult problem. To elevate the standpoint of something like the personhood or spirit of human beings, as a move in a direction away from the tendency toward the loss of humanity, is fundamentally and essentially indispensable to the proper mode of being for humans. This is why ethics, art, philosophy, and so on have great significance. And it is possible to draw a fundamental line around the domain of such things that resist the control of science. It has been thought that we can furthermore discern a relationship with God as absolute person or absolute spirit at the root of this domain of the personal and the spiritual, and that only on the basis of this religious relationship can the person or spirit of human beings be provided with an unshakable foundation. The orientation opposing the governance of science has for the most part found its impetus in the domain of religion. As a result, resistance to the loss of humanity has, until now, assumed the form of setting limits to the scientific standpoint from a position based upon the domain of religious matters. It probably goes without saying that traces of this kind of effort can be seen throughout the history of philosophy from Descartes onwards. And these efforts have been undertaken with due cause to the extent that what we call personhood or spirit constitutes the core of true humanity.

However, as stated earlier, our image of the natural world has undergone drastic changes as a result of the natural science that has been with us since early modern times, and the world has come to appear completely unfeeling and utterly *indifferent*[1] to human concerns. The world has become something that transects the personal relationship between God and human beings. As a result, things like the divine order of the world and the providence of history, and even the existence of God itself, have become distant notions. Human beings are becoming increasingly indifferent to such notions and even to their own humanity. Human beings continue to be dehumanized and mechanized. Faced with such a situation, we cannot but conclude that we are up against something beyond solution from the standpoint of personhood or spirit, or of the personal relationship between God and human beings. Here, as I touched upon earlier, it becomes necessary for a new site to open

---

[1] "indifferent" is written in English in the original text (translator).

up, a site of trans-personhood that transcends the standpoint of personhood or spirit, a site that is conversely the only sort of site where something like personhood or spirit can manifest as such. In the past, owing to the apprehension of an element of trans-personhood in God, we were able to recognize a personal-impersonal quality in regard to God's omnipresence in the world, or God's indiscriminate love or "completeness" that makes the sun rise for good and evil human beings alike. Eckhart's account of an absolute nothing as the "essence" of the personal God is also indicative of this standpoint. He conceived of this as a site of absolute negation, lying immediately beneath our own subjectivity, that breaks through even subjectivity as personhood, and at the same time also as the site of absolute affirmation wherein our personhood becomes manifest; in short, he thought of it as the site of absolute of death-qua[*soku*]-life [死即生]. This site, in truth, cannot lie on the far side [彼岸] as utterly transcendent to us, but rather must lie on our near side [此岸] that is even nearer than what we ordinarily think of as our selves. What Eckhart called "detachment" [離脱], that is, a transcendence that is a freeing not only from the self and the world but even from God—what he described as a flight from God for the sake of God—must lie upon our near side that is absolutely transcendent. He himself stated that the root of God lies within the self, even closer to the self than the self itself. This point emerges with greater clarity in the standpoint of what is referred to in Buddhism as "emptiness" [空]. "Emptiness" is where we become manifest just as we are as concrete human beings, that is, as individual human beings not only with personhood but also with bodies, and at the same time it is also where everything around us becomes manifest just as it is. As I have stated before, this can also be regarded as the sort of place where "the renewal of the universe with one's great death" [大死一番乾坤新たなり] simultaneously signifies the rebirth of the self. While it may be called a "rebirth", this is where the self's original countenance [本来の面目] appears as it is. It signifies the return of the self to its original self as it truly is. Is it not indeed the case that only by coming back to this standpoint that the relationship we referred to earlier, in which submission to the rule of the laws of nature is immediately an emancipation from it, obtains for the first time? And does it not then follow that the possibility of the existence of human beings properly obtains only as this relationship properly becomes possible? To put it another way, do we not find here for the first time a standpoint that could truly overcome the situation in which that relationship is perverted by the governance of science and we lose our humanity, and furthermore a standpoint that can properly overcome the nihilism appearing as a result of this perversion? In what follows I will attempt to address the question of how we might consider these things.

Earlier I said that emptiness is the site of absolute transcendence, is furthermore a site opened not upon the far side but on our near side that is nearer to us even than ourselves, and that its disclosure signifies a conversion that can be described as absolute death-qua[*soku*]-life. We must consider this death-qua[*soku*]-life as thoroughly as possible. Even in the past, many religions have spoken of living by dying; examples of this include dying in one's finite life to live an eternal life, dying as oneself to live in God, and so on. But as I have stated before, in such cases the emphasis is placed on the side of life. What is referred to as "soul" [魂] or "spirit [mind]" or "person", too, has long been viewed principally from the side of life. In the orientation of life biological life was seen as one step beyond inanimate matter. And from there this orientation was thought of as ascending further to the dimension of soul, spirit, and person, and then crossing over with a single leap to the standpoint of religion as the personal relationship between God and human beings. In contrast, the orientation toward death, passing through personhood, spirit, soul, and [biological] life, ultimately returns to inanimate matter. There everything is seen as based on, and reducible to, materiality. The scientific viewpoint, at its root, is established in this orientation. And, as discussed above, with a single leap in the same direction, meaninglessness and nihility are disclosed at the root of all things and at the root of life itself, and nihilism then emerges from this awareness.

Of course, it goes without saying that in actuality it is not so clear-cut as this brief sketch I have just outlined. For example, to the extent that it is believed, as in the case of Christianity, that everything was created out of nothing, the personal relationship between God and human beings is established as a salvation in which this nihility is destroyed and eternal life is bestowed from beyond [God]. This salvation carries the significance of living by dying, and thus contains an element that cannot be dealt with simply as belonging to the orientation of life. And when human beings try to be completely on their own as finite beings without God, this nihility or death that absolutely separates human beings and God appears in their self-awareness as the sin of rebellion against God. Sin is, as it were, nihility or death appearing in sublimated form for self-aware beings. The root of this "original sin" takes hold not only in the spirit or personhood of "natural" human beings, but extends into their soul and biological life as well. As the forgiveness of this sin, salvation is therefore also an overcoming of nihility or death in this primordial sublimated and comprehensive form. We can speak of living by dying in this more fundamental sense as well. What I referred to earlier as the orientation of life can open up the world of religion only by overcoming death in its depths, and this is also why I said earlier that therein lies a leap. Conversely, in the orientation of death, even when we say that meaninglessness and nihility open up at the root of all things and at the root of life itself, this does not simply mean that God is missing and only the nihility of creation out of nothing remains. Nor does it simply mean the realization of nihility lying behind the "being" of finite beings. If that is all it signifies, it does not pass beyond traditional nihilism [虚無主義].[2] In contemporary nihilism [ニヒリズム], however, as I have said before, this nihility stretches, so to speak, into the site of God's being, and in this way becomes an abyss. And upon this godless nihility that has become an abyss, all life, not only biological life and souls, but even spiritual and personal life, manifests the form of something

---

[2] Here Nishitani uses 虚無主義, the standard Japanese translation of "nihilism", while in the following sentence he uses ニヒリズム, a phonetic transcription of the English word "nihilism" (translator).

fundamentally meaningless. At the same time, it is furthermore claimed that human beings can only truly become free and independent and become true subjects when they resolutely ground themselves upon this abyssal nihility. In other words, nihility is here taken to be the site of ecstatic [脱自的] transcendence of human existence, that is, the site where existence is established. Here existence, by assuming responsibility for itself, attempts to create anew the meaning of being and of life itself where it has exhausted them to their meaninglessness and nihility. Or, in other words, it attempts to draw forth the strength to affirm life as it is in its absurdity from the passion that maintains its stance without covering over the absurdity of life. Generally speaking, here it is an image of the "overman" or an image of the "human being" that is held up in place of the "image of God" as the intentional object immanent to human beings. But in any case, within nihilism [ニヒリズム] as existence there is something that cannot be defined simply as an orientation toward death. There is a sense in which nihility becomes the basis of a new (realistic) mode of being, and death becomes the basis of a new and different way of living. This is also why I said earlier that nihilism appears through a leap beyond the orientation toward death where the perspective of science was generated. In short, whether in the orientation toward life or toward death, the situation is far from simple.

That being said, however, I think it is indeed possible to say that traditional religion, broadly speaking, has been oriented towards life as its principle axis, while the line connecting the scientific point of view and nihilism [ニヒリズム] takes the orientation towards death as its principle axis. This should become all the more evident by contrasting them with the standpoint of "emptiness" mentioned earlier.

As I have said before, all things in their genuine form of suchness [如実相] can be seen as emerging, so to speak, at the intersection between the orientation toward life and the orientation toward death. All things can be seen, as it were, as a kind of double exposure of life and death, being and nihility. By this I do not mean to assert, as has been claimed since Plato, that things in the sensible world are, as a "mixture" of being and non-being, transient entities undergoing change. Nor am I saying that being and non-being are mixed within things as though constituting quantitative parts. Nor again, of course, am I saying that death is realized where life runs out or that nihility appears when being is extinguished. I am saying that life to all extents is life and death to all extents is death, and yet they become manifest as a single "thing", so that the aspect of life, remaining the aspect of life just as it is, can at the same time also be seen as the aspect of death. In this sense we can probably refer to this state of affairs as life-qua[*soku*]-death, death-qua[*soku*]-life. If so, it should naturally be possible to conceive of a way of proceeding that sees the actual form of this kind of "thing" without turning away from it, in accordance with this very form that to all extents is life-qua[*soku*]-death and death-qua[*soku*]-life. We can describe the two orientations discussed above as addressing the actual form of "things", one taking an orientation toward life as its principle axis and the other the orientation toward death. On the one hand there is thus the perspective of upward development, ascending from life and soul toward spirit or personhood. At its extremity, the "death" implied in everything from spirit or personhood to soul and life is realized as sin (as so-called "original sin" in Christianity) in the sense of rebellion against God, who is absolute life. At the same time the standpoint of personal communion with God as the overcoming of death by passing through its depths manifests in a leap. On the other hand, another perspective is formed that attempts to reduce everything to material relationships. At its extremity, the "life" implied in everything from life, soul, and spirit to personhood is realized as meaninglessness. At the same time the standpoint of existence within nihilism [ニヒリズム] as the overcoming of this meaninglessness by passing through its depths manifests in a leap. But what happens if we proceed thoroughly in accordance with the very form of "things" mentioned above, that is, of life-qua[*soku*]-death and death-qua[*soku*]-life? If indeed a leap is possible here, it is surely neither in the direction of development upwards toward personhood nor downwards in the direction of reduction toward materiality. It would instead have to be a leap that would be realized, so to speak, with the very form of "things" that is life-qua[*soku*]-death and death-qua[*soku*]-life directly underfoot. Here a viewpoint should appear that is completely different from those that would distinguish various levels or dimensions between materiality and personhood, and is therefore distinct from the viewpoint of "ascending" to higher levels or of "reduction" to foundations. It should then be possible to conceive of a standpoint in which personhood and materiality, usually considered to be altogether mutually exclusive, can shed themselves of these fixed ideas normally attached to them and thereby allow themselves to be seen through the sort of double exposure mentioned above. We might describe this standpoint as one of absolute "equality", in which personhood, while seen as personhood just as it is, is nonetheless seen as equal to material things, and material things, while seen as material things just as they are, are nonetheless seen as equal to personhood. What permits this is nothing other than the standpoint of "emptiness". But what is the meaning of this statement? Why is this the standpoint of "emptiness"? Here it is necessary to have in mind from the start the distinction between the standpoint of nihility on which nihilism is based and the standpoint of "emptiness".

As I have already noted, the traditional view of the person [人格] has looked upon the person from [the perspective of] the person itself. Or rather, the person has been grasping itself from [the perspective of] itself. The view of the person up until now has been established with this self-centered grasp of the person as its core. But it can also be said that this way of looking at the person, or indeed the self-grasping of the person itself, is already a kind of captivity or self-attachment. I have discussed the standpoint of the absolute nothing, the standpoint of "emptiness", as a standpoint that breaks through such self-attachment, thereby negating the self-centered grasp of the person. I have also discussed how the person becomes manifest in the form of suchness, as a true *reality*, only in unison with the absolute nothing (see my essay "Shūkyō ni okeru jinkakusei to hijinkakusei" [「宗教における人格性と非人格性」 "Personhood and non-Personhood in Religion"]. Moreover, this standpoint of the absolute nothing does not lie on the far side of what we customarily call our own personhood or ego, but rather on their near side.

It is, so to speak, the absolute "near side". This "emptiness" is not the same as the nihility [虚無] found in nihilism.

Earlier I said that in modern nihilism nihility has deepened into an abyss, and by this I meant that the nihility awakened at the root of the world and the self has extended into the place of God. Nihilism's claim was that only by standing upon this nihility could human beings be truly autonomous and free. It saw that by means of the subjectivization of the abyss of nihility, a place had opened up at the root of the self-existence of human beings, a place that, going beyond the constraints of the divine order that had previously been thought to essentially govern the self, allowed nothing to preside over it, not even God. And it was perceived that here the autonomy of human beings truly obtains for the first time. The anxiety of having nothing to rely on, the instability of being deprived of any fixed, stable foundation, was directly transformed into the standpoint of creative freedom that is not fixed upon anything existing. Nihility became a site of ecstatic self-detachment [脱自性] for the self-existence of human beings, and nihilism became an existential standpoint. Yet the representation of "the nothing" [無] in nihilism still shows traces of its reification as a "thing" that is not [無]. Of course, to the extent that nihilism is an existential standpoint, a standpoint in which nihility has been subjectivized, we cannot say that this nihility is being conceived as a "thing" that is not [無] as though it were some objective entity. Here the conception of the nothing, or its representation, is not the issue. Nihilism is thoroughly based on the *real* [リアル] experience of nihility awakened at the root of the being of things and of ourselves. It is a standpoint in which we ourselves act as if we have fully become nihility, a standpoint that can be described as the *realization* [リアリゼーション] of nihility in the sense mentioned earlier. Notwithstanding this, however, here nihility is still being seen as lying at the root of self-existence and as the "groundlessness" (*Grundlosigkeit*) of being from the side of self-existence. This means that nihility is being seen as lying outside of the "being" of the self, and thus as that which is apart from or other than "being". We notice this point of view, for example, even in Heidegger's talk of the being of the self as "suspended [差し懸けられて]" in the nothing. And the very discussion of the "abyss" of nihility, too, already indicates this viewpoint. In Heidegger's case, the nothing does indeed still retain the traces of its representation as a "thing" that is not. But as I have said previously, the representation of the nothing is not the issue. On the contrary, it is rather that we encounter the nihility opening up at its root when standing upon the being of the self, a nihility indeed truly emerging as an abyss upon which that being is suspended. The issue is that here nihility is thoroughly nihility for self-being, and thus the nihility one encounters when standing on the side of being. From here it follows that nihility is being represented as that which is absolutely other than, and outside of, being. The ordinary way of thinking that simply opposes the nothing to being, taking it as a negative concept vis-a-vis being, still leaves its traces here. The Western view of the nothing has so far failed to escape this way of thinking. When we speak of "emptiness", however, we can discern therein a fundamental difference.

"Emptiness" only becomes emptiness when it empties itself of the standpoint that represents it as some "thing" that is emptiness. This means that emptiness, instead of being posited as simply outside of or distinct from being, is realized as that which is one with being, or as self-identical to being. Phrases such as "being-qua[*soku*]-nothing" or "form is [*soku*] this very emptiness" [色即是空] do not mean that what is initially conceived *to be* on the one hand and what is conceived *to not be* on the other hand have then been joined together. On the contrary, being-qua[*soku*]-nothing means that by taking this "qua [*soku*]" as our standpoint we view being as being and nothing as nothing. Ordinarily, of course, we take a standpoint confining us to being to view being as mere being. It thus follows that nihility emerges when this standpoint is broken through and negated. But this standpoint of nihility once again is a standpoint confined to the nothing to view the nothing merely as the nothing. In other words, this too is a standpoint that needs to be negated. Emptiness then emerges as a standpoint of complete non-attachment liberated from this two-fold confinement.

Viewed in terms of this process, emptiness is the completion of an orientation toward negation. As a standpoint that has negated nihility as the negation of being, we can also describe it as the absolute transcendence of being. This transcendence is the absolute negation of the standpoint confined to being, a separation from this standpoint. In this sense we can also speak of "emptiness" as completely "outside" of, and absolutely other than, the standpoint confined to being. But this is not to say that emptiness is some thing "outside" of, or distinct from, being. In spite of its utter transcendence of the standpoint confined to being, or indeed precisely because of this, it can only arise in self-identity with being. Thus even when described as transcendence, it does not entail a departure toward some transcendent "thing" called "emptiness" or "nothingness". This is also why I earlier spoke of it as lying on "the near side" that is even "nearer" than what we ordinarily regard as the ego. Emptiness, or the nothing, is not the sort of thing we can turn to face. It is not something can be discerned in front of us as opposite to us or something that, in general, can be represented as an object. On the contrary, it slips away as soon as we adopt such a stance [toward it]. It has already been noted that the ego as subject cannot be viewed as an object at all. Nevertheless there is a tendency within the self to incessantly view itself as a "thing" called "I". This tendency is inherent in the essence of the self as self-consciousness. This is why we can say that the emergence of the standpoint of existence in ecstasy [of the self] suspended upon nihility as a truly subjective standpoint of self-being [自己存在] was a great step forward. And if there still remain traces even in this standpoint, as mentioned earlier, of the representation of the nothing that posits it as a "thing" that is not, then the standpoint of emptiness, as a standpoint that transcends that standpoint of subjective nihility, and, furthermore, as a standpoint that has transcended toward the "near side", is a standpoint that absolutely cannot be objectified.

Therefore, even what we have called the abyss of nihility is in fact realized only within emptiness. And its representation itself as this abyss is also only possible on the basis of emptiness. In this sense, just as nihility is an abyss for that which exists, we can say that emptiness is an abyss for this abyss of nihility. For example, just as we can imagine a bottomless ravine to be in fact within the endless expanse of the heavens [天空], nihility is likewise within emptiness [空]. In this case, however, the heavens are not simply something stretching far above the ravine, but the place where the earth, ourselves, and the countless stars and planets exist and move. They are below the ground we stand on and even further below the bottom of the ravine. If Heaven is where the omnipresent God resides, then Heaven must exist even below bottomless Hell. Heaven would then be to Hell an abyss. In the same sense, emptiness is an abyss to the abyss of nihility. At the same time, it is moreover something that opens up more on the "near side" and is more immediate than what we call ego or subject. But just as we ordinarily overlook this fact as we move about within the heavens, in the sense I described above, and only gaze at the sky above our heads, likewise we fail to realize emptiness is itself even more on the "near side" than our selves.

On the basis of the fundamental difference I have just stated between the standpoint of emptiness and contemporary nihilism [ニヒリズム], the standpoint of emptiness is not an atheism in the same sense that nihilism is an atheism. And even less is it akin to the atheism of positivism or materialism, which embarks on a course completely distinct from that of nihilism. (Indeed, within the standpoint of emptiness that speaks of being-qua[*soku*]-nothing or form-qua[*soku*]-this very emptiness [色即是空], there is an aspect that, while negatively transcending nihilism on the one hand and positivism and materialism on the other, at the same time harnesses the fundamental orientations and impetus that these opposing standpoints contain at a more fundamental locus than either of them alone, and sublates them into one. This is something I will address later.) It goes without saying, however, that while the standpoint of emptiness is not atheism in the ordinary sense of the word, neither is it so-called theism. Earlier I mentioned the case of Eckhart as one instance in the West of a standpoint that does not belong to either pole of the opposition between atheism and theism. When he grasps the personal relationship between God and human beings as a living relationship between the "image of God" within the soul and its "original image", refers to the completely "imageless (*bildlos*)" godhood [godhead] or the "essence" of God beyond all forms as the "nothing", and goes on to consider how the soul returns to itself and attains absolute freedom only by becoming completely one with this "nothingness" of godhood, this is neither mere theism, nor, of course, mere atheism. (For this reason it has sometimes been misunderstood as being pantheism.) This "nothing", as the "ground" of the personal God, constitutes the background of God that is the "far side" [彼岸]. And yet it is realized as immediately "my ground", lying, so to speak, in the foreground of the self that is the "near side" [此岸]. We can see here in Eckhart's thought as well the turn toward the standpoint I described earlier as the absolute near side. And the standpoint of emptiness is the standpoint that emerges when this turn has been accomplished with decisive clarity. Transcendence toward the far side has, of course, been discussed even in the Buddhism that preaches the standpoint of emptiness. But this transcendence toward the far side is realized as the opening up of a horizon that transcends the opposition between near and far as these terms are ordinarily construed, and in this sense ought to be called the "absolute near side". The distinction of Buddhism may be that it is the religion of the absolute near side. Already in the case of Eckhart, the "nothing" found where "the root of God is my root, the root of myself is God's root" is the site where the personal relationship between God and human beings obtains. The manifestation [現相] (or visible form [見相], *Bild*) of all that exists, including God, appears on the basis of the "nothing". All of what is represented as God, the soul, and their relationship, is possible only on the basis of this "nothing". It is the same with the standpoint of emptiness. I stated above that only in emptiness can the abyss of nihility be realized and only on the basis of emptiness can it be represented as an abyss. Only on the site of this same emptiness, moreover, can God in personal form and human beings and their relationship be realized, and only here can their representations take form. This standpoint of emptiness, furthermore, is one that opens up in the absolute "near side" of what is referred to as our self or subjectivity.

Nishitani Keiji (1900–1990). Born in Ichikawa Prefecture. Became an instructor at Kyoto University in 1932 (full professor in 1943) after graduating from Kyoto Imperial University's Faculty of Letters and teaching at Dai-san High School. After reaching the age of retirement, became a professor at Ōtani University. Writings include *Kongenteki shutaisei no tetsugaku* [[『根源的主体性の哲学』 *The Philosophy of Originary Subjectivity*] (Kōbundō Shobō, 1940), *Nihirizumu* [[『ニヒリズム』*Nihilism*] (Kōbundō, 1949), and *Shūkyō towa nanika* [[『宗教とは何か』*What is Religion?*] (Sōbunsha, 1961). "Nihility and Emptiness" was first published in *Gendai shūkyō kōza* [[『現代宗教講座』 *Lectures on Contemporary Religion*] Vol. 4 (Sōbunsha, 1961) in 1955 and was later included in *What is Religion?* It is also included in *Nishitani Keiji chosakushū* [[『西谷啓治著作集』 *Collected Writings of Nishitani Keiji*] Vol. 10 (Sōbunsha).

Chapter 16
Philosophy of Overcoming Nihilism

[ニヒリズム超克の哲学]

Keta Masako

16.1 Life and Writings

Nishitani Keiji was born in Ushitsu, in the town of Noto, Fugeshi District, Ishikawa Prefecture on February 27th, 1900 (the 33rd year of the Meiji period), the only child of his father, Nishitani Yonejirō, and his mother, Kayo. Ushitsu was a harbor town on Toyama Bay in the northern part of the Noto Peninsula, and the Nishitanis, who ran a kimono shop, were one of its older families. When Keiji was six years old his family moved to Tokyo because of a business dispute between his father and grandfather, but his memories of the time spent surrounded by nature in the depths of the Noto peninsula were etched deeply into his young mind.[1]

In 1912 Keiji entered Waseda middle school, but two incidents then marred his otherwise unconstrained student life blessed by unique educators.[2] One was his father dying of tuberculosis when he was fourteen years old, and the other was contracting tuberculosis himself at the age of seventeen and having to forego entering Dai-ichi [The First] High School in order to undergo treatment. Fortunately he recovered quickly and was able to enter Dai-ichi High School's Section One German law course. Years later Nishitani would say of this Dai-chi High School period, "At that time I endured an excessive degree of anguish caused by various events occurring around me. An

---

Translated from the Japanese by Robert Chapeskie and revised by John W. M. Krummel.

[1]Quotations from the 26 Volumes of Nishitani Keiji chosakushū [『西谷啓治著作集』 Collected Writings of Nishitani Keiji] (Sōbunsha, 1986~1995) are cited by volume and page number only. See Vol. 21, p. 155f.
[2]See Sasaki Tōru, *Nishitani Keiji – sono shisaku he no dōhyō* [『西谷啓治 – その思索への道標』 *Nishitani Keiji: Signposts to his Thought*], Hōzōkan, 1986.

M. Keta (✉)
Professor Emeritus, Kyoto University, Kyoto, Japan
e-mail: m-keta@zeus.eonet.ne.jp

unshakeable despair took root at my utmost core, everything seemed to be false and empty, and an infinitely desolate wind blew through the interior of my spirit".[3] But his time at Dai-ichi High School was also the period during which he encountered his lifelong mentor, Nishida Kitarō, and which decided the course of his life. "It is a rare happiness to encounter someone who summons you to greater heights, someone who lays down a path leading you to yourself, someone who can be a mentor in the true sense of the word. I had a profound sense that in accidentally stumbling across [Nishida's] *Shisaku to taiken* [『思索と体験』 *Contemplation and Experience*] I had just found such happiness".[4]

Guided by this encounter, in 1921 (the 10th year of the Taishō period) Nishitani enrolled in the philosophy program of Kyoto Imperial University's Faculty of Literature to major in philosophy under Nishida. As classmates enrolled in the philosophy program at the time, his seniors were the likes of Mutai Risaku, Miyake Gōichi, Miki Kiyoshi, Tanikawa Tetsuzō, Kimura Motomori, and Kōsaka Masaaki and his juniors included Shimomura Toratarō, Tanaka Michitarō, Karaki Junzō, and Kōyama Iwao. His graduation thesis was "Sheringu no zettaiteki kannenron to beruguson no junsui keiken" [「シェリングの絶対的観念論とベルグソンの純粋経験」 "Schelling's Absolute Idealism and Bergson's Pure Experience"], and the study of Schelling became the starting point of Nishitani Keiji's philosophical inquiry.

After graduating he taught at the Kyoto Technological Higher School and Dai-san [The Third] High School before returning to Kyoto University as a lecturer in 1932 (the seventh year of the Shōwa period) when he was thirty-two years old. Beginning in 1937 he spent two years studying diligently under Heidegger at the University of Freiburg in Germany. *Kongenteki shutaisei no tetsugaku* [『根源的主体性の哲学』 *The Philosophy of Originary Subjectivity*] (Kōbundō Shobō), the opening essay of which, "Niiche no tsaratsusutora to maisutaa ekkuharutoi" [「ニイチェのツァラツストラとマイスター・エックハルト」 "Nietzsche's Zarathustra and Meister Eckhart"], was written during his stay in Germany, was released the year after his return and became his first published work.

A major incident then occurred in the midst of this stable scholarly life. In 1947 (the 22nd year of the Shōwa period), Nishitani was designated unfit for the teaching profession and resigned from Kyoto University. His banishment from teaching continued for five years, but his research activities during this period were more vigorous than ever, and the results of his studies on mysticism, which became an important pillar in the formation of his thought, were published in 1948 (the 23rd year of the Shōwa period) under the title *Kami to zettaimu* [『神と絶対無』 *God and Absolute Nothing*] (Kōbundō Shobō). His *Nihirizumu* [『ニヒリズム』 *Nihilism*] (Kōbundō), published the following year (1949) (Shōwa 24), was also an important work that traced the genealogy of European nihilism in Nietzsche, Stirner, and Heidegger, and investigated "the meaning of nihilism for us".

---

[3] *Collected writings* Vol. 9, p. 17.
[4] Ibid., pp. 16–17.

After returning to Kyoto University, too, he continued to release important works on a regular basis. *Shūkyō towa nanika – shūkyō ronshū I* [『宗教とは何か – 宗教論集 I』 *What is Religion? Essays on Religion I*] (Sōbunsha), published in 1961 (the 36th year of the Shōwa period) became one of Nishitani's major works. The year after its publication (1962) this book was translated into English and German, and as a result Nishitani Keiji came to attract international interest as the philosopher of religion of the Kyoto School and successor to Nishida.

After retiring from Kyoto University at the designated age he transferred to Ōtani University, and his investigations gradually came to be focused more directly on Buddhism. Particularly important writings from this period are collected in *Zen no tachiba – shūkyō ronshū II* [『禅の立場 – 宗教論集 II』 *The Standpoint of Zen: Essays on Religion II*] (Sōbunsha, 1986). His work at Ōtani University, while taking various forms, continued until his final years. He passed away in 1990 (the 2nd year of the Heisei period) at the age of ninety.

16.2 Philosophy and Zen

In order to grasp the overall picture of Nishitani Keiji's thought, we first need to examine the relationship between philosophy and Zen in his work.

Nishitani states in his later years that a vague interest in Zen had already sprouted in him "during the period stretching from the end of middle school to high school"[5] thanks to the works of Natsume Sōseki, and he read whatever writings of Suzuki Daisetsu he could get his hands on. His interest in Zen continued after this period as well, but his engagement with this subject was always in the form of reading related texts. As he began the life of a student specializing in Western philosophy, however, "in the midst of studying the thought of various philosophers I came to feel a void within myself".[6] This was a "feeling that none of the thought of the philosophers that had piqued my interest up to that point and that I had studied and ought to have acquired had in a true sense become a part of me, or the feeling that even while internalizing a certain amount of information or knowledge my own feet were not firmly planted on the ground".[7] He came to feel that there was no way out of this situation other than Zen, and that there was nothing left for him to do but engage in its practice. Thus at the age of thirty-three he began practicing Zen at the Meditation Hall of Shōkoku Temple in Kyoto.[8] He would later

---

[5]Vol. 11, p. 6.

[6]Ibid., p. 7.

[7]Ibid., pp. 7–8.

[8]See Ueda Shizuteru, "Nishitani Keiji – Shūkyō to hishūkyō no aida" [西谷啓治 – 宗教と非宗教の間」 "Nishitani Keiji: Between Religion and Irreligion"] (Nishitani Keiji (author), Ueda Shizuteru (editor), *Shūkyō to hishūkyō no aida* [『宗教と非宗教の間』*Between Religion and Irreligion*], Iwanami Shoten, 1996).

state that through this practice he somehow managed to extricate himself from this crisis.

Nishitani repeatedly asserts that Zen is "before philosophy" and also "after philosophy". What does this mean?

Firstly, this can be said to refer to Nishitani's personal journey, described above, from Zen (before philosophy) to philosophy, and from philosophy back to Zen (after philosophy). This is also indicative of the fact that Zen is something that arises from an even deeper place in human nature than philosophy. Secondly, it refers to the fact that in Nishitani's thought philosophy is something established as an undertaking spanning two flanks of Zen, and that the standpoint of Zen is mediated by philosophy. In other words, on the one hand, in order to convey the standpoint of Zen to the contemporary world, he calls for shattering Zen's rejection of intellectual cognition, reflecting Zen in the standpoint of philosophy, and conducting a deep inquiry from the standpoint of philosophy into the intellectual investigations of Zen. On the other hand, he holds that unless it steps outside of the framework of previous notions of philosophy and takes up the standpoint of Zen as a "path of philosophical self-awakening," philosophy cannot be preserved.

Nishitani is not attempting to connect philosophy and Zen in a slipshod manner. Instead we ought to say that his work contains the motif of having no choice but to find some route [between them] where they are not unrelated despite their clear distinction, and to excavate this place where they may be connected. This motif is "nihilism" [ニヒリズム]. He describes the starting point of his own philosophy as "nihilism of the form that, while preceding philosophy, contains in its essence a transition to the dimension of philosophy".[9]

That nihilism precedes philosophy means that, as the suffering of human beings found in being alive itself, it is an affair of the dimension of religion. This in turn means that the resolution of nihilism is only possible in the dimension of religion. That this nihilism also contains in its essence a transition to the dimension of philosophy, however, results from the fact that this nihilism is not a question of nihility [虚無] as it is ordinarily understood, but rather one in which "nihility has reappeared in the dimension of religion where ordinary nihility is overcome, or in a dimension equally high (or deep)".[10] In other words, nihilism includes doubt concerning ethics and religion, and this doubt demands a transition to philosophy.

The form Nishitani Keiji's thought takes as a whole is a path that sets out toward philosophy from a nihilism preceding philosophy and then takes a detour around philosophy to head toward religion. Nishitani himself says that his philosophical inquiry developed in three fundamental directions as it followed this path. "Accordingly, the fundamental directions proceeding from it are: 1. To trace the course of the philosophical development of the standpoint of nihilism itself; 2. To philosophically and critically investigate the various issues of ethics and religion; and 3. To search for a path to the overcoming of nihilism through nihilism itself.

---

[9]Vol. 20, p. 186.
[10]Ibid., p. 189.

These three thread-lines are naturally interwoven as one".[11] He then describes the fundamental task running through philosophical investigations interwoven as one to be "the overcoming of nihilism through nihilism". We can say that each of his studies, which together encompass a wide range of content and form a massive body of work that fills the twenty-six volumes of his collected writings, is positioned somewhere within these three directions and has been thought through with this fundamental task in mind.

But the establishment of his philosophy, an undertaking spanning the two wings of Zen (religion), cannot be adequately explained by the fact that it takes this sort of thing as its task. The necessity of this being adopted as the proper standpoint of philosophy must be clarified philosophically. I think we can discern this in his essay "Rekishitekinaru mono to sententekinaru mono" [「歴史的なるものと先天的なるもの」 "The Historical and the A Priori"] included in *Kongenteki shutaisei no tetsugaku* [『根源的主体性の哲学』 *Philosophy of Originary Subjectivity*].

In this essay, Nishitani distinguishes two meanings of "being" [*sonzai* 存在], and, borrowing Meinong's terms, calls them *Sosein* (*sōzon* [相存、form being or being-as]) and *Dasein* (*genzon* [現存、actual being or being-there]) and examines them as follows.[12] From the fact alone that a certain something combines particular qualities to exist in such and such a form (*Sosein*), it does not follow that it actually is or was (*Dasein*). The form of being of a given entity [存在者], that is, *Sosein*, is distinct from its being itself, that is, *Dasein*, and thus to inquire into the cause of *Sosein*, that is, the cause that unified a certain particularity, and to search for the source of *Dasein* are clearly different undertakings. As a result, when we seek the "origin" of the emergence of a certain historical actuality we must always seek two "origins". The "origin" of its *Sosein* is the "cause" (in its early modern sense) of the emergence of this entity on the basis of historical causal relations and can be traced back indefinitely within the causal sequence of history. The "origin" of its *Dasein*, on the other hand, is the root source (ἀρχή) of this entity's being itself,[13] and is not something that falls within history. For Nishitani, philosophy was a special field of study that seeks this "origin" of *Dasein*, and he understood Aristotle's *Metaphysik* to be just this sort of field of study as well.

Nishitani then asserts that we have no choice but to conceive that this "origin" of *Dasein* lies in the pre-temporal ontological structure of human beings who possess the freedom to spontaneously act and emerge from within themselves and who are ceaselessly creating history anew.[14] In other words, what we might call a particular *Konstellation* (arrangement of various moments) within the structural links of human existence can be thought to be the a priori of the being-there [*gensonzai* 現存在 *Dasein*] of the kind of actual circumstances of history corresponding to it, but this *Konstellation* includes an impulse of movement in a certain originary direction,

---

[11] Ibid., pp. 191–192.
[12] Vol. 1, p. 193.
[13] Ibid., p. 194.
[14] Ibid., p. 201.

and across the interior of this tendency stretches a *Form* that includes all of the potential directions for the realization of this tendency. This *Form* is transcendental and static insofar as it unifies the infinite potential directions of dynamism from its interior, and it is immanent and dynamic insofar as it can only manifest through and within this dynamism, this dynamism manifests as a demand from the source, and this demand from the source gives birth to, and continues to enliven, the actual circumstances through experience and practice that are its realization.

The a priori of the actual circumstances of history never appears in actuality unadorned. What constitutes the *Index* of this *Konstellation* is generally a "demand from the source" of a specific type. The demand from the source throws open a horizon at our feet that ought to be filled in both directions toward and away from the source that is making the claim.[15] If we assume that ideas and actual circumstances can be dialectically mediated only through practice or within practice, then the "demand from the source", as the source of practice, is a spark shooting out where ideas and actual circumstances cut into each other.[16] On the one hand this is the starting point of experience and practice analogous to the "original bodhisattva mind" [発菩提心 *hotsubodaishin*, "the decision to pursue enlightenment"], while on the other hand it is at the same time the point at which ideas touch the actual world, and as such constitutes the center point in the dialectic of practice between ideas and actuality.[17]

In many of Nishitani's studies, such as those discussed above, we can discern the state of philosophy that attempts to arrive at the source of being itself, taking as a clue the demand from the source that operates from within our own selves, by the method of investigating its horizon opened at our feet. This approach incorporates within it a fundamental critique of the philosophy of contemplation that has occupied the mainstream in the tradition of Western philosophy, and of the academic attitude that looks at its object from the position of a third party. The *Idealität* [ideality] of ideas, when relating to the presence [現在性] of actual practice, is grasped as something absolute. (When Nishitani explicates this standpoint of philosophy, we cannot help but note the important role played by his study of Aristotle. By this I do not mean that his standpoint takes Aristotelian philosophy as its foundation, but rather that it takes as its foundation what became apparent to him through his study of Aristotelian philosophy.)

Within the "demand from the source", philosophy and religion clearly overlap as material. The difference between them appears to be formed by the fact that they confront in different ways the empty space in need of filling that expands below this demand, while at the same time it seems that here a relationship is produced between philosophy and religion in which their attitudes can shift reciprocally and freely. When investigating the "demand from the source", what Nishitani adopts as its model is "religious demand". Religious demand is one conspicuously concrete

---

[15]Ibid., p. 207.
[16]Ibid., p. 208.
[17]Ibid., p. 208.

16 Philosophy of Overcoming Nihilism

fact among demands from the source, and we may view religion itself as one conspicuous actual circumstance of history. Incidentally, the theme of nihilism is also nothing other than one actual circumstance of the history of the "demand from the source".

Nishitani's philosophy is characterized by this sort of deep internal affinity toward religion and a tense relationship in which it is prevented from letting itself slide into this affinity. This is the standpoint of "originary subjectivity". "Originary subjectivity" is the standpoint in which autonomous reason as the standpoint of the moderns and faith as the standpoint of the medievals are dialectically unified, and is "a standpoint that began within modernity but belongs to the next generation".[18] Nishitani's philosophy is the line traced by a sincere inquiry pursued from this standpoint. This is perhaps the reason that his philosophy neither forms a system nor is completed by a single logic.

16.3 What is Religion?

The book in which Nishitani squarely addresses the standpoint of philosophy described above is *What is religion?* This title, which at first glance suggests an introductory text on religion, is full of a sense of "asking the question on my own and seeking its solution on my own". This becomes the posture of "subjectively examining, in the person of my present self, the 'origin' in human beings from which what we call religion emerges.[19]

Running through this book's reflections is the intention to "dig up the roots of human existence through issues thought to lie buried in the roots of the historical domain referred to as 'modernity', and at the same time to search once more for the wellspring of 'reality' [実在] (*reality*)".[20] Nishitani was keenly aware of the fact that the issue of religion as it is found within us exists in the historical circumstances referred to as "modernity", and as a result his reflections here became "reflections of one placed upon an unsettled and mobile zone of negotiation straddling both religion and anti-religion or non-religion".[21] This unsettled zone of negotiation is the place where the "philosophy of religion" resides.

In the modern period, what came to have *real* meaning was not some particular religion but the universal concept of "religion" itself, and this inevitably led to the establishment of the "philosophy of religion". In this book Nishitani is undoubtedly engaging in his own philosophy of religion. But since previous standpoints of the philosophy of religion have been based on things "immanent" to human beings, such as reason, intuition, and emotion, he concludes that they have been rendered

---

[18]Vol. 1, p. 82.
[19]Vol. 10, p. 4.
[20]Ibid., p. 4.
[21]Ibid., p. 4.

impossible by the emergence of Nietzsche's standpoint of nihilism, and he attempts to develop his stance on this ground where earlier standpoints of the philosophy of religion have been torn apart or broken through. It appears that by emerging at this point where they have been torn apart or broken through, Nishitani's philosophy of religion overcomes the character, belonging to previous approaches to the philosophy of religion, of being a branch of philosophy. The standpoint of Nishitani's philosophy that in its essence comes into contact with religion as described above may, to begin with, be something that could be described as a "philosophy of religion". But it was guided by an unwavering pursuit of the question, "What is the subject of philosophy?" One might perhaps say that in Nishitani the philosophy of religion is philosophy in its essential sense.

To ask "What is religion?" in the historical epoch called "modernity" is synonymous with ascertaining the source of the occurrence of nihilism and seeking a way to overcome it. And what Nishitani Keiji reached in his attempt to take up the task of overcoming nihilism, "from the most comprehensive and originary site", was the standpoint of "emptiness". *What is Religion?* is a book in which Nishitani, through the standpoint of "emptiness", vigorously takes up the subject of overcoming nihilism. As such it is regarded as his most important work.

This book is comprised of six chapters of essays. "Nihility and Emptiness", included here, is the third of these but marks the first time that the standpoint of "emptiness" is presented. In the first chapter preceding it, "Shūkyō to wa nanika" [「宗教とは何か」 "What is Religion?"], and Chap. 2, "Shūkyō ni okeru jinkakusei to hijinkakusei" [「宗教における人格性と非人格性」 "Personhood and Non-Personhood in Religion"], Nishitani gives a historical and comprehensive explanation of the nature of the standpoint of nihilism that has become an issue in the contemporary world and how religion, in particular Christianity, has confronted the issue of nihility. In Chap. 4, "Kū no tachiba" [「空の立場」 "The Standpoint of Emptiness"], Chap. 5, "Kū to toki" [「空と時」 "Emptiness and Time"], and Chap. 6, "Kū to rekishi" [「空と歴史」 "Emptiness and History"], as is already evident from their titles, Nishitani describes in detail the nature of the standpoint of "emptiness" and examines how it overcomes nihilism. "Nihility and Emptiness" is accordingly positioned as the book's pivot and is the essay in which its main subject is thrust into view.

16.4 Nihilism and Science

In "Nihility and Emptiness", Nishitani argues that the standpoint of nihilism emerges when taking a leap from the extremity of the scientific standpoint that attempts to see everything by reducing it to material relationships. This argument can be summarized as follows.

The basis for regarding the standpoint of science as absolute truth lies in the complete objectivity of the laws of nature. The laws of nature govern the way of being of all "things", from inanimate objects to human beings, in each of their various dimensions. In the case of human beings these laws manifest in action while being refracted within knowledge. This manifestation is technology, and therein these laws manifest at the site where knowledge and action operate as one in their development. In cases where this knowledge becomes scientific, technology becomes mechanistic technology that includes scientific knowledge. In this mechanistic technology the governing power of the laws of nature reaches its greatest depth, but in proportion to this the power of "things" that makes use of these laws also manifests more deeply. When this stage is reached a reversal in the relationship between the laws of nature and "things" arises. In other words, the relationship in which human beings govern the laws of nature through the laws of nature governing the work and daily activities of human beings themselves reverses into a relationship at a more fundamental level where these human beings who govern the laws of nature are conversely once again governed by the laws of nature. This is nothing other than the situation described as the trend toward the mechanization of the internal life and social relationships of human beings, or the trend toward the loss of humanity. And just as the mechanization of humanity is a reversal of the governance of human beings over the laws of nature, a reversal also arises in the governance of the laws of nature over human beings. This manifests as a situation in which the governance of these laws of nature, at the deep extremity of this governance within human beings, opens up a mode of being for human beings in which it is as if they stood completely outside the laws of nature. This human mode of being, put simply, is the way of being where, at its root, nihility opens; it is the way of being of a subject who, while standing upon nihility, pursues his/her desires without restraint. We can call this mode of being "nihilism without self-awareness".

This nihility is something that will naturally enter a human being's awareness when he/she faces up to his/her own existence without deceit. The affirmative nihilism found in existentialism that plants itself upon nihility with self-awareness expresses an effort to escape from this pitfall of inversion into which human beings have presently fallen. But at the same time because this nihility is something opened by this inversion, and the pit that opens at the bottom of this inversion is nothing other than nihility itself, to the extent that one plants oneself upon nihility one cannot really escape this inversion. Nihilism, with its awareness of nihility, is a standpoint that contains this kind of dilemma.

Not only is this approach to nihilism without equal when compared to the understanding of nihilism among thinkers of the West, it is indeed an intellectual achievement of the highest order equipped with its own unique perspective. Nishitani was able to understand nihilism, not simply as a mood, emotion, or intellectual trend, but as a fundamental phenomenon rooted deeply in European culture because this understanding was based on an outstanding critique of science.

This is the reason that in the midst of reading about how Nishitani understands nihilism we cannot help but confirm our own exhaustion in keeping up with the transformations of scientific civilization.

Nishitani attempted to elucidate how nihility opens at the root of the mode of being of human beings who live in a modern scientific technological civilization by looking for its causes. Here we see the conviction that one can discern the true state of nihilism by tracing its historical origin. This conviction includes the belief that by this method one can ascertain the essence of modern science, one fundamental factor that gave rise to various contemporary issues, and the consequences it has brought to contemporary society. But we would probably have to say that that the transformations of the world during the latter half of the twentieth century caused by contemporary technology have moved well beyond the understanding of science as it was grasped by Nishitani. Not only have scientific knowledge and technology moved beyond our control to control us in turn, they have also led to our dismantling as governing and governed entities. We are now, in a manner of speaking, no more than fragments of ourselves. If the conviction that we had fully ascertained the consequences of science turns out to be hollow, so too must be our conviction that we had grasped the true form of nihilism. Nihilism reveals the uncanniness of nihility not being overturned by the uncovering of its origin.

Nevertheless, even if this shows that Nishitani's approach to nihilism possesses certain historical limitations, it does not necessarily mean that his approach was inadequate. The question here is certainly not whether or not he was able to perfectly foresee, in the manner of a prophet, the consequences that would be brought about by science and scientific technology. The convictions found in Nishitani's understanding of nihilism point to the existence, within his thought developed by having lived through nihilism, of what we might describe as the soundness of comportment to "things". His having confronted nihilism with this soundness is what makes Nishitani's understanding of nihilism original. And when we have no choice but to abandon grasping the true form of nihilism by clarifying its historical origins, Nishitani's understanding of nihilism tells us what we have lost.

This something that we have lost is connected to that which gives us the sense, when comparing their thought, that Nishitani's thinking is somehow more contemporary than that of Nishida Kitarō. Within Nishitani's thought there is indeed nested what may be referred to as a certain exhaustion of existence, and by means of it his contemplation both serves as an excellent guide to Nishida's more rigid philosophy and allows us to see him as a philosopher of deeper empathy for us living in the contemporary world.

16.5 The Standpoint of "Emptiness"

So what is it that gives rise to this soundness of comportment to "things" in Nishitani's thought? Put simply, it is the religious and cultural tradition of the East with Buddhism at its core. On the one hand, taking this tradition of the East as an intellectual setting made it possible to consider the intellectual tradition of Europe as a whole by providing a position outside of Europe, while on the other hand it also allowed for an understanding of the "nothing [無]" that, on the basis of a deep internalization of Buddhist thought, goes beyond the trajectory of previous philosophy. And this also ties in to the standpoint of "emptiness".

To press onward with thought in direct confrontation with the genuine form of the self and the world is something that is no longer so easy for us to do in the 21st century.

Nishitani's analysis of the relationship between religion and science makes evident how necessary the "advent" of nihilism was within the intellectual tradition that has created the framework of modern civilization. And he says that the reverse course in opposition to the dominance of science had for the most part found its impetus in the domain of religion. The standpoint of religion hitherto had been founded upon the personal relationship between human beings and God, conceiving both in terms of personhood:

> ...[T]hrough natural science since early modern times, our image of the natural world has undergone drastic changes, and the world has come to appear as a completely unfeeling world utterly *indifferent*[22] to human concerns. It has become something that transects the personal relationship between God and human beings. [...] Faced with such circumstances, we cannot avoid concluding that something is emerging that cannot possibly be solved from the standpoint of person or spirit, or the standpoint of the personal relationship between God and human beings. Here, as I once touched upon, it becomes necessary for a site to open up, a site of trans-personhood that transcends the standpoint of things such as personhood or spirit, a site that is conversely the only sort of site where things such as personhood and spirit can manifest as personhood and spirit.[23]

Nishitani states that what most clearly emerges at this site is the standpoint of what Buddhism refers to as "emptiness", and that this is "the standpoint that can truly overcome nihilism." Emptiness is thus constantly being clarified in contrast to the standpoint of nihilism that had emerged as a leap from the previous standpoints of religion and the scientific point of view. As a result, the standpoint of emptiness, along with being characterized as the site where the personal relationship between God and human beings is negated and transcended, is also characterized as the site where one is freed of the remaining traces of nihilism that has subjectified the abyss of nihility to become an existential standpoint. These traces are the traces of a way of thinking that simply contrasts the nothing with being as a negative concept in opposition to it.

Nishitani notices something in common with this standpoint of emptiness in what is expressed by Eckhart's term "detachment". What is spoken of as the standpoint of emptiness is not something found only within Buddhism, but something that can obtain within the history of other religions as well. That "the self returns to its original self just as it is" is something universal to all human existence. The idea that the site where "the self returns to its original self just as it is" lies not in the direction of the "absolutely transcendent far side," but rather opens even more on the "near side" than what we ordinarily think of as the "self" is indeed a part of the Buddhist tradition. But "the self returning to its original self just as it is" is not something shackled to a particular religious denomination or sect. This is the place of thought in Nishitani's philosophy of religion. By securing this place of thought

---

[22]"Indifferent" is written in English in the original text (translator).
[23]Ibid., p. 101.

that is the philosophy of religion, Nishitani was able to deal freely in the language of Buddhism. Even in cases where he is thinking by discussing the scriptures of Buddhism and using Buddhist terminology, such contemplation can best be characterized neither as Buddhist thought nor as Buddhist philosophy but rather as the philosophy of religion.

Nishitani discusses the standpoint of emptiness in a variety of ways. On the one hand he explains it by making extensive use of the concepts of Western philosophy, and on the other he expresses it directly through the words of Buddhist figures, for example, "separated by an eternity, yet not apart even for the slightest duration; always standing face to face, yet not being face to face even for an instant" [億劫相別れて而も須臾も離れず、尽日相対して而も刹那も対せず]. But the true apex of Nishitani's thinking may be found, for example, in the following simple manner of narration:

> But what sort of thing is this abyss of nihility in reality that estranges us even from what is closest to us? It lies behind all things of the world. Even galaxies and nebulae, for example, cannot escape from within nihility. And this cosmic nihility is the same nihility that separates us from one another. We might even say that at the bottomless rupture lying between us as we chat cheerfully with one another, galaxies are expanding and nebulae are spiraling. This means that each of us sitting face to face with one another in a room are, in a manner of speaking, standing outside of the entire universe. In other words, we sit across from each other as bodies-and-minds [*shinjin* 身心] manifesting atop an abyss of nihility, the extent of which is unknowable. This is what the abyss of nihility means.
>
> If emptiness proves to be an abyss even to this abyss of nihility, then what has just now been said about the abyss of nihility can be said with true absoluteness about emptiness.... And yet, contrary to the place of nihility, wherein this absolute rupture is immediately also a desolate abyss that estranges everything existing from one another, at the site of emptiness this absolute rupture immediately signifies also our most intimate encounter with everything that exists. Emptiness is the site where both that which in the ordinary sense is furthest away, that which is even hostile, and that which is most intimate can be equally encountered in their essence...[24]

Before Nishitani, had anyone ever spoken of such ultimate matters with such delicate and, furthermore, precise eloquence while situated within the setting of philosophy?

We can perhaps say that Nishitani was the first to introduce, through the task of overcoming nihilism, the modern concept of "history" into the intellectual context of emptiness or the nothing of Mahāyāna [大乗]. The consequence of this was the opening of a new line of development within the thinking of emptiness itself, and at the same time a presentation of Mahāyāna emptiness in a manner more easily comprehensible for people around the world. We can regard Nishitani's philosophy as having opened up a more flexible and elastic relationship between Buddhism and philosophy.

We must take note, however, that Nishitani's approach to speculation that attempts to constantly gaze at, and break through, the root of historical epochs does

---

[24]Ibid., pp. 114–115.

not permit us to be satisfied with his thought and remain content with it. It is extremely doubtful whether the standpoint of emptiness constitutes a way of thinking that overcomes nihilism in the same way vis-à-vis the nihilism that has been advanced today; to begin with, contemporary nihilism contains an aspect that resists any attitude of "overcoming". The nature of Nishitani's philosophy itself urges us to confront these new challenges.

Keta Masako Professor Emeritus, Kyoto University. Major works: *Nishida Kitarō "Zen no kenkyū"* [『西田幾多郎『善の研究』』 *Nishida Kitarō "An Inquiry into the Good"*] (Kōyōshobō, 2011), *Nihirizumu no shisaku* [『ニヒリズムの思索』 *Contemplation of Nihilism*] (Sōbunsha, 1999), *Shūkyō keiken no tetsugaku: jyōdokyō sekai no kaimei* [『宗教経験の哲学:浄土教世界の解明』*Philosophy of Religious Experience: An Elucidation of the World of Pure Land Buddhism*] (Sōbunsha, 1992).

Part IX
Supplementary Essay

Chapter 17
The Kyoto School and the Issue of "Overcoming Modernity"

[京都学派と「近代の超克」の問題]

Kosaka Kunitsugu

The term "Kyoto School" appears to possess a kind of ambivalent meaning. In an affirmative or positive sense it is the appellation of perhaps the only school of philosophy that can be said to be representative of modern Japan, the group of philosophers that has attracted attention in Europe and America since the war as the *Kyoto school* or *Kyoto Schule*. Briefly stated, it is an attempt to express an Eastern (or Japanese) way of thinking and seeing things based on the Buddhist philosophical tradition through the use of the terms, concepts and logical framework of Western philosophy. And as an antithesis to the Western way of thinking and seeing things, we might add that it occupies an important position in terms of comparative thought. In particular, it presents a completely different way of thinking to that of the Western tradition in regard to the fundamental issues of philosophy, such as reality (the absolute), history (time), the relationship between the universal and the individual, dialectics, and so on. In this sense the philosophy of the Kyoto School possesses an extremely positive significance as the mediator of an encounter between Buddhist thought and Western philosophy, a significance the importance of which is equal to, or perhaps even greater than, the earlier encounter between Greek philosophy and Christianity. And this significance will presumably only increase with time.

On the other hand, however, the term "Kyoto School" also bears a negative connotation tied to the abhorrent experience of the war. Today, many of the thinkers who belong to the Kyoto school, beginning with Nishida Kitarō, have been stamped with the label of having been collaborators in Japan's activities during World War II. In particular, the theory of "overcoming modernity" that they advocated has been denounced as rejecting modern Western democracy and liberalism, providing a theoretical foundation for Japanese nationalism and the conception of the "Greater

---

Translated from the Japanese by Robert Chapeskie and revised by John W. M. Krummel.

K. Kosaka (✉)
Nihon University, Tokyo, Japan
e-mail: kosaka.kunitsugu@nihon-u.ac.jp

East Asia Co-prosperity Sphere", and endorsing the war as a means of promoting these ideas. After the war many of them were in fact purged from public office for this reason. Is there any real basis for this negative image that has become attached to the Kyoto School? What is the true nature of the theory of "overcoming modernity" that its members advocated? And how is this theory of "overcoming modernity", which can be described as the dark side of Kyoto School thought, connected to the philosophy of the "absolute nothing" or the absolute dialectic that was its bright side?

When discussing the issue of "overcoming modernity", to begin with we need to clarify what exactly "modernity" is. To what does "modernity", here the object of "overcoming", refer? And in conjunction with this, at the same time we also need to consider the identity of the subject who overcomes modernity. Some people may say the answer is obvious: modernity is the modernity of the West, and the subject who overcomes this modernity is we ourselves. Nothing could be more straightforward.

But is it really so simple and straightforward? For even if we assume that modernity is the modernity of the West and thus modernization is Westernization, the content implied by the words "modernization" and "Westernization" is quite diverse, including such elements as rationalism, individualism, capitalism, liberalism, democracy, and so on. Shimomura Toratarō writes that the word "modernization" "takes as its moments citizenship as its social structure, democracy as its political idea, capitalism as its economic structure, liberalism and individualism as its social thought, and empiricism (positive empirical science) as its intellectual idea",[1] and here we might also add the moments of "secularism as its form of religion and rationalism as its idea of value".

In this way a variety of different moments are included within terms like modernization or Westernization. When one speaks of overcoming modernity, therefore, the semantic content of this phrase is not necessarily self-evident, nor must it necessarily imply a comprehensive negation of modernization or Westernization as a whole. When one reads the writings of Nishida Kitarō or Miki Kiyoshi, for example, hardly any negative views concerning science or technology (symbols of modernity) are to be found. On the contrary, Nishida and Miki take science and technology to be important moments of what they call the "logic of form" [形の論理].[2] This is evinced by the fact that their discourse on technology is

---

[1]Shimomura Toratarō, "Nihon no kindaika ni okeru tetsugaku ni tsuite" [「日本の近代化における哲学について」 "On Philosophy in the Modernization of Japan"], *Shimomura Toratarō chosakushū*『下村寅太郎著作集』 Collected Writings of Shimomura Toratarō] Vol. 3, Misuzu Shobō, 1990, p. 537.

[2]Regarding Nishida Kitarō's and Miki Kiyoshi's approach to technology, see my *Nishida Kitarō – sono shisō to gendai*『西田幾多郎 — その思想と現代』 *Nishida Kitarō: His Thought and Today*], Minerva Shobō, 1995, pp. 170–175; and "Nishida Kitarō to Miki Kiyoshi" [「西田幾多郎と三木清」 "Nishida Kitarō and Miki Kiyoshi"] in *Nishida Kitarō o meguru tetsugakusha gunzō* [『西田幾多郎をめぐる哲学者群像』 *The Group of Philosophers Surrounding Nishida Kitarō*], Minerva Shobō, 1997, pp. 233–238.

a major element of the idea of "active intuition" [行為的直観] or of the "logic of imagination" [構想力の論理]. On this point their approach is in contrast to the "critical theory" of Horkheimer, who critiques modern science and technology as products of "instrumental reason" (*instrumentelle Vernunft*), as well as to the stance of the existentialists who denounced them as factors in human alienation.

In contrast to the thought of Nishida Kitarō and Tanabe Hajime, in which the issue of nihilism as a consequence of the rationalism and secularism of Western modernity is for the most part not made into an object of serious consideration, for Nishitani Keiji the issue of nihilism and its overcoming serve as the starting point for the formation of his thought. In this regard, at least, the thought of Nishitani belongs to the lineage of Nietzsche and Heidegger rather than to that of Nishida and Tanabe. In this way, even when speaking of the critique or overcoming of modernity we see a marked contrast between the claims of existentialist philosophers, such as Nietzsche and Heidegger, or the Frankfurt School, centered around Horkheimer and Adorno, and the claims of the Kyoto School. And even among those belonging to the Kyoto School we can recognize subtle differences and discrepancies in their focus of interest and points of emphasis.

Similarly, the identity of the subject of overcoming modernity is not so self-evident either. If we assume that modernity is the modernity of the West and thus modernization means Westernization, then it must be the non-West, and in particular a non-West where modernization is most advanced, namely Japan, that overcomes modernity. And in this sense one can indeed say that the identity of the subject of this overcoming of modernity is self-evident. On the other hand, however, if the modernization of Japan is nothing other than the Westernization of Japan, then a modernized Japan is a Westernized Japan, and in this sense it can no longer be said to be non-West. It therefore follows that overcoming modernity, whether in the West or in Japan, must not mean overcoming modernity from the outside but rather breaking out of modernity from within. In other words, it must possess the meaning of overcoming oneself. "Modernity is we ourselves, and the overcoming of modernity is the overcoming of ourselves".[3] As a result, if we take overcoming modernity to mean the overcoming of modernity as an other (in relation to oneself) it cannot be said to be the overcoming of modernity in its truest sense.

Strictly speaking, we [Japanese] have received the *outcome* of Western modernization, not the *process* of modernization. We simply transplanted its fruits without historically experiencing the modernization of the West. Even though we use the same word "modernization," there is thus naturally a difference in character between the modernization of the West and that of Japan. The modernization of Japan is, so to speak, like the grafting of a new sapling onto an old tree, not something acquired through our own effort, and it is therefore inevitable that there

---

[3] Shimomura Toratarō, "Kindai no chōkoku no hōkō [「近代の超克の方向」] "The Course of Overcoming Modernity"], Kawakami Tetsutarō and Takeuchi Yoshimi eds., *Kindai no chōkoku* [『近代の超克』 *Overcoming Modernity*], Fuzanbō hyakkabunko 23, p. 113.

remains within it elements external (to ourselves). If we receive only its fruits, omitting its spirit, these fruits will not be made our own without difficulty. This is indeed the case. But even if it was an adoption of modernization as mere fruits [of someone else's labor], through this act of reception we are, without a doubt, placed within modernization. We are by no means outside of it. Overcoming modernity, accordingly, must at the same time be accompanied by a critique of our selves who are within modernization. In considering the issue of overcoming modernity, whether or not this kind of self-awareness is present on our side is a very important issue. To adopt Western modernization on the one hand while critiquing it and attempting to overcome it as something extrinsic to ourselves on the other is a contradiction. And in this sense we must conclude that the identity of the subject in the overcoming of modernity is not so self-evident.

So far I have examined what modernity is and who the subject of its overcoming might be. The answers to these questions are not as self-evident as is generally believed. They contain a variety of complex elements, ambiguities, and contradictions. This is perhaps particularly true when it comes to the discourse on "overcoming modernity" in Japan. For modernity is to us both ourselves and not ourselves. As I noted above, we received Western modernization as a finished product. We did not historically experience and achieve the modernization of the West in our own country, but rather simply dropped its outcome into our own particular milieu. Discarding its internal spirit or *ethos*, we adopted only its external institutions and technics. Modernization thus never became our own flesh and blood in a true sense. It possessed the contradictory character of being both completely internal and yet completely external. In short, it was not something of our own creation but rather something borrowed. This is why the discourse on "overcoming modernity" in our country is easily tied to restorationism or ultranationalism. In our country, the overcoming of modernity tends to take the form of the negation of modernity from outside of modernity and not the form of breaking through modernity from within. This kind of tendency is notably apparent in the assertions of the Japanese Romantic school represented by Yasuda Yojūrō and Kamei Katsuichirō. To them overcoming modernity meant "the end of the logic of civilization and enlightenment".[4] Clearly in their minds the subject of the overcoming of modernity is positioned outside of modernity.

The discourse on "overcoming modernity" in our country seems to contain this sort of contradiction and absurdity. At the same time, we also have to bear in mind the historical fact that the theme of "overcoming modernity" in our country sprang up like mushrooms after the rain to become widely discussed during the period between the Sino-Japanese War and World War II. This demonstrates that in large part the arguments over "overcoming modernity" were colored by politics. We can indeed say that this was a reflection and product of the political, economic and

---

[4] See Yasuda Yojūrō, "Bunmei kaika no ronri no shūen [「文明開化の論理の終焉」 "The End of the Logic of Civilization and Enlightenment"] (*Yasuda Yojūrō zenshū* 『保田与重郎全集』 *Complete Works of Yasuda Yojūrō*], Kōdansha, 1985–1989, Vol. 7), pp. 11–21.

military circumstances into which Japan had been placed at the time. At the very least, such historical circumstances were certainly a factor. This should be evident from the fact that the discourse on "overcoming modernity" in Japan was oriented toward the criticism of Anglo-American imperialism, colonialism, liberalism, individualism and utilitarianism. For example, if we look at the theories of "overcoming modernity" advocated by those of the Kyoto School, the bulk of their critiques were directed toward Anglo-American imperialism and colonialism or utilitarianism and individualism, or in other words, critiques of nations with which Japan was at the time locked in an intense struggle, and made almost no mention of France, while sympathy was directed towards Germany and Italy which were lagging behind in their modernization.[5] So while it may have been a critique of Western modernity, it was in fact a critique of modernity whose scope was severely limited and whose content was circumscribed.

From this sort of political perspective, the defect of the discourse on "overcoming modernity" was its tendency to limit its object in practice to Anglo-American modernity despite proclaiming a critique of Western modernity as a whole, and to criticize the imperialism of the West on the one hand while turning a blind eye toward Japan's own imperialism, or indeed even justifying and glorifying it, on the other. This tendency was manifest in the discursive tone that emphasized the unique character of Japan's position in history. On the one hand those who engaged in this discourse (particularly the advocates of the "philosophy of world history") criticized Anglo-American imperialist behavior as colonialism or aggression, while on the other hand they attempted to justify similar behavior engaged in by Japan under the pretext of the emancipation of Asia. To be sure, the conception of the Greater East-Asia Co-prosperity Sphere contained the idea of emancipating oppressed peoples, and as a world historical idea it may indeed have had positive significance as a driving force in history.

Nevertheless, emphasizing the unique position of Japan and attempting to justify Japan's imperialistic behavior in the name of this cause was never going to win widespread approval. Using imperialism to restrain imperialism is a contradiction. No amount of emphasizing the unique character of Japan was ever going to dissolve this contradiction in the least. True resolution of this contradiction could perhaps have been found in an approach that theorized Japan's actions as having been driven by necessity in the direction of world history, and that universalized and rationalized these actions as possessing a global and moral character. In short, rather than treating Japan and its actions as special or unique, it was only by universalizing them that this contradiction could potentially have been resolved.

Yet this was precisely the point that was given most glaringly short shrift in the discourse on "overcoming modernity". While by its nature logic is something that must possess universality, the proponents of "overcoming modernity" on the

---

[5]For example, see the series of round-table discussions between Kōsaka Masaaki, Nishitani Keiji, Kōyama Iwao, and Suzuki Shigetaka published in *Chūōkōron*『中央公論』 *Central Review*]. These round-table discussions were published in book form as *Sekaishiteki tachiba to nihon*『世界史的立場と日本』 *The World-Historical Standpoint and Japan*], Chūōkōronsha, 1943.

contrary emphasized particularity. As a result their discourse became mystical rather than logical. In the midst of such circumstances, Nishida Kitarō, as an exception to this trend, stressed that the spirit of the "imperial way" [*kōdō* 皇道] or "[all] eight directions under one roof" [*hakkō ichiu* 八紘一宇] must possess a global and universal nature. But in the end the "Principle of a New World Order" advocated by Nishida was no more than an idea that was never realized. While it had been composed in response to a request of politicians of the day, in practice its spirit was never brought to life. Was this in the end merely a case of politics being politics and thought being thought? Or was there some kind of flaw within Nishida's thought itself? This point is worth examining.

Looking at the Kyoto School philosophers' discourse on "overcoming modernity", its content can be broadly divided into two categories: those focusing mainly on perspectives of culture, and those adopting perspectives that are political or pertain to the philosophy of history. The former can be seen in the thought of Nishida Kitarō and Miki Kiyoshi and the latter in the thought of Kōsaka Masaaki, Nishitani Keiji, and Kōyama Iwao. Needless to say, it is not as though there were no historical-philosophical or political-philosophical perspectives in Nishida's and Miki's discourse on "overcoming modernity", and no comparative cultural perspectives in the discourse of the proponents of the so-called "philosophy of world history". For example, Nishida's essays such as "Kokka riyū no mondai" [「国家理由の問題」 "The Problem of the Reason of the State [*Staatsräson*]], "Sekai shinchitsujo no genri" [「世界新秩序の原理」 "The Principle of a New World Order"], and "Kokutai" [「国体」 "National Polity"] can be described as theories of modernization from the perspective of the philosophy of history and political philosophy, and Kōyama's *Bunka ruikeigaku kenkyū* [『文化類型学研究』 *Studies on Cultural Typology*] (1941), as its title indicates, addressed modernization from a comparative cultural perspective. Nevertheless, however, we can see a clear difference in where they put their emphasis, and this difference is decisive in determining the character of their approaches to "overcoming modernity".

Nishida Kitarō, Watsuji Tetsurō, and Miki Kiyoshi were all basically "philosophers of culture", and as a result their discourse on modernization for the most part took a comparative cultural perspective. Although Nishida did not specifically discuss "overcoming modernity" in a direct manner, he does occasionally touch on this topic, such as in the address, "Gakumonteki hōhō" [「学問的方法」 "The Method of Academic Inquiry"] (October 1937) delivered at a public lecture organized by the Ministry of Education's Agency of Education and Learning; "Nihon bunka no mondai" [「日本文化の問題」; "The Problem of Japanese Culture"], a "Monday Lecture" organized by Kyoto Imperial University's Students' Association [*Gakuyū-kai* 学友会] (April and May 1938); a broadly revised and expanded version of this lecture, *Nihon bunka no mondai* [『日本文化の問題』 *The Problem of Japanese Culture*] (Iwanami Shinsho, March 1940); "Rekishi tetsugaku ni tsuite" [「歴史哲学について」 "On the Philosophy of History"] (January 1941), a lecture given in the presence of the emperor; "Kokka riyū no mondai" [「国家理由の問題」 "The Problem of the Reason of the State [*Staatsräson*]"] (*Tetsugaku kenkyū* [『哲学研究』 *Philosophical Studies*],

September 1941); "Sekai shinchitsujo no genri" [「世界新秩序の原理」 "The Principle of a New World Order"] (May 1943), written in response to a request from the National Policy Research Institute [国策研究会 Kokusaku kenkyūkai]; and "Kokutai" [「国体」 "National polity"] (Tetsugaku kenkyū [『哲学研究』 Philosophical Studies], September 1944), written in response to a request from Morita Jūjirō. What Nishida consistently asserts in all of these lectures, talks, and writings is not that we ought to circumscribe Japanese culture or the Japanese spirit within a particular region called Japan, but instead that we ought to universalize and globalize it, and to this end it must first and foremost possess a scientific and logical nature.

What was important to Nishida was not to emphasize the particularity of the Japanese spirit and set it up in opposition to the universal and modern Western spirit, but on the contrary to broaden it into a world-historical principle as a particularity that subsumes the universal or a particularity that universalizes itself. And to this end the Japanese spirit had to have an academic and theoretical character. Against the general trend of the period that emphasized the particularity of one's own culture or spirit and attempted to mystify it instead of treating it theoretically, Nishida pursued the Japanese spirit's scientific and logical qualities as far as he could. This is particularly important to bear in mind when considering his discourse on "overcoming modernity". Nishida sought this global, universal, logical, and scientific nature not only in the domain of culture or spirit, but at the same also in political slogans such as the "imperial way" [kōdō 皇道], "[all] eight directions under one roof" [hakkō ichiu 八紘一宇], and the "Greater East-Asia Co-prosperity Sphere". His discourse on "overcoming modernity" is thus completely unrelated to ultra-nationalism, totalitarianism, and restorationism of the ultra-Right.

For example, in his Monday Lecture "The Problem of Japanese Culture", Nishida says more or less the following. In the past the "world" was something like an idea conceived only in our heads, but today it has become an actuality. Japan must therefore be truly nationalistic as a Japan of this world. True nationalism, however, must not be something "backward-looking" that returns to ancient traditions or emphasizes its [the nation's] particularity, but on the contrary something with a "forward looking" character that steps forward assertively into the global arena to contribute to the creation of global culture. What becomes an issue here is how we [Japanese], who had for a long time, in a state of national isolation, grown accustomed to our own isolated culture being for private use, are to assimilate global culture now that we have encountered it, and what sort of attitude we are to take towards it. In this situation the worst response is eclecticism, the paradigmatic example of which is "wakon-yōsai [和魂洋才 Japanese soul, Western knowledge]". As Japanese culture up to now has been a culture that had not yet encountered the scientific spirit, the spirit of "wakon-yōsai" will either be defeated by the scientific spirit or cause the degeneration of science into something unscientific or pseudoscientific. Nishida cites "Japanese science", a buzzword at the time, as a prime example of this.

What then was the most desirable attitude? Nishida states that it is to cease flaunting a narrow-minded Japanism, thoroughly empty oneself, and rally the various cultures of the world together, thereby becoming the focal point around which a new synthetic culture is created. In his view, there is, so to speak, a "primal culture" [原文化] at the root of the world's cultures, and Eastern culture and Western culture can be seen as developments of this "primal culture" in distinct directions. The original characters of Eastern culture and Western culture are such that they ought to be mutually complementary, not such that one is superior to the other or one must be integrated into the other. What is important is instead to uncover the broader and deeper roots that run through both Eastern culture and Western culture, and from there to shine a new light on both cultures. Nishida argued that this is precisely the world-historical role Japan (being well versed in both cultures) bears today.

In this way, Nishida's theory of "overcoming modernity" was not one that preached a regression to traditional culture, nor one that asserted the negation and overcoming of Western culture, nor even one that sought to synthesize or unify both cultures. Instead, it strove to uncover the deeper and greater foundation common to both cultures and to shine a new light from this origin on both cultures as they exist today. For Nishida, "overcoming modernity" was nothing other than for both cultures, while maintaining their unique characteristics, to develop in new directions by being illuminated in a new light emanating from this common foundation. Nishida, taking the spirit or culture of Japan as his model, lays out this new course in *Nihon bunka no mondai* [*The Problem of Japanese Culture*] as the development of "the logic of the mind" [心の論理] as opposed to "the logic of things". I do not have enough space to go into this in detail here,[6] but its main points can be summarized as follows.

Generally speaking, the scientific spirit can be described as the spirit that "goes to the truth of things" or the spirit "devoted to the truth of things". We can think of two directions in which to proceed towards the truth of things. One is the direction "from the environment to the subject" and the other is the opposite direction "from the subject to the environment". "From the environment to the subject" means that "the environment becomes the subject by negating itself in a self-contradictory manner", and "from the subject to the environment" means, conversely, that "the subject becomes the environment and becomes things by negating itself in a self-contradictory manner".[7] Nishida calls the former "the logic of things" and the latter "the logic of the mind".[8] The logic of things attempts to approach the truth of things by taking things as its objects, but this logic fails to truly grasp the mind (the subject). It is impossible to dispel the image of the mind as always outside of things

---

[6]See my "Sensō to tetsugakusha – kindai nihon tetsugaku no unmei" [「戦争と哲学者 — 近代日本哲学の運命」 "War and Philosophers: the Destiny of Modern Japanese Philosophy"] (*Kenkyū kiyō* [『研究紀要』 *Research Bulletin*] (Nihon daigaku keizaigaku kenkyū kai [日本大学経済学研究会 *Nihon University Economics Research Association*]), Vol. 30, 2000).

[7]Nishida Kitarō, *Nihon bunka no mondai* [『日本文化の問題』 *The Problem of Japanese Culture*] (*Nishida Kitarō zenshū* [西田幾多郎全集 *Complete Works of Nishida Kitarō*], Iwanami Shoten, Vol. 12) pp. 345–346.

[8]Ibid., p. 289.

and observing the world of things from this external vantage point. Nishida states that in general Western logic possesses this kind of dualistic or subjectivist flaw.

In contrast to this approach, the logic of the mind is a logic that takes the mind (the subject) as its object and pursues the truth, but in this logic what exists is only the mind (the subject), and the world of things is found at the bottom [底] of this subject's self-negation. We can say that it is this sort of world seen at the bottom of the subject's absolute self-negation that is the world that truly encompasses all things, but in India this "logic of the mind" remained a mere subjective experience (states of mind) and was not concretely developed into the world of things. Strictly speaking, therefore, we should say not that the logic of the mind existed in the East but rather that this is where its germination occurred. As the course Japanese culture ought to take, Nishida thus advocates proceeding further without halting this sort of logic of the mind at the level of mere experience, and from there entering into the world of the truth of things and thereby truly becoming creative elements of the creative world. This is the idea of "active intuition" [行為的直観] that he discusses. Put simply, "active intuition" is "to see by becoming a thing, and to do by becoming a thing". To put it another way, it is "to act as if one is that thing". It is the spirit of "entering the world of things and looking at things from among things", rather than "looking at things from outside of things" as in the logic of things.[9] On this basis Nishida asserts that it is only upon this standpoint of the absolute negation of the subject that the world becomes truly creative through its contradictory self-identity as environment-qua-subject and subject-qua-environment.

Nishida's theory of politics and view of history takes this kind of theory of culture as its foundation. What he consistently asserts is that the construction of a new Japan should be considered not separately from the construction of a new world but rather as part of it. We can say that the assertion of this sort of globality is the polar opposite of the assertions of the nationalists and ultra-nationalists of the period. Nishida says, "What must be cautioned against more than anything is the subjectivization [*shutaika* 主体化] of Japan. That would be nothing more than the transformation of the imperial way [皇道] into military rule [覇道]". On the contrary, "We must contribute to the world by discovering, in the depths of our own historical development, the principle of the self-formation of the contradictory self-identical world itself. This would be an exhibition of imperial rule and the true meaning of '[all] eight directions under one roof' [*Hakkō ichiu* 八紘一宇]".[10]

This idea, expressed in *The Problem of Japanese Culture*, was consistently maintained in Nishida's later writings on politics and current affairs. In "Rekishitetsugaku ni tsuite" [「歴史哲学について」 "On the Philosophy of History"], for example, Nishida asserts that the nationalism of today, when the whole world has truly become one world, must not be a nationalism in the sense of each nation turning back in on itself, but rather a nationalism in the sense of each country occupying its own position within this world, or, in other words, a

---

[9]Ibid., p. 380.
[10]Ibid., p. 341.

nationalism in the sense of each country becoming global. In "The Problem of the Reason of the State [*Staatsräson*]" he claims that a nation is a form of the historical world's individual self-awareness, and the place of self-awareness of the history-forming self [歴史形成的自己]. In "The Principle of a New World Order" he states that if the 18th century was the era of the self-awareness of the individual and the 19th century was the era of the self-awareness of the nation, the 20th century is the era of the self-awareness of the world, and then asserts that in this era of the self-awareness of the world each nation, while remaining true to itself, must transcend itself to form the world-of-worlds [*sekaiteki sekai* 世界的世界]. In "National Polity" he then further claims that national polity is the form in which the historical world individualizes itself. What can be seen in common throughout these texts is a stance that attempts to conceive the nation, national polity, or nationalism not from the side of the self but rather from the side of the world as its creative formative element.

This kind of stance has nothing to do with hyper-nationalism or ultra-nationalism. On this point we must say that the post-war criticism of Nishidian philosophy is therefore completely groundless. Unless one attempts to intentionally distort Nishida's assertions, it is quite impossible to see him as a collaborator in the war. His thought exhibits cosmopolitanism in its true sense and is the polar opposite of ultranationalism.

Nevertheless, it is not as though there were no aspects at all within Nishida's conception of an "absolute nothing" that sees everything as the manifestation of the "eternal now" (absolute present) that could be used, counter to his intentions, by right-wing ideologues. For example, Nishida understood the Imperial Household as the absolute present or absolute nothing that encompasses both past and future. Naturally, Nishida was not saying that the imperial family as an actuality is directly equivalent to the absolute nothing, but rather that as an idea it ought to be so or must be so. At the same time, however, he was also advocating "idea-qua-actuality" and "actuality-qua-idea"—that is, "absolutely contradictory self-identity"—and thus, unbeknownst to Nishida himself, his thought harbored the risk of regarding the actual Imperial Household in itself as the absolute nothing. But to regard the Imperial Household as the absolute nothing would lead to regarding the actual Japan not as a particular but as a universal, and thus to seeing it as an absolute. Instead of seeing Japan as one particular nation, it would position Japan as the "nation of nations". To try to make Japan a paradigm of what a nation ought to be is fine, but when this becomes an attempt to position the actual Japan as the "nation of nations" it is problematic. As a cultural concept this would not be a problem, but when it comes to political actuality it leaves a lot of room for problems to arise. Nishida's standpoint of absolutely contradictory self-identity that endlessly attempts to enfold and position all things within itself carries the risk of confusing the world of religious self-awareness and the world of historical actuality, or, to put it more simply, the ideal world and the actual world. Nishida himself consistently placed culture at the foundation of politics and the state, but an ideal and contemplative culture will inevitably be swallowed up by actual political mechanics and the trickery they employ. It is similar to the situation of someone stuck in a bog who sinks deeper and deeper the harder he struggles to reach the bank. And indeed it is precisely this point that sealed the fate and epitomized the tragedy of Nishida Kitarō, who was essentially a philosopher of culture, and of his philosophy.

Kuno Osamu has stated that as means of resistance available to oppressed intellectuals during the war, "What remained was either the path of devoting all of one's responsibility to preparing for after the war while remaining silent...or the path of devoting all of one's responsibility to the war and plotting a transformation of the war's meaning"[11] In the final analysis we can say that the path chosen by Tanabe Hajime was the former while the path chosen by Nishida Kitarō and Miki Kiyoshi was the latter.

In the late 1930s Tanabe published a series of essays referred to as "The Logic of Species" [*Shu no ronri* 「種の論理」]. The logic of species was a logic of social existence that assigns the human race (states), ethnicity, and the individual person to what in logic is referred to as genus, species, and individual respectively, and asserts that actual societies are established through mutual mediation—or absolute mediation in the sense that it does not admit a single immediate entity—in the self-negation of these three elements. This was originally a scheme to realize a rational nation-state of the human race through the mediating acts via self-negation of free individuals while distinguishing itself from the ethno-nationalism and totalitarianism popular at the time, but it gradually came to advocate reduction or consolidation of individuals into the (ethnic) nation-state as a whole-qua-individual, substratum-qua-subject [基体即主体].[12]

In October of 1941, however, after publishing "Kokka no dōgisei" [「国家の道義性」 "Morality of the State"], "Shisō hōkoku no michi" [「思想報国の道」 "The Way of Intellectual Patriotism"], and "Jitsuzon gainen no hatten" [「実存概念の発展」 "The Development of the Concept of Existence"], Tanabe, in what may have been a conscious decision, ceased all writing activities and fell silent. The duration of this silence perfectly corresponds to that of "the Great Asian War" (the Pacific War). Although we cannot gauge Tanabe's true thoughts during this period, in the preface to *Zangedō toshite no tetsugaku* [『懺悔道としての哲学』 *Philosophy as Metanoetics (the Way of Repentance)*], published after the war, Tanabe himself writes,

> ...[A]t the same time that I, too, needless to say, had to taste this kind of general national suffering, as someone who participates in thinking, I also had to experience in addition a special kind of anguish. This was the anguish of being stuck between on the one hand the understanding that to the extent that one has studied philosophy at all and is in a position to respond in thought to the nation one ought, even if it displeases the current government, to

---

[11] Kuno Osamu, "Kōki" [「後記」; "Postscript"] (*Miki Kiyoshi zenshū* [『三木清全集』 *Complete Works of Miki Kiyoshi*]) Iwanami Shoten, Vol. 14).

[12] Tanabe himself acknowledges that the logic of species, contrary to its original intention, possessed a tendency to absolutize the nation and assimilate into it the individual's freedom. *Shu no ronri no benshōhō* [『種の論理の弁証法』 *The Dialectic of the Logic of Species*] (*Tanabe Hajime Zenshū* [『田辺元全集』 *Complete Works of Tanabe Hajime*], Chikuma shobō, Vol. 7) p. 253.

offer one's opinion of the government in plain words in regard to the nation's policy concerning intellectual scholarship, and that, considering these critical times that do not permit a day's postponement, to be silent when there is something one ought to say concerning the policies of the administration would be disloyal to the nation, and on the other hand a self-restraint based on the idea that activities that may be undertaken as a matter of course in peacetime have the danger during wartime of exposing domestic thinking to division in the face of enemy and to that extent ought not to be permitted, and finding myself unable to decide between them.[13]

According to Tanabe's own account, finding himself completely at a loss in the face of this internal contradiction between conflicting poles and having no choice but to give up on himself completely, a resolution to repent on behalf of his powerless self that was unable to do what was right and to thoroughly examine this self then arose within him. The content of this self-awareness of repentance was described in *Philosophy as Metanoetics* [*the Way of Repentance*], and can be described as a philosophy that took the standpoint of an absolute other-power [絶対他力] rather than the standpoint of self-power [自力] adopted in previous philosophical approaches and completely rejected the workings of the self. Here it is not the self but repentance that philosophizes, and in this sense we can say it is "philosophy that is not philosophy, reborn anew out of what remains after the rejection of previous philosophy."[14] Philosophy as the way of repentance is not philosophy conducted with one's own power [self-power], but philosophy that the self is made to engage in through an other-power that awakens the self to its powerlessness, transforms it by turning it toward repentance, and thereby causes the self to start afresh. Tanabe refers to this other-power as the "absolute nothing", "great compassion" [大悲], "nothing-qua-love" [無即愛], and so on. Reflecting from this vantage point that the species in "the logic of species" had not yet penetrated the nothing-like character that is the foundation of repentance, he developed it after the war as "the logic of species as the mediation of the negative turn of (the individual's) death and resurrection [死復活]."[15]

If philosophy fundamentally takes the standpoint of reason, the way of repentance takes the standpoint of a thoroughgoing critique of reason. To put it another way, it is a philosophy that has been resurrected once every standpoint and method of philosophy has been rejected as powerless. To clarify this concept, Tanabe applies the translation *Metanoetik* to the term "*zange-dō* [the way of repentance]", and states that since *Metanoetik* also means *Meta-Noetic* (to transcend rational knowing) the way of repentance is at the same time the way of transcending rational knowledge. The way of repentance, while as *metanoia* is the self-awareness of the

---

[13]Tanabe Hajime, *Zangedō toshite no tetsugaku* [『懺悔道としての哲学』 *Philosophy as Metanoetics*] (*Zenshū* [『全集』 *Complete Works*] Vol. 9), p. 3.

[14]Ibid., p. 4.

[15]Tanabe Hajime, *Shu no ronri no benshōhō* [『種の論理の弁証法』 *The Dialectic of the Logic of Species*] (*Zenshū* [『全集』 *Complete Works*] Vol. 7), p. 259.

path of repentance and regret, as *metanoesis* is also the self-awareness of the transcendence of rational knowledge,[16]

Here I will not examine the validity of these views expressed by Tanabe.[17] What is important for us is that to Tanabe this way of repentance was indeed the way of "overcoming modernity". Like Nishida, Tanabe did not specifically discuss the overcoming of modernity. Nevertheless, as Kawakami Tetsutarō has pointed out, at the time the phrase "overcoming modernity" was a kind of "watchword", striking a chord whenever it was uttered and evoking a common feeling or image in anyone who heard it.[18] Thus in Tanabe's case the answer to the problem of "overcoming modernity", which in its broad sense had served as a kind of keynote within intellectual circles at the time, is presented in *Philosophy as Metanoetics*, a book written after a five-year silence. The way of repentance he arrived at through turning around at the limits of despair, anguish, and the awareness of his own powerlessness during the war, was literally a path of repentance or regret, but at the same time it was also an awareness of the limits of modern reason and a path to overcoming them.

When people speak of "overcoming modernity," the semantic content of this phrase is not necessarily uniform,[19] its meaning or content differs depending on the person employing it. This is readily apparent when we look at the assertions of Miki Kiyoshi and the advocates of "philosophy of world history" whom we will examine next. But for Tanabe, who had personally experienced the peeling apart of autonomous reason, it was both the way of repentance and at the same time the transcendence of modern rational knowledge, or, in other words, the way of transcending rational knowledge. And insofar as a Mahāyāna Buddhist awareness, that is, the self-awareness of absolute nothing, was adopted as the foundation of this sort of overcoming of modernity, Tanabe's philosophy shares an entirely common basis with that of Nishida.

If Tanabe Hajime chose "the path of devoting all of one's responsibility to preparing for after the war while remaining silent" as the means of resisting fascism, Miki Kiyoshi chose "the path of devoting all of one's responsibility to the war and plotting a transformation of the war's meaning". This can be seen in the abundance of current affairs pieces he wrote during the Showa teens [1935–1945]. In the midst of the gradually *fascisizing* social conditions, he stood firm at the very edge of what

---

[16] See Tanabe Hajime, *Zangedō toshite no tetsugaku* [『懺悔道としての哲学』 *Philosophy as Metanoetics*] (*Zenshū* [『全集』 *Complete Works*] Vol. 9) pp. 8–9.

[17] See Nishitani Keiji, "Tanabe tetsugaku ni tsuite [「田辺哲学について」 "On the Philosophy of Tanabe"] (in *Nishitani Keiji chosakushū* [『西谷啓治著作集』 *Collected Writings of Nishitani Keiji*], vol. 9), and Tsujimura Kōichi, "Tanabe tetsugaku ni tsuite [「田辺哲学について」 "On the Philosophy of Tanabe"] (in *Tanabe Hajime* [『田辺元』], *Gendai nihon shisō taikei* [『現代日本思想大系』 *Systems of Contemporary Japanese Thought*] Vol. 23, Chikuma Shobō).

[18] Kawakami Tetsutarō and Takeuchi Yoshimi eds., *Kindai no chōkoku* [『近代の超克』 *Overcoming Modernity*], Toyamabō hyakkabunko 23, p. 171.

[19] Takeuchi Yoshimi, "Kindai no chōkoku" [「近代の超克」 ; "Overcoming Modernity"] *Nihon to Ajia* [『日本とアジア』 *Japan and Asia*], Chikuma Gakugeibunko) p. 162.

was permitted by the authorities and society at the time and continued his forlorn resistance to a quite harrowing degree. But as a whole this was a process of defeat and failure involving a gradual but unavoidable retreat. Here we can perhaps obtain a clear sense of the fate of those living in this period in which resistance was impossible even for someone of Miki's abilities.[20]

In the process of this resistance, what then were Miki's own thoughts concerning the overcoming of modernity?

In 1938, Miki became a member of the Shōwa Kenkyū-kai [昭和研究会 Showa Research Association]. The Shōwa Kenkyū-kai was an association formed by Gotō Ryūnosuke, a close friend of Konoe Fumimaro from their days at Kyoto Imperial University, in order to draw up policies in areas such as diplomacy, national defense, economics, society, education, administration, and so on in anticipation of a future Konoe government.[21] In order to accomplish its intended goals, this association established several specialized research groups, and Miki, having become chair of the "cultural research group", put together "Shin nihon no shisō genri" [「新日本の思想原理」 "The Principles of Thought for a New Japan"] (January, 1939) and "Kyōdōshugi no tetsugakuteki kiso – Shin nihon no shisō genri zokuhen" [「協同主義の哲学的基礎 ─ 新日本の思想原理　続編」 "Philosophical Foundations of Cooperatism: Principles of Thought for a New Japan, Part Two"] (September, 1939). These were of course the product of collaborative discussions and cannot be said to express the thoughts of Miki as an individual, but since Miki himself was the one who wrote them we can presumably see them as reflecting his own ideas.

In these texts Miki seeks the meaning of the Sino-Japanese conflict in the unification of East Asia. This unification, however, is not intended to isolate East Asia from the rest of the world;, on the contrary, he states that it is a unification required in order for the world to become truly global. According to Miki, the world of today can no longer remain at mere ethnic nationalism, and the overcoming of modern globalism must be made manifest through its divisive formation into even larger units (economic blocks or spheres) that transcend each race or ethnicity. Within this context, the East Asian community must serve a signpost on the road to this new world order. The culture of the East Asian community must therefore contain within itself that which can become global principles in the new stage of world history.[22] Up to this point Miki's assertions mostly coincide with those of

---

[20]See Kuno Osamu, "Kōki" [「後記」 "Postscript"] (*Miki Kiyoshi Zenshū* [『三木清全集』 *Complete Works of Miki Kiyoshi*], Vol. 14). See also Masuda Keizaburō, "Kōki" [「後記」 "Postscript"] (Vol. 17).

[21]Concerning the circumstances of the establishment of the Shōwa Kenkyū-kai and the content of its activities, see Sakai Saburō, *Shōwa kenkyūkai—aru chishikijin shūdan no kiseki* [『昭和研究会 ─ ある知識人集団の軌跡』 *The Showa Research Association: Traces of a Group of Intellectuals*] (TBS Buritanika, 1979)] for the details.

[22]See Miki Kiyoshi, "Shin nihon no shisō genri" [「新日本の思想原理」 "Principles of Thought for a New Japan"] (*Zenshū* [『全集』 *Complete Works*], Vol. 17) pp. 507–513.

Nishida, but we can recognize elements unique to the former in his ideas concerning these global principles.

According to Miki, Eastern culture in general is a culture of *Gemeinschaft* (communal society) based on various ethical human relationships. In order for it to dispel the feudal elements within itself, it is important for it to incorporate modern the Western culture of the *Gesellschaft* (interest society) characterized by individualism, liberalism, and rationalism. And the new culture that has, so to speak, synthesized or unified these cultures of *Gemeinschaft* and *Gesellschaft* must then become the culture of the East Asian community in order to constitute a global principle. Miki sought the foundations for this sort of new worldview in the principles of cooperatism [協同主義]. Because the East Asian community implies ethnic cooperation it transcends mere ethno-nationalism, but at the same time this community must recognize the individuality of each ethnic group within it. Because totalitarianism can easily lead to closure and become exclusivist or self-righteous, the principle of East Asian thought must not be a totalitarianism of this sort but rather the cooperatism of ethnic cooperation. It must recognize the freedom and individuality of the individual and possesses a public and global nature.

Cooperatism takes the standpoint of the whole by negating individualism, but unlike mere totalitarianism conceives this whole developmentally by stages. This cooperation must begin with the cooperation of the citizens of a nation, extend to cooperation within East Asia, and ultimately develop into cooperation throughout the world. Moreover, this cooperatism must not be based on a cooperation that maintains the status quo but rather a reformist cooperation. And it must not be a coercive cooperation enforced from above but rather a voluntary cooperation arising from below. Miki adds that this kind of cooperatism is indeed that which takes what he calls the "thinking of form" [形の思想] as its fundamental principle.

While liberalism demands that which is abstract and universal, totalitarianism is likewise abstract but in its emphasis on particularity. At the heart of cooperatism is the thought of form, and form is neither simply universal nor particular but their unification. And in contrast to classism [階級主義] that one-dimensionally takes a spatial viewpoint, the form that is esteemed in the thought of cooperatism is form only as the unity of the spatial and the temporal. The new order of East Asia views regional principles as important, but it is also based on temporally developing principles. Whether planned economies or national organization, they are issues of historical form. These forms are imagined as unities of the spatial and the temporal.[23]

In this way Miki conceives what he refers to as the "logic of form" as indicating the course that "overcoming modernity" ought to take. But form here is neither the form [形相] (*eidos*) of eidology (*Eidologie*) nor the form [形態] (*morphē*) of morphology (*Morphologie*). This is "not simply form [形式], but something that

---

[23] Miki Kiyoshi, "Shin nihon no shisō genri zokuhen" [「新日本の思想原理 続編」 "Principles of Thought for a New Japan, Second Part"] (*Zenshū* 『全集』 *Complete Works*], Vol. 17) pp. 582–583.

gives life to the content within itself, the internal unity of content itself".[24] It is not an eternally unchanging essence but rather form that continues to be formed historically, not a form that brings death but rather one that bestows life. Moreover, it is not form as seen from the standpoint of contemplation but form that is formed from the standpoint of action.[25] Briefly stated, it is "form without form" or "formless form". It is that which gives birth to all sorts of forms, without itself having form. In taking the standpoint of the nothing and the standpoint of action in this way, Miki's approach to "overcoming modernity" is commensurate with those of Nishida and Tanabe. By taking the standpoint of Buddhistic nothing and reconstructing it as something active and practical rather than leaving it as something merely mental and contemplative, all of these thinkers sought a path to overcoming the Western and the modern.

Regarding the Great East Asia War (the Pacific War), Nishida was negative and pessimistic from the start.[26] Tanabe maintained his silence. Miki endeavored to shift its meaning.[27] In contrast, the proponents of the "philosophy of world history" were extremely positive and enthusiastic. From 1941 to 1942, Kōsaka Masaaki, Nishitani Keiji, Kōyama Iwao, and Suzuki Shigetaka held three round-table discussions under the auspices of the magazine *Chūōkōron* [『中央公論』 *Central Review*] and published the results under the title, *Sekaishiteki tachiba to nihon* [『世界史的立場と日本』*The Standpoint of World History and Japan*], writing in its preface, "along with believing that the truth of Japan is distinctly unfolding before our eyes through the Great East Asia War, we are convinced that by putting this truth into practice the distortion of actuality will be corrected"[28] and declaring, "December 8th was thus the day we Japanese citizens felt our own *moralische Energie* most vividly".[29]

These thinkers were in agreement in viewing the war as a manifestation of (what [Leopold von] Ranke calls) *moralische Energie* (moral life-force), in understanding it as a struggle to create a new world order, that is, as an epochal war that was attempting to transcend the modern world, in positioning Japan as having been

---

[24]Miki Kiyoshi, *Tetsugaku nyūmon* [『哲学入門』 *Introduction to Philosophy*] (*Zenshū* [『全集』 *Complete Works*], Vol. 7) pp. 114–115.

[25]See my *Nishida Kitarō o meguru tetsugakusha gunzō* [『西田幾多郎をめぐる哲学者群像』 *The Group of Philosophers Surrounding Nishida Kitarō*], Minerva Shobō, 1997, pp. 223–225, 233–235.

[26]See Aihara Shinsaku, "Sensei ni yotte yokensareta nihonminzoku no unmei" [「先生によって予見された日本民族の運命」 "The fate of the Japanese People as Predicted by *Sensei* [my teacher]"] (in *Nishida sunshin sensei hen'ei* [『西田寸心先生片影』 *A Glimpse of Professor Nishida Sunshin*], Reimei Shobō, 1949), and my "Sensō to tetsugakusha – kindai nihon tetsugaku no unmei [「戦争と哲学者 — 近代日本哲学の運命」 "War and Philosophers: the Destiny of Modern Japanese Philosophy"].

[27]See Miki Kiyoshi, "Senji ninshiki no kichō [「戦時認識の基調」 "The Fundamental Tone of Wartime Consciousness"] (*Zenshū* [『全集』 *Complete Works*], Vol. 15) pp. 459–477.

[28]Kōsaka Masaaki, Nishitani Keiji, Kōyama Iwao, and Suzuki Shigetaka, *Sekaishiteki tachiba to nihon* [『世界史的立場と日本』 *The World Historical Standpoint and Japan*], Chūōkōronsha, 1943, p. 6.

[29]Ibid., p. 139.

given the mission and role of a world historical ethnos in the establishment of this new world order, and, finally, in regarding it as a total war that was at the same time both a military conflict and an intellectual conflict, and asserting that the basis upon which this intellectual conflict ought to be waged was a higher level moral dimension that transcended the mere opposition of good and evil to make use of even the latter, in other words, the standpoint of the Mahāyāna [*Daijō*大乗, "Greater vehicle"].

According to the advocates of the "philosophy of world history",[30] the primary aim of the Great East Asia War was the liberation of East Asia from Anglo-American imperialism, but this liberation of East Asia would inevitably lead to the construction of a new order for East Asia, and this construction of a new order for East Asia would in turn develop into the construction of a new order for the world. In other words, this war was a war fought to bring about a great turn in world history that would herald the end of modernity, a turn that would involve the overcoming of the Anglo-Saxon order and the overturning of the Versailles system. And its leading ethnos was Japan. The actions of Japan therefore had to possess a global, and at the same time moral, nature. The proponents of this philosophy sought this worldview in the standpoint of a subjective nothing that negates evil but also, so to speak, "makes use" of it by leaving it in its place without opposing it.

Insofar as these philosophers emphasized the special position of Japan in the Great East Asia War political elements were stronger than cultural elements in their critique of modernization, and to the extent that they took an affirmative stance toward the war these thinkers differed from Nishida, Tanabe, and Miki. This was one factor in their being banished from their official positions for a certain period after the war had ended. Yet if we calmly analyze their high-spirited assertions, we can see that what they were aiming at in the end was neither the execution nor glorification of the war, but rather its idealization. This is made clear, for example, by their repeated assertions that the actions of Japan in its world-historical role must be those which possess globality and morality.

After the war, in "Sekaishi no rinen" [「世界史の理念」 "The Idea of World History]", an article with the same title as one he had written during the war, Kōyama Iwao writes, "I do not think what I took to be the fundamental idea of world history was mistaken. For I was not conceiving an idea that could be swayed

---

[30]"Philosophy of world history" is a general term for philosophy that deals with the fundamental concept of world history that first became a reality in contemporary times. It was advocated by members of the Kyoto School such as Kōsaka Masaaki, Kōyama Iwao, and Nishitani Keiji.

Kōsaka Masaaki, *Minzoku no tetsugaku* [『民族の哲学』 *Philosophy of Ethnos*] (Iwanami Shoten, 1942), *Rekishi tetsugaku josetsu* [『歴史哲学序説』 *Introduction to the Philosophy of History*] (Iwanami Shoten, 1943).

Kōyama Iwao, *Sekaishi no tetsugaku* [『世界史の哲学』 *Philosophy of World History*] (Iwanami Shoten, 1942), *Nihon no kadai to sekaishi* [『日本の課題と世界史』 *The Task of Japan and World History*] (Kōbundō, 1943).

Nishitani Keiji, *Sekaikan to kokkakan* [『世界観と国家観』 *View of the world and View of the State*] (Kōbundō, 1941), "Sekaishi no tetsugaku" [「世界史の哲学」 "Philosophy of World History"] (*Sekaishi no riron* [『世界史の理論』 *A Theory of World History*], Kōbundō, 1944).

by whether there is a war or not or by who won and who lost".[31] I believe these words came not from any posturing or bravado on Kōyama's part, but in fact reflected his undisguised true feelings. He had indeed explained the moral life-force (*moralische Energie*) in terms of the "clear bright mind" [清明心] of antiquity, *bushidō*, and Fujita Tōko's [poem] "*Tenchi seidai no ki*" [天地正大の気 Great and righteous spirit of heaven and earth], but far from being simple restorationism or ultranationalism, he discussed it as that which ought to form the basis of the spirit of "[all] eight directions under one roof" [*hakkō ichiu*] that "permits all nations and peoples their place" [*banpō chōmin* 万邦兆民]. After the war Kōyama delved deeper into this principle and presented it as an "ethics of place" that overcomes utilitarian ethics and the ethics of Kantian personalism representative of the modern West by integrating them.[32] We can see therein a consistency of thought that stands in contrast to the many progressive intellectuals [formerly right-wing intellectuals] who made spectacular, or perhaps merely shrewd, about-faces after the war.

Despite differences in strength and depth the theme of "overcoming modernity" ran through the thought of all of the members of the Kyoto School as a kind of keynote, and they were all in agreement in attempting to accomplish this overcoming through the Mahāyāna Buddhist worldview and the self-awareness of what they referred to as the absolute nothing, and in believing that this was something with a strongly active and ethical character and at the same time a strongly logical (or trans-logical in the sense of transcending Western logic) character. We can easily discern these characteristics in Nishida Kitarō's "active intuition" and "logic of the mind/heart" [心の倫理], Tanabe Hajime's "way of repentance" and "logic of absolute mediation", Miki Kiyoshi's "logic of imagination" and "logic of form", and Kōyama Iwao's "principle of call and response" [呼応の原理] and "ethics of place".

Upon reflection, the issue of "overcoming modernity" in Japan was an issue of overcoming modernity in two senses. Firstly, on the grounds that modernity was Western modernity and modernization was Westernization, the issue of overcoming modernity had to have the sense of overcoming the Western and modern worldview. Secondly, however, if Japan's modernization was advanced through the adoption and transplantation of the fruits of Western modernization, then the issue of overcoming modernity had to be one that critically examines this mode of the modernization of Japan itself. Moreover, these two factors are of an inseparable nature. The first issue and the second issue are distinct avenues of inquiry and at the same time blend into one. The issue of overcoming modernity is a particularly Japanese issue, and also a universally global issue. It is therefore of central importance that an issue that is very Japanese at the same time possesses a global

---

[31]Kōyama Iwao, "Sekaishi no rinen" [「世界史の理念」 "The Concept of world history"], *Risō* [『理想』 *Ideals*], Vol. 217, June 1951.

[32]See my "Kōyama Iwao to tokoro no rinri" [「高山岩男と所の倫理」 "Kōyama Iwao and the Ethics of Place"] (in *Kindai nihon ni okeru rinri kyōiku kenkyū* 『近代日本における倫理教育研究』 *Studies of Ethical Education in Modern Japan*], Nihondaigaku Kyōiku Seido Kenkyūjo, 2000).

nature, and that the particular can subsume the universal or universalize itself. One can probably say that the thought of the members of the Kyoto School has provided one approach to resolving the issue of "overcoming modernity" in both of the above senses. In short, it was to attempt to overcome the various problems posed by modernity by reconstructing, or rather deconstructing, the idea of the nothing found in Mahāyāna Buddhism. The issue then is whether or not the conception of subjective or absolute nothing they proposed frees itself from the Mahāyāna Buddhist character that forms its basis, in particular its mental or experiential character, to come to possess instead a truly active or historical-formative character. Regarding this point, my own view is quite negative.[33] And in this sense we must say that the issue of overcoming modernity remains unresolved.

Takeuchi Yoshimi writes, "As an occurrence 'overcoming modernity' has passed. But as an idea it has not passed".[34] I think this is indeed the case. The issue of "overcoming modernity" as an idea must therefore be discussed anew. Surely, however, it is necessary to discuss this issue on a more universal cultural basis than the narrow scope afforded by the kind of political ideology understood by Takeuchi Yoshimi and those involved in the post-war debate over "overcoming modernity". And in this regard, is there not indeed a need to seriously reengage and reexamine the philosophy of the Kyoto school?

Kosaka Kunitsugu Professor Emeritus, Nihon University. Major works: *Nishida tetsugaku no kisō – shūkyōteki jikaku no ronri*〚西田哲学の基層――宗教的自覚の論理〛 *The Substratum of Nishidian Philosophy: the Logic of Religious Self-awareness*] (Iwanami Shoten), *Nishida Kitarō no shisō*〚西田幾多郎の思想〛 *The Thought of Nishida Kitarō*] (Kōdansha), *Nishida Kitarō kenkyū shiryō shūsei*〚西田幾多郎研究資料集成〛 *A Collection of Nishida Kitarō Research Materials*] (Editor/annotator, Kress Shuppan).

---

[33] See my "Sensō to tetsugakusha – kindai nihon tetsugaku no unmei" [「戦争と哲学者 ― 近代日本哲学の運命」 "War and Philosophers: the Destiny of Modern Japanese Philosophy]".
[34] Takeuchi Yoshimi, op. cit., p. 162.

Chapter 18
The Identity of the Kyoto School: A Critical Analysis

John C. Maraldo

In the past three decades in the West, literature about the Kyoto School and translations of its writings have proliferated.[1] Yet the very scholarship that perpetuates the name has also created confusion about its reference. Which thinkers belong to the "Kyoto School"? What do they have in common? Do they represent something we can call Eastern philosophy, which pursues a way of thinking fundamentally different from that of the West? Is the core of that alternative philosophy, or alternative rationality, a notion of absolute nothingness with roots in Buddhism? Is Kyoto School philosophy an expansion of Buddhism that opens it to interreligious dialogue, or a retraction into cultural nationalism that closes thought off from criticism? In my view, the very question of the identity of the Kyoto School, far from being merely a conventional matter of a name, opens up a range of

---

An abbreviated version of the first part of this article appeared as "The Kyoto School: Overview" in *Japanese Philosophy: A Sourcebook*, eds. James W. Heisig, Thomas P. Kasulis, & John C. Maraldo (Honolulu: University of Hawai'i Press, 2011), 639–645.

[1]Recent collections with commentary include the section on the Kyoto School in *Japanese Philosophy: A Sourcebook*; *Die Philosophie der Kyoto-Schule: Texte und Einführung*, ed. Ryōsuke Ōhashi (Freiburg & München: Karl Alber Verlag, 1990, 2nd edition 2011); *Textos de la filosofía japonesa moderna*, vol. I, translated and edited by Agustín Jacinto Z. (Zamora, Mexico: El Colegio de Michoacán, 1995); and *Sourcebook For Modern Japanese Philosophy: Selected Documents*, translated and edited by David A. Dilworth & Valdo H. Viglielmo, with Agustin Jacinto Zavala (Westport, Connecticut & London: Greenwood Press, 1998). Recent monograph studies and translations of Kyoto School philosophers in Spanish, German, English, French and Italian are too numerous to be listed here. For an excellent survey and analysis, see Bret W. Davis, "The Kyoto School", *The Stanford Encyclopedia of Philosophy* (Summer 2010 Edition), Edward N. Zalta (ed.), URL = <http://plato.stanford.edu/archives/sum2010/entries/kyoto-school/>.

J. C. Maraldo (✉)
University of North Florida, Jacksonville, USA
e-mail: jmaraldo.unf.edu@gmail.com

questions that concern the very meaning and scope of philosophy. The following essay attempts not to offer definitive answers to these questions, but to show why they arise and what import they have. My intention is to encourage more thorough investigation of each of these issues, and others as well.

18.1 The Question of Identity: Who Belongs to the Kyoto School?

Historically, we know that the name "Kyoto School" most likely originates with Tosaka Jun's description in 1931 of certain philosophers associated with Nishida Kitarō.[2] Tosaka's description was more critical than complimentary; the very name "Kyoto School" carried an ideological tone that was meant to indicate its rightist political tendencies. At the time, of course, Tosaka could not anticipate that a much larger group would come to be associated with the name he gave, and that he himself would sometimes be included in the "Kyoto School."

What criteria do scholars use to include some thinkers and exclude others? I would name six criteria, each of which involves a stance toward a matter that could be understood as relatively independent of the School. Moreover, in forging the identity of the Kyoto School, these criteria have usually been invoked implicitly and selectively, in various combinations, rather than consciously and cumulatively. Because of the selective and variable way that the criteria have been employed, there has been no agreement on which thinkers count as members. In this sense, the Kyoto School comprises something like a "fuzzy set" that has indefinite boundaries and varying degrees of membership.

18.2 Six Criteria Used to Identify the Kyoto School

Perhaps the only feature common to all identifications of Kyoto School members is their *connection with Nishida,* the so-called founder who had no intention of founding a "school." Nishida himself stands both within the School and outside it, depending on one's viewpoint. On the one hand, Nishida's philosophy is its own towering achievement, and can be understood and interpreted independently of almost all interpretations and work by others aligned with the Kyoto School. The one exception is the work of Tanabe, whose criticisms so influenced Nishida's development that their philosophies grew partially in reaction to one another. (For this reason, Tanabe is sometimes considered the co-founder of the School.) On the

---

[2]"Kyōto gakuha no tetsugaku" [The Philosophy of the Kyoto School], in *Tosaka Jun Zenshū* [『戸坂潤全集』 *Collected Works of Tosaka Jun*] III (Tokyo: Keisō shobō, 1966), pp. 171–176.

other hand, considered as the founder (or co-founder) of the Kyoto School, Nishida belongs within the School of thinkers who have been inspired by his thought.

As a common factor, however, this inspiration is highly ambivalent and of varying degrees. Some thinkers, like Tanabe, were younger colleagues intensely involved in studying Nishida's works and appropriating them critically, adapting some ideas and rejecting others. Tanabe was more Nishida's critic than his follower; yet all commentators include him in the Kyoto School. On the other hand, those who appreciated and appropriated Nishida's ideas are not necessarily included in the School. Nishida's friend D. T. Suzuki is one example. Another is Watsuji Tetsurō, who went to Kyoto Imperial University at Nishida's invitation to teach ethics from 1925 to 1934. Watsuji's major work, *Ethics*, written mostly after he left Kyoto for Tokyo Imperial University, still clearly draws upon Nishida for many of its key ideas.[3] Yet another example is Kuki Shuzō, who began teaching at Kyoto Imperial University in 1929 upon Nishida's recommendation, and whose 1932 book *The Problem of Contingency* shows the unmistakable influence of Nishida's thought. Some thinkers often included in the School, such as Tosaka, Miki, Nishitani, Hisamatsu Shinichi, and Shimomura Toratarō were direct students of Nishida. But their stance toward the master varied from Tosaka's rejection to Nishitani's creative reception to Shimomura's uncritical celebration. Other students are rarely treated as members, such as Mutai Risaku (1890–1974) Sera Hisao (1888–1973), and Kimura Motomori.

In short, the connection to Nishida counts in practice as a necessary criterion for membership in the Kyoto School, but it alone is not sufficient. Other factors count as well. For example, certain students of Nishida's students are considered Kyoto School members because of their appreciative interpretations and extensions not only of Nishida's philosophy, but also of the Zen tradition. They include Hisamatsu disciples Abe Masao and Tsujimura Kōichi as well as Nishitani's student, Ueda Shizuteru. The stance toward Zen Buddhism is crucial enough to function as a separate criterion, and will be mentioned below.

The *second criterion* that is often used, at least implicitly, to identify Kyoto School thinkers is their *association with Kyoto University*. Some scholars name only people who had a teaching position with Kyoto University, or even more narrowly, only those who held a chair in philosophy proper (so-called "pure philosophy") or in philosophy of religion. In fact, however, the designations of the chairs and the alliances of chair holders are far from simple. There is not room here for a detailed history of Kyoto University positions. Suffice it to say that not all who

---

[3]Several key ideas in Watsuji's books on ethics bear the unmistakable influence of Nishida and a deep affinity with the ideas of other recognized Kyoto School philosophers. We find in Watsuji's ethics the ideas that the truly Absolute cannot exclude the relative, that Buddhist emptiness applies to social realities as well as to individual entities; that self-negation defines the nature of the self; that factors which define entities come in contradictory pairs such as "independent and at the same time not independent" (reminiscent of the so-called logic of *soku-hi*), and that to be human means to be a unity of contradictories between self and other, reminiscent of Nishida's "contradictory self-identity".

succeeded Nishida and Tanabe in the chair for philosophy, or who followed Nishitani in the chair for religion, count as Kyoto School members; while others who held a position outside these chairs (such as Suzuki Shigetaka), or even outside Kyoto University (such as Abe Masao) often do count as members. The relevant factor seems to be the person's stance toward Nishida, or inclusion by way of other criteria. For these reasons, the second criterion, which taken alone is perhaps the weakest, is also a matter of a stance, and not merely of a university position.

The *third criterion* involves a *stance toward Japanese and Eastern intellectual traditions.* Unlike other modern and contemporary philosophers in Japan who eschew their "own" Japanese tradition and devote themselves entirely to an imported "western" philosophy, those associated with the Kyoto School appropriated the insights and texts of "the East" in their encounter with western thought. Their stance toward the spiritual heritage and institutions of the East, particularly of Japan, is attentive and appreciative, rather than negligent or negative. Yet it is the evaluation of this stance that in recent times has most divided the supporters and the critics of the Kyoto School. Supporters have described it as a group of the world's first thinkers to be thoroughly immersed in both European and East Asian traditions. Some commentators have used the positive stance toward "Far Eastern" traditions as a criterion to exclude Tosaka from the Kyoto School; others use it to include D. T. Suzuki. Critics, on the other hand, have identified Kyoto School philosophers by their use (or purported misuse) of both European and Asian sources, considering them eclectics who commingle and conflate ideas of historically separate origin. But both critics and commentators who use the third criterion to identity the Kyoto School rely upon a general opposition between Japan or "the East," on one side, and "the West" on the other. This alleged opposition will become more questionable as we look at the remaining criteria and the unresolved issue of tradition.

Sometimes identifications of the Kyoto School entail tradition in a more specific manner, as extending in one of two directions: toward the future of the nation and toward the Buddhist heritage of the past. The direction of the future of the nation actually involved a *stance toward three inter-related matters: Marxism, the nation-state, and the Pacific War.* This stance, as broad as it is, counts as *the fourth criterion* for identifying the Kyoto School. Marxism was a powerful influence on first and second generation Kyoto School figures. Students of Nishida like Tosaka and Miki are often excluded from the School, or at least considered its left wing, because of their pro-Marxist stance.[4] Nishida and his followers rejected the Marxist interpretation of history and culture but were still deeply affected by it. Marxist currents in the 1920s and 1930s undoubtedly helped turn Tanabe's interest to history, and they form the background of his ideas of historical mediation and the

---

[4] Ōhashi Ryōsuke explicitly excludes Miki because of his conversion to Marxism; see *Die Philosophie der Kyoto-Schule*, 1990, p. 12, note 5. For an exposition that differentiates Miki's position and criticizes other Kyoto School thinkers, see Najita, Tetsuo & H.D. Harootunian, "Japanese revolt against the West: political and cultural criticism in the twentieth century," in Peter Duus, ed., *The Cambridge History of Japan*, vol. 6 (Cambridge, 1988), pp. 740ff.

"logic of species." Nishida felt compelled to address the problems of the historical and social dimensions of reality largely because of Tosaka's and Tanabe's criticisms of him. He formed his notions of poiesis, production, and action in counter-distinction to Marxist ideas.

In the late 1930s and early 1940s, with Marxist ideas on one side and rightist extremism on the other, thinkers associated with Nishida took an overt stance toward the Japanese nation-state and the Pacific War. In fact, that stance comprises a rather broad spectrum of attitudes. If there is a common factor, it is the conviction that a new world order was needed in which the East would have its rightful place alongside the West in the new "world-historical world." Supporters of the School judge this conviction as legitimate; critics condemn it as naive at best, imperialist at worst. More specifically, supporters say Nishida and Tanabe tired to present the Japanese government with a third possibility for national identity and global presence, neither Marxist nor ultranationalist; but critics see their efforts as justifying the Pacific War. Whatever the judgment, the political stance of thinkers who in the 1930s and 1940s invoked the idea of a world-historical world became a common criterion for identifying them as the Kyoto School.

The *fifth criterion* in common use to designate the Kyoto School is its *stance toward Buddhist tradition, and toward religion in general*. The theme of religion as representing humankind's most powerful and profound demands is common to many Kyoto School writers. Zen and True Pure Land Buddhism, in particular, but Christianity as well, exemplify religion for these thinkers. Nishida's Zen practice is often named as a source of his conception of "pure experience." Hisamatsu, who spoke of a religion of awakening and a philosophy of awakening, was a practicing Zen master. Tsujimura and Ueda have offered philosophical interpretations of Zen texts and have drawn upon Zen in interpreting Meister Eckhart and Martin Heidegger. Kyoto School thinkers have found in Zen and Mahayana traditions not only a source of personal spirituality but also a resource for philosophical reasoning and even for large-scale social problems. The Buddhist logic of *soku-hi* (即非), *śūnyatā*, and self-negation provide the basis (or field) that enables cultural and national renewal (D. T. Suzuki), the overcoming of nihilism (Nishitani), or a human community beyond national egoism (Abe). Other Kyoto School thinkers such as Tanabe, Takeuchi, and even Miki, turned principally to the True Pure Land tradition of Buddhism. Nishida's and Nishitani's writings on religion referred to True Pure Land faith as well, and they advanced interpretations that undermine any fundamental difference between P ure Land faith and Zen practice, or between "other-power" and "self-power."[5]

Many Kyoto School thinkers also deeply appreciated Christianity and sought a common ground between it and Buddhism. Tanabe gained a deep appreciation of Christianity in the final stage of his career. In his 1948 book, *The Dialectics of*

---

[5]See for example chapter four of Nishida's "The Logic of *Topos* and the Religious Worldview," trans. Michiko Yusa, *The Eastern Buddhist* 19(2): 1–29 & 20(1): 81–119; and Nishitani Keiji, *Religion and Nothingness* (Berkeley: University of California Press, 1982), pp. 261–262.

Christianity, he gave it a Buddhist interpretation, and proclaimed himself "ein werdender Christ"if never "ein gewordener Christ."[6] Nishida himself at the end of his life had located the negation and the expression of the Absolute in Christianity as well as Buddhism. Nishitani's *Religion and Nothingness* is permeated with both critical and appreciative discussions of Christian ideas and doctrines. The concern to find a common meeting ground between Buddhism and Christianity, in the mysticism of Eckhart or the kenotic understanding of Christ, for example, describes some of the work of Ueda and Abe respectively. Both continue in an intensified manner the efforts of their teacher Nishitani, and his teacher Nishida, to demonstrate that the modern world is a global area of religious encounter. As we shall see, the representation of religion, Buddhism, and Christianity in Kyoto School thinkers is controversial today, but it is undeniable that there is a religious, specifically Buddhist core that identifies almost all of them.

The *sixth criterion* is a *stance toward the notion of absolute nothingness*. The invocation of this key idea is almost an ID tag for differentiating Kyoto School thinkers for others. Yet the meaning of *absolute nothingness* is problematic, and the stance of various Kyoto School writers toward this idea is varied. The relevant Buddhist notion of nothingness (*mu* 無) of course can be traced back far earlier than the twentieth-century Kyoto School, but Nishida and Kyoto School thinkers gave it a novel explanatory role. Nishida took the experiential and practice-oriented thrust of the *mu* of Zen texts and redirected it toward a philosophical account of the world. Absolute nothingness is the ultimate *topos* (*basho* 場所) of historical reality in all its immediacy and its resistance to objectification. Tanabe criticized its designation as a place (*basho*) but retained the notion to describe the working of absolute mediation. Hisamatsu and his followers made it synonymous with the "formless Self" and invoked it as the notion that differentiated the East from the West. Nishitani later shifted it again to its traditional Buddhist roots when he replaced it with the notion of *śūnyatā* (*kū* 空 in Japanese) as distinguished from nihility (虛空). Whether these various permutations of absolute nothingness retain a univocal meaning is a question we shall take up next. But whatever its answer, it is clear that the central role of this term in various thinkers frequently serves to identify them as Kyoto School members.

We may now describe in more detail some of the issues that the six criteria leave unresolved.

---

[6]*Kirisutokyō no benshō* [『キリスト教の弁証』 *Dialectics of Christianity*], *Tanabe Hajime Zenshū* [『田辺元全集』 *Complete Works of Tanabe Hajime*] X (Tokyo: Chikuma Shobō, 1963), p. 261.

18.3 Absolute Nothingness: Sign of the East's Unique Contribution, or Floating Signifier?

What exactly do the terms "nothingness" and "absolute nothingness" in Kyoto School thinkers signify? How have these terms functioned to identify their particular contribution and to differentiate it from so-called western philosophy, or perhaps even from the predominant meaning of philosophy in general?

Kyoto School thinkers often emphasize that absolute nothingness means "neither being nor nonbeing," a description we find for example in the Creation Hymn of the tenth book of the Rig Veda. They also often use the term in place of the Buddhist *śūnyatā*. Yet in the history of ideas, nothingness (*mu* 無) does not seem to be an equivalent to Buddhist *śūnyatā* (*kū* 空). The Chinese Taoist tradition set 無 in opposition to 有 (being or having), so that the Sino-Japanese term *mu* seems more akin to the Sanskrit term *abhava* (nonbeing), as opposed to *bhava* (being). The specification of nothingness as "absolute" may help to differentiate it from mere nonbeing. But it does not resolve the ambiguity between the pre-Buddhist sense of "neither being nor nonbeing" on the one hand, and the Buddhist sense of emptying everything of self-subsistent "own being" (*svabhāva*), on the other.

Nishitani's book *Religion and Nothingness* seems to offer some clarification. The first two chapters distinguish the relative nothingness or "nihility" that denotes the "not" or the negation of being, and that remains a mere concept, from the absolute nothingness that must be realized in actual life (and death) through self-negation. For the most part, Sartre's *néant* and even Heidegger's *Nichts* count as relative nothingness for Nishitani. Nishitani does find an approximation to the kind of lived nothingness that he has in mind in Meister Eckhart. Eckhart says that the *Gottheit* which must be discovered in the human soul is beyond all modes of being; it is purely nothing, or "the nothingness of the absolute" in Nishitani's rendition. This captures both the sense of "beyond being and nonbeing," and the sense of a lived realization via negation of self. This latter sense connects absolute nothingness to Buddhist *śūnyatā*, and in the later chapters of his book Nishitani prefers the Buddhist term, *kū*. Yet there are problems with this developing interpretation. First is the question whether Eckhart can so easily be buddhacized, his *lauter nichts* turned into "the nothingness of the absolute," and his German writings separated from his Latin texts that are more Christological. Another problem is whether Nishitani has done justice to Heidegger's notion of *Nichts*, which is formulated within the ontological difference between Being (*Sein*) and beings (*Seiende*). Surely Heidegger's *Nichts* cannot be equated with Buddhist *śūnyatā*, but because of the ontological difference, *Nichts* also cannot be relegated to nonbeing as opposed to being. Heidegger once remarked that *Nichts* is what *Sein* looks like when it is not differentiated from *Seiendes*, when *Seiendes* is taken as all there is.[7]

---

[7]Martin Heidegger, "Was ist Metaphysik?" in Gesamtausgabe Band 9: *Wegmarken* (Frankfurt: Vittorio Klostermann, 1976), p. 103. Attempts to maintain the distinct notion of absolute nothingness in Zen and Nishida, while fully acknowledging Heidegger's ontological difference, can be

In mid-career Nishida as well, the meanings of *mu* are not clearly distinguishable from the senses of nothingness found in western philosophy, and invite further investigation. For example, when Nishida writes of consciousness as a place of nothingness, he invokes a sense of nonbeing or no thing that he himself finds in western thinkers as early as the Pseudo-Dionysius (although of course there is no equivalent notion of consciousness in Dionysius). In order to differentiate Nishida's meaning from western conceptions such as Sartre's nothingness (*néant*), commentators like Abe emphasize that Nishida means "consciousness that is now conscious." Nishida also writes of consciousness as nothingness in the sense of an immediacy that can never be objectified, in contrast to objectified being. Later Kyoto School thinkers such as Nishitani and Abe have especially emphasized non-objectifiablity. But this theme also occurs in twentieth-century western philosophy. It is not obvious that Nishida's meaning differs from Husserl's sense of consciousness as primal streaming (*Ur-Strömen*) or as living present (*lebendige Gegenwart*). The theme of an immediacy anterior to intentional consciousness, or a matrix anterior to representation, is also found in French philosophers such as Emmanuel Levinas and Michel Henry. And the possibility of a non-objectifying thinking in general is a question that Heidegger addresses.[8] Instead of assuming that Nishida and Kyoto School thinkers, on the one side, mean something fundamentally different than "western" philosophers on the other, it would be more fruitful to consider them together and to investigate their notions of nothingness, non-objectifiablity, and immediacy in detail.

The meaning and role of nothingness were also disputed within the Kyoto School, particularly between Nishida and Tanabe, as is well known. Tanabe accused Nishida of "intutionism" or merely contemplative philosophy rooted in the experience of nothingness. This very formulation implies that nothingness is somehow the object of an experience. Tanabe's objection also implies that Nishida's philosophy of nothingness lacks an account of action and creation. Both of these implications would be inimical to Nishida and in fact do not accord well with his later philosophy.[9] Tanabe himself did eventually invoke the notion of absolute nothingness, for example, as a kind of ultimate ground (or *Abgrund*) for artistic creativity. But he continued to differ from Nishida. At first he insisted that any unmediated relation with absolute nothingness is impossible; every relation is disrupted by other relationships and hence requires a logic of absolute mediation, a

---

seen in essays by Tsujimura Kōichi: "Die Seinsfrage und das absolute Nichts - Erwachen," in *Transzendenz und Immanenz*, ed. D. Papenfuß & J. Söring (Stuttgart, 1977); and "Die Wahrheit des Seins und das absolute Nichts," in *Die Philosophie der Kyoto-Schule*, pp. 441–454. John C. Maraldo, "Rethinking God: Heidegger in the Light of Absolute Nothing, Nishida in the Shadow of Onto-Theology, in *Religious Experience and the End of Metaphysics*, Jeffrey Bloechl, ed. (Indiana University Press, 2003), pp. 31–49, contrasts Heidegger's and Nishida's notions of nothingness.

[8] See Martin Heidegger, *Wegmarken*, pp. 68–77.

[9] See John C. Maraldo, "Metanoetics and the Crisis of Reason: Tanabe, Nishida, and Contemporary Philosophy" in *The Religious Philosophy of Tanabe Hajime: The Metanoetic Imperative*. Taitetsu Unno & James W. Heisig, eds. (Berkeley: Asian Humanities Press, 1990), pp. 235–255.

logic of species or intermediaries that come between nothingness as a universal and the individual self. Eventually Tanabe proposed that there is a way to absolute nothingness mediated by faith or the act of metanoia. The relationship between Nishida's and Tanabe's dialectics deserves further questioning. So also does the relation between any sense of experience (including pure experience) on the one hand and nothingness on the other. (Can nothingness be said to be an experience? an object of experience? the ground of experience? the subjectivity behind experience?) And the claim that some uniform concept of absolute nothingness is a notion common to all Kyoto School thinkers is likewise disputable.

In Nishida at least, the non-objectifiable, immediate, and living character of nothingness leads to the possibility of understanding it as a positive (non-)principle of creativity. This creativity became a prominent theme in Nishida's later writings, where he called the "historical world" a place of nothingness and wrote of it as the field of interacting individual selves, each in continual formation, "from something created to something creating." Continuing this sense of nothingness, Hisamatsu and Nishitani used words like "living," "free," and "concrete" to characterize what they respectively called oriental nothingness and absolute nothingness. From a logical point of view, however, it seems ill-spoken to predicate any qualities at all to nothingness. We might be able to argue that creativity and freedom presuppose a sense of nothingness, just as we can assert that the Buddhist sense of the co-dependent origination of all things presupposes *śūnyatā*. But to say that such matters depend on nothingness or *śūnyatā* is not yet to qualify nothingness or *śūnyatā*. The logic and semantics of nothingness, which did concern Nishida, call for much more investigation.

A similar issue remains to be explored when "nothing" is used in the sense of "without ground" or "without reason." For example, Nishida refers to both world and self as without ground, and Ueda refers to the emergence of all phenomena as "without reason." Ueda shows that this notion can be found in thinkers such as Angelus Silesius and Heidegger.[10] Indeed, Heidegger's entire project of overcoming what he calls "onto-theology," that is, overcoming philosophy as discourse that seeks ultimate grounds or reasons, may be a counterpart to the Kyoto School project of pioneering a philosophy that arises from a sense of nothingness as absence of ultimate ground or reason. Their projects are of course not identical. Heidegger sought to overcome philosophy with "thinking" (*Denken*), insofar as the (western) philosophical tradition was directed to beings (*Seiende*) in oblivion of Being (*Sein*). Nishida and others in the Kyoto School sought not to overcome the "eastern" tradition of nothingness but to raise it to the level of philosophical discourse, where that logic or discourse seeks the relevant place (*basho*) or field (*ba*) of all phenomena rather than their ultimate ground. Yet both projects seek an alternative to a philosophy of beings and to a logic of ultimate grounds, and seem comparable in this respect. This matter deserves further research.

---

[10]Ueda Shizuteru, "The Zen Buddhist Experience of the Truly Beautiful," *The Eastern Buddhist* XXII, 1 (Spring 1989), pp. 1–36.

Kyoto School thinkers like Hisamatsu, Shimomura, and Abe use the qualification of nothingness as "absolute" (*zettai*) to differentiate it from western conceptions. Hisamatsu in particular made popular the notion of an "oriental nothingness" that is uniformly and fundamentally distinct from all "western" conceptions of nothingness which in comparison are merely relative.[11] In the light of the different senses of nothingness in Nishida alone, not to speak of the entire "East," Hisamatsu's analysis is not very persuasive. Nevertheless, his point, like Shimomura's and Abe's, is not simply that the western notions involve a relative nothingness, but also that the sense of absolute in the East is different. The usual sense of *zettai*, as a translation of "absolute," opposes it to "relative." Nishida plays upon the more literal sense of *zettai* (絶対) as that which roots out or overcomes (絶やす) all opposition (対) and in this way transcends the relative. If a supposed absolute stands opposed to things (as its objects) then it is relative (*sōtai* 相対), literally, mutually opposing. On the other hand, a mere transcendence of oppositions, such as a passive harmony, would be a mere nothing without creative power. Hence the self-contradictory nature of the absolute for Nishida: it must relate to the relative without opposing it and without being reduced to it. This is a very powerful notion of absolute, but is it really without precedent in western philosophers? In Hegel, for example, the Absolute does not exclude contingency or the relative, nor does it merely transcend oppositions to achieve a passive harmony. The difference between Nishida's "place of nothingness" (*mu no basho*) and Hegel's Absolute Spirit may be evident, but not the difference between their basic senses of "absolute."

In summary, it might be the case that "absolute nothingness" functions as a "floating signifier" (a term used by Claude Levi-Strauss) which is not attached to any particular meaning. Presumably, however, it is more than an empty signifier, a mere absence of meaning. In that case, the unresolved questions that arise concerning the issue of nothingness are these: (1) what is the relation between the (absolute) nothingness of the Kyoto School and Buddhist *śūnyatā*? (2) Is there a notion of (absolute) nothingness that is a common denominator of Eastern thought? (3) Is there a uniform sense of (absolute) nothingness in the Kyoto School philosophers who invoke the term? (4) Is Nishida's sense of nothingness (and of absolute) different from all senses of nothingness (and senses of absolute) in western philosophy? (5) What are the different senses of nothingness in Nishida's philosophy, and how do they relate to the notion of experience? Finally, (6) does a philosophy of nothingness, in some sense at least, place the very nature of philosophy in question, insofar as philosophy means the grounding of whatever is? And if it does, is it fundamentally different in direction from Heidegger's attempt to

---

[11]Hisamatsu's essay has been translated into English as "The Characteristics of Oriental Nothingness" in *Philosophical Studies of Japan* 2 (1960), pp. 65–97; and into German as *Die Fülle des Nichts. Vom Wesen des Zen* (Stuttgart: Neske, 1994).

overcome metaphysics as onto-theology, or of more recent (western) thinkers who would overcome philosophies of substantial being? Such questions must be pursued in detail if we are to understand the significance of "absolute nothingness" for philosophy—or against philosophy—today.

18.4 Kyoto School: Contemporary Buddhist Philosophy or Eclectic Idealism?

Kyoto School thinkers who are read in translation outside Japan today, such as Nishida, Tanabe, Hisamatsu, Nishitani, Abe, Takeuchi, and Ueda, are often regarded as contemporary Buddhist philosophers. Their thought is obviously informed by Buddhist traditions, and by their own Buddhist practice; but they are also "free thinkers" who are not bound to any sense of orthodoxy or orthopraxis. On the one hand, then, they serve as resources for philosophers and theologians outside Japan who want to learn what Buddhism teaches and how Buddhists think. Some of them, most of all Abe Masao, have participated directly in the continuing interreligious dialogue between Buddhists and Christians or Jews.[12] In the United States and Canada, they have probably had a stronger impact on theologians and scholars of religion than on any other group; and in Europe, especially Germany, they are becoming increasingly known among philosophers precisely for their Buddhist approach to philosophical problems. On the other hand, scholars of Buddhism outside Japan often regard them as less than ideal representatives of the Buddhist tradition. To such scholars, most Kyoto School thinkers appear to be biased toward the Zen tradition, or rather toward a very particular understanding of that tradition that does not pay sufficient attention to its diversity and historicity. In addition, they are judged too eclectic, mixing their selective Buddhist thought with existentialist philosophy or German idealism.

Two issues related to the Buddhist identity of Kyoto School philosophers can test their relevance for current debates in religious studies, especially in Great Britain and North America. First is the issue of how to understand the role of experience in religion. The most influential works for readers of English, Nishida's *Inquiry into the Good*, Tanabe's *Philosophy as Metanoetics*, and Nishitani's *Religion and Nothingness*, all urge that religion, when it is correctly understood on the basis of personal experience and not of abstract reason, gives access to true reality. This conviction permeates all their major works and works of other Kyoto School thinkers, even when, like later Nishida, they replace the term "experience" with other terms, and even when, like Nishitani, they question the meaning of

---

[12]Abe has published and written for several volumes on interreligious dialogue, including *The Emptying God: A Buddhist-Jewish-Christian Conversation*, eds. John B. Cobb, Jr. & Christopher Ives (New York, 1990); *Buddhism and Interfaith Dialogue* (Honolulu, 1995); and *Divine Emptiness and Historical Fullness: A Buddhist-Jewish-Christian Conversation With Masao Abe* (Trinity Press International, 1995).

"personal." In varying degrees their works appeal to the kind of Buddhist non-duality that early Nishida found in "pure experience" prior to the division between subject and object. The controversial relation between religion and experience is at the heart of this first issue. At its broadest, this issue includes the question whether religion should be understood in terms of experience at all—especially when other, more public religious phenomena such as ritual, scripture, art, etc. are relatively ignored.

Even if we grant that experience in some sense underlies all such phenomena and renders them meaningful, then significant questions still arise. Is there really such a thing as "pure experience" that cannot be attributed to human subjects in their particularity? Most philosophers and scholars of religion today insist that all experience is inevitably conditioned by such factors as one's language, past history, culture, and gender. Does "pure experience"in early Nishida (or "active-intuition" in later Nishida) imply an experiencing/intuiting that is immediate and unconditioned by such factors, or does he propose an alternative sense of experience, in which "pure" or "direct" does not necessarily mean "unmediated"? Does Tanabe's "meta-noesis" preserve a mediated quality of experience while still undermining duality? Nishitani's "realization of reality" is clearly non-dual; it is at the same time a self's understanding or appropriation and reality's actualization of itself. But is this "realized reality" so basic as to be unconditioned by a particular language, culture, or body? And is it so basic that it underlies all so-called world religions, or even all of Buddhism? These questions touch upon the very universality of the concepts of religion and experience. Indeed, some scholars go so far as to question the legitimacy of the very concept of "experience."[13] "Experience" itself is regarded as a mythical construct. A closer examination of Kyoto School works, and not simply the most influential ones already translated, can contribute much to the resolution of these various questions.

The second related issue concerns not only the Buddhist identity of Kyoto School philosophers but the very identity of Buddhism. Should Buddhism itself be thought of as a loose cluster of traditions, some of which are no longer living and others of which still live in practice and thought? Do these traditions maintain in common a core that identifies them as distinctively Buddhist? Ironically, one Kyoto School thinker who finds a common core in all Buddhism, Takeuchi Yoshinori,[14] appears to buddhologists as someone who has thoroughly infected his Buddhism with twentieth century existentialism. What is at stake here is the possibility of a philosophy that could still be called Buddhist while growing in quite new directions and even incorporating non-Asian concepts and ways of thinking. Whereas almost all scholars of Buddhism recognize its potential for change, transplantation, and

---

[13]See two articles by Robert Sharf, "Buddhist Modernism and the Rhetoric of Meditative Experience," *Numen* vol. 42 (1995), and "Experience" In *Critical Terms for Religious Studies*, Mark C. Taylor, ed. (Chicago: University of Chicago Press, 1998).

[14]See especially his book in English, *The Heart of Buddhism* (New York: Crossroad, 1983, 2nd edition 1991).

adaptation in its 2500-year history, only a few seem willing to allow Buddhism to grow in new, "westernized" forms.

Yet that prospect evokes serious problems about the Buddhist identity of the Kyoto School. Why is it that buddhologists join many western-trained philosophers in their appraisal of Nishida and Tanabe as late-born Hegelians? On what "field" would the identity and difference of Nishida's thought be visible to such scholars? In the case of Nishitani, his own avowed standpoint of non-duality has not assured his readers of his difference from a monist and pantheist philosophy based on an experience of absolute oneness. Is yet another standpoint needed in order to differentiate these thinkers from the western sources they invoke and criticize? These questions become particularly pressing for theologians and philosophers who wish to find new ways to speak and think of God.[15] Persuasive demonstrations of the particular contributions of Kyoto School thinking to this endeavor remain an important task.

18.5 World Philosophers or Japanists? the Place of Kyoto School Philosophers in the World Today

Intellectual historians and philosophers outside Japan have paid a great deal of attention to Kyoto School thought about culture and politics. Their concerns relate most closely with the stance of Kyoto School thinkers toward Japanese tradition, and toward Marxism, the nation-state, and the Pacific War. The stance toward Japanese and Asian tradition entails the issue of nationalism in several ways. Consider first the link with the question of originality. The claim is often made that the Kyoto School is the only original philosophical school in Japan. Not satisfied with western formulations and solutions of philosophical problems, it drew from both Asian traditions and western philosophy, and creatively expressed something distinctively Japanese in its thought. This claim already links originality with nationality. Indeed, many Kyoto School philosophers have made a concerted effort

---

[15]See particularly the discussions between Abe and Christian and Jewish theologians in the books edited by Abe mentioned above. Critical expositions of Nishitani and Tanabe in German also address this challenge: Hans Waldenfels, *Absolutes Nichts. Zur Grundlegung des Dialoges zwischen Buddhismus und Christentum* (Freiburg: Herder, 1976), translated into English by J. W. Heisig as *Absolute Nothingness: Foundations for a Buddhist-Christian Dialogue* (New York: Paulist Press, 1980); and Johannes Laube, *Dialektik des absoluten Vermittlung. Hajime Tananbes Religonsphilosophie als Beitrag zum "Wettstreit der Liebe" zwischen Buddhismus und Christentum.* (Freiburg: Herder, 1984). The problem of God is one of the major issues discussed in two volumes of critical essays, *The Religious Philosophy of Nishitani Keiji*, Taitetsu Unno, ed. (Berkeley: University of California Press, 1989); and *The Religious Philosophy of Tanabe Hajime*, Taitetsu Unno and James W. Heisig, eds. (Berkeley: University of California Press, 1990). For a philosopher's attempt to relate Nishida to the question of God, see also Robert E. Carter's book, *The Nothingness Beyond God: An Introduction to the Philosophy of Nishida Kitarō* (New York, 1989, second edition 1998).

to show what Japanese "ways of thinking" have to offer. Only Tosaka seems to have taken a critical stance toward this tendency.[16]

Aside from the question of originality, Kyoto School authors may have stressed Japan-ness and "things Japanese" for good reasons: In the modern world among industrialized nations, Anglo-American and European thought has predominated and has resulted in a kind of colonization of thought. That predominance followed upon a long history of western hegemony and political colonization of other countries. As a counterbalance to western cultural domination, some thinkers more or less associated with the Kyoto School, such as D. T. Suzuki and Hisamatsu, presented the allegedly unique achievements of Japanese culture, which they linked particularly with Zen.[17] Their appraisal of Japan and the East has recently met with sharp criticism, directed also at other Kyoto School figures such as Nishida and Nishitani insofar as they too represented the ways of the East as an alternative to western rationality. The Kyoto School is accused of producing *nihonjinron*, the theory of the uniqueness of the Japanese, and of perpetrating "reverse orientalism." That is, they have allegedly not only treated "the East" in over-generalized terms, idealizing and "essentializing" a diverse group of cultures and traditions; they have also placed Japanese culture at the apex and attributed its superiority to the Zen way.[18]

To a certain extent, however, the demand for generalized views about the Japanese is kept alive by American and European expectations. On the other hand, the cultural diversity so celebrated today can also be stereotyped. What is needed is both a debunking of stereotypes and a retrieval of insights that are significant for current issues today, such as the issue of mutliculturalism and interculturality. Recently, western scholars of Nishida have made attempts to relate his views of an interrelated multi-national world to the contemporary problem of multicultural nation-states in a post-colonial world.[19]

---

[16]*Nihon idiorogi ron* [『日本イデオロギー論』Japanese Ideology, 1935 and 1936], in *Tosaka Jun Zenshū* [『戸坂潤全集』*Collected Works of Tosaka Jun*] II.

[17]Two books in English have been particularly influential: D. T. Suzuki's *Zen and Japanese Culture*, and Hisamatsu's *Zen and the Fine Arts*. The more recent work of Ōhashi Ryōsuke, *Nihon-tekina mono, Yōroppa-tekina mono* [『日本的なもの、ヨーロッパ的なもの』Things Japanese, Things European] (Tokyo: Shinchōsha, 1992) continues this avocation.

[18]See, for example, the critique of Bernard Faure, "The Kyoto School and Reverse Orientalism, "in *Japan in Traditional and Postmodern Perspectives,* eds. Charles Wei-shun Fu & Steven Heine (Albany: State University of New York Press., 1995); Robert Sharf, "The Zen of Japanese Nationalism, "in *Curators of the Buddha: The Study of Buddhism Under Colonialism*, ed. Donald s. Lopez, Jr. (Chicago: University of Chicago Press, 1995). These essays are relevant as well for the issue of the Kyoto School presentation of Buddhism.

[19]See, for example, Agustín Jacinto Zavala, "Lógica tópica y cultura occidental: Doce problemas en el estudio de una cultura diversa," *Relaciones* 12, 48 (1991), pp. 137–155; Elmar Weinmayr, "Europäische Interkulturalität und japanische Zwischen-Kultur," *Philosophisches Jahrbuch* 100, 1 (1993); John C. Maraldo, "The Problem of World Culture: Towards an Appropriation of Nishida's Philosophy of Nation and Culture," *The Eastern Buddhist* 28/2 (Fall 1995), pp. 183–197; Yoko Arisaka, "Beyond'East and West': Nishida's Universalism and Postcolonial Critique," *The Review of Politics* 59, 3 (summer 1997), pp. 541–560; and Rolf Elberfeld, *Nishida Kitarō (1870–1945):*

Kyoto School thinkers sought not only to counterbalance western cultural domination, but also to overcome western political hegemony. Nishida, and even more so his close followers, advocated the specialness not only of Japanese culture but also of the nation-state of Japan, that is, of the *kokutai*, an imperialist designation for the nation of Japan. They proposed that the special mission of Japan was to stand up for the East and usher the world into a new era of global history. In this new, truly "world-historical world," each nation-state had its own mission to pursue, but it was Japan alone that could demonstrate this principle of a new world order to the West. The advocacy of Japan as a special culture or nation has made Nishida's 1940 essay, "The Problem of Japanese Culture,"[20] controversial, and the roundtable talks of Nishitani, Kōyama, Kōsaka and Suzuki Shigetaka in 1941–1942[21] particularly notorious. Rightly or wrongly, intellectual historians have used this advocacy more than anything to identity the thought of the Kyoto School, and the ensuing controversy about its nationalism has recently intensified.[22] Today there are renewed calls worldwide for an accountability of Japanese colonialism and imperialism, and so the problem of the Kyoto School stance remains a live issue. Beyond the question of any possible culpability during the War, the question of another kind of complicity is also relevant: the complicity of intellectuals not by actions that perpetrate evils nor by a passivity that tolerates evils, but rather by effect of a rhetoric that can easily be misused.[23]

The broader issue, however, concerns not only any past complicity of Kyoto School thinkers in the Pacific War. It also concerns the present world domination of technological and capitalistic culture—and here the stance toward the future of the nation and the world is still relevant. Today, problems that motivated Japanese Marxists are not moot, despite the fall of the Soviet Union and communist regimes. Those problems pertain to the link between pervasive consumerism and social

---

Das Verstehen der Kulturen: Modern japanische Philosophie und die Frage nach der Interkulturalität (Amsterdam & Atlanta: Editions Rodopi, 1999).

[20]Nishida's draft of 1943 on the principle of a new world order has also received attention for this advocacy; see the translation and commentary of Yoko Arisaka, The Nishida Enigma: 'The Principle of the New World Order,'"*Monumenta Nipponica* 51, 1 (1996), pp. 81–105.

[21]See *Japanese Philosophy: A Sourcebook*, 1059–1077, for a translation of excerpts of these roundtable talks, published in *Chūōkōron*[『中央公論』],

[22]For a range of differing judgments, see Christopher Goto-Jones, ed., *Repoliticizing the Kyoto School as Philosophy* (London & New York: Routledge, 2008); and James W. Heisig & John C. Maraldo, eds., *Rude Awakenings: Zen, the Kyoto School, and the Question of Nationalism* (Honolulu: University of Hawai'i Press, 1995). The literature on this topic is now quite extensive; some of it is listed in my review article: John C. Maraldo, "The War Over the Kyoto School," *Monumenta Nipponica* 61, 3 (Autumn 2006), 375–406. Graham Parkes gives a spirited defense of Kyoto School Philosophers in "Heidegger and Japanese Fascism: An Unsubstantiated Connection," in *Japanese and Continental Philosophy" Conversations with the Kyoto School*, Bret W. Davis, Brian Schroeder, & Jason W. Wirth, eds. (Bloomington: Indiana University Press, 2011), pp. 247–265.

[23]As early as 1935, in the aforementioned essay on Japanese ideology, Tosaka made a distinction between the essence and the effect of an ideology, saying that although Nishida's philosophy was not fascist in essence, it could have a fascist effect. See *Tosaka Jun Zenshū* II, p. 342.

injustice. Kyoto School thinkers seem aloof from a concern with social justice; perhaps they have considered the whole notion of justice a questionable part of western conceptuality. During the War, however, some of them did concern themselves with overcoming (European) modernity in a way that is relevant to recent discussions about Eurocentrism and technological culture. Overcoming modernity is still an issue discussed today in Japan and elsewhere, particularly as it touches upon the possibility of an alternative to western forms of modern rationality in an age of globalization.[24] Is there such a thing as a distinct Asian (or Japanese) rationality that can serve to rectify the western rationality that has subjugated the earth, and can Kyoto School philosophy help articulate it?

In the end, we seem to face a dilemma: should Kyoto School thinkers count as Japanists who have continually championed their own nation or culture, or as international thinkers who have attempted to bridge different intellectual traditions? Are they nationalists who would remain rooted in Japan, or world philosophers who can cross-fertilize the intellectual soil of different nations and cultures? The answer may depend more on their readers than on their writings, that is, on the ways that readers resist or appropriate their work. The answer, again, may be neither Japanist nor internationalist. We may come to recognize world philosophers as people who speak to others out of a particular tradition, rather than as those who would pretend a view from nowhere.

John C. Maraldo Professor Emeritus, University of North Florida. Major works: *Japanese Philosophy: A Sourcebook* (ed. by J. W. Heisig, T. P. Kasulis, and J. C. Maraldo, University of Hawai'i Press, 2011), *Rude Awakenings* (ed. by J. W. Heisig and J. C. Maraldo, University of Hawai'i Press, 1995), *Der hermeneutische Zirkel: Untersuchungen zu Schleiermacher, Dilthey und Heidegger* (Alber, 1974).

---

[24]Much recent literature in Japanese re-assesses the July, 1942 colloquium on "overcoming modernity" in which Nishitani, Suzuki Shigetaka, and Shimomura took part. Excerpts from the text of the colloquium are translated in *Japanese Philosophy: A Sourcebook*, pp. 1078–1084. Recent conferences have also revived the theme. For example, it was discussed as a current task at a January, 2000 symposium in Tokyo on "Japan with World History, 1850–2000, which also mentioned the Kyoto School. In October 1997, an international colloquium in Paris discussed the "logique de lieu et dépassement de la modernité." For general discussions, see *Postmodernism and Japan: Post-contemporary Interventions*, eds. Masao Miyoshi & H. D. Harootunian (Durham, North Carolina, 1989); and Kōjin Karatani, "Wo liegt der Ursprung der Moderne—Interview von Steffi Richter," *Deutsche Zeitschrift für Philosophie* 44,6 (1996), pp. 1007–1019.

Index

A
Abe, Masao, 255, 256, 258, 260, 262, 263
absolute mediation (絶対媒介). *See* mediation
absolute nothing (絶対無). *See* nothing
action, 9, 12, 17, 18, 28–30, 36, 47, 52, 59, 60, 63, 64, 68, 71, 72, 75, 76, 85, 141, 145, 148, 157
active intuition (行為的直観), 14, 241
Adorno, Theodor, 235
Akamatsu, Tsunehiro, 77
Anderson, Benedict, 45
Angelus Silesius, 261
An Inquiry into the Good (善の研究), 65, 150
anthropology, 68, 69, 98, 124
antinomy
   absolute antinomy, 150, 154–156
Arakawa, Ikuo, 73
Aristotle, 7, 9, 17, 18, 21, 36, 38, 50, 58, 59, 62, 82, 167, 174, 221, 222
Augustine, 39

B
Bacon, Francis, 84
Baumgarten, Alexander Gottlieb, 61, 63, 64
being, 3, 7–10, 12, 19, 21, 26, 28–31, 34, 36, 38, 44, 47–51, 53, 61, 62, 66, 69, 71, 75, 81–83, 85–87, 91, 93–95, 97, 100, 104, 105, 109–116, 118, 120, 130, 140, 141, 143, 144, 146–148, 150, 153, 154, 156, 158, 169, 171, 173, 177, 184, 195, 201, 203, 204, 206, 210, 211, 213, 214, 220, 221, 224, 225, 227, 238, 243, 259, 262, 263
being-qua [soku]-nothing, 140, 141, 214, 215
Bergson, Henri, 45, 201

body
   social body, 63, 69
Body and Spirit (身体と精神), 112, 124, 126–128, 133
Böhme, Jakob, 84
Bourdieu, Pierre, 74
Buddha, 144–146, 158, 159
Buddhism, 149, 152, 164, 209, 215, 219, 226–228, 253, 255, 257, 263–265
Burckhardt, Jacob, 184, 191–193

C
Campanella, Tommaso, 84
Cassirer, Ernst, 62
Cauchy, Augustin Louis, 175
Christ, Jesus, 142, 191, 258
Clarifying the Meaning of the Logic of Species (種の論理の意味を明らかにす), 44
Comte, Auguste, 46, 174
contradiction
   absolute contradiction, 147, 153
criticism
   radical criticism, 89, 94, 106
culture
   eastern culture, 22, 61, 139, 143, 152, 240, 247
   western culture, 22, 82, 143, 152, 240, 247

D
De Anima, 7
Democritus, 167
Descartes, 12, 109, 172, 175, 208
dialectic, 27, 30, 32, 33, 38, 40, 51, 60, 127, 222, 234
Dilthey, Wilhelm, 68, 194

Dōgen, 145
dropping away of body and mind (身心脱落), 144, 145
Durkheim, Émile, 45, 46

E
Eckhart, Meister, 209, 215, 218, 257–259
Einstein, Albert, 99, 185
emptiness (空), 144, 145, 155, 209, 212–214, 216, 224, 227, 228
eternal now (absolute present), 242
Euclid (Eukleides), 174
experience
  fundamental experience, 69, 89, 168
  pure experience, 14, 16, 21, 257, 261, 264
expression, 17, 31, 39, 51, 63, 110–113, 116, 119, 128, 180, 204, 258
expressive love (表現愛), 119, 123, 124, 126, 127, 129

F
FAS, 156, 157, 159
Fichte, 113, 122, 123, 125
Fichte, Johann Gottlieb, 14, 113, 125, 127, 132
field of consciousness (意識の野), 5–7, 9, 10, 12
Ford, Henry, 83
form, 5–11, 18, 19, 22, 26, 28–31, 33, 35, 36, 51, 57–61, 63, 64, 69, 72, 74–76, 86, 113, 126, 131, 135, 144, 148, 158, 163, 165, 166, 177–179, 188, 199, 205, 210, 212, 219, 220, 222, 227, 242, 248, 265, 268
formless self (無相の自己), 149, 155, 156, 158, 258
Francis of Assisi, 190
Frankfurt school, 235
From that which Acts to that which Sees (働くものから見るものへ), 14
Fujita, Masakatsu, 22
Fujita, Tōko, 250
Funayana, Shin'ichi, 98

G
Gemeinschaft, 247
Gemeinschaft und Gesellschaft, 27, 247
Gesellschaft, 247
Geulincx, Arnold, 110
Gotō, Ryūnosuke, 246

H
Hatano, Seiichi, 65
Hayashi, Hachizō, 150

Hegel, G.W.F., 28, 36, 38, 47–49, 51, 53, 59, 63, 64, 85, 101, 127, 173, 193, 262
Heidegger, Martin, 21, 50, 51, 58, 66, 68, 213, 218, 235, 257, 259, 260, 262
Henry, Michel, 260
Hisamatsu, Shin'ich, 149–159, 195, 255, 257, 258, 261–263, 266
historical materialism, 43, 58, 66, 68
Historical Materialism and Contemporary Consciousness (唯物史観と現代の意識), 58, 66
Hobbes, Thomas, 48
Homer, 81
Horkheimer, Max, 235
human nation, 28, 43, 47
Husserl, Edmund, 50, 260

I
idea, 3, 6, 7, 9, 11, 12, 14–19, 22, 25, 28, 29, 31, 34, 44, 48, 50–53, 59, 60, 68, 71, 73, 101, 104, 110, 112, 113, 116–118, 127, 134, 164, 166–168, 171, 180, 222, 234, 235, 237–239, 244, 246, 249, 256, 258, 259
Iemura, Seiichi, 186
Ikegami, Shōzan, 151
imagination, *See* 'logic of imagination'
Imaizumi, Motoji, 149
imperialism, 237, 249, 267
intellectual history, 66, 89, 164, 166, 168, 170, 171, 176, 178, 187–192
intuition, 11, 12, 14–17, 26, 45, 60, 61, 76, 179–181, 223
Intuition and Reflection in Self-awareness (自覚における直観と反省), 100
Iwanami, Shigeo, 66, 90, 91, 93, 98, 124, 238

J
Jellinek, Georg, 28
Joyce, James, 81

K
Kakehashi, Akihide, 96–98
Kamei, Katsuichirō, 236
Kant, Immanuel, 11, 51, 58, 62–65, 72, 99, 100, 110, 113, 117, 127, 172, 174, 175, 180, 181
Kantian school, 6
Karaki, Junzō, 218
Kawakami, Tetsutarō, 187, 245
Keta, Masako, 229
Kimura, Motomori, 123–129, 131–133, 186, 218, 255

Index

Kobayashi, Hideo, 187
Konoe, Fumimaro, 67, 246
Kosaka, Kunitsugu, 251
Kōsaka, Masaaki, 123, 186, 218, 238, 248, 267
Kōyama, Iwao, 13, 14, 186, 218, 238, 248–250, 267
Kuki, Shūzō, 255
Kultur, 165, 166
Kuno, Osamu, 243

L

Lask, Emil, 6, 8, 9, 12
Le deux sources de la morale et de la religion, 26, 45
Leibniz, Gottfried Wilhelm, 68, 172, 175, 180, 186, 191, 193
Leonardo da Vinci, 190
Lévinas, Emmanuel, 260
Lévi-Strauss, Claude, 73
Lévy-Bruhl, Lucien, 26, 45
life
  expressive life, 111–113, 116–120, 128, 129, 134
life-qua[*soku*]-death, 211, 212
Locke, John, 48
logic
  logic of form (形の論理), 58–60, 64, 68, 234, 247, 250
  logic of imagination (構想力の論理), 59–64, 71, 75, 76, 250
  logic of species (種の論理), 25, 30, 32, 38, 39, 41, 43, 44, 46–51, 53, 243, 244, 257, 261
  logic of the mind (心の論理), 240, 241, 250
  placial logic (場所的論理), 16
  predicate-oriented logic (述語的論理), 22
logos, 39, 58, 62, 64, 69–74, 98
Lotze, Hermann, 3

M

machinery, 202–206
Mahāyāna Śraddhotpāda Śāstra (大乗起信論), 145
making (ποίησις), 59
Malebranche, Nicolas, 110
Maraldo, John C., 268
Marx, Karl, 66, 68, 69, 71, 97
Marxism, 43, 49, 67–69, 71, 97, 101, 256, 265
mathematics, 33, 34, 53, 92, 93, 95, 164, 167, 168, 170–173, 175–179, 181, 185, 186, 188, 190, 191, 194
mediation

absolute mediation, 32, 38, 39, 44, 51, 52, 243, 250, 258, 260
Meier, Georg Friedrich, 62
Meier, Heinrich, 62
Meinong, Alexius, 221
metanoetics (懺悔道), 44, 243, 244
metaphysics, 10, 31, 50, 53, 58, 86, 99, 101, 105, 139, 142–144, 146, 152, 167, 168, 170, 174–178, 181, 199, 263
Michelangelo, 114, 127
Miki, Kiyoshi, 65–77, 96, 98, 105, 234, 238, 246, 247, 256, 257
mind-tea (心茶), 157–159
Miyake, Gōichi, 218
modernity
  overcoming modernity, 48, 187, 233–240, 245, 247, 250, 251, 268
monad, 68, 180
Mori, Ōgai, 65
Morita, Jūjiro, 239
Mūlamadhyamakakārikā - śāstra (中論), 145
Mutai, Risaku, 123, 218, 255
myth, 26, 45, 58, 61, 63, 72–74

N

Nakaoka, Narifumi, 53
Napoléon Bonaparte, 49
nationalism
  ultra-nationalism, 100, 239, 242
nature
  historical nature, 119, 120, 128–131, 134
  laws of nature, 120, 200–207, 209, 224, 225
negation
  absolute negation, 27–32, 35–38, 40, 41, 46, 52, 53, 144, 154, 155, 209, 214, 241
  negation of negation, 11
Neo-Kantian school, 66, 68, 93, 94, 99–101
Newton, Isaac, 175, 180, 189, 193
Nietzsche, Friedrich, 27, 46, 68, 218, 224, 235
nihilism, 154, 155, 206–215, 218, 220–229, 235, 257
  crypto- nihilism, 206
nihility
  standpoint of nihility, 212, 214
Nihility and Emptiness (虚無と空), 224
Nishida, Kitarō, 4, 12–19, 21, 22, 65, 75, 77, 96, 125, 128, 131, 150, 151, 183, 184, 186, 193, 218, 219, 226, 235, 238–242, 245, 247, 248, 254, 255, 257, 258, 260–262, 264, 266, 267
Nishidian Philosophy (西田哲学), 13, 15, 59, 89, 128, 129, 189, 193, 242

Nishikawa, Tomio, 106
Nishitani, Keiji, 96, 123, 184, 186, 190, 217–224, 226–228, 235, 255, 257–261, 263–267
nothing (無)
    absolute nothing (絶対無), 22, 140, 147, 153, 154, 209, 212, 218, 234, 242, 244, 245, 250, 259–261, 263
    eastern nothing (東洋的無), 143, 144, 149, 151, 152, 157
    oppositional nothing (対立的無), 10–12
    true nothing (真の無), 9–11

O

Ōbaku, Kiun, 145, 146
Odysseia, 81
Ōhashi, Ryōsuke, 194
Ōkōchi, Masatoshi, 83
Ōnishi, Masamichi, 135
overcoming modernity. *See* "modernity"

P

Pacific War, *See* war
Pascal, Blaise, 58, 62, 66, 68, 98
Pathos, 58, 62, 64, 68, 70, 72–75, 98, 118
pedagogy, 123, 125, 131, 134, 135
Phänomenologie des Geistes, 51
philosophy
    eastern philosophy, 143, 172, 253
    Nishidian philosophy, 13, 15, 59, 89, 128, 129, 189, 193
    philosophy of awakening (覚の哲学), 149, 151, 157, 257
    western philosophy, 125, 143, 152, 171, 186, 219, 222, 228, 233, 259, 260, 262, 265
Philosophy as Metanoetics (懺悔道としての哲学), 243, 245, 263
Philosophy of History (歴史哲学), 57, 68, 69, 71, 72, 75, 76, 185, 238, 241
Philosophy of the History of Science (科学史の哲学), 184, 186–188, 191
physics (Physik), 168, 176
place (basho, 場所)
    place of forms (形相の場所), 7
    place of emplacement (於てある場所), 9, 11
    place of nothing (無の場所), 10, 12, 19, 260–262
    place of true nothing (真の無の場所), 12
placial logic (場所的論理). *See* 'logic'
Plato, 3, 33, 50, 51, 82, 109, 167, 174, 175, 211
predicate-oriented logic. *See* 'logic'
Principia philosophiae, 175

Principle of a New World Order (世界新秩序の原理), 238, 239, 242, 267
production, 59, 63, 64, 68, 70–72, 74, 75, 77, 83, 85–87, 90, 92, 103, 104, 111, 166, 257
Pseudo-Dionysius, 260
pure experience (純粋経験). *See* 'experience'
Pythagorean school, 170, 179

R

radical criticism, *See* 'criticism'
reality
    true reality, 41, 212, 263
Record of Linji (臨済録), 148
religion of awakening (覚の宗教), 149, 151, 152, 157, 257
Ribot, Théodule, 62
Rickert, Heinrich, 15, 66, 68, 101
Rig Veda, 259
Roosevelt, Franklin, 44
Rousseau, Jean-Jacques, 109

S

Saint-Simon, Claude, 84
Sartre, Jean-Paul, 259, 260
Scheler, Max, 68
Schelling, F.W.J., 33, 36, 84, 218
Sein und Zeit, 50, 68
self-alienation, 33–35, 38, 52, 53
self-awareness (自覚), 7, 14, 16–18, 22, 31, 35, 36, 40, 41, 81, 111, 117–119, 123, 124, 127, 131, 142, 150, 156, 166, 170, 171, 177, 186, 207, 210, 225, 236, 242, 244, 245, 250
self-inhabitation (自家止住), 35, 53
self-negation, 27, 32, 34–38, 47, 52, 120, 141, 156, 241, 243, 257, 259
Sera, Hisao, 255
Shimazaki, Tōson, 65
Shimomura, Toratarō, 183–194, 196, 255, 262
Simmel, Georg, 68
Sōda, Kichirō, 15, 19
soku (即), 47, 53, 178, 257
species. *See* 'logic of species'
    species society (種的社会), 26, 27, 35, 45
    species substratum (種的基体), 25, 26, 32–34, 36, 41, 46, 52
Speusippus, 175
Spinoza, Baruch de, 109, 172
spirit
    historical spirit, 85, 86, 102
    scientific spirit, 84–87, 89, 90, 93, 94, 98, 106, 239, 240
    technological spirit, 81–89, 94, 104, 106

Index 273

state
    ethnic state, 25, 28–30, 44, 48–50
Stirner, Max, 218
subject/object opposition, 7, 8
subjectivity
    originary subjectivity (根源的主体性), 218, 221, 223
subject-object unity, 11, 61
sublation (Aufheben), 29
substratum (ὑποκείμενον), 17, 18, 21, 25, 26, 28, 30–32, 34–38, 40, 46–50, 52
Suetsuna, Joichi, 188
Suzuki, Daisetsu, 219, 255–257, 266
Suzuki, Shigetaka, 248, 256, 267

T
Takeda, Atsushi, 196
Takeuchi, Yoshimi, 251, 257, 263
Takeuchi, Yoshinori, 264
Tanabe, Hajime, 43–53, 85, 91–93, 97, 132, 184, 189, 190, 193, 235, 243–245, 248, 254, 256–258, 260, 261, 264, 265
Tanaka, Michitarō, 218
Tanikawa, Tetsuzō, 218
technology, 58, 60, 61, 70, 72, 74, 76, 77, 81–85, 87, 90, 92, 94, 102–104, 106, 187, 202, 208, 225, 226, 234, 235
Tetens, Johann Nikolaus, 62
Thales, 81, 167
The Critique of Pure Reason, 172
The Dialectic of the Logic of Species (種の論理の弁証法), 43
The Doctrine of the Mean (中庸), 131
The Hit of a Chisel (一打の鑿), 126, 127
The Logic of Imagination (構想力の論理), 57–64, 68, 70, 72–74
The Logic of Social Being (社会存在の論理), 25, 32, 33, 51
The Logic of Species and the Schema of the World (種の論理と世界図式), 52
The Marxist Form of Anthropology (人間学のマルクス的形態), 98
The Metaphysical Element of the East (東洋的に形而上的なるもの), 140, 144, 146, 147, 152, 153, 157
The Odyssey, 81
The Philosophy of Originary Subjectivity (根源的主体性の哲学), 218
The Problem of Japanese Culture (日本文化の問題), 238–241, 267

The Social Ontological Structure of Logic (論理の社会存在論的構造), 33
The Study of Man in Pascal (パスカルに於ける人間の研究), 58, 66
The Way of the Absolute Subject (絶対主体道), 149, 151–153, 157
The World of Burckhardt (ブルクハルトの世界), 184, 191, 192
Timeaus, 3, 33
Tomonaga, Shin'ichirō, 188
Tönnies, Ferdinand, 27
Tosaka, Jun, 89–95, 97, 98, 100–106, 254, 255, 257, 266
totemism, 26, 45
trans-oppositional object, 6
Tsujimura, Kōichi, 255, 257

U
Über das Wesen der menschlichen Freiheit, 33
Ueda, Shizuteru, 123, 255, 257, 258, 261, 263

V
Vienna circle (Wiener Kreis), 34, 53, 99

W
wabi-tea (佗茶), 158, 159
war
    Pacific War, 92, 187, 243, 248, 256, 257, 265, 267
    World War II, 43, 92, 187, 233, 236
Watsuji, Tetsurō, 92, 105, 238, 255
way of the absolute subject (絶対主体道), 149, 152, 153, 157
Weierstraß, Karl, 175
Wells, Herbert George, 84
What is religion? (宗教とは何か), 219, 223, 224
What is the Technological Spirit? (技術的精神とは何か), 90
will to power, 27, 46, 47
world-historical world, 257, 267

Y
Yasuda, Yojyurō, 236

Z
Zen, 14, 22, 151, 155, 157–159, 219–221, 255, 257, 258, 266

Printed by Printforce, the Netherlands